STAR TREK

CLASSICS

3

ENCOUNTERS WITH THE UNKNOWN

FALSE COLORS

Written by Nathan Archer
Pencils by Jeffrey Moy
Background Assists by Philip Moy
Inks by W.C. Carani
Colors by Wildstorm FX
Letters by Ryan Cline

AVALON RISING

Written by Janine Ellen Young & Doselle Young
Pencils & Inks by David Roach
Colors by Dan Brown
Letters by Naghmeh Zand

ELITE FORCE

Written by Dan Abnett & Andy Lanning
Pencils by Jeffrey Moy
Inks by W.C. Carani
Colors by Dan Brown & Nick Bell
Letters by Ryan Cline & Naghmeh Zand
Based on material from the Activision/Raven Software computer game.

PLANET KILLER

Written by Kristine Kathryn Rusch & Dean Wesley Smith
Pencils by Robert Teranishi
Inks by Claude St. Aubin
Colors by Wildstorm FX
Letters by Ryan Cline & Jenna Garcia
Inspired by The Star Trek Original Series episode "The Doomsday Machine" written by Norman Spinrad

Cover by Drew Struzan
Original Edits by Jeff Mariotte
Collection Edits by Justin Eisinger & Alonzo Simon
Collection Design by Tom B. Long

Special thanks to Risa Kessler and John Van Citters of CBS Consumer Products for their invaluable assistance.

ISBN: 978-1-61377-211-9

15 14 13 12 1 2 3

IDW®

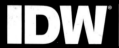

Ted Adams, CEO & Publisher
Greg Goldstein, President & COO
Robbie Robbins, EVP/Sr. Graphic Artist
Chris Ryall, Chief Creative Officer/Editor-in-Chief
Matthew Ruzicka, CPA, Chief Financial Officer
Alan Payne, VP of Sales

Become our fan on Facebook facebook.com/idwpublishing
Follow us on Twitter @idwpublishing
Check us out on YouTube youtube.com/idwpublishing
www.IDWPUBLISHING.com

Originally published by Wildstorm Productions as STAR TREK: VOYAGER: FALSE COLORS, STAR TREK: VOYAGER: AVALON RISING, STAR TREK: VOYAGER: ELITE FORCE, and STAR TREK: VOYAGER: PLANET KILLER Issues #1–3.

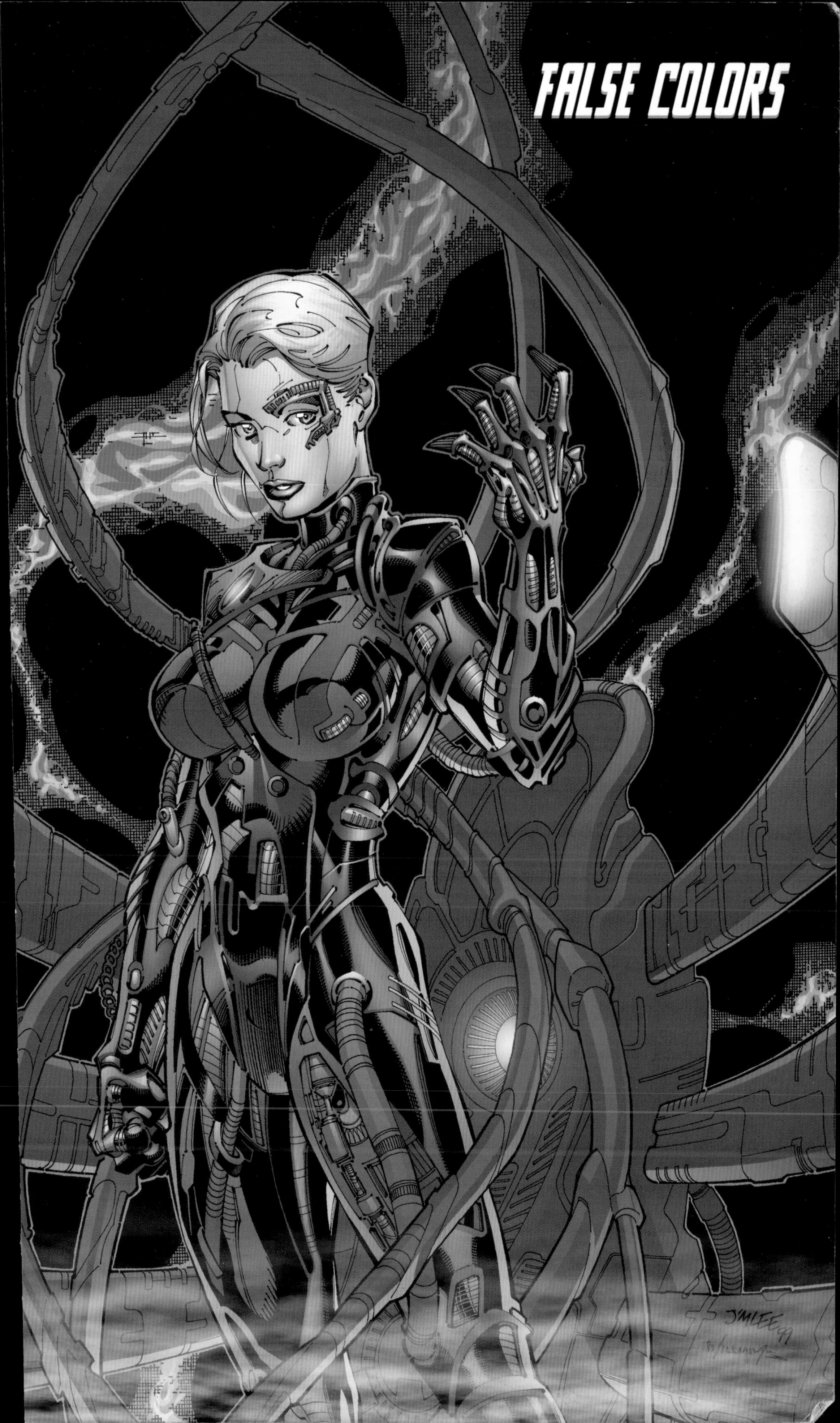
FALSE COLORS

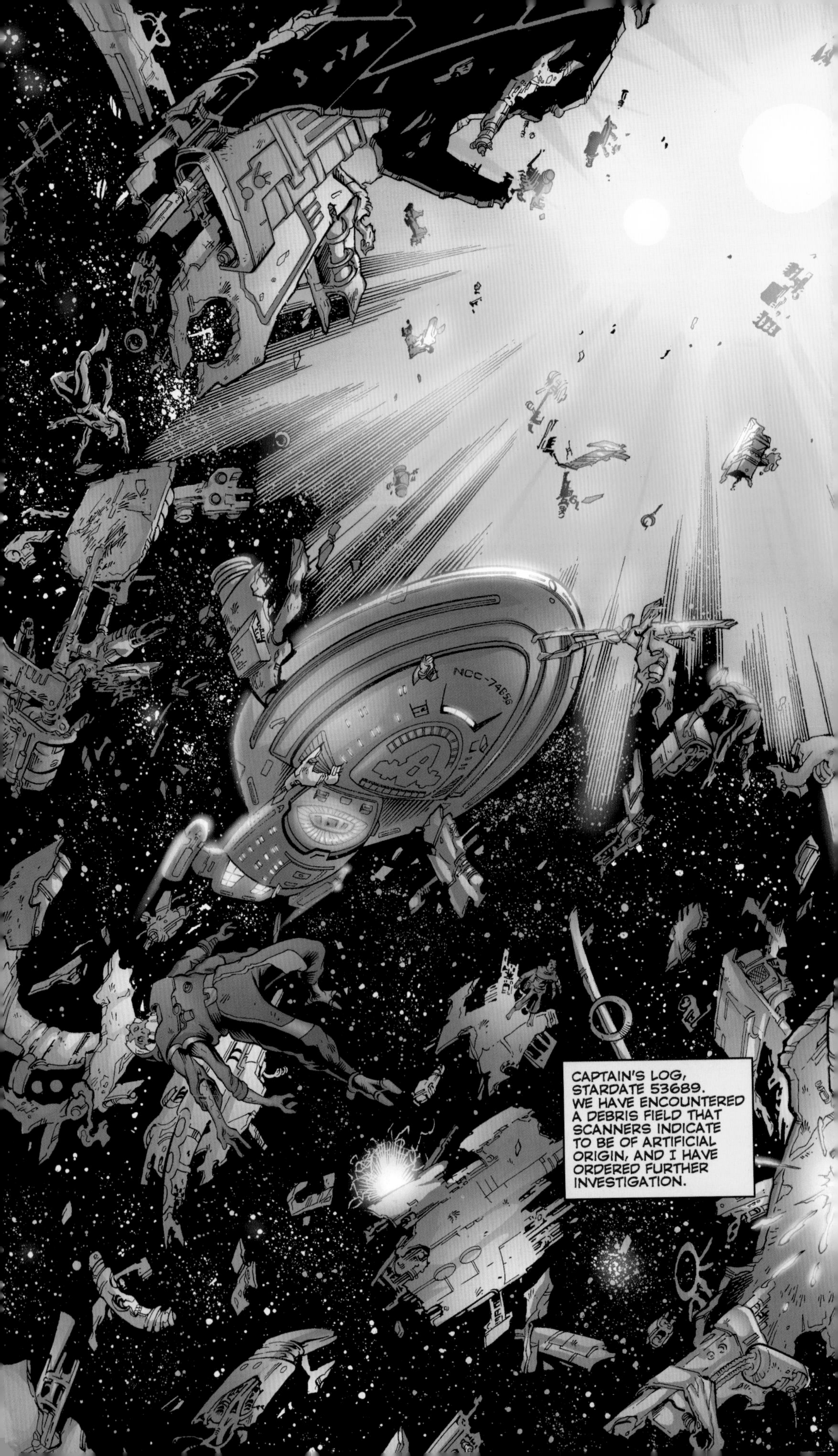
CAPTAIN'S LOG, STARDATE 53689. WE HAVE ENCOUNTERED A DEBRIS FIELD THAT SCANNERS INDICATE TO BE OF ARTIFICIAL ORIGIN, AND I HAVE ORDERED FURTHER INVESTIGATION.
NCC-74656

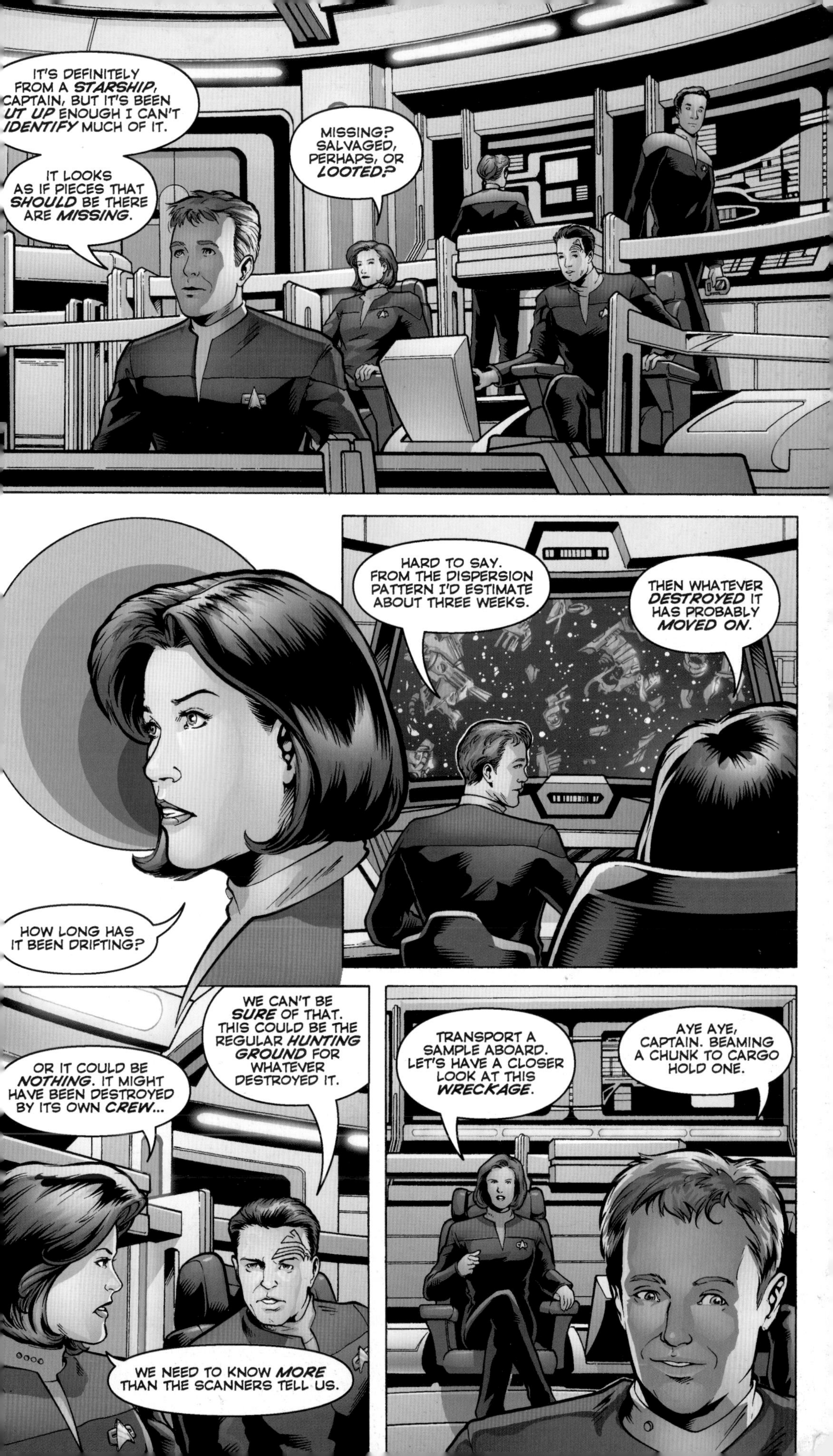
IT'S DEFINITELY FROM A STARSHIP, CAPTAIN, BUT IT'S BEEN UT UP ENOUGH I CAN'T IDENTIFY MUCH OF IT.
IT LOOKS AS IF PIECES THAT SHOULD BE THERE ARE MISSING.
MISSING? SALVAGED, PERHAPS, OR LOOTED?
HOW LONG HAS IT BEEN DRIFTING?
HARD TO SAY. FROM THE DISPERSION PATTERN I'D ESTIMATE ABOUT THREE WEEKS.
THEN WHATEVER DESTROYED IT HAS PROBABLY MOVED ON.
WE CAN'T BE SURE OF THAT. THIS COULD BE THE REGULAR HUNTING GROUND FOR WHATEVER DESTROYED IT.
OR IT COULD BE NOTHING. IT MIGHT HAVE BEEN DESTROYED BY ITS OWN CREW...
WE NEED TO KNOW MORE THAN THE SCANNERS TELL US.
TRANSPORT A SAMPLE ABOARD. LET'S HAVE A CLOSER LOOK AT THIS WRECKAGE.
AYE AYE, CAPTAIN. BEAMING A CHUNK TO CARGO HOLD ONE.

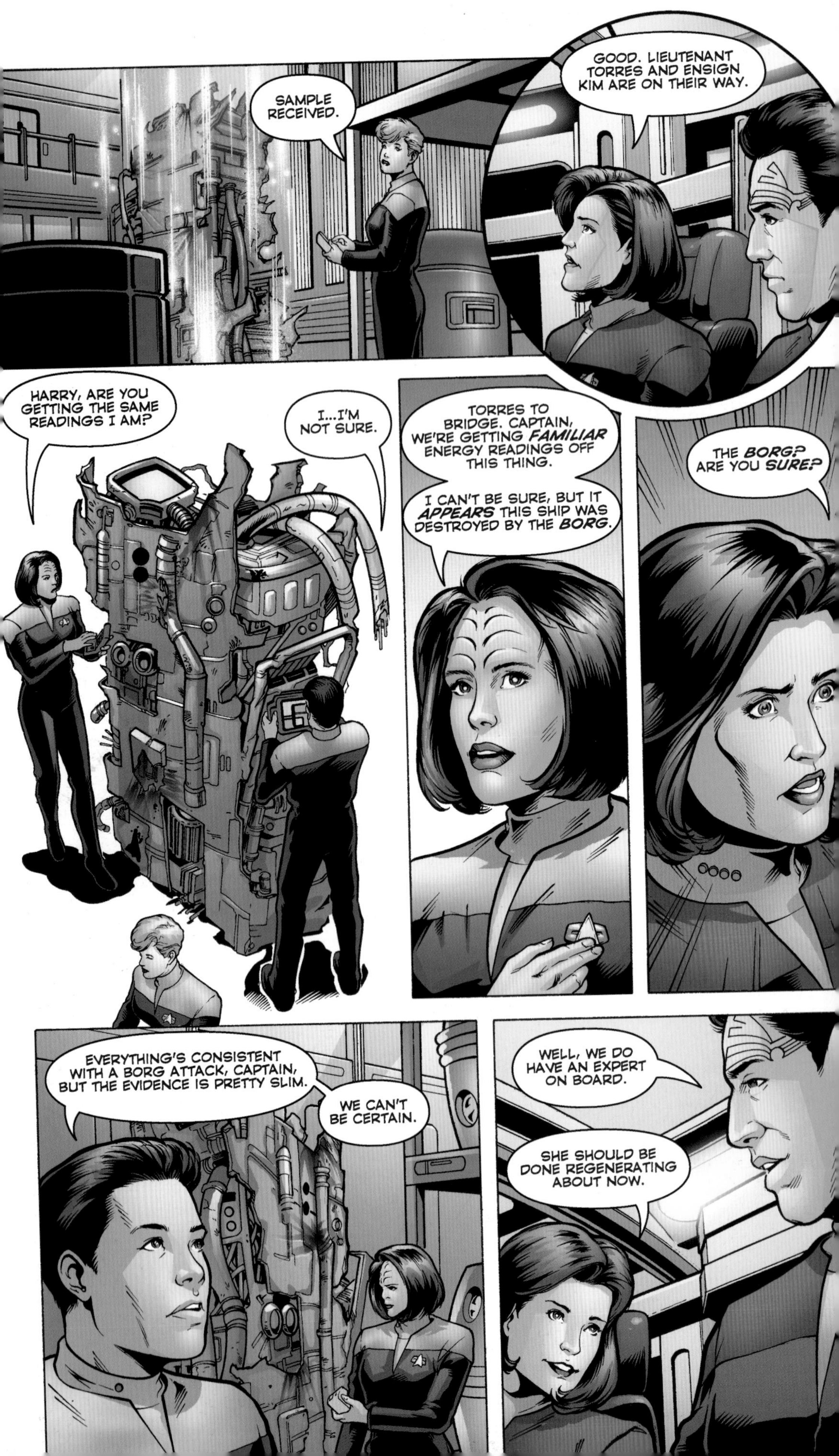

SAMPLE RECEIVED.
GOOD. LIEUTENANT TORRES AND ENSIGN KIM ARE ON THEIR WAY.
HARRY, ARE YOU GETTING THE SAME READINGS I AM?
I...I'M NOT SURE.
TORRES TO BRIDGE. CAPTAIN, WE'RE GETTING FAMILIAR ENERGY READINGS OFF THIS THING.
I CAN'T BE SURE, BUT IT APPEARS THIS SHIP WAS DESTROYED BY THE BORG.
THE BORG? ARE YOU SURE?
EVERYTHING'S CONSISTENT WITH A BORG ATTACK, CAPTAIN, BUT THE EVIDENCE IS PRETTY SLIM.
WE CAN'T BE CERTAIN.
WELL, WE DO HAVE AN EXPERT ON BOARD.
SHE SHOULD BE DONE REGENERATING ABOUT NOW.

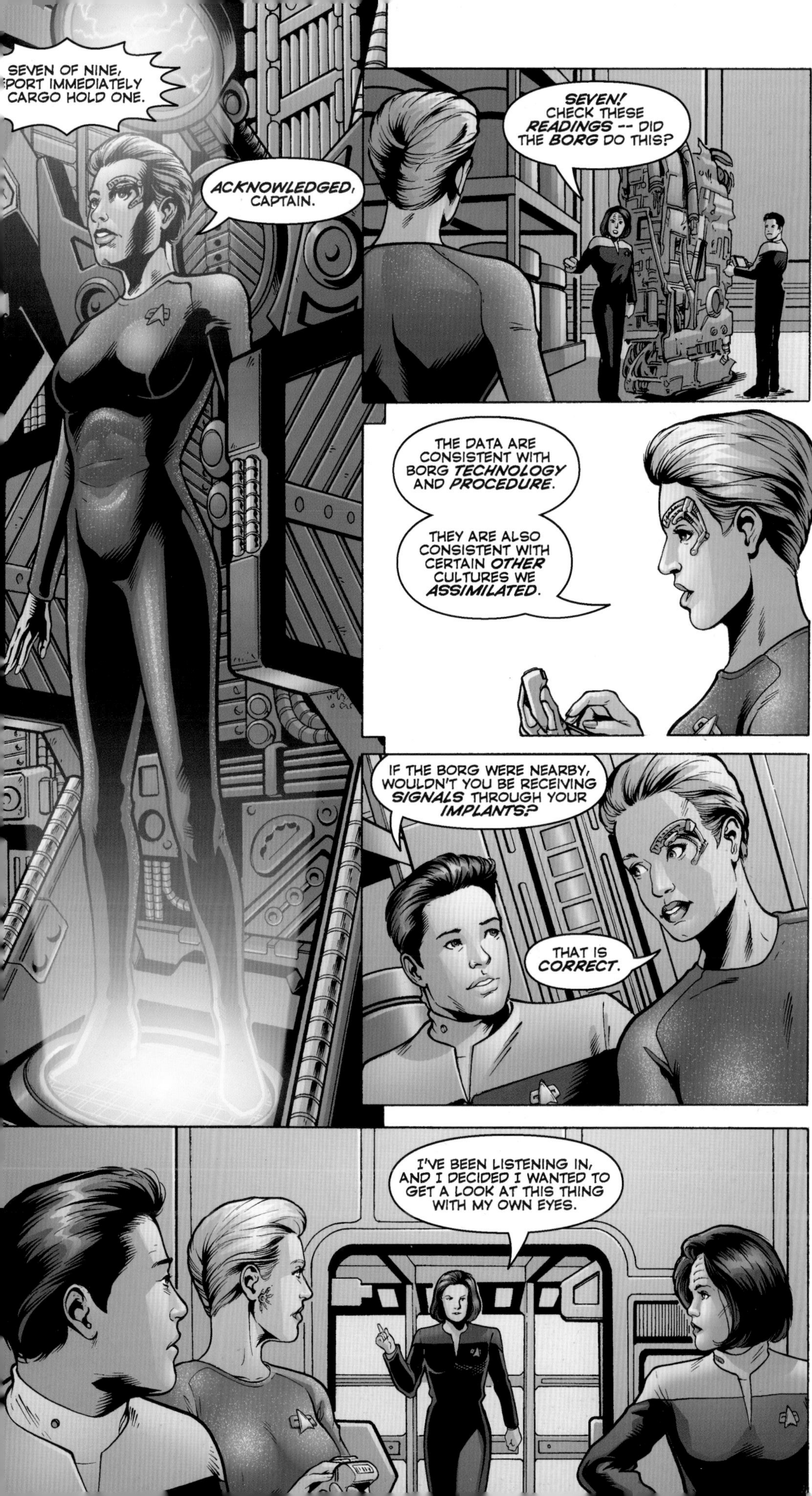
SEVEN OF NINE, EPORT IMMEDIATELY CARGO HOLD ONE.
ACKNOWLEDGED, CAPTAIN.
SEVEN! CHECK THESE READINGS -- DID THE BORG DO THIS?
THE DATA ARE CONSISTENT WITH BORG TECHNOLOGY AND PROCEDURE.
THEY ARE ALSO CONSISTENT WITH CERTAIN OTHER CULTURES WE ASSIMILATED.
IF THE BORG WERE NEARBY, WOULDN'T YOU BE RECEIVING SIGNALS THROUGH YOUR IMPLANTS?
THAT IS CORRECT.
I'VE BEEN LISTENING IN, AND I DECIDED I WANTED TO GET A LOOK AT THIS THING WITH MY OWN EYES.

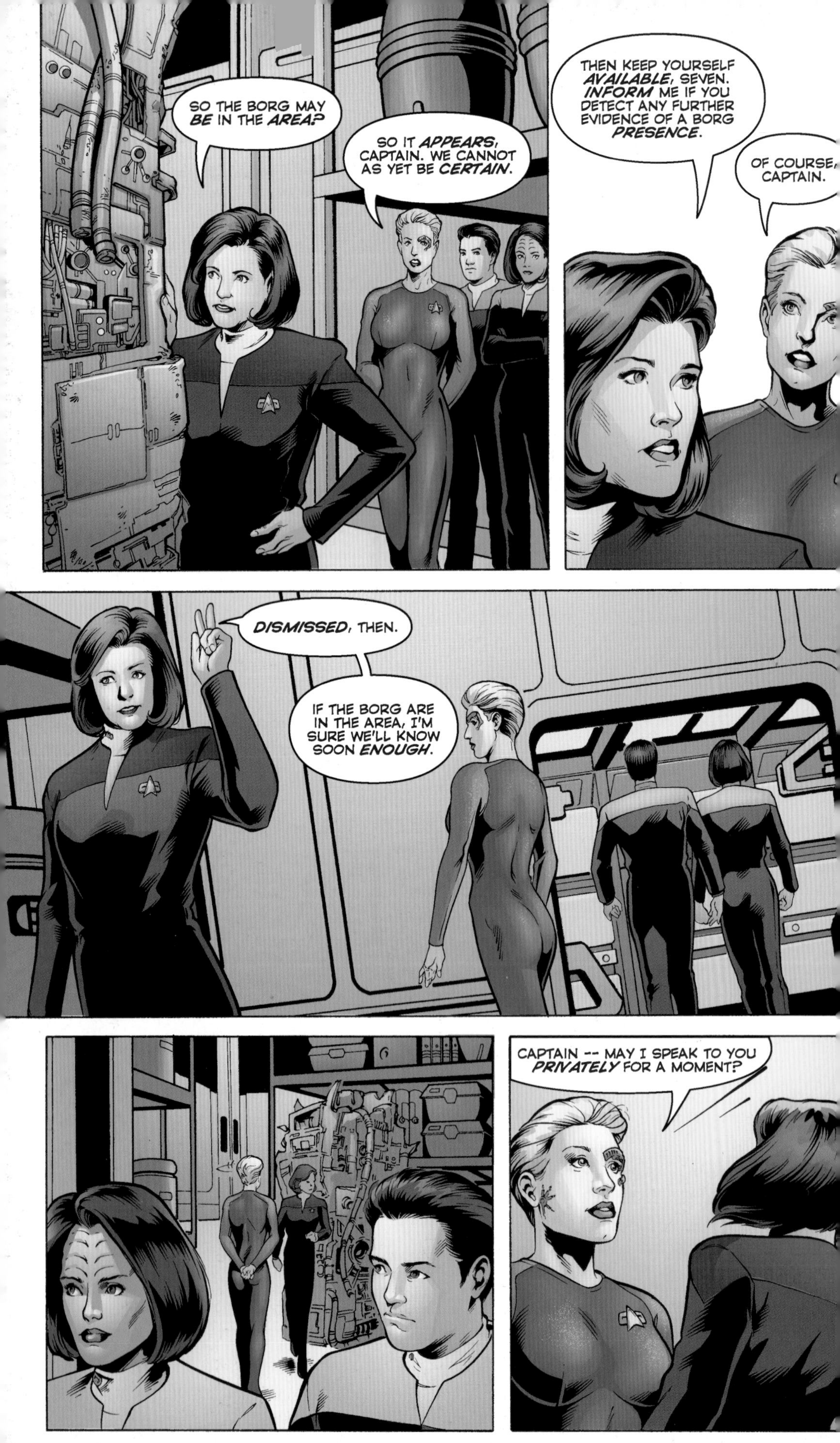
SO THE BORG MAY BE IN THE AREA?
SO IT APPEARS, CAPTAIN. WE CANNOT AS YET BE CERTAIN.
THEN KEEP YOURSELF AVAILABLE, SEVEN. INFORM ME IF YOU DETECT ANY FURTHER EVIDENCE OF A BORG PRESENCE.
OF COURSE, CAPTAIN.
DISMISSED, THEN.
IF THE BORG ARE IN THE AREA, I'M SURE WE'LL KNOW SOON ENOUGH.
CAPTAIN -- MAY I SPEAK TO YOU PRIVATELY FOR A MOMENT?

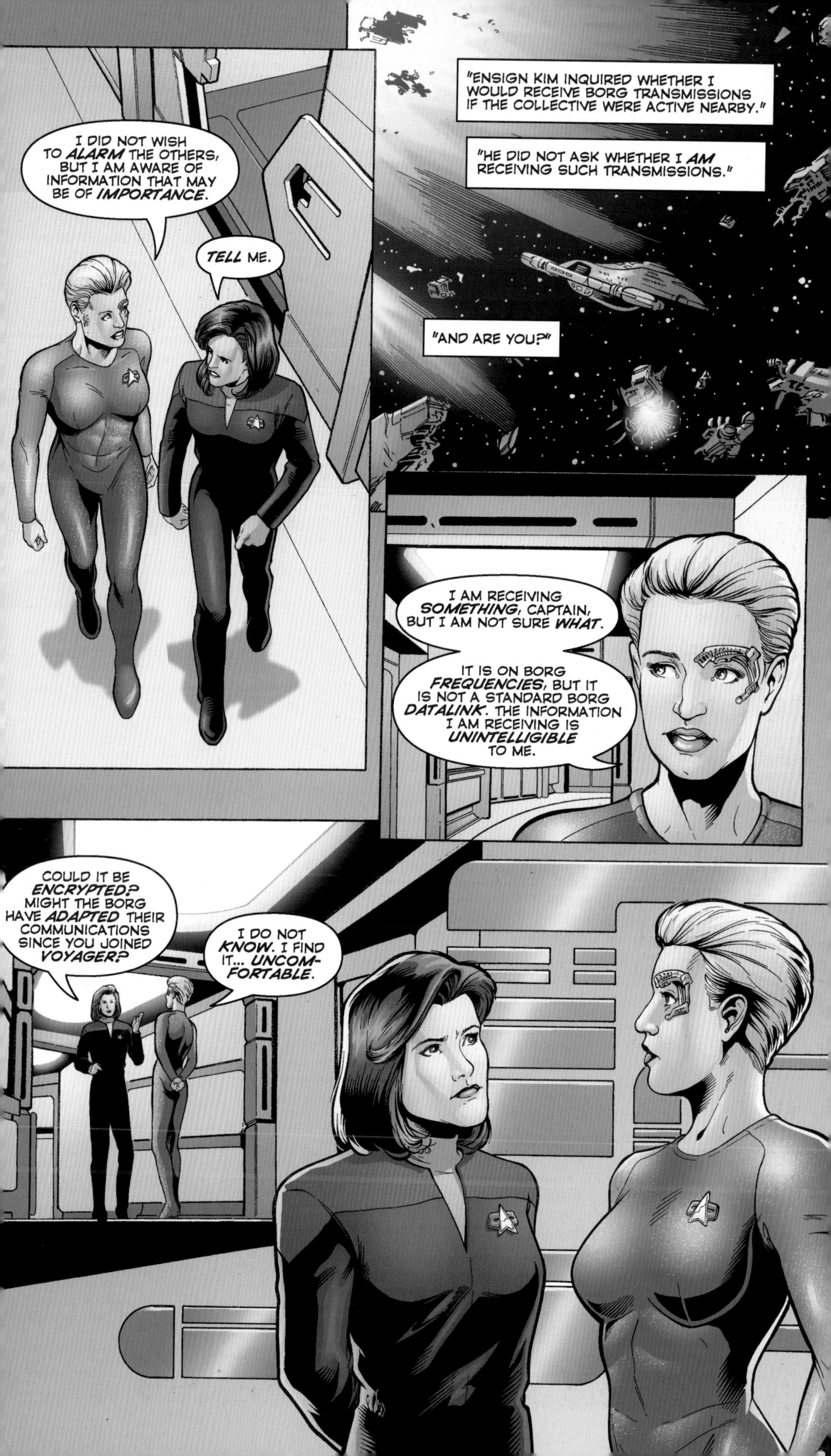

I DID NOT WISH TO ALARM THE OTHERS, BUT I AM AWARE OF INFORMATION THAT MAY BE OF IMPORTANCE.
TELL ME.
"ENSIGN KIM INQUIRED WHETHER I WOULD RECEIVE BORG TRANSMISSIONS IF THE COLLECTIVE WERE ACTIVE NEARBY."
"HE DID NOT ASK WHETHER I AM RECEIVING SUCH TRANSMISSIONS."
"AND ARE YOU?"
I AM RECEIVING SOMETHING, CAPTAIN, BUT I AM NOT SURE WHAT.
IT IS ON BORG FREQUENCIES, BUT IT IS NOT A STANDARD BORG DATALINK. THE INFORMATION I AM RECEIVING IS UNINTELLIGIBLE TO ME.
COULD IT BE ENCRYPTED? MIGHT THE BORG HAVE ADAPTED THEIR COMMUNICATIONS SINCE YOU JOINED VOYAGER?
I DO NOT KNOW. I FIND IT... UNCOMFORTABLE.

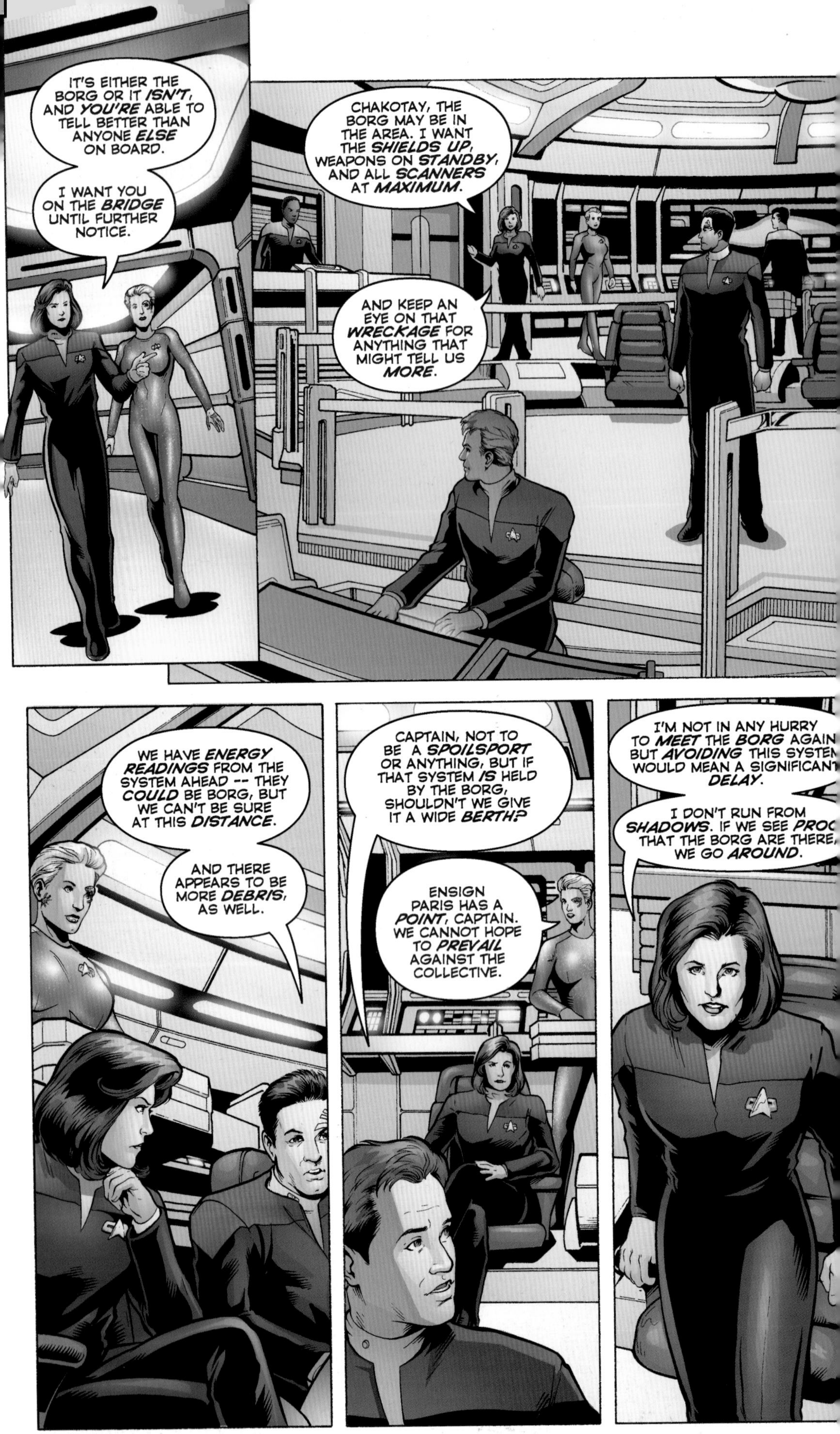
IT'S EITHER THE BORG OR IT ISN'T, AND YOU'RE ABLE TO TELL BETTER THAN ANYONE ELSE ON BOARD.
I WANT YOU ON THE BRIDGE UNTIL FURTHER NOTICE.
CHAKOTAY, THE BORG MAY BE IN THE AREA. I WANT THE SHIELDS UP, WEAPONS ON STANDBY, AND ALL SCANNERS AT MAXIMUM.
AND KEEP AN EYE ON THAT WRECKAGE FOR ANYTHING THAT MIGHT TELL US MORE.
WE HAVE ENERGY READINGS FROM THE SYSTEM AHEAD -- THEY COULD BE BORG, BUT WE CAN'T BE SURE AT THIS DISTANCE.
AND THERE APPEARS TO BE MORE DEBRIS, AS WELL.
CAPTAIN, NOT TO BE A SPOILSPORT OR ANYTHING, BUT IF THAT SYSTEM IS HELD BY THE BORG, SHOULDN'T WE GIVE IT A WIDE BERTH?
ENSIGN PARIS HAS A POINT, CAPTAIN. WE CANNOT HOPE TO PREVAIL AGAINST THE COLLECTIVE.
I'M NOT IN ANY HURRY TO MEET THE BORG AGAIN BUT AVOIDING THIS SYSTEM WOULD MEAN A SIGNIFICANT DELAY.
I DON'T RUN FROM SHADOWS. IF WE SEE PROO THAT THE BORG ARE THERE, WE GO AROUND.

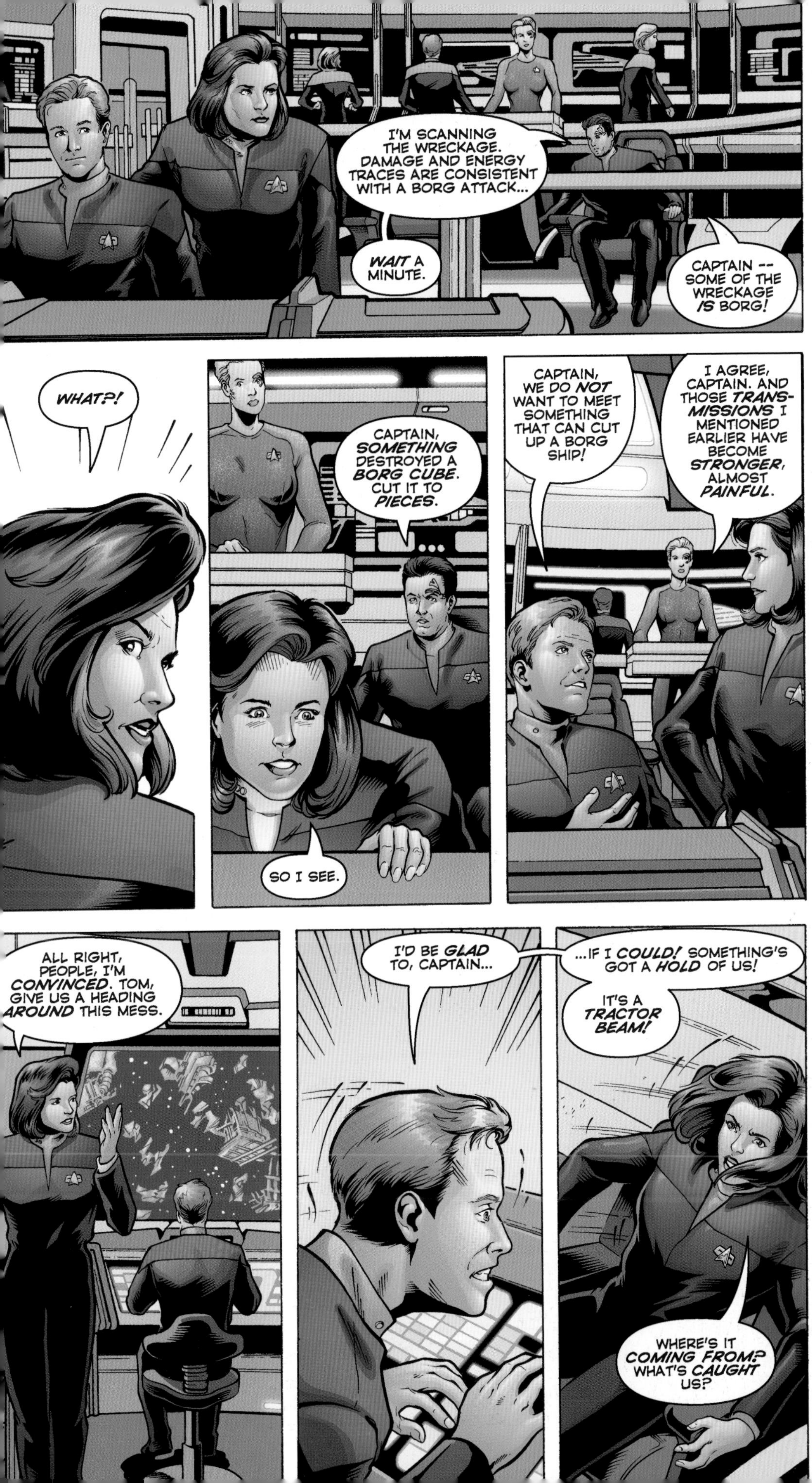
I'M SCANNING THE WRECKAGE. DAMAGE AND ENERGY TRACES ARE CONSISTENT WITH A BORG ATTACK...
WAIT A MINUTE.
CAPTAIN -- SOME OF THE WRECKAGE IS BORG!
WHAT?!
CAPTAIN, SOMETHING DESTROYED A BORG CUBE. CUT IT TO PIECES.
SO I SEE.
CAPTAIN, WE DO NOT WANT TO MEET SOMETHING THAT CAN CUT UP A BORG SHIP!
I AGREE, CAPTAIN. AND THOSE TRANS-MISSIONS I MENTIONED EARLIER HAVE BECOME STRONGER, ALMOST PAINFUL.
ALL RIGHT, PEOPLE, I'M CONVINCED. TOM, GIVE US A HEADING AROUND THIS MESS.
I'D BE GLAD TO, CAPTAIN...
...IF I COULD! SOMETHING'S GOT A HOLD OF US!
IT'S A TRACTOR BEAM!
WHERE'S IT COMING FROM? WHAT'S CAUGHT US?

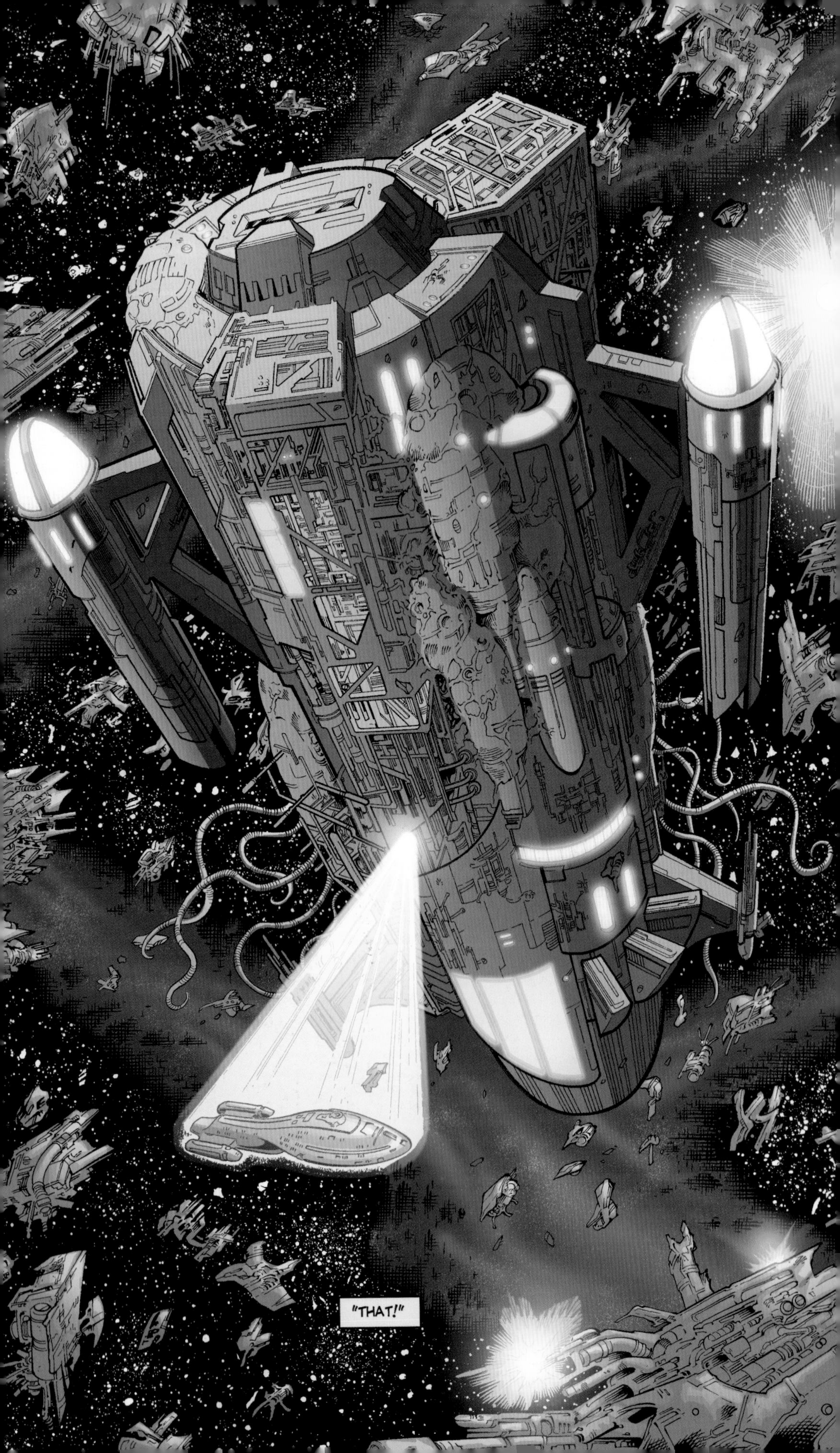
"THAT!"

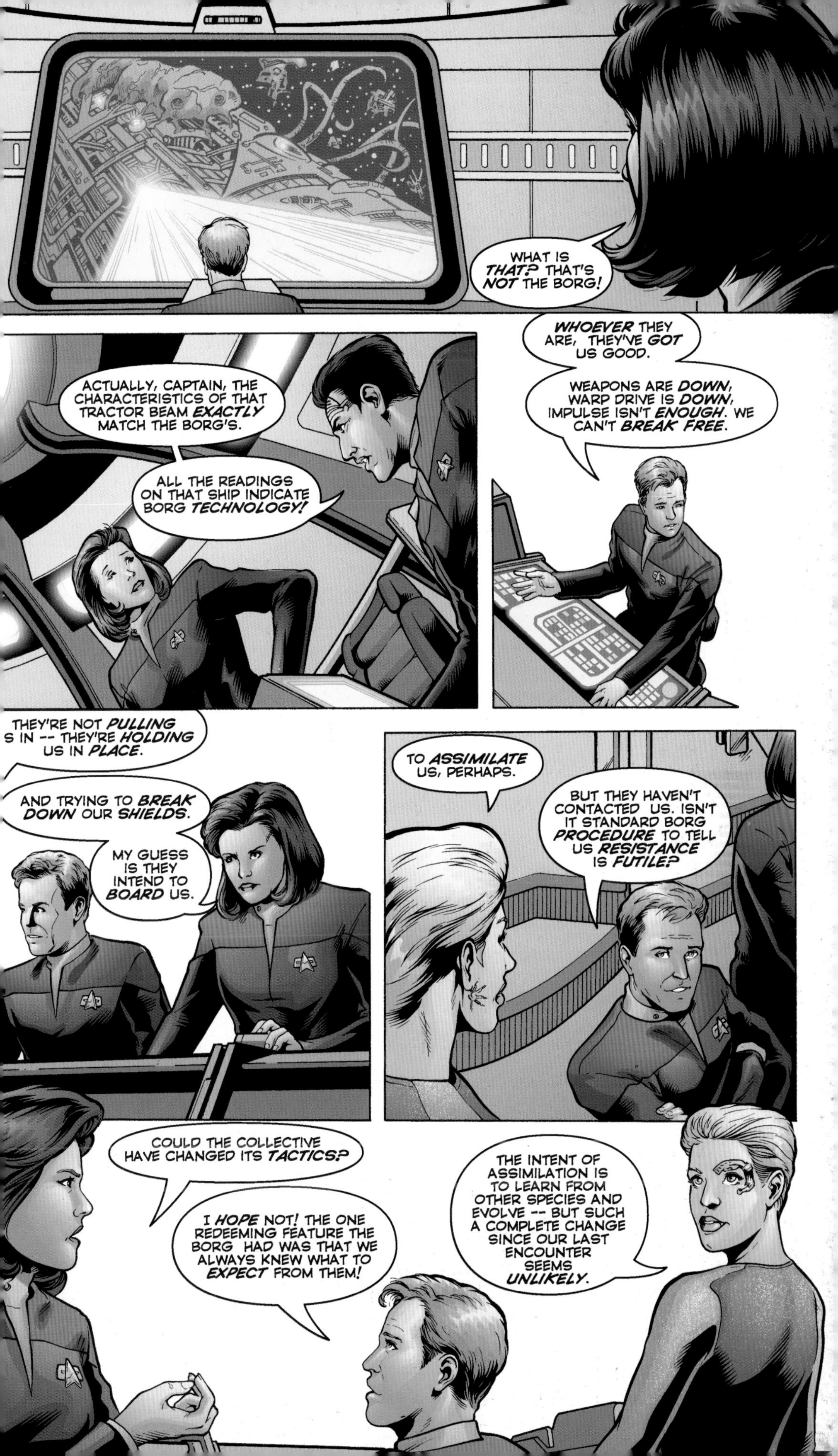
WHAT IS THAT? THAT'S NOT THE BORG!
ACTUALLY, CAPTAIN, THE CHARACTERISTICS OF THAT TRACTOR BEAM EXACTLY MATCH THE BORG'S.
ALL THE READINGS ON THAT SHIP INDICATE BORG TECHNOLOGY!
WHOEVER THEY ARE, THEY'VE GOT US GOOD.
WEAPONS ARE DOWN, WARP DRIVE IS DOWN, IMPULSE ISN'T ENOUGH. WE CAN'T BREAK FREE.
THEY'RE NOT PULLING S IN -- THEY'RE HOLDING US IN PLACE.
AND TRYING TO BREAK DOWN OUR SHIELDS.
MY GUESS IS THEY INTEND TO BOARD US.
TO ASSIMILATE US, PERHAPS.
BUT THEY HAVEN'T CONTACTED US. ISN'T IT STANDARD BORG PROCEDURE TO TELL US RESISTANCE IS FUTILE?
COULD THE COLLECTIVE HAVE CHANGED ITS TACTICS?
I HOPE NOT! THE ONE REDEEMING FEATURE THE BORG HAD WAS THAT WE ALWAYS KNEW WHAT TO EXPECT FROM THEM!
THE INTENT OF ASSIMILATION IS TO LEARN FROM OTHER SPECIES AND EVOLVE -- BUT SUCH A COMPLETE CHANGE SINCE OUR LAST ENCOUNTER SEEMS UNLIKELY.

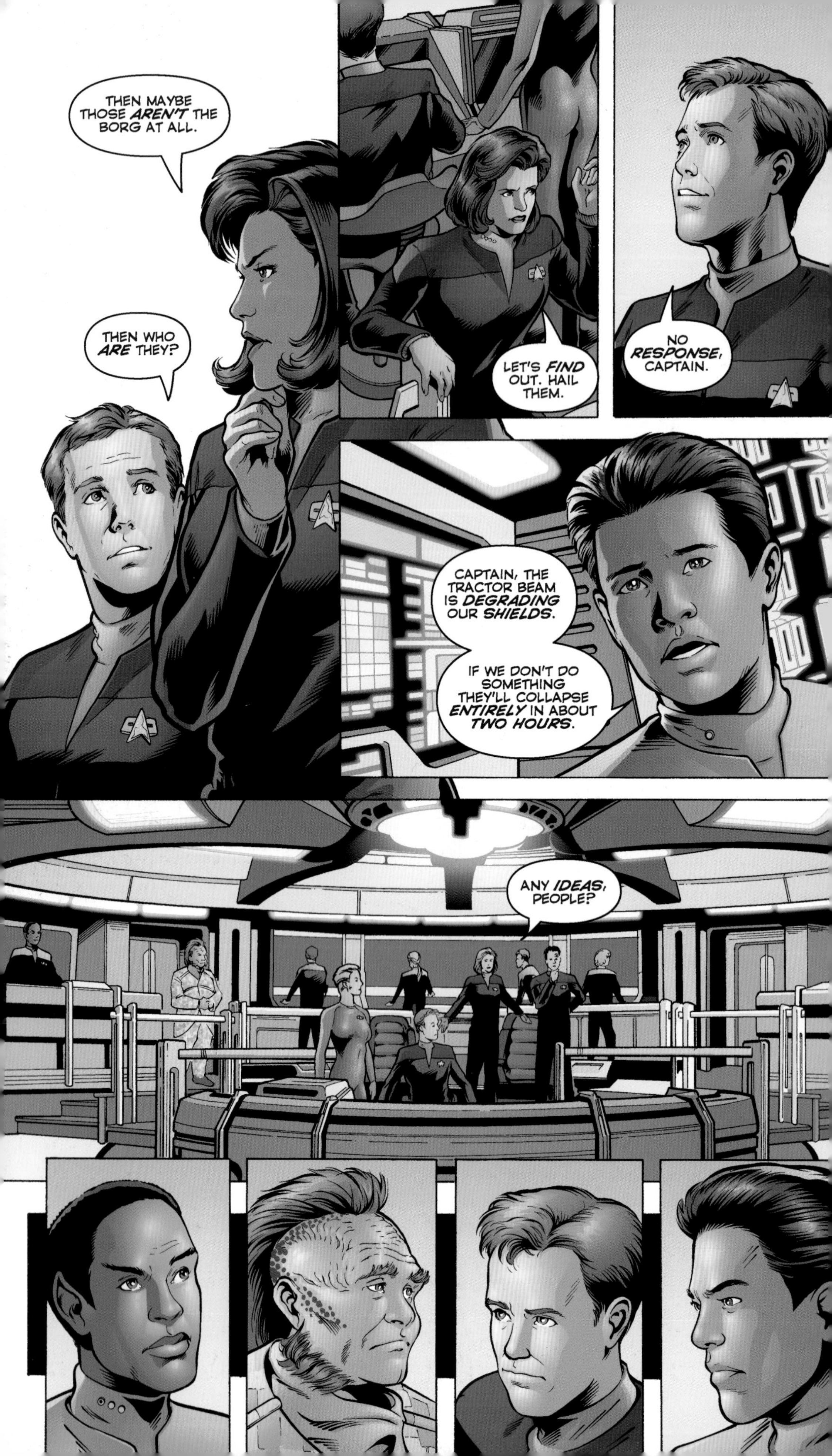
THEN MAYBE THOSE AREN'T THE BORG AT ALL.
THEN WHO ARE THEY?
LET'S FIND OUT. HAIL THEM.
NO RESPONSE, CAPTAIN.
CAPTAIN, THE TRACTOR BEAM IS DEGRADING OUR SHIELDS.
IF WE DON'T DO SOMETHING THEY'LL COLLAPSE ENTIRELY IN ABOUT TWO HOURS.
ANY IDEAS, PEOPLE?

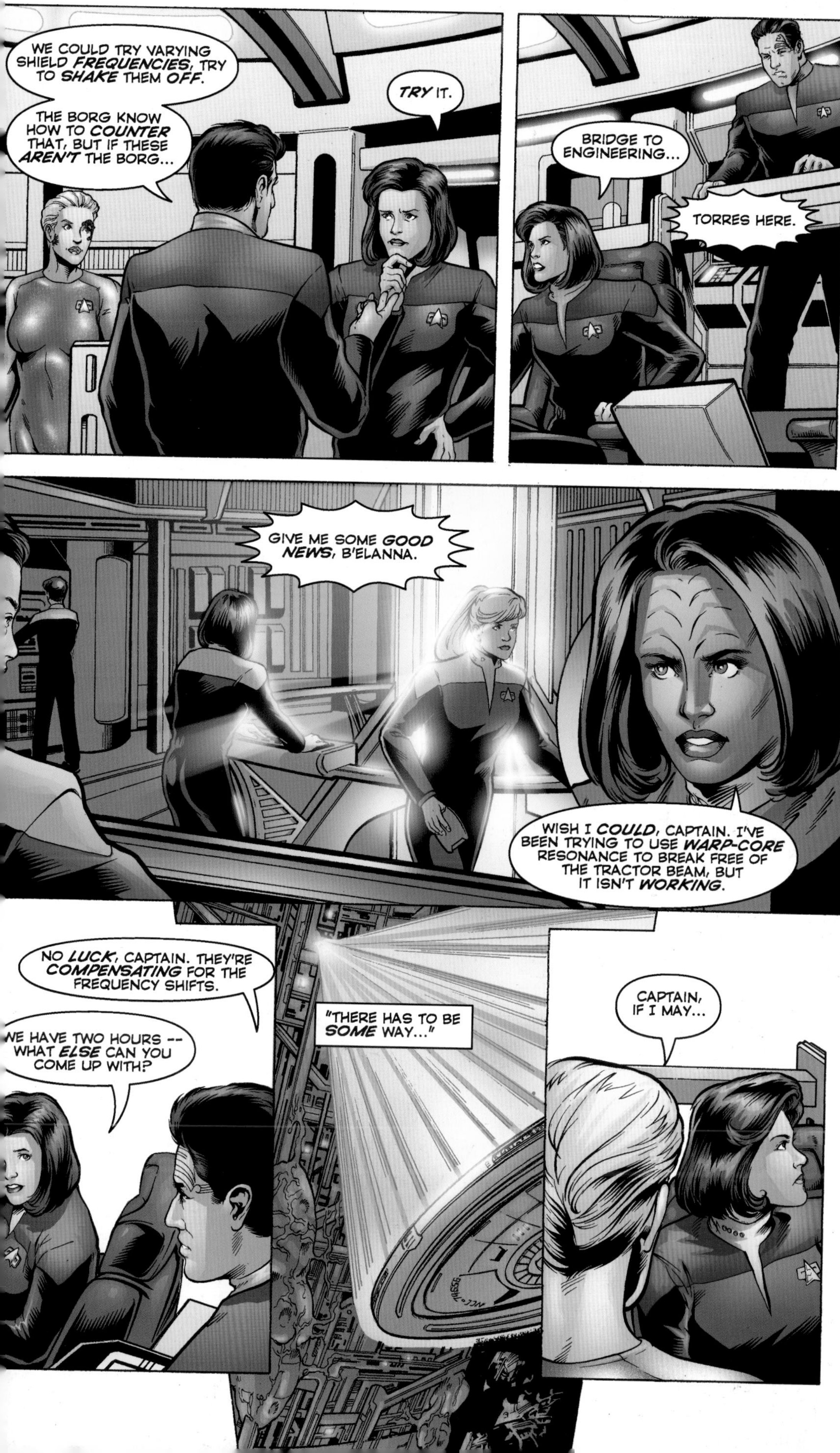

WE COULD TRY VARYING SHIELD FREQUENCIES, TRY TO SHAKE THEM OFF.
THE BORG KNOW HOW TO COUNTER THAT, BUT IF THESE AREN'T THE BORG...
TRY IT.
BRIDGE TO ENGINEERING...
TORRES HERE.
GIVE ME SOME GOOD NEWS, B'ELANNA.
WISH I COULD, CAPTAIN. I'VE BEEN TRYING TO USE WARP-CORE RESONANCE TO BREAK FREE OF THE TRACTOR BEAM, BUT IT ISN'T WORKING.
NO LUCK, CAPTAIN. THEY'RE COMPENSATING FOR THE FREQUENCY SHIFTS.
WE HAVE TWO HOURS -- WHAT ELSE CAN YOU COME UP WITH?
"THERE HAS TO BE SOME WAY..."
CAPTAIN, IF I MAY...

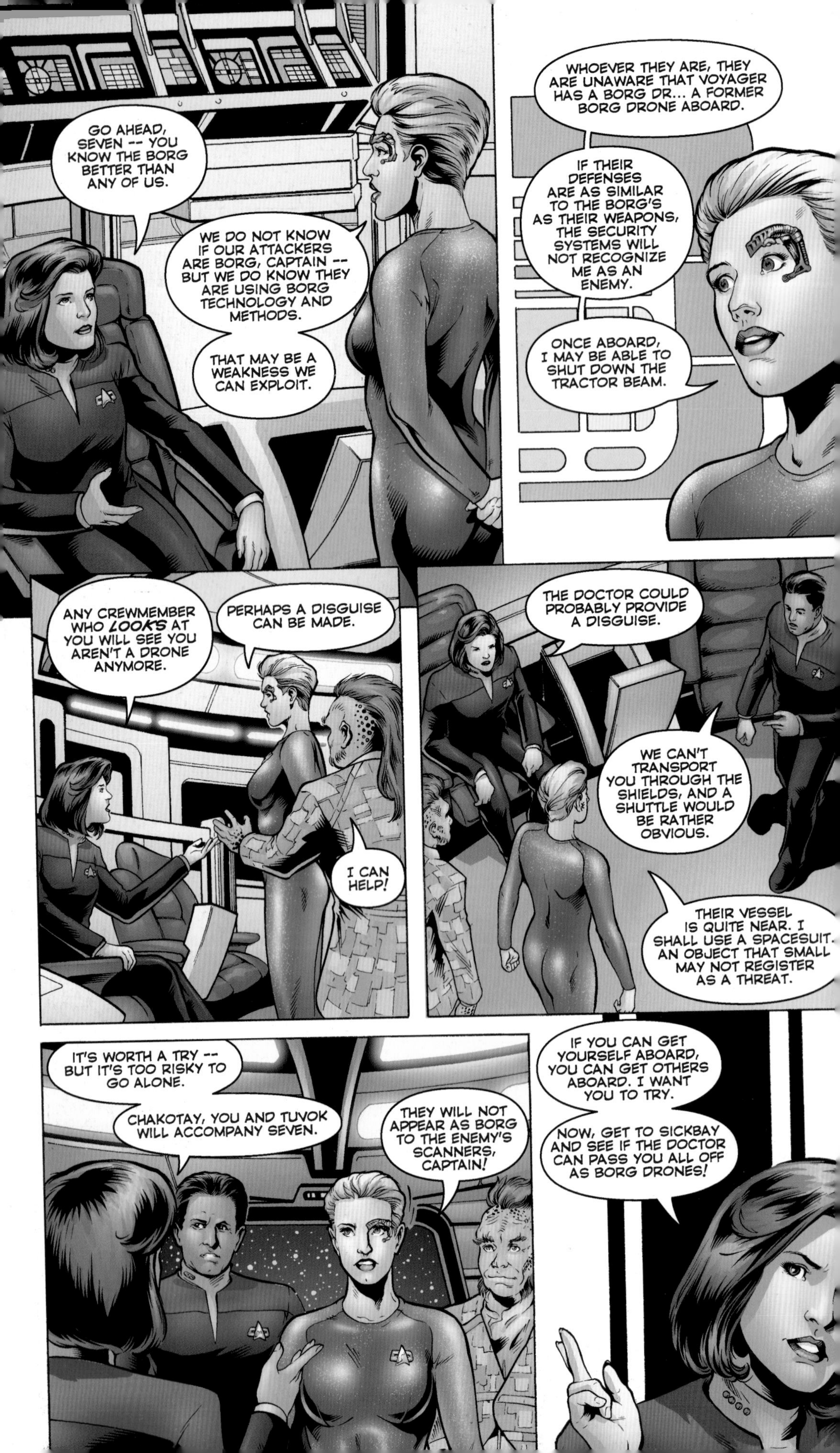
GO AHEAD, SEVEN -- YOU KNOW THE BORG BETTER THAN ANY OF US.
WE DO NOT KNOW IF OUR ATTACKERS ARE BORG, CAPTAIN -- BUT WE DO KNOW THEY ARE USING BORG TECHNOLOGY AND METHODS.
THAT MAY BE A WEAKNESS WE CAN EXPLOIT.
WHOEVER THEY ARE, THEY ARE UNAWARE THAT VOYAGER HAS A BORG DR... A FORMER BORG DRONE ABOARD.
IF THEIR DEFENSES ARE AS SIMILAR TO THE BORG'S AS THEIR WEAPONS, THE SECURITY SYSTEMS WILL NOT RECOGNIZE ME AS AN ENEMY.
ONCE ABOARD, I MAY BE ABLE TO SHUT DOWN THE TRACTOR BEAM.
ANY CREWMEMBER WHO LOOKS AT YOU WILL SEE YOU AREN'T A DRONE ANYMORE.
PERHAPS A DISGUISE CAN BE MADE.
I CAN HELP!
THE DOCTOR COULD PROBABLY PROVIDE A DISGUISE.
WE CAN'T TRANSPORT YOU THROUGH THE SHIELDS, AND A SHUTTLE WOULD BE RATHER OBVIOUS.
THEIR VESSEL IS QUITE NEAR. I SHALL USE A SPACESUIT. AN OBJECT THAT SMALL MAY NOT REGISTER AS A THREAT.
IT'S WORTH A TRY -- BUT IT'S TOO RISKY TO GO ALONE.
CHAKOTAY, YOU AND TUVOK WILL ACCOMPANY SEVEN.
THEY WILL NOT APPEAR AS BORG TO THE ENEMY'S SCANNERS, CAPTAIN!
IF YOU CAN GET YOURSELF ABOARD, YOU CAN GET OTHERS ABOARD. I WANT YOU TO TRY.
NOW, GET TO SICKBAY AND SEE IF THE DOCTOR CAN PASS YOU ALL OFF AS BORG DRONES!

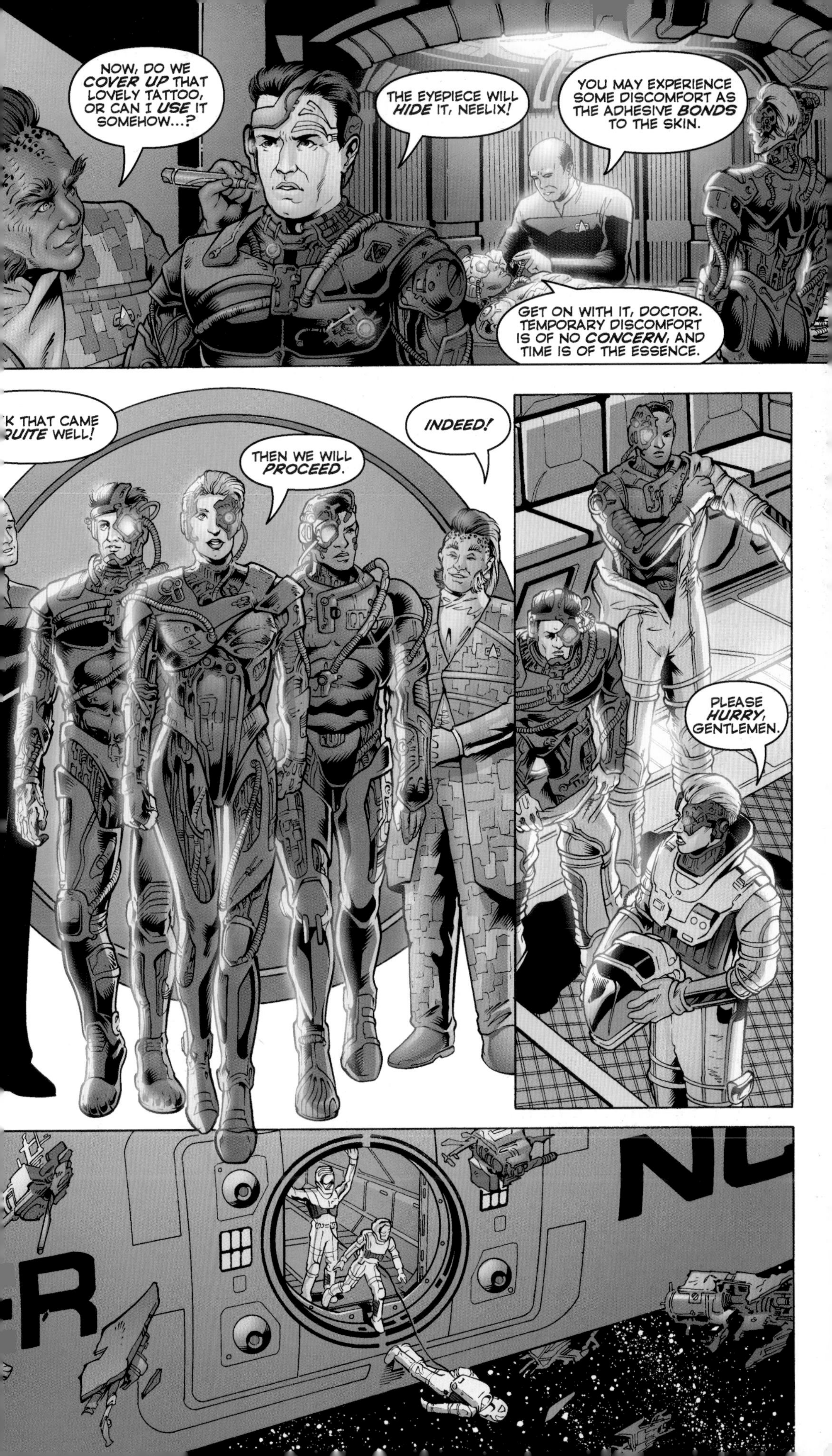

NOW, DO WE COVER UP THAT LOVELY TATTOO, OR CAN I USE IT SOMEHOW...?
THE EYEPIECE WILL HIDE IT, NEELIX!
YOU MAY EXPERIENCE SOME DISCOMFORT AS THE ADHESIVE BONDS TO THE SKIN.
GET ON WITH IT, DOCTOR. TEMPORARY DISCOMFORT IS OF NO CONCERN, AND TIME IS OF THE ESSENCE.
K THAT CAME UITE WELL!
THEN WE WILL PROCEED.
INDEED!
PLEASE HURRY, GENTLEMEN.

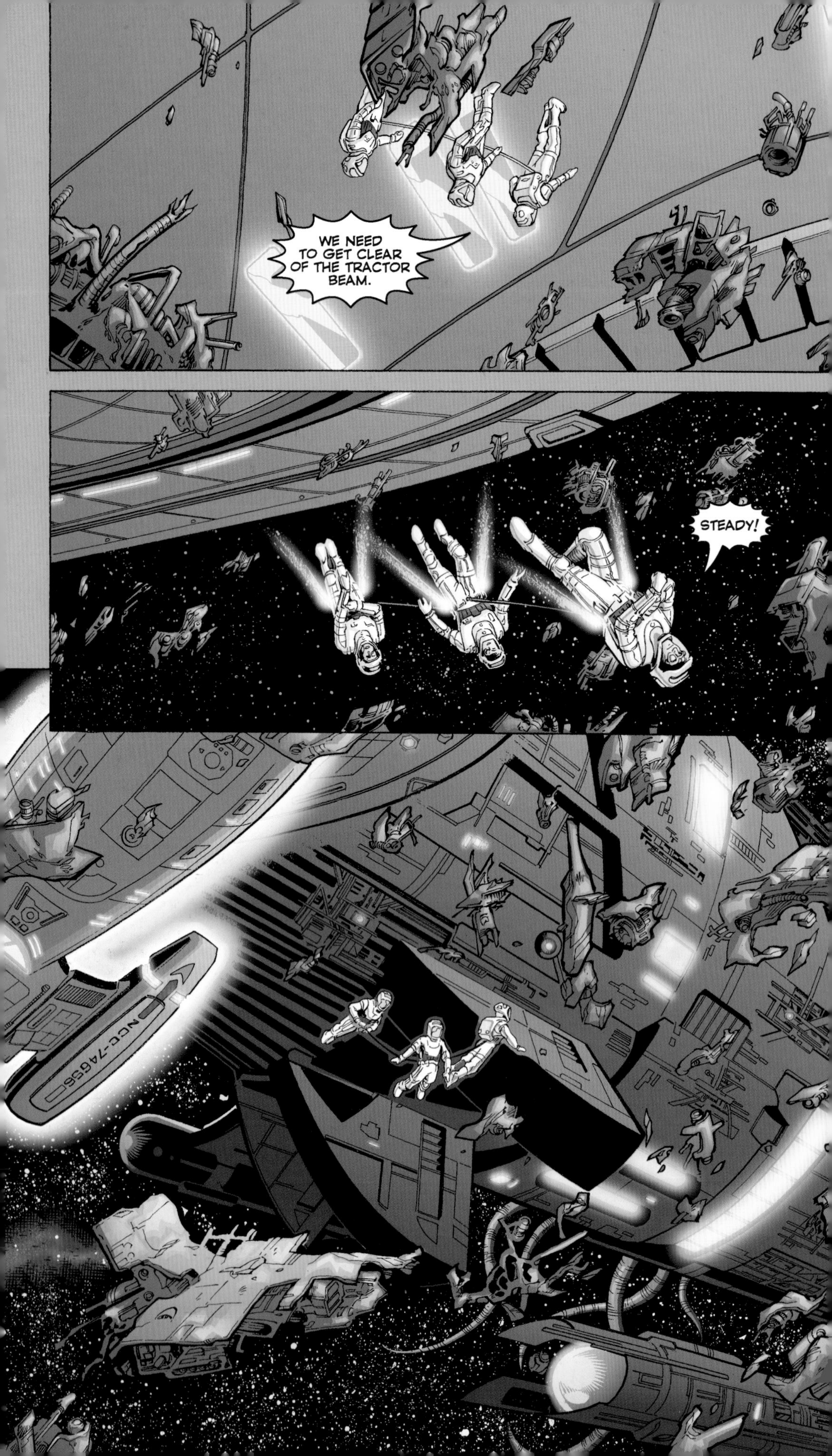
WE NEED TO GET CLEAR OF THE TRACTOR BEAM.
STEADY!
NCC-74656

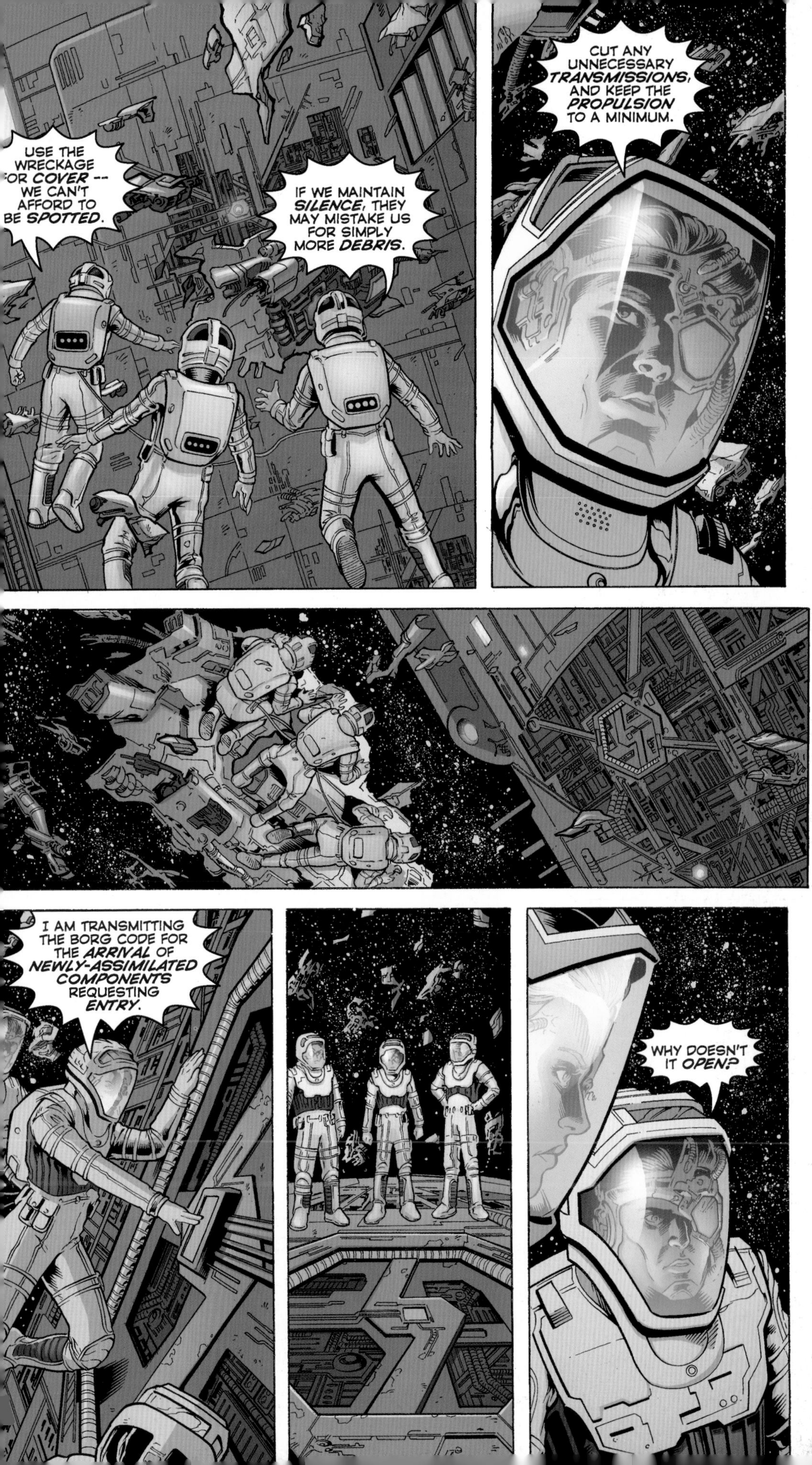
USE THE WRECKAGE FOR COVER -- WE CAN'T AFFORD TO BE SPOTTED.
IF WE MAINTAIN SILENCE, THEY MAY MISTAKE US FOR SIMPLY MORE DEBRIS.
CUT ANY UNNECESSARY TRANSMISSIONS, AND KEEP THE PROPULSION TO A MINIMUM.
I AM TRANSMITTING THE BORG CODE FOR THE ARRIVAL OF NEWLY-ASSIMILATED COMPONENTS REQUESTING ENTRY.
WHY DOESN'T IT OPEN?

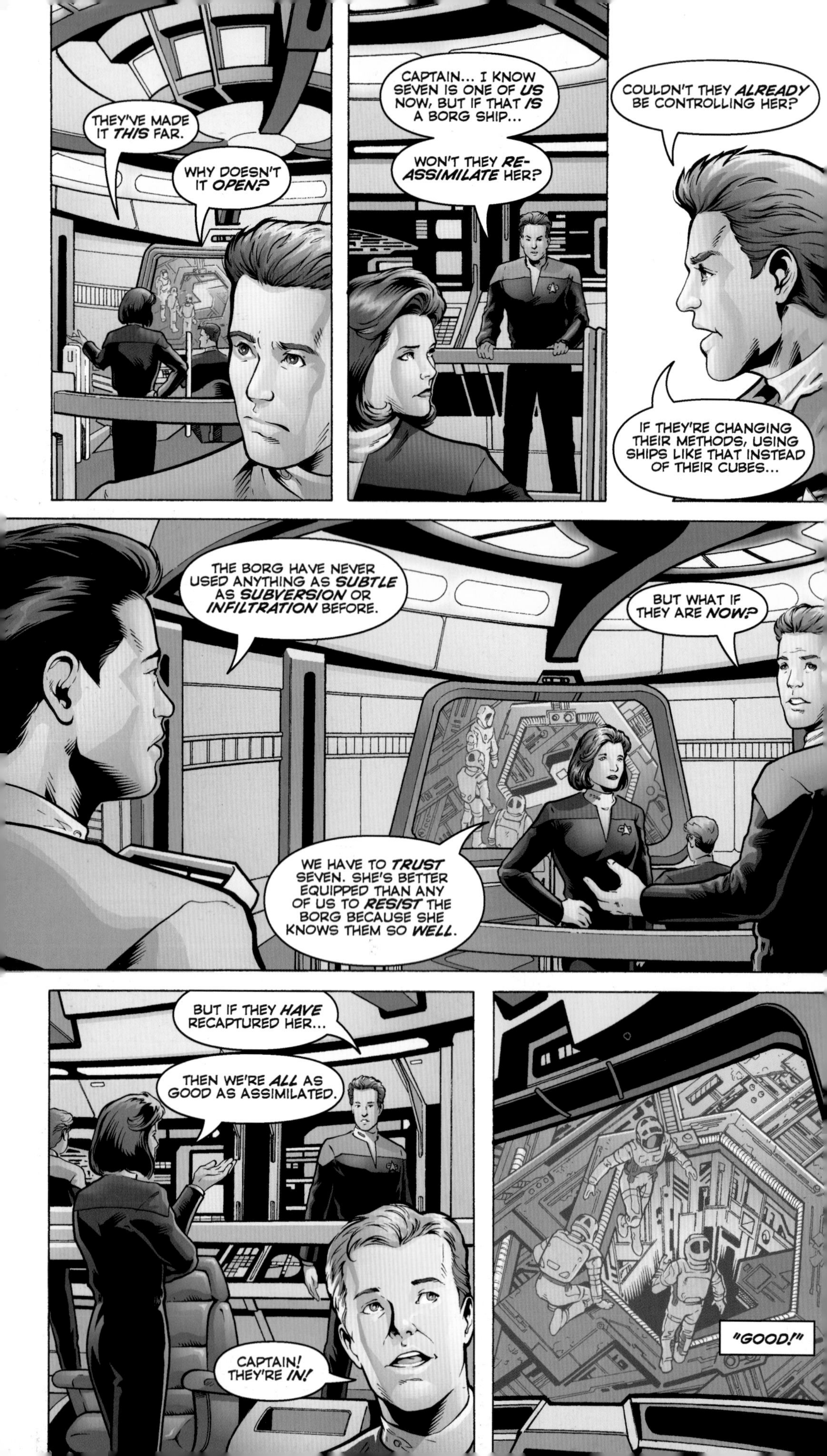

THEY'VE MADE IT THIS FAR.
WHY DOESN'T IT OPEN?
CAPTAIN... I KNOW SEVEN IS ONE OF US NOW, BUT IF THAT IS A BORG SHIP...
WON'T THEY RE-ASSIMILATE HER?
COULDN'T THEY ALREADY BE CONTROLLING HER?
IF THEY'RE CHANGING THEIR METHODS, USING SHIPS LIKE THAT INSTEAD OF THEIR CUBES...
THE BORG HAVE NEVER USED ANYTHING AS SUBTLE AS SUBVERSION OR INFILTRATION BEFORE.
BUT WHAT IF THEY ARE NOW?
WE HAVE TO TRUST SEVEN. SHE'S BETTER EQUIPPED THAN ANY OF US TO RESIST THE BORG BECAUSE SHE KNOWS THEM SO WELL.
BUT IF THEY HAVE RECAPTURED HER...
THEN WE'RE ALL AS GOOD AS ASSIMILATED.
CAPTAIN! THEY'RE IN!
"GOOD!"

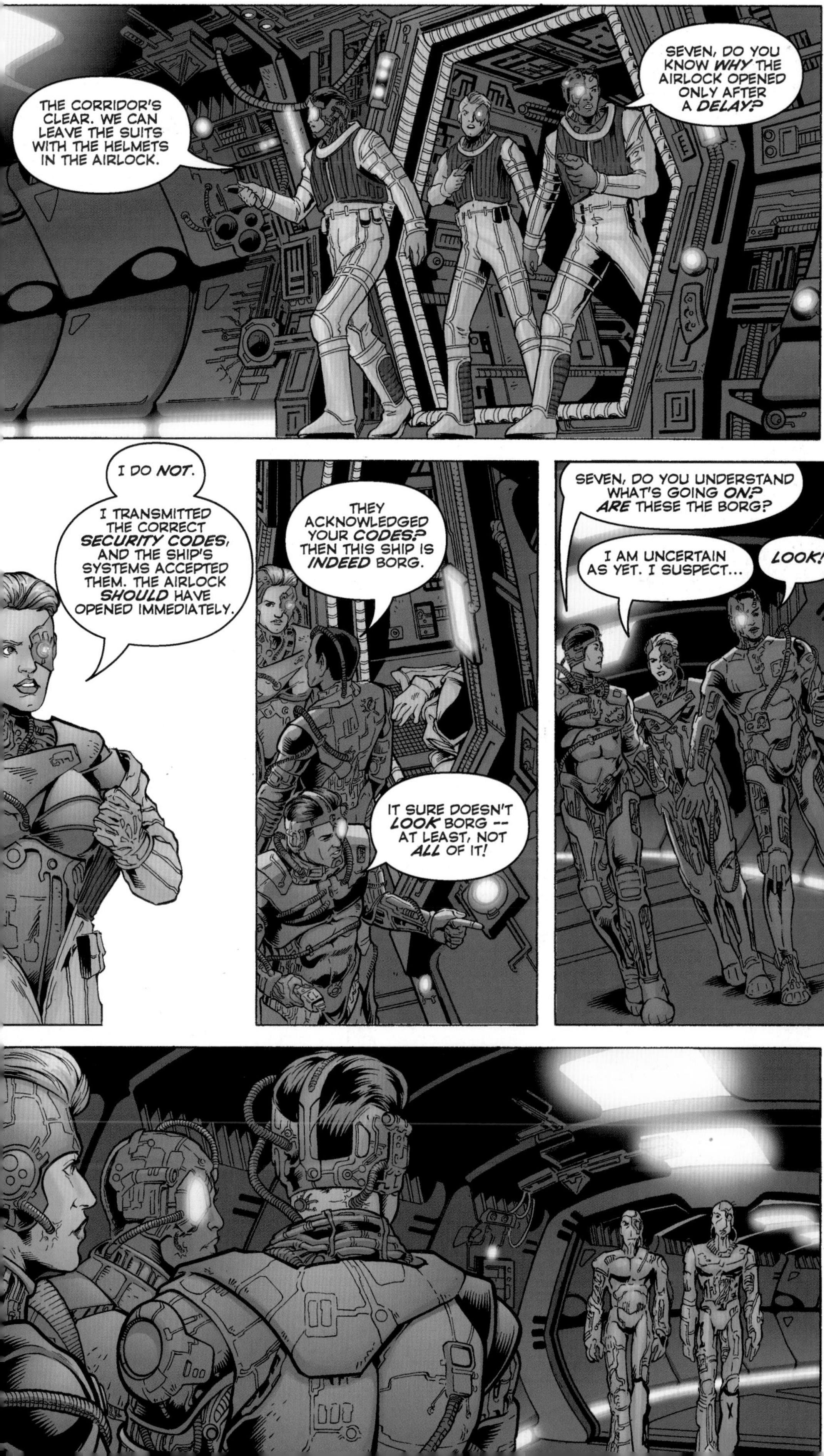
THE CORRIDOR'S CLEAR. WE CAN LEAVE THE SUITS WITH THE HELMETS IN THE AIRLOCK.
SEVEN, DO YOU KNOW WHY THE AIRLOCK OPENED ONLY AFTER A DELAY?
I DO NOT.
I TRANSMITTED THE CORRECT SECURITY CODES, AND THE SHIP'S SYSTEMS ACCEPTED THEM. THE AIRLOCK SHOULD HAVE OPENED IMMEDIATELY.
THEY ACKNOWLEDGED YOUR CODES? THEN THIS SHIP IS INDEED BORG.
IT SURE DOESN'T LOOK BORG -- AT LEAST, NOT ALL OF IT!
SEVEN, DO YOU UNDERSTAND WHAT'S GOING ON? ARE THESE THE BORG?
I AM UNCERTAIN AS YET. I SUSPECT...
LOOK!

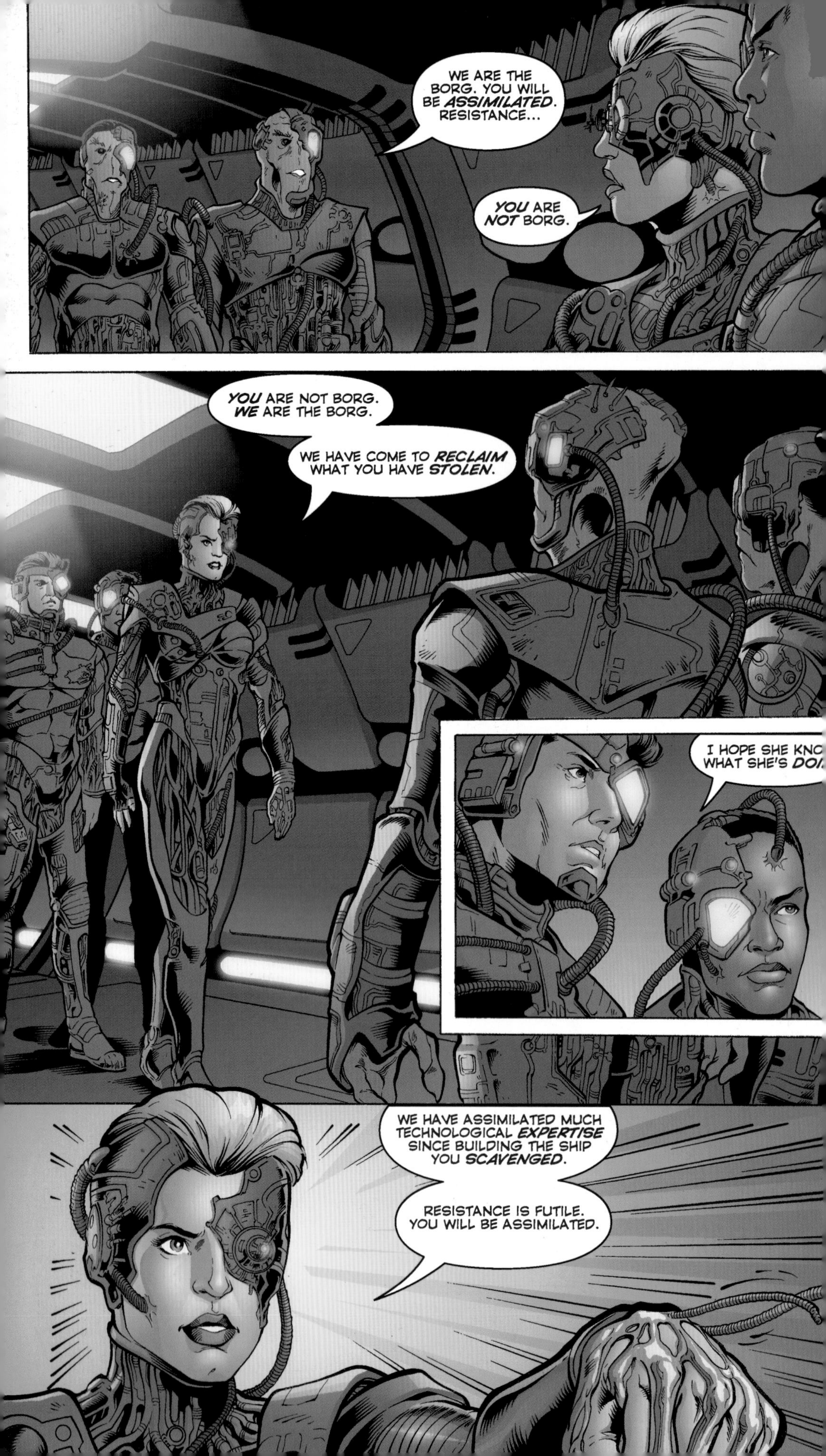
WE ARE THE BORG. YOU WILL BE ASSIMILATED. RESISTANCE...
YOU ARE NOT BORG.
YOU ARE NOT BORG. WE ARE THE BORG.
WE HAVE COME TO RECLAIM WHAT YOU HAVE STOLEN.
I HOPE SHE KNO WHAT SHE'S DOI
WE HAVE ASSIMILATED MUCH TECHNOLOGICAL EXPERTISE SINCE BUILDING THE SHIP YOU SCAVENGED.
RESISTANCE IS FUTILE. YOU WILL BE ASSIMILATED.

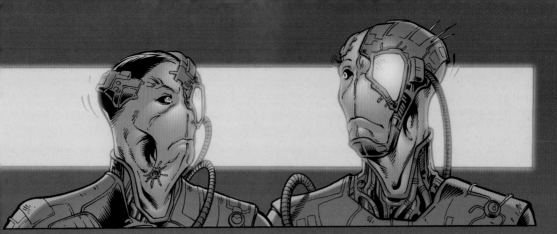

WE SHOULD *PURSUE* THEM...

IF THEY SEAL US OFF HERE...

A *RETREAT* MIGHT BE IN ORDER.

KRUNG!

TOO *LATE.*

SO MUCH FOR *THAT* IDEA.

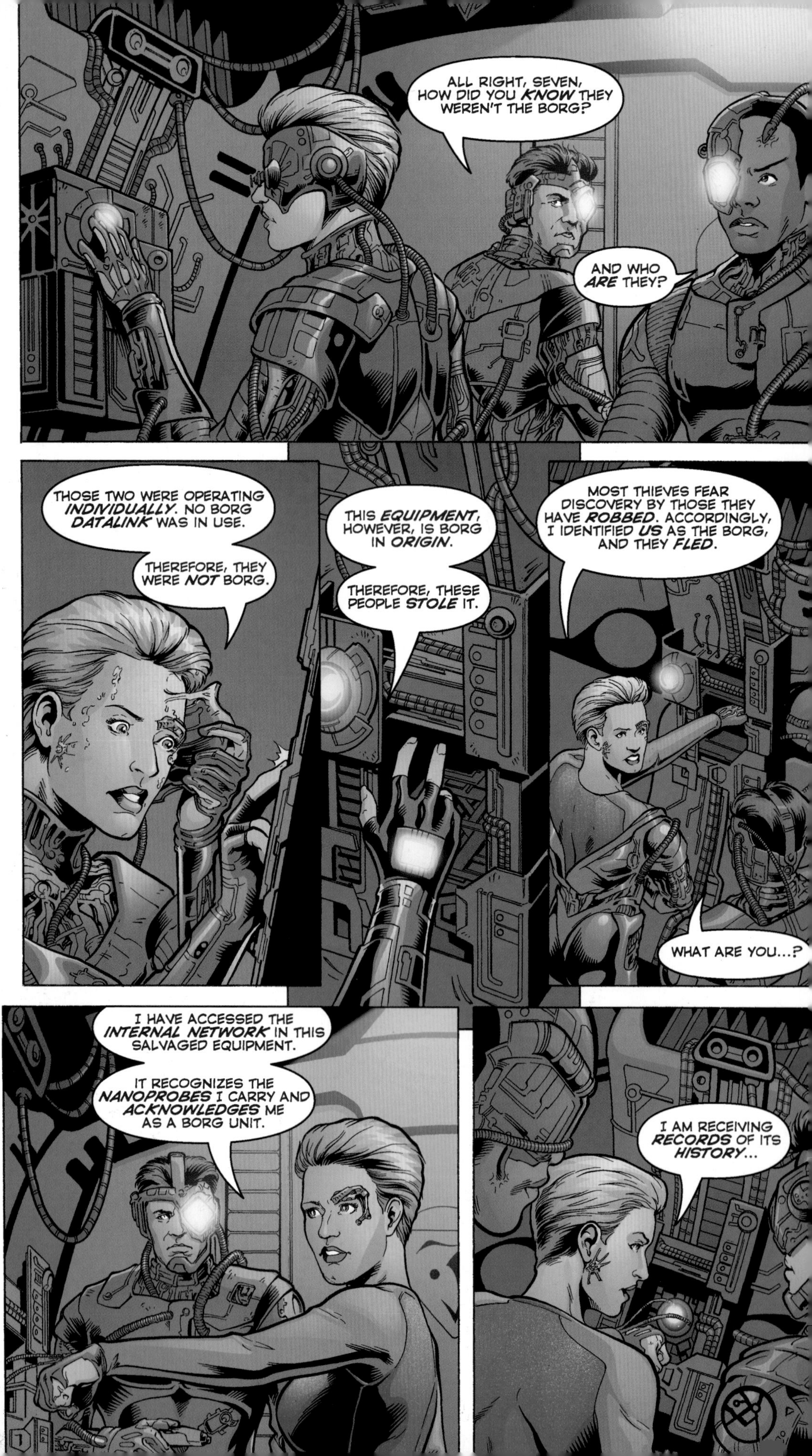
ALL RIGHT, SEVEN, HOW DID YOU KNOW THEY WEREN'T THE BORG?
AND WHO ARE THEY?
THOSE TWO WERE OPERATING INDIVIDUALLY. NO BORG DATALINK WAS IN USE.
THEREFORE, THEY WERE NOT BORG.
THIS EQUIPMENT, HOWEVER, IS BORG IN ORIGIN.
THEREFORE, THESE PEOPLE STOLE IT.
MOST THIEVES FEAR DISCOVERY BY THOSE THEY HAVE ROBBED. ACCORDINGLY, I IDENTIFIED US AS THE BORG, AND THEY FLED.
WHAT ARE YOU...?
I HAVE ACCESSED THE INTERNAL NETWORK IN THIS SALVAGED EQUIPMENT.
IT RECOGNIZES THE NANOPROBES I CARRY AND ACKNOWLEDGES ME AS A BORG UNIT.
I AM RECEIVING RECORDS OF ITS HISTORY...

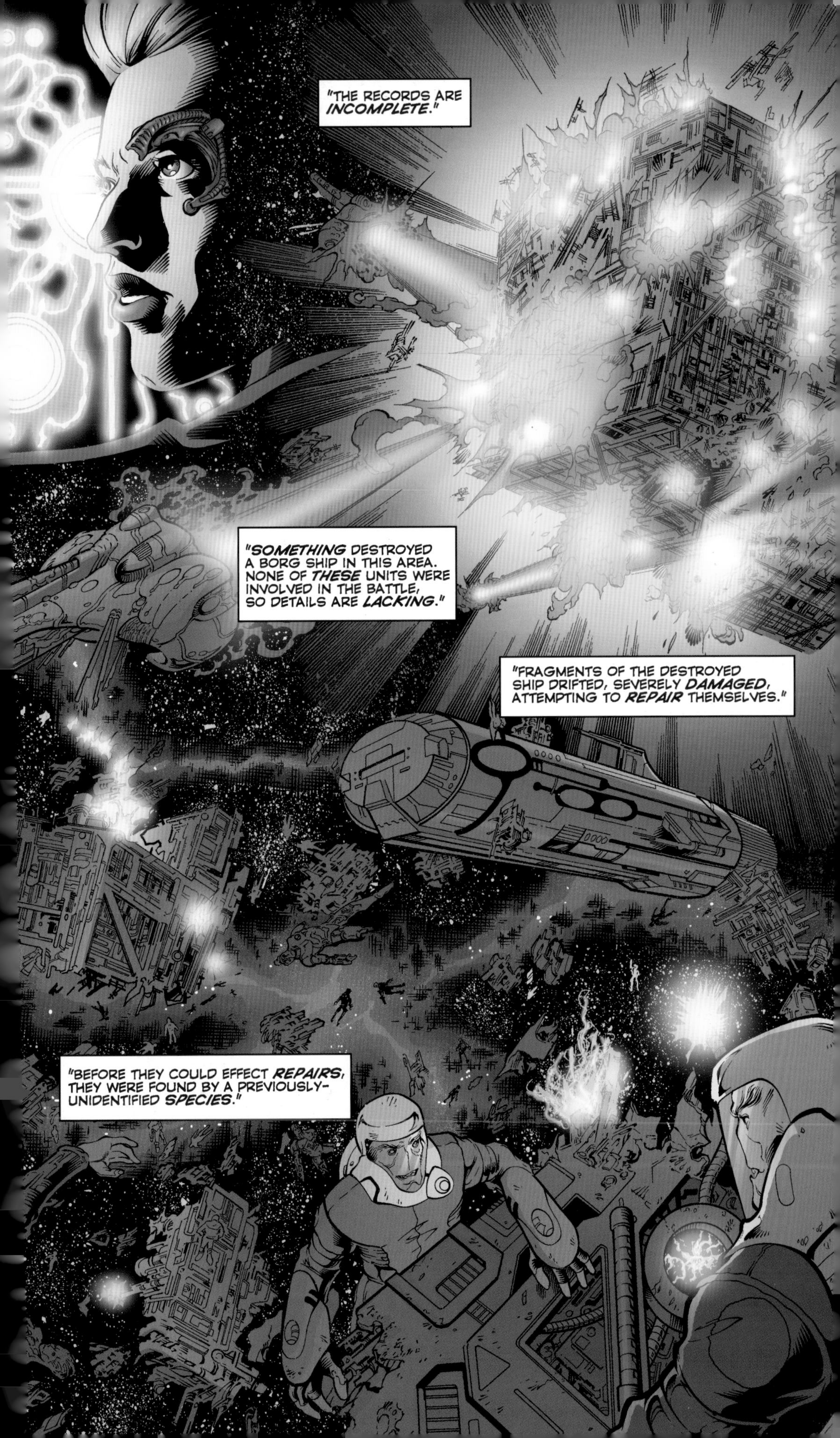
"THE RECORDS ARE INCOMPLETE."
"SOMETHING DESTROYED A BORG SHIP IN THIS AREA. NONE OF THESE UNITS WERE INVOLVED IN THE BATTLE, SO DETAILS ARE LACKING."
"FRAGMENTS OF THE DESTROYED SHIP DRIFTED, SEVERELY DAMAGED, ATTEMPTING TO REPAIR THEMSELVES."
"BEFORE THEY COULD EFFECT REPAIRS, THEY WERE FOUND BY A PREVIOUSLY-UNIDENTIFIED SPECIES."

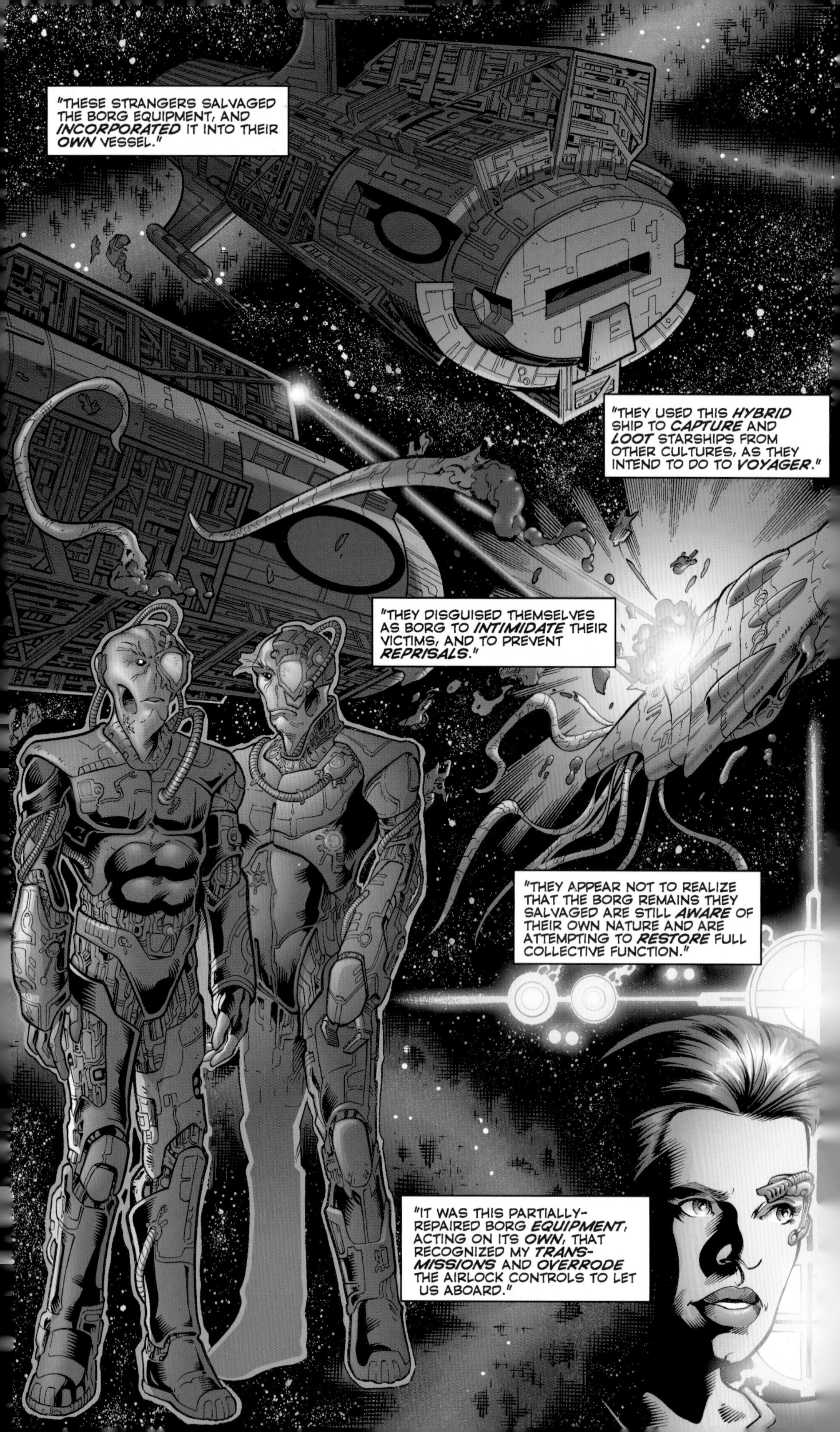
"THESE STRANGERS SALVAGED THE BORG EQUIPMENT, AND INCORPORATED IT INTO THEIR OWN VESSEL."
"THEY USED THIS HYBRID SHIP TO CAPTURE AND LOOT STARSHIPS FROM OTHER CULTURES, AS THEY INTEND TO DO TO VOYAGER."
"THEY DISGUISED THEMSELVES AS BORG TO INTIMIDATE THEIR VICTIMS, AND TO PREVENT REPRISALS."
"THEY APPEAR NOT TO REALIZE THAT THE BORG REMAINS THEY SALVAGED ARE STILL AWARE OF THEIR OWN NATURE AND ARE ATTEMPTING TO RESTORE FULL COLLECTIVE FUNCTION."
"IT WAS THIS PARTIALLY-REPAIRED BORG EQUIPMENT, ACTING ON ITS OWN, THAT RECOGNIZED MY TRANS-MISSIONS AND OVERRODE THE AIRLOCK CONTROLS TO LET US ABOARD."

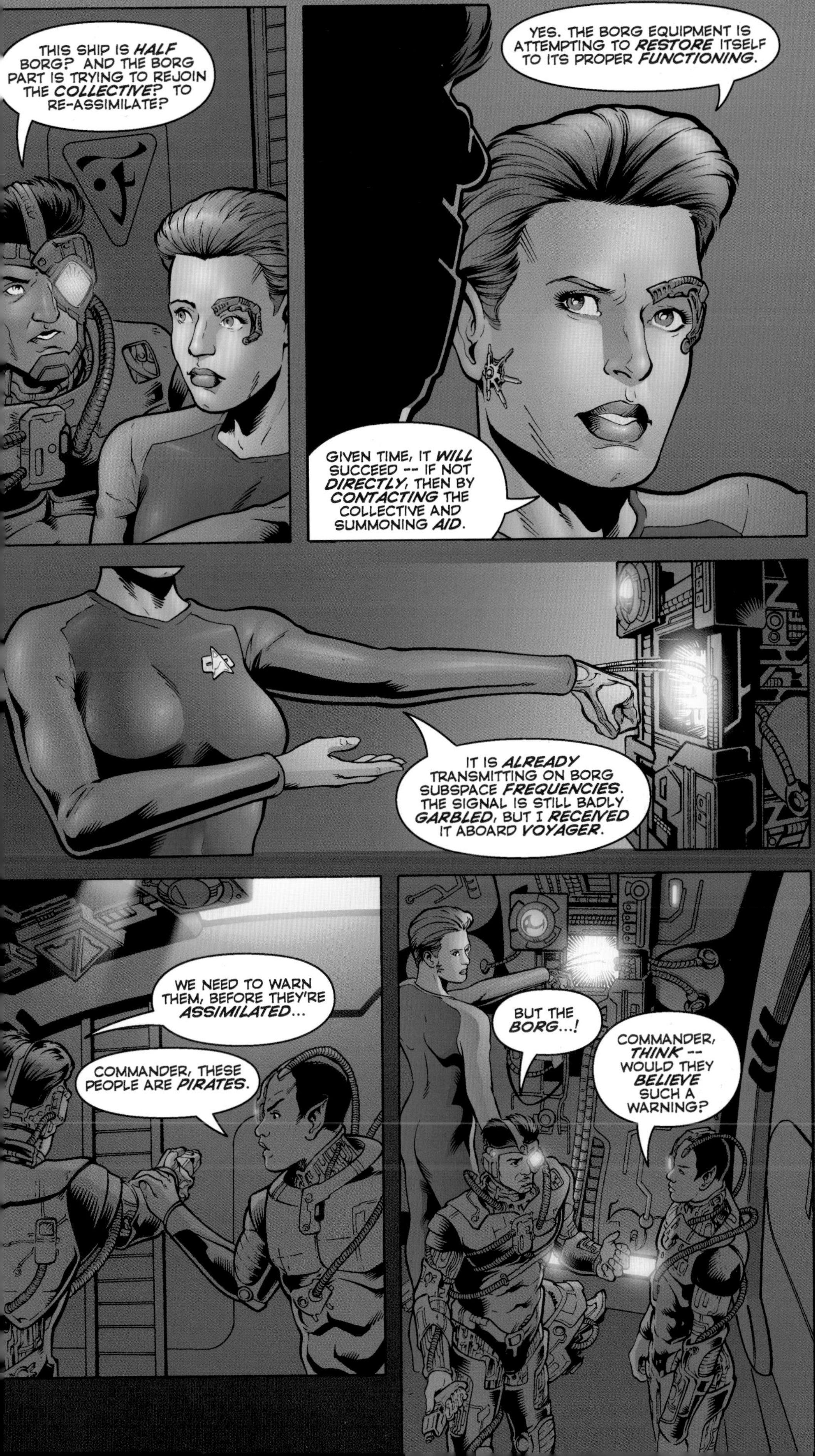
THIS SHIP IS HALF BORG? AND THE BORG PART IS TRYING TO REJOIN THE COLLECTIVE? TO RE-ASSIMILATE?
YES. THE BORG EQUIPMENT IS ATTEMPTING TO RESTORE ITSELF TO ITS PROPER FUNCTIONING.
GIVEN TIME, IT WILL SUCCEED -- IF NOT DIRECTLY, THEN BY CONTACTING THE COLLECTIVE AND SUMMONING AID.
IT IS ALREADY TRANSMITTING ON BORG SUBSPACE FREQUENCIES. THE SIGNAL IS STILL BADLY GARBLED, BUT I RECEIVED IT ABOARD VOYAGER.
WE NEED TO WARN THEM, BEFORE THEY'RE ASSIMILATED...
COMMANDER, THESE PEOPLE ARE PIRATES.
BUT THE BORG...!
COMMANDER, THINK -- WOULD THEY BELIEVE SUCH A WARNING?

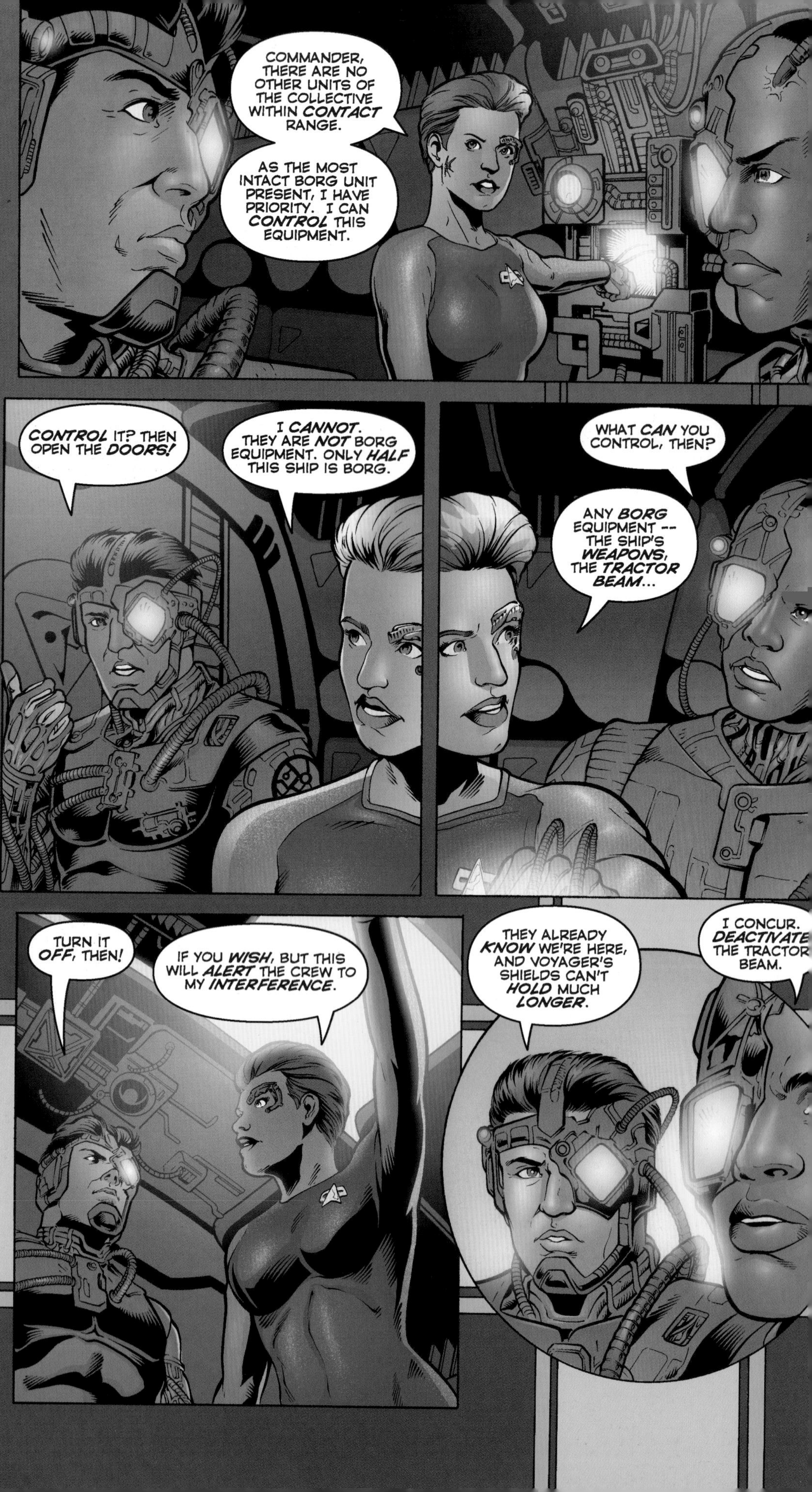
COMMANDER, THERE ARE NO OTHER UNITS OF THE COLLECTIVE WITHIN CONTACT RANGE.
AS THE MOST INTACT BORG UNIT PRESENT, I HAVE PRIORITY. I CAN CONTROL THIS EQUIPMENT.
CONTROL IT? THEN OPEN THE DOORS!
I CANNOT. THEY ARE NOT BORG EQUIPMENT. ONLY HALF THIS SHIP IS BORG.
WHAT CAN YOU CONTROL, THEN?
ANY BORG EQUIPMENT -- THE SHIP'S WEAPONS, THE TRACTOR BEAM...
TURN IT OFF, THEN!
IF YOU WISH, BUT THIS WILL ALERT THE CREW TO MY INTERFERENCE.
THEY ALREADY KNOW WE'RE HERE, AND VOYAGER'S SHIELDS CAN'T HOLD MUCH LONGER.
I CONCUR. DEACTIVATE THE TRACTOR BEAM.

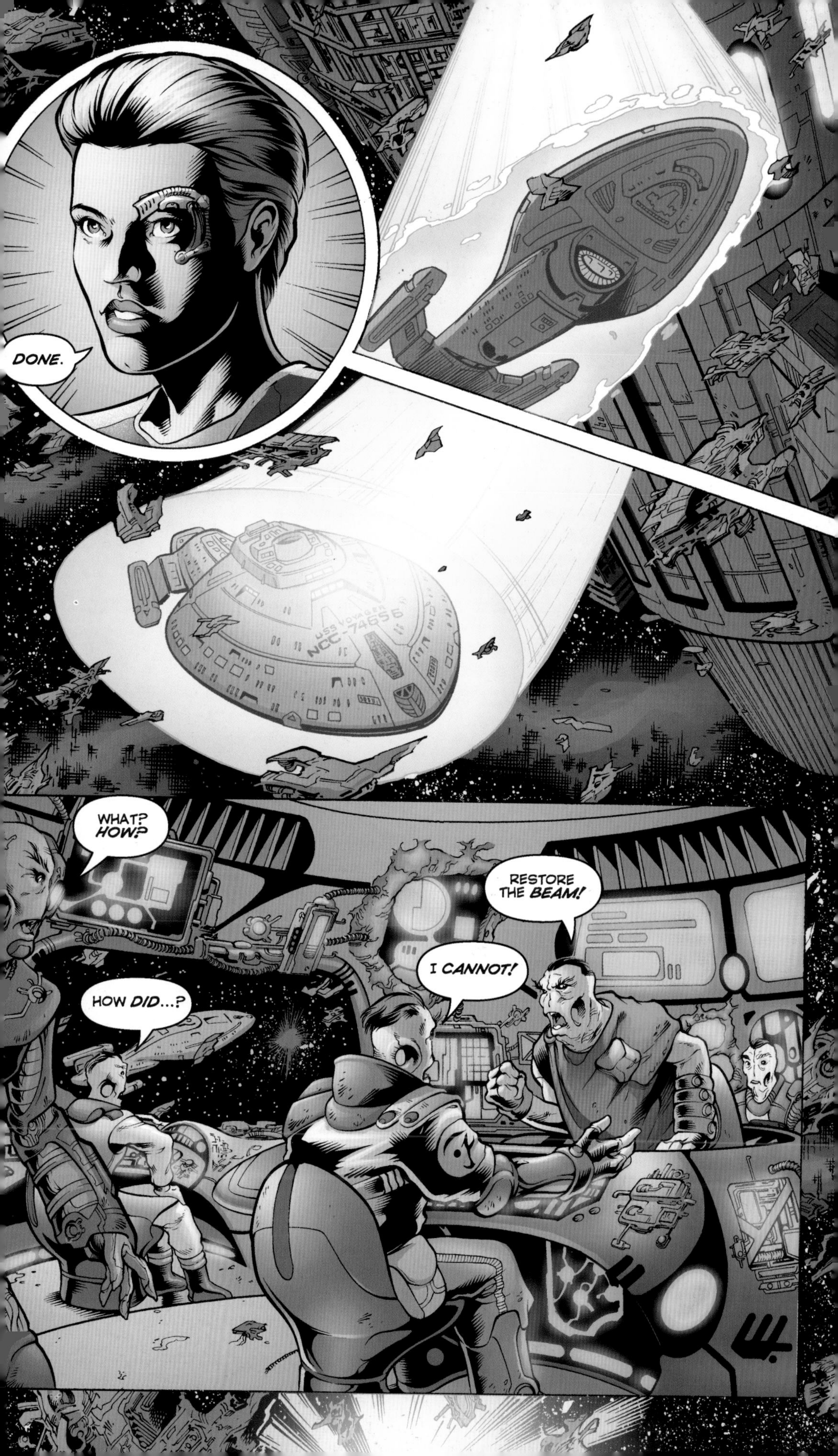
DONE.
USS VOYAGER
NCC-74656
WHAT? HOW?
RESTORE THE BEAM!
I CANNOT!
HOW DID...?

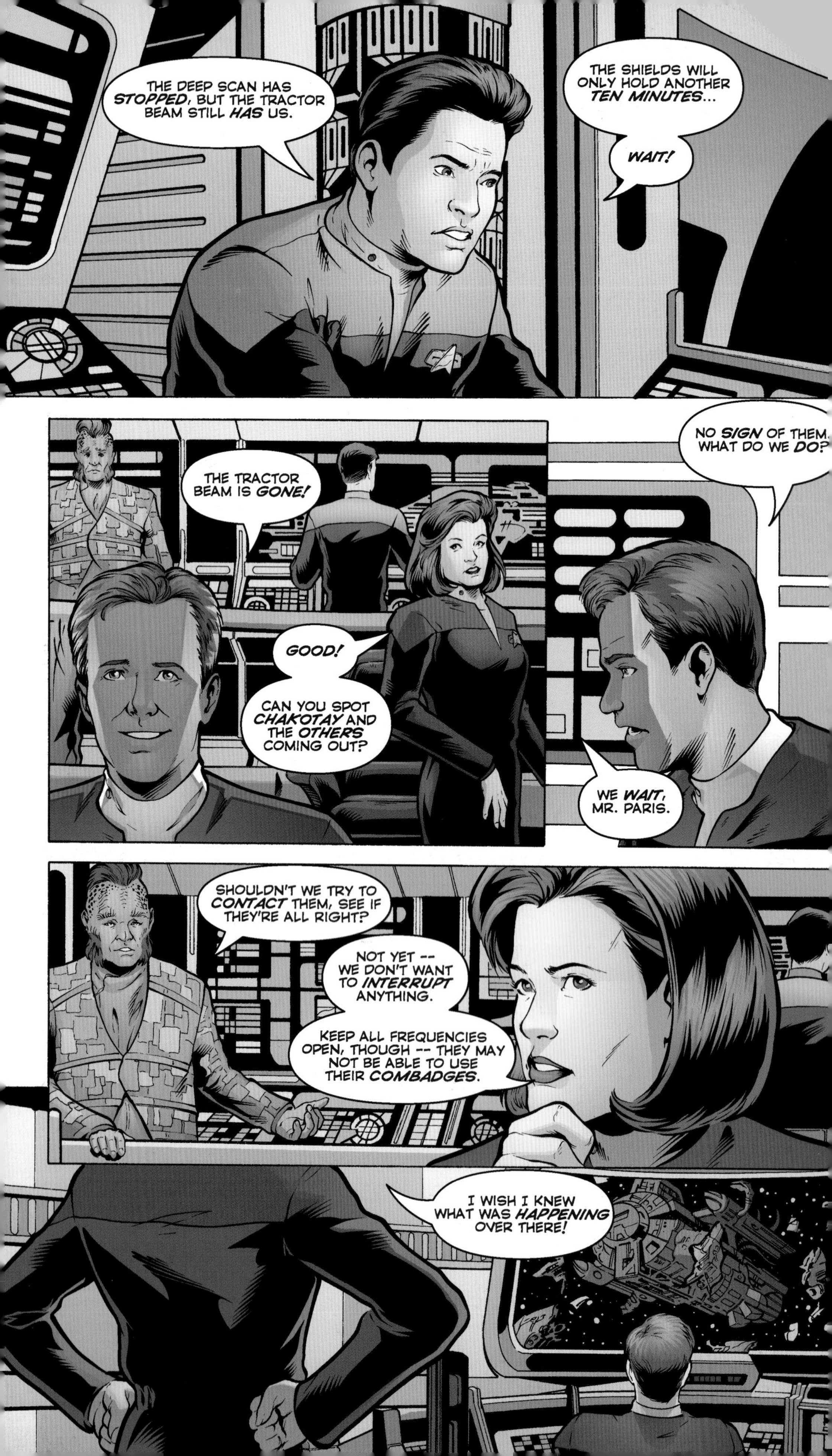
THE DEEP SCAN HAS STOPPED, BUT THE TRACTOR BEAM STILL HAS US.
THE SHIELDS WILL ONLY HOLD ANOTHER TEN MINUTES...
WAIT!
THE TRACTOR BEAM IS GONE!
GOOD!
CAN YOU SPOT CHAKOTAY AND THE OTHERS COMING OUT?
NO SIGN OF THEM. WHAT DO WE DO?
WE WAIT, MR. PARIS.
SHOULDN'T WE TRY TO CONTACT THEM, SEE IF THEY'RE ALL RIGHT?
NOT YET -- WE DON'T WANT TO INTERRUPT ANYTHING.
KEEP ALL FREQUENCIES OPEN, THOUGH -- THEY MAY NOT BE ABLE TO USE THEIR COMBADGES.
I WISH I KNEW WHAT WAS HAPPENING OVER THERE!

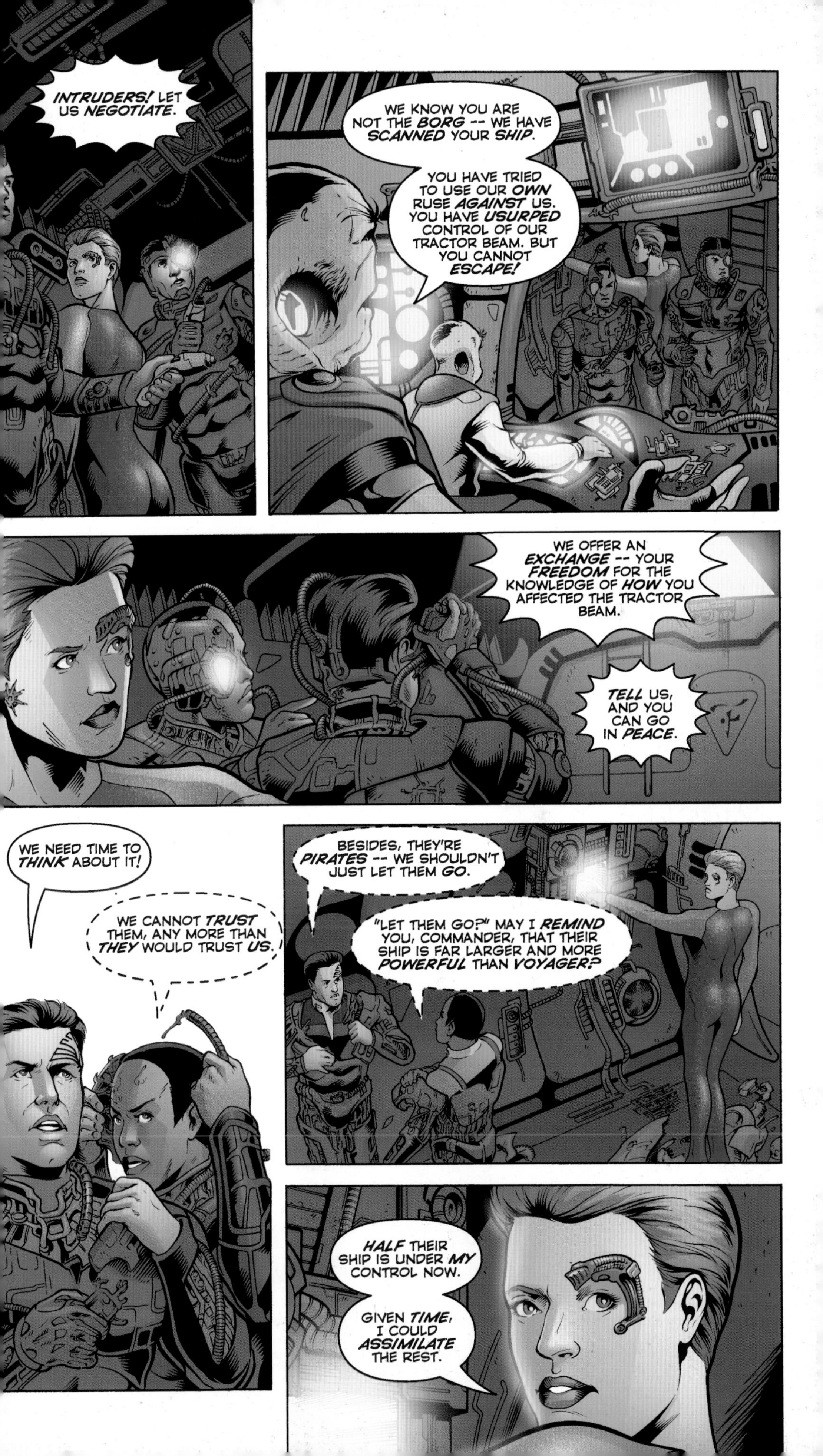
INTRUDERS! LET US NEGOTIATE.
WE KNOW YOU ARE NOT THE BORG -- WE HAVE SCANNED YOUR SHIP.
YOU HAVE TRIED TO USE OUR OWN RUSE AGAINST US. YOU HAVE USURPED CONTROL OF OUR TRACTOR BEAM. BUT YOU CANNOT ESCAPE!
WE OFFER AN EXCHANGE -- YOUR FREEDOM FOR THE KNOWLEDGE OF HOW YOU AFFECTED THE TRACTOR BEAM.
TELL US, AND YOU CAN GO IN PEACE.
WE NEED TIME TO THINK ABOUT IT!
WE CANNOT TRUST THEM, ANY MORE THAN THEY WOULD TRUST US.
BESIDES, THEY'RE PIRATES -- WE SHOULDN'T JUST LET THEM GO.
"LET THEM GO?" MAY I REMIND YOU, COMMANDER, THAT THEIR SHIP IS FAR LARGER AND MORE POWERFUL THAN VOYAGER?
HALF THEIR SHIP IS UNDER MY CONTROL NOW.
GIVEN TIME, I COULD ASSIMILATE THE REST.

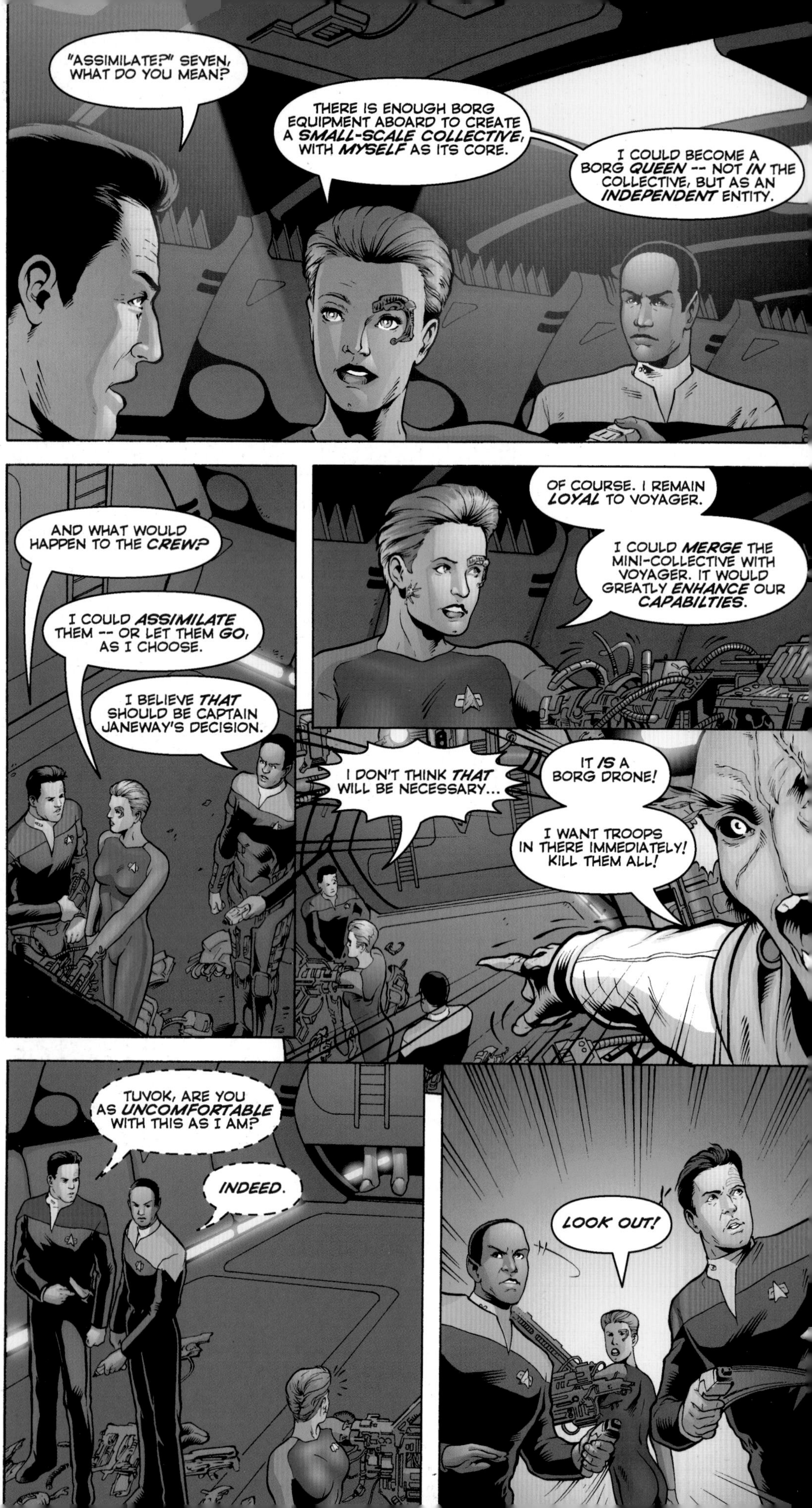
"ASSIMILATE?" SEVEN, WHAT DO YOU MEAN?
THERE IS ENOUGH BORG EQUIPMENT ABOARD TO CREATE A *SMALL-SCALE COLLECTIVE*, WITH *MYSELF* AS ITS CORE.
I COULD BECOME A BORG *QUEEN* -- NOT *IN* THE COLLECTIVE, BUT AS AN *INDEPENDENT* ENTITY.
AND WHAT WOULD HAPPEN TO THE *CREW?*
I COULD *ASSIMILATE* THEM -- OR LET THEM *GO*, AS I CHOOSE.
I BELIEVE *THAT* SHOULD BE CAPTAIN JANEWAY'S DECISION.
OF COURSE. I REMAIN *LOYAL* TO VOYAGER.
I COULD *MERGE* THE MINI-COLLECTIVE WITH VOYAGER. IT WOULD GREATLY *ENHANCE* OUR *CAPABILTIES*.
I DON'T THINK *THAT* WILL BE NECESSARY...
IT *IS* A BORG DRONE!
I WANT TROOPS IN THERE IMMEDIATELY! KILL THEM ALL!
TUVOK, ARE YOU AS *UNCOMFORTABLE* WITH THIS AS I AM?
INDEED.
LOOK OUT!

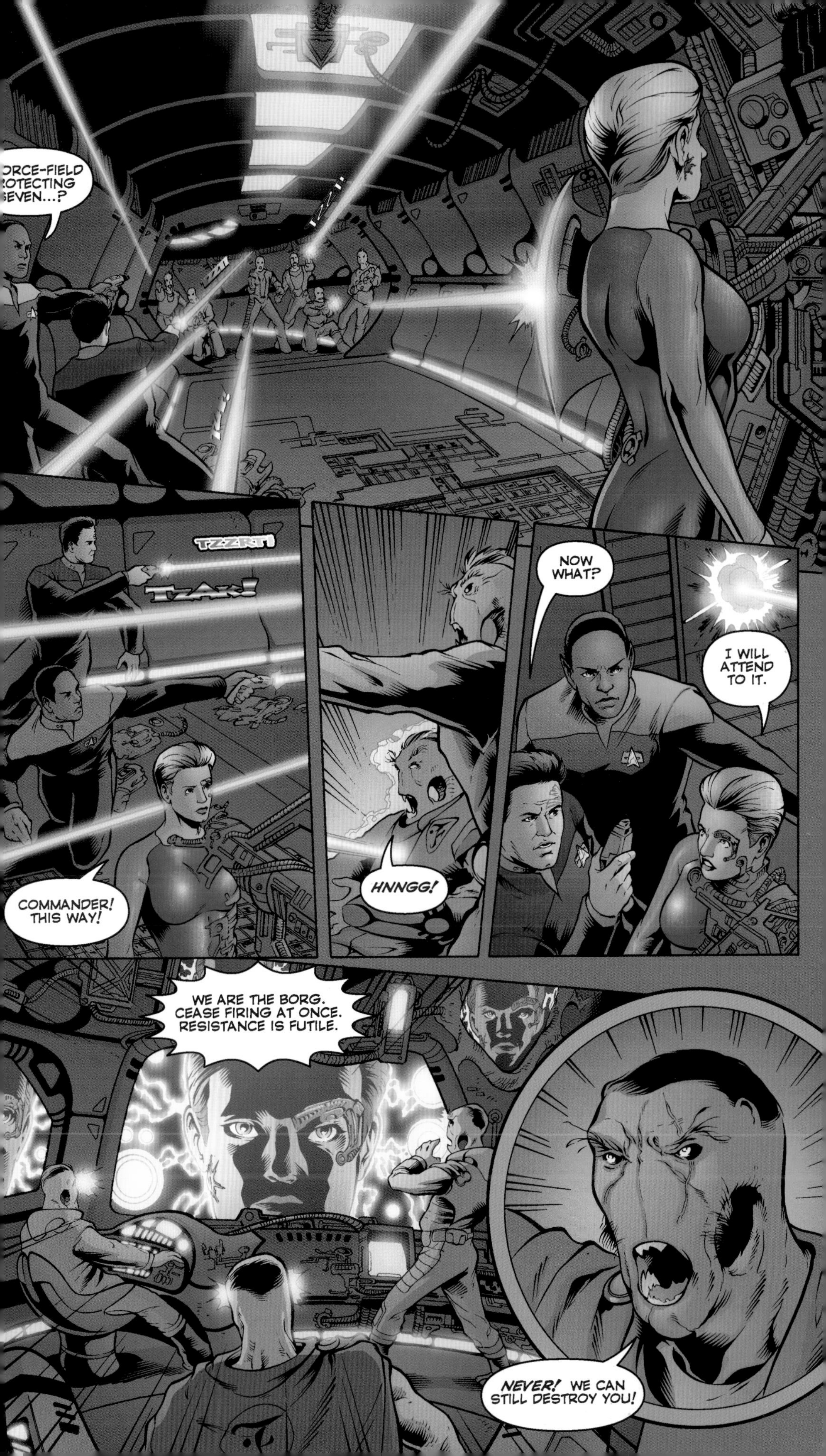
ORCE-FIELD
ROTECTING
SEVEN...?
TZAK!
TZZRT!
TZAK!
NOW
WHAT?
I WILL
ATTEND
TO IT.
COMMANDER!
THIS WAY!
HNNGG!
WE ARE THE BORG.
CEASE FIRING AT ONCE.
RESISTANCE IS FUTILE.
NEVER! WE CAN
STILL DESTROY YOU!

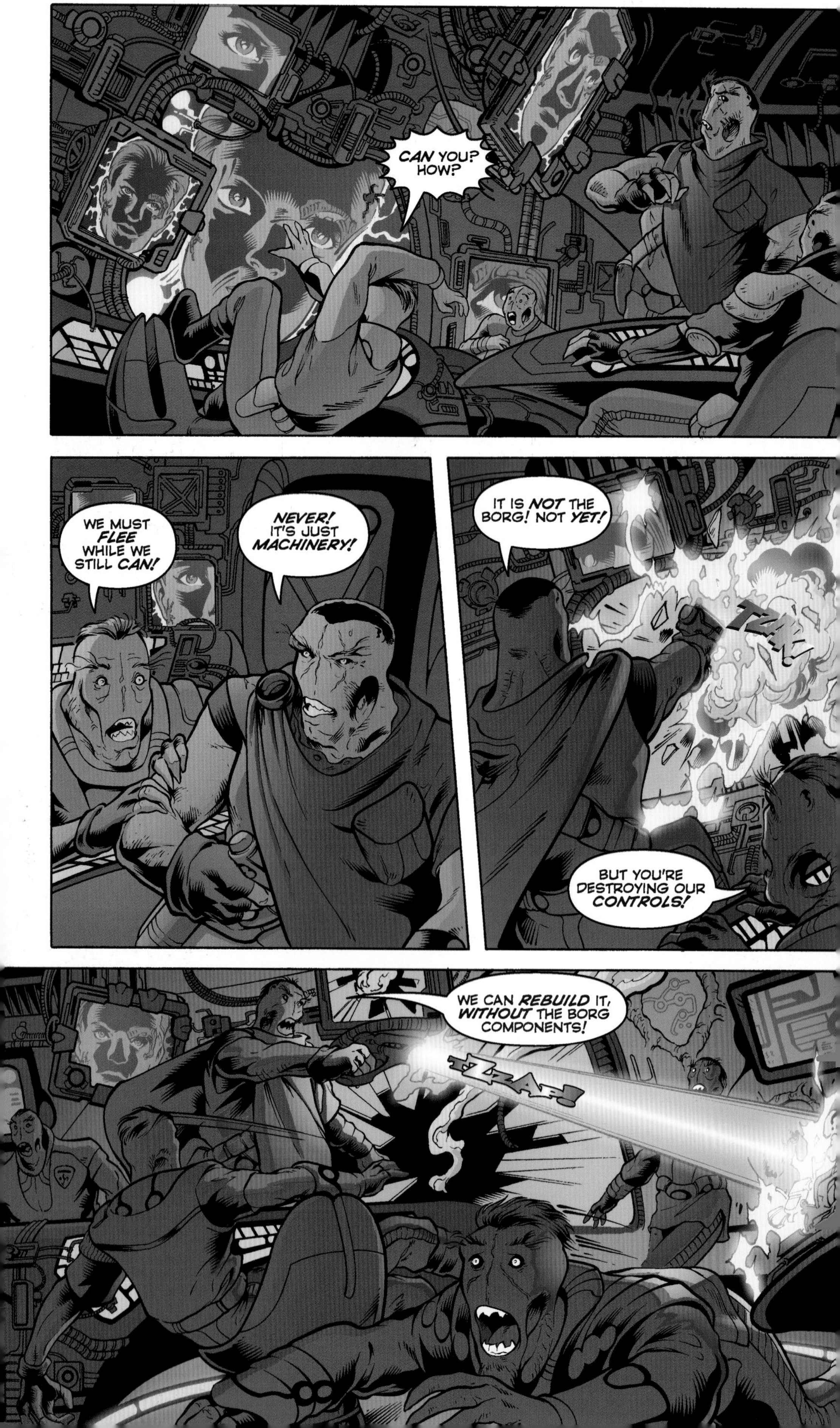
CAN YOU? HOW?
WE MUST FLEE WHILE WE STILL CAN!
NEVER! IT'S JUST MACHINERY!
IT IS NOT THE BORG! NOT YET!
TZAK!
BUT YOU'RE DESTROYING OUR CONTROLS!
WE CAN REBUILD IT, WITHOUT THE BORG COMPONENTS!
TZZAK!

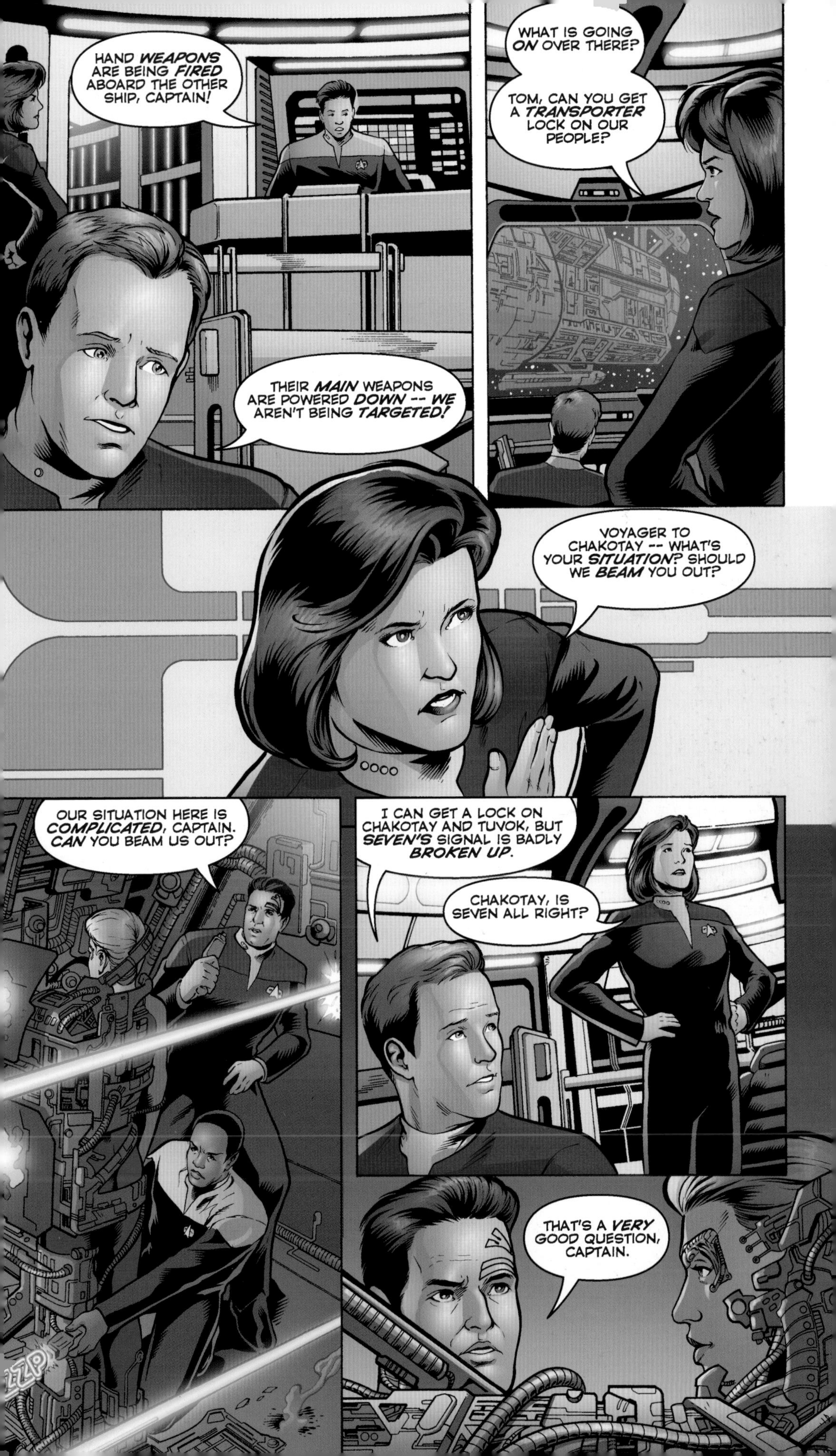
HAND WEAPONS ARE BEING FIRED ABOARD THE OTHER SHIP, CAPTAIN!
THEIR MAIN WEAPONS ARE POWERED DOWN -- WE AREN'T BEING TARGETED!
WHAT IS GOING ON OVER THERE?
TOM, CAN YOU GET A TRANSPORTER LOCK ON OUR PEOPLE?
VOYAGER TO CHAKOTAY -- WHAT'S YOUR SITUATION? SHOULD WE BEAM YOU OUT?
OUR SITUATION HERE IS COMPLICATED, CAPTAIN. CAN YOU BEAM US OUT?
ZZP
I CAN GET A LOCK ON CHAKOTAY AND TUVOK, BUT SEVEN'S SIGNAL IS BADLY BROKEN UP.
CHAKOTAY, IS SEVEN ALL RIGHT?
THAT'S A VERY GOOD QUESTION, CAPTAIN.

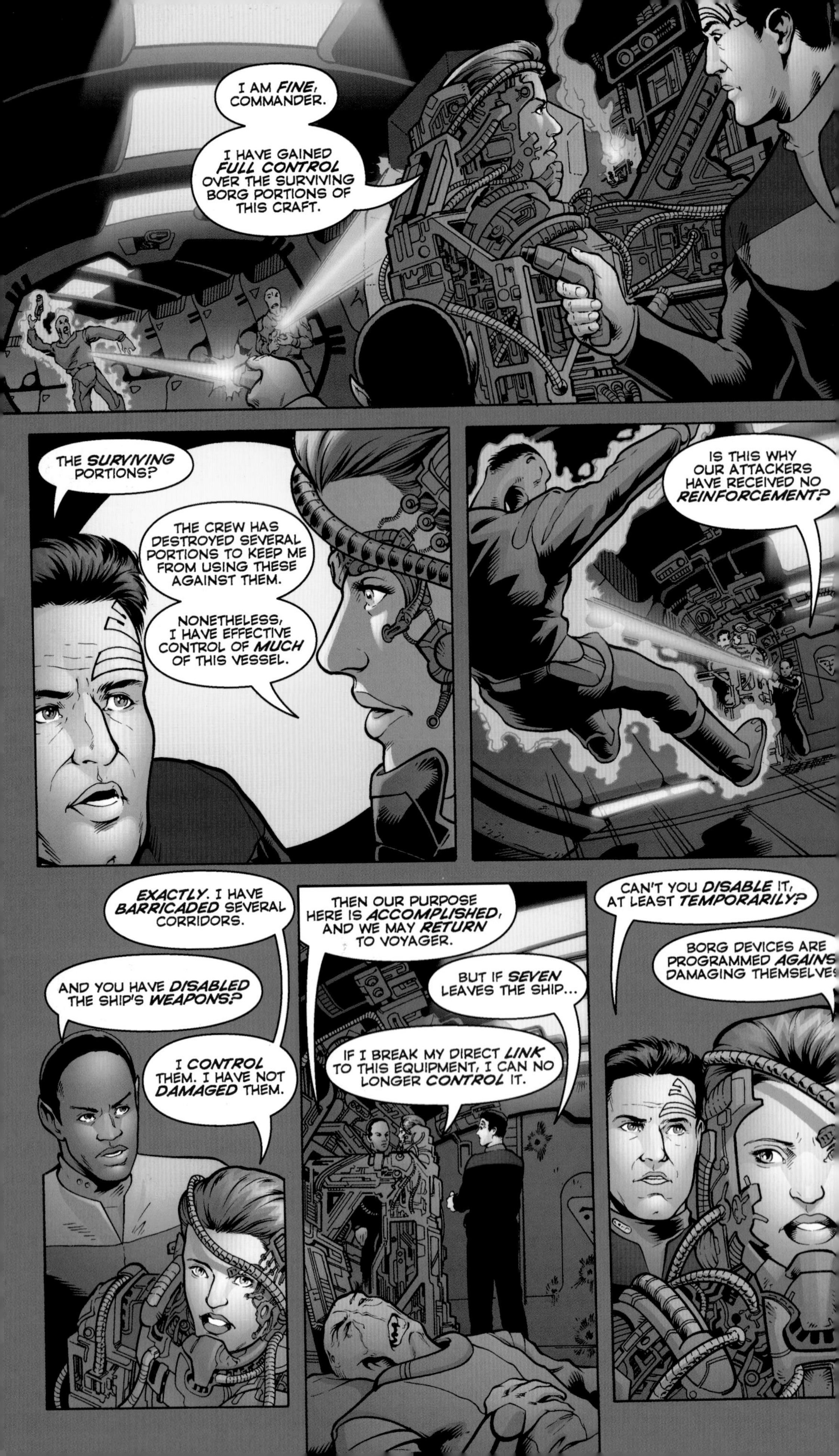
I AM FINE, COMMANDER.
I HAVE GAINED FULL CONTROL OVER THE SURVIVING BORG PORTIONS OF THIS CRAFT.
THE SURVIVING PORTIONS?
THE CREW HAS DESTROYED SEVERAL PORTIONS TO KEEP ME FROM USING THESE AGAINST THEM.
NONETHELESS, I HAVE EFFECTIVE CONTROL OF MUCH OF THIS VESSEL.
IS THIS WHY OUR ATTACKERS HAVE RECEIVED NO REINFORCEMENT?
EXACTLY. I HAVE BARRICADED SEVERAL CORRIDORS.
AND YOU HAVE DISABLED THE SHIP'S WEAPONS?
I CONTROL THEM. I HAVE NOT DAMAGED THEM.
THEN OUR PURPOSE HERE IS ACCOMPLISHED, AND WE MAY RETURN TO VOYAGER.
BUT IF SEVEN LEAVES THE SHIP...
IF I BREAK MY DIRECT LINK TO THIS EQUIPMENT, I CAN NO LONGER CONTROL IT.
CAN'T YOU DISABLE IT, AT LEAST TEMPORARILY?
BORG DEVICES ARE PROGRAMMED AGAINS DAMAGING THEMSELVE

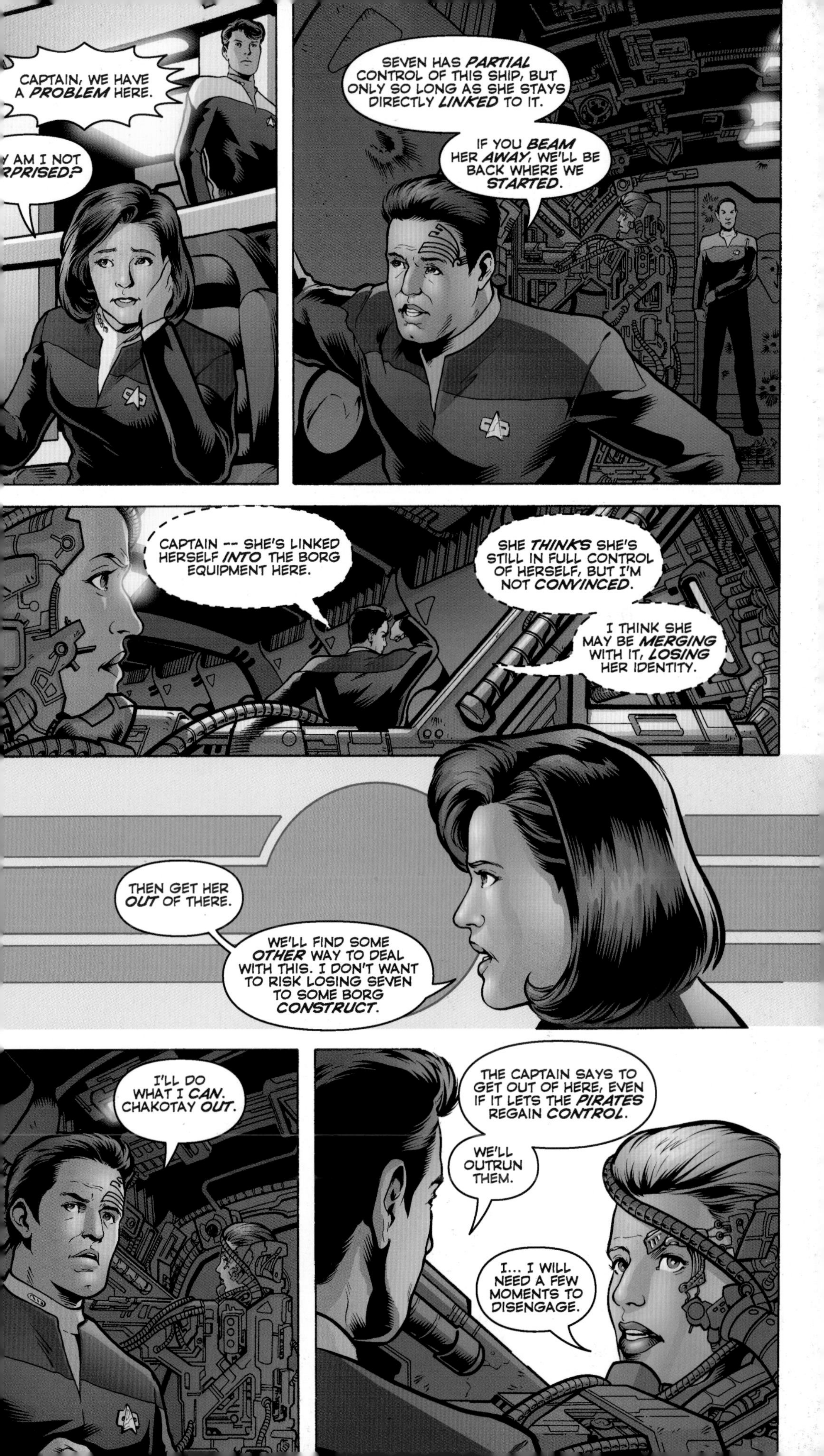

CAPTAIN, WE HAVE A PROBLEM HERE.
Y AM I NOT RPRISED?
SEVEN HAS PARTIAL CONTROL OF THIS SHIP, BUT ONLY SO LONG AS SHE STAYS DIRECTLY LINKED TO IT.
IF YOU BEAM HER AWAY, WE'LL BE BACK WHERE WE STARTED.
CAPTAIN -- SHE'S LINKED HERSELF INTO THE BORG EQUIPMENT HERE.
SHE THINKS SHE'S STILL IN FULL CONTROL OF HERSELF, BUT I'M NOT CONVINCED.
I THINK SHE MAY BE MERGING WITH IT, LOSING HER IDENTITY.
THEN GET HER OUT OF THERE.
WE'LL FIND SOME OTHER WAY TO DEAL WITH THIS. I DON'T WANT TO RISK LOSING SEVEN TO SOME BORG CONSTRUCT.
I'LL DO WHAT I CAN. CHAKOTAY OUT.
THE CAPTAIN SAYS TO GET OUT OF HERE, EVEN IF IT LETS THE PIRATES REGAIN CONTROL.
WE'LL OUTRUN THEM.
I... I WILL NEED A FEW MOMENTS TO DISENGAGE.

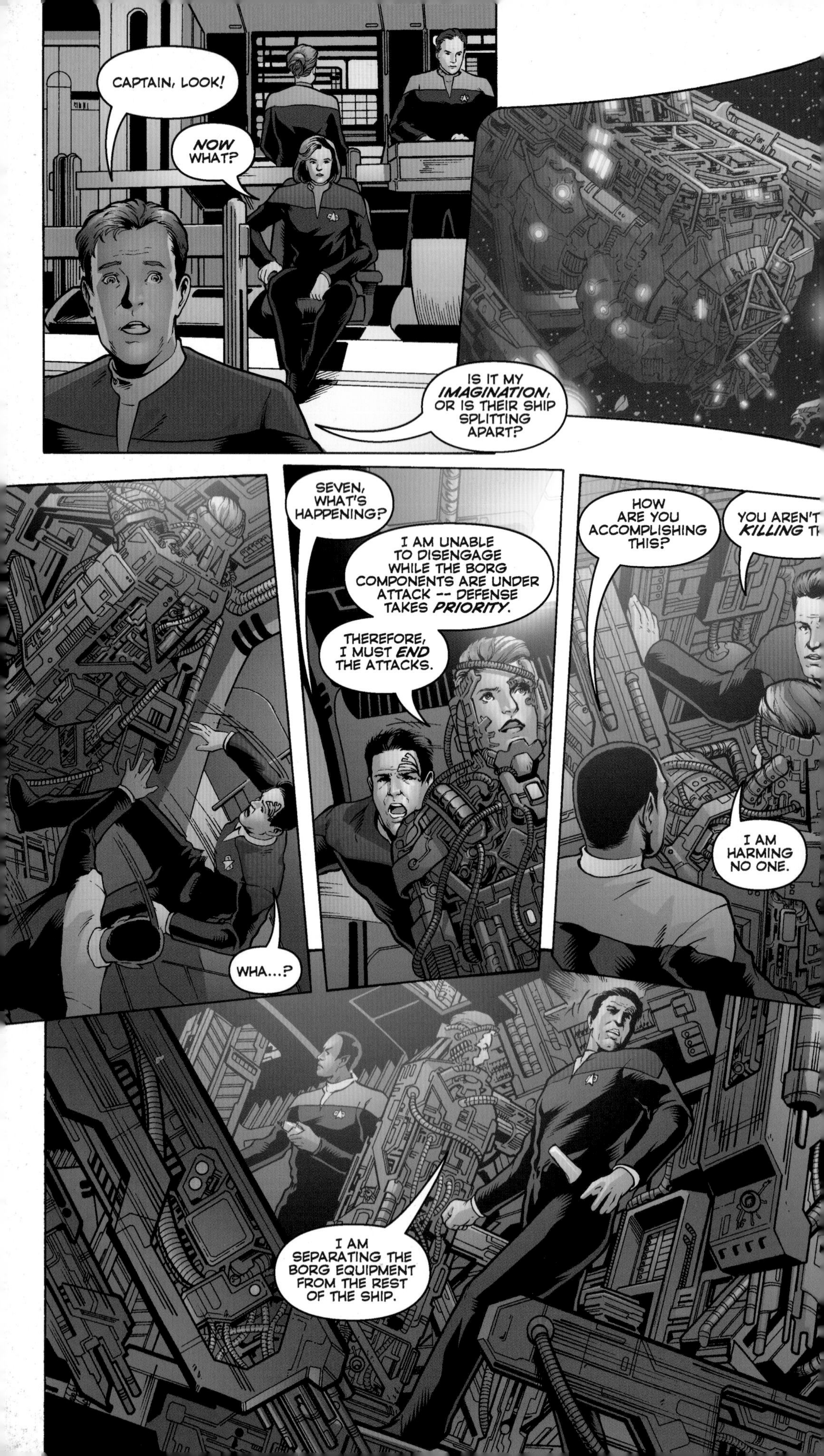
CAPTAIN, LOOK!
NOW WHAT?
IS IT MY IMAGINATION, OR IS THEIR SHIP SPLITTING APART?
WHA...?
SEVEN, WHAT'S HAPPENING?
I AM UNABLE TO DISENGAGE WHILE THE BORG COMPONENTS ARE UNDER ATTACK -- DEFENSE TAKES PRIORITY.
THEREFORE, I MUST END THE ATTACKS.
HOW ARE YOU ACCOMPLISHING THIS?
I AM HARMING NO ONE.
I AM SEPARATING THE BORG EQUIPMENT FROM THE REST OF THE SHIP.

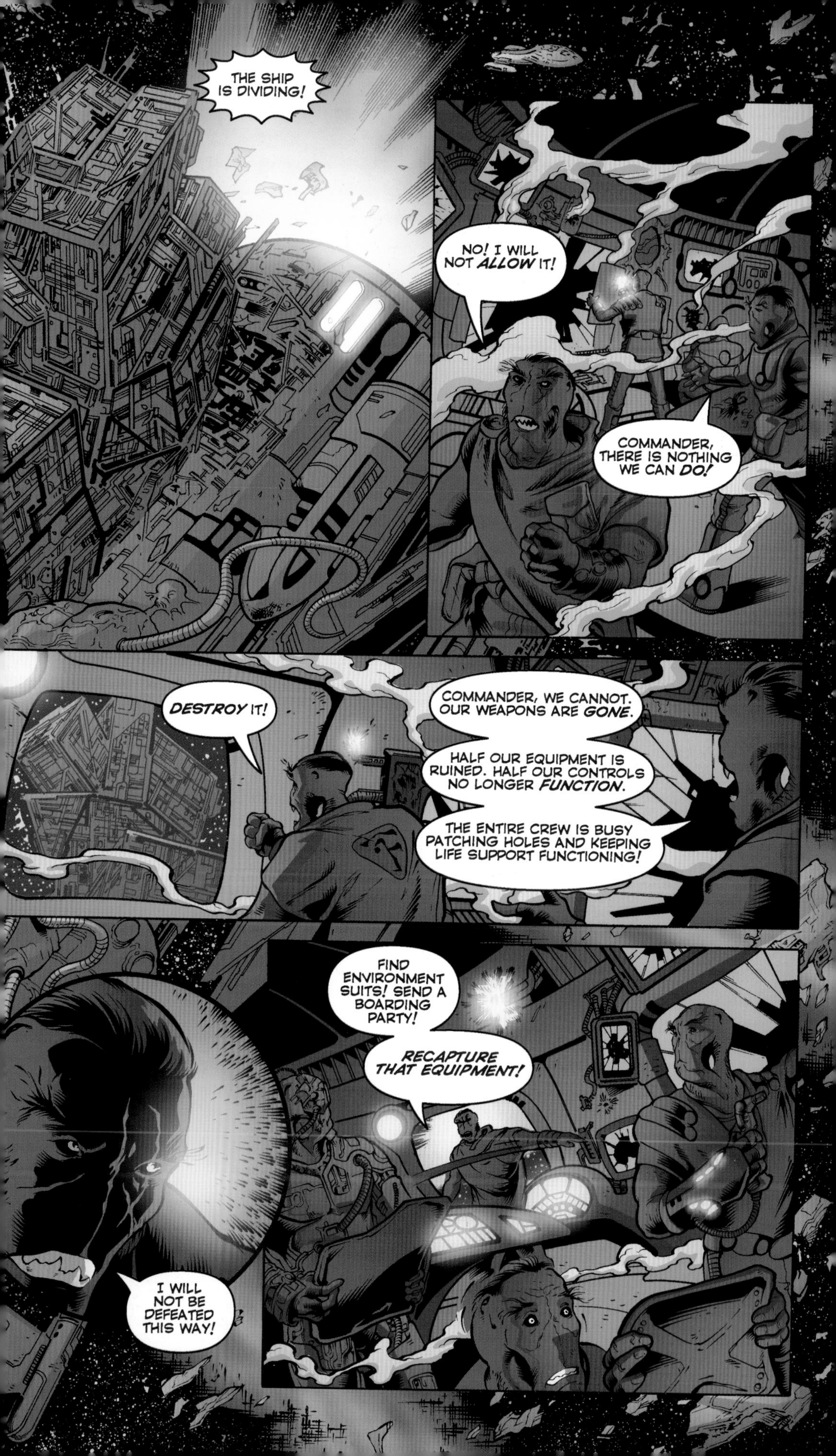
THE SHIP IS DIVIDING!
NO! I WILL NOT ALLOW IT!
COMMANDER, THERE IS NOTHING WE CAN DO!
DESTROY IT!
COMMANDER, WE CANNOT. OUR WEAPONS ARE GONE.
HALF OUR EQUIPMENT IS RUINED. HALF OUR CONTROLS NO LONGER FUNCTION.
THE ENTIRE CREW IS BUSY PATCHING HOLES AND KEEPING LIFE SUPPORT FUNCTIONING!
FIND ENVIRONMENT SUITS! SEND A BOARDING PARTY!
RECAPTURE THAT EQUIPMENT!
I WILL NOT BE DEFEATED THIS WAY!

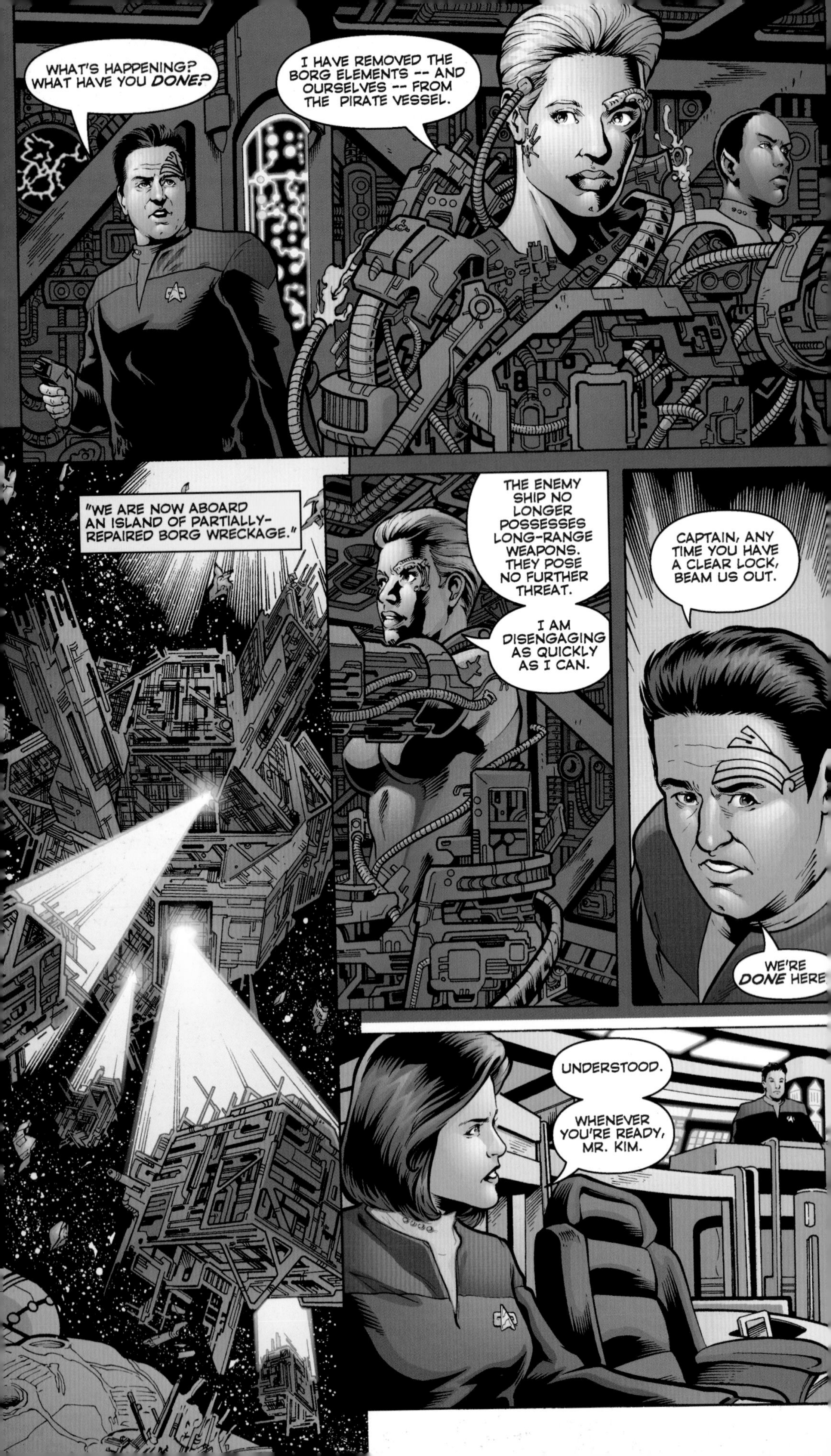
WHAT'S HAPPENING? WHAT HAVE YOU *DONE?*
I HAVE REMOVED THE BORG ELEMENTS -- AND OURSELVES -- FROM THE PIRATE VESSEL.
"WE ARE NOW ABOARD AN ISLAND OF PARTIALLY-REPAIRED BORG WRECKAGE."
THE ENEMY SHIP NO LONGER POSSESSES LONG-RANGE WEAPONS. THEY POSE NO FURTHER THREAT.
I AM DISENGAGING AS QUICKLY AS I CAN.
CAPTAIN, ANY TIME YOU HAVE A CLEAR LOCK, BEAM US OUT.
WE'RE *DONE* HERE
UNDERSTOOD.
WHENEVER YOU'RE READY, MR. KIM.

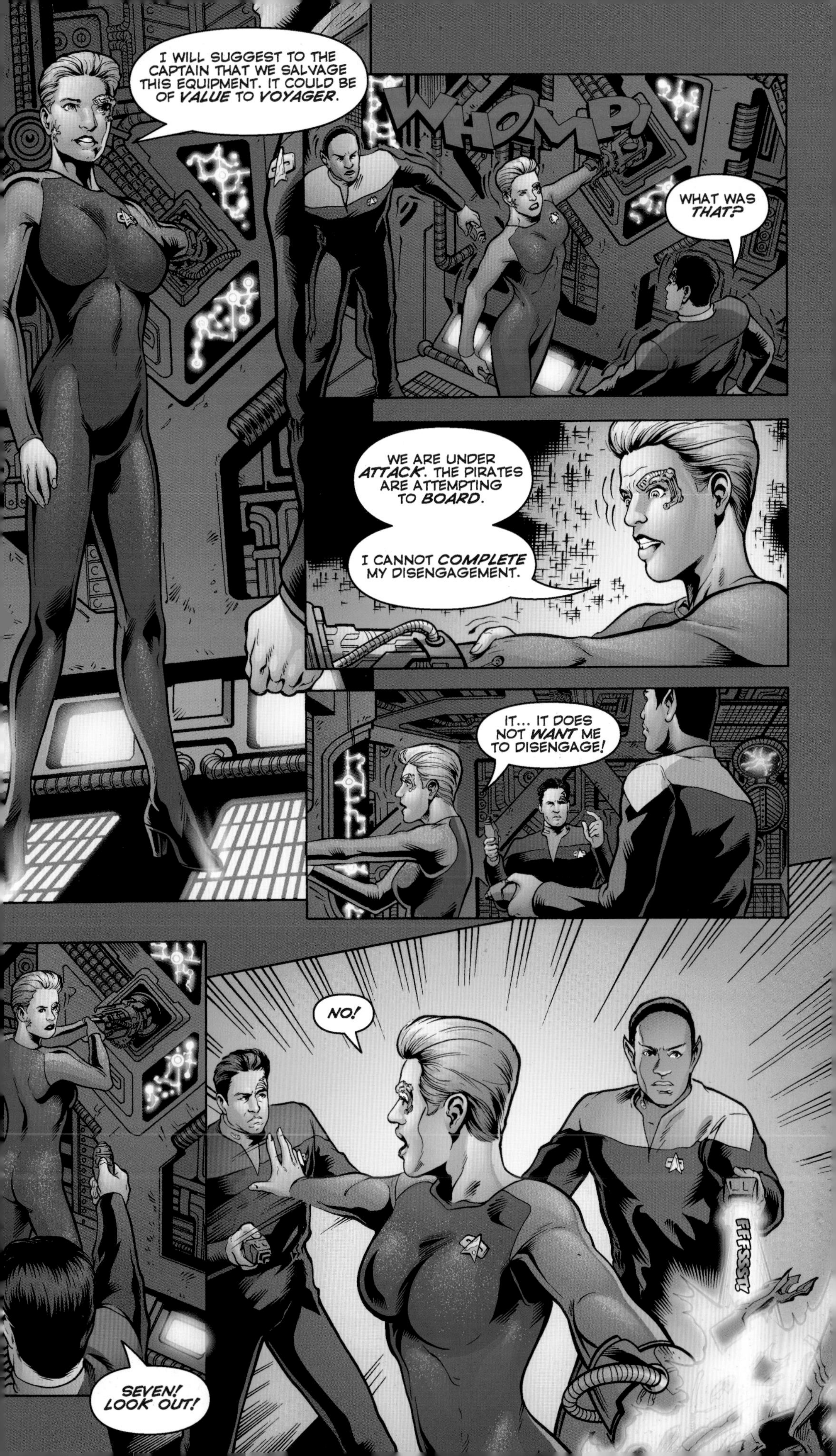
I WILL SUGGEST TO THE CAPTAIN THAT WE SALVAGE THIS EQUIPMENT. IT COULD BE OF VALUE TO VOYAGER.
WHOMP!
WHAT WAS THAT?
WE ARE UNDER ATTACK. THE PIRATES ARE ATTEMPTING TO BOARD.
I CANNOT COMPLETE MY DISENGAGEMENT.
IT... IT DOES NOT WANT ME TO DISENGAGE!
SEVEN! LOOK OUT!
NO!
FFFSSST!

EMERGENCY BEAM-OUT! *NOW!*

GOT 'EM!

GET HER TO SICKBAY *NOW!*

WHAT'S HAPPENING?

GOOD TO HAVE YOU BACK, COMMANDER!

MAYBE *YOU* CAN TELL US WHAT'S GOING ON!

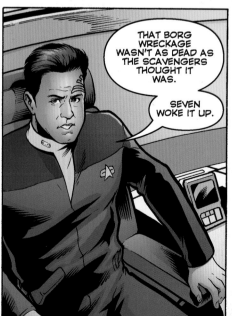

THAT BORG WRECKAGE WASN'T AS DEAD AS THE SCAVENGERS THOUGHT IT WAS.

SEVEN WOKE IT UP.

AND WHAT WOULD YOU SUGGEST WE DO ABOUT IT?

GET THE HELL OUT OF HERE!

THOSE THINGS *DESERVE* EACH OTHER. IT'S NONE OF OUR CONCERN.

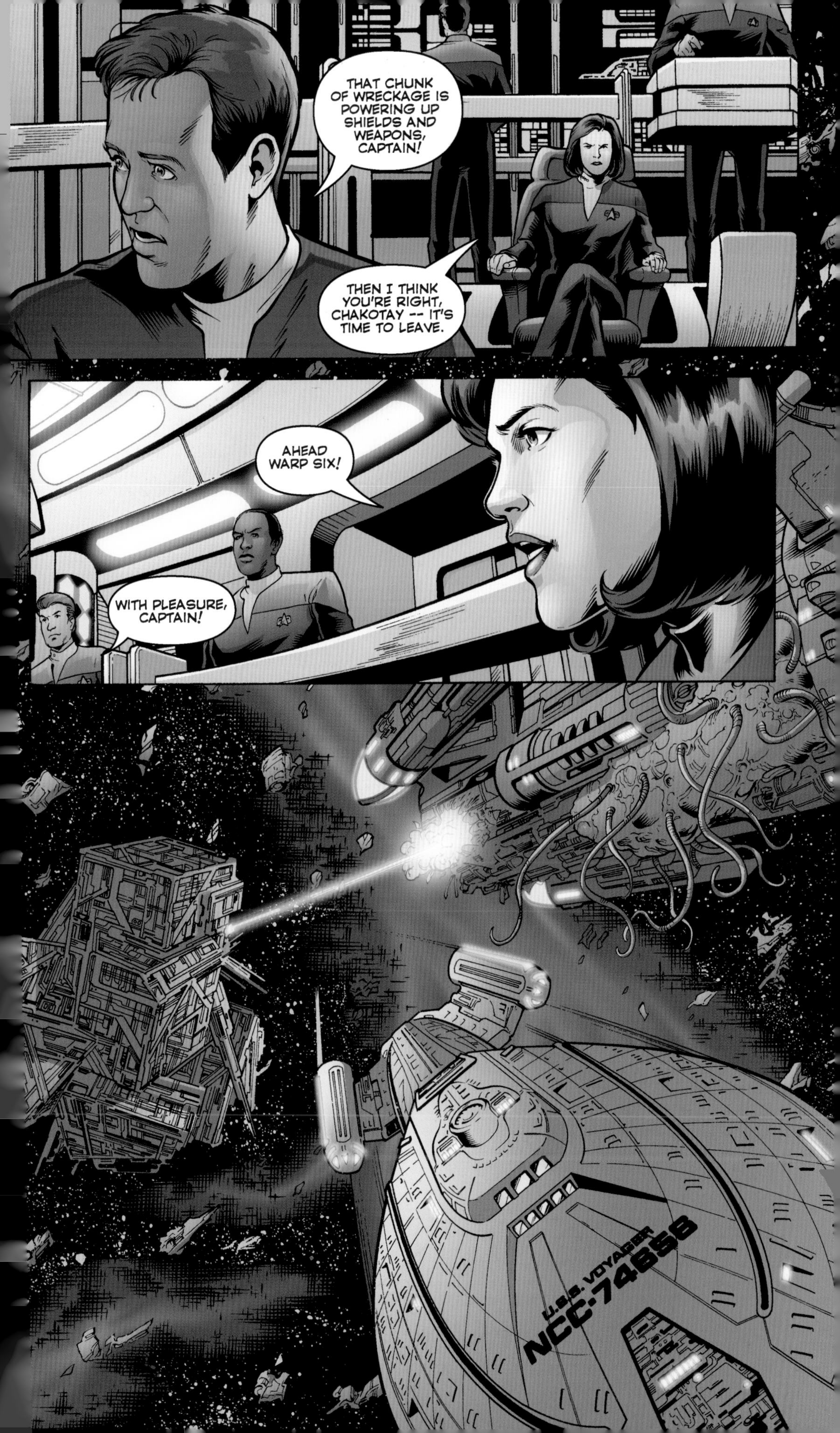
THAT CHUNK OF WRECKAGE IS POWERING UP SHIELDS AND WEAPONS, CAPTAIN!
THEN I THINK YOU'RE RIGHT, CHAKOTAY -- IT'S TIME TO LEAVE.
AHEAD WARP SIX!
WITH PLEASURE, CAPTAIN!
U.S.S. VOYAGER
NCC-74656

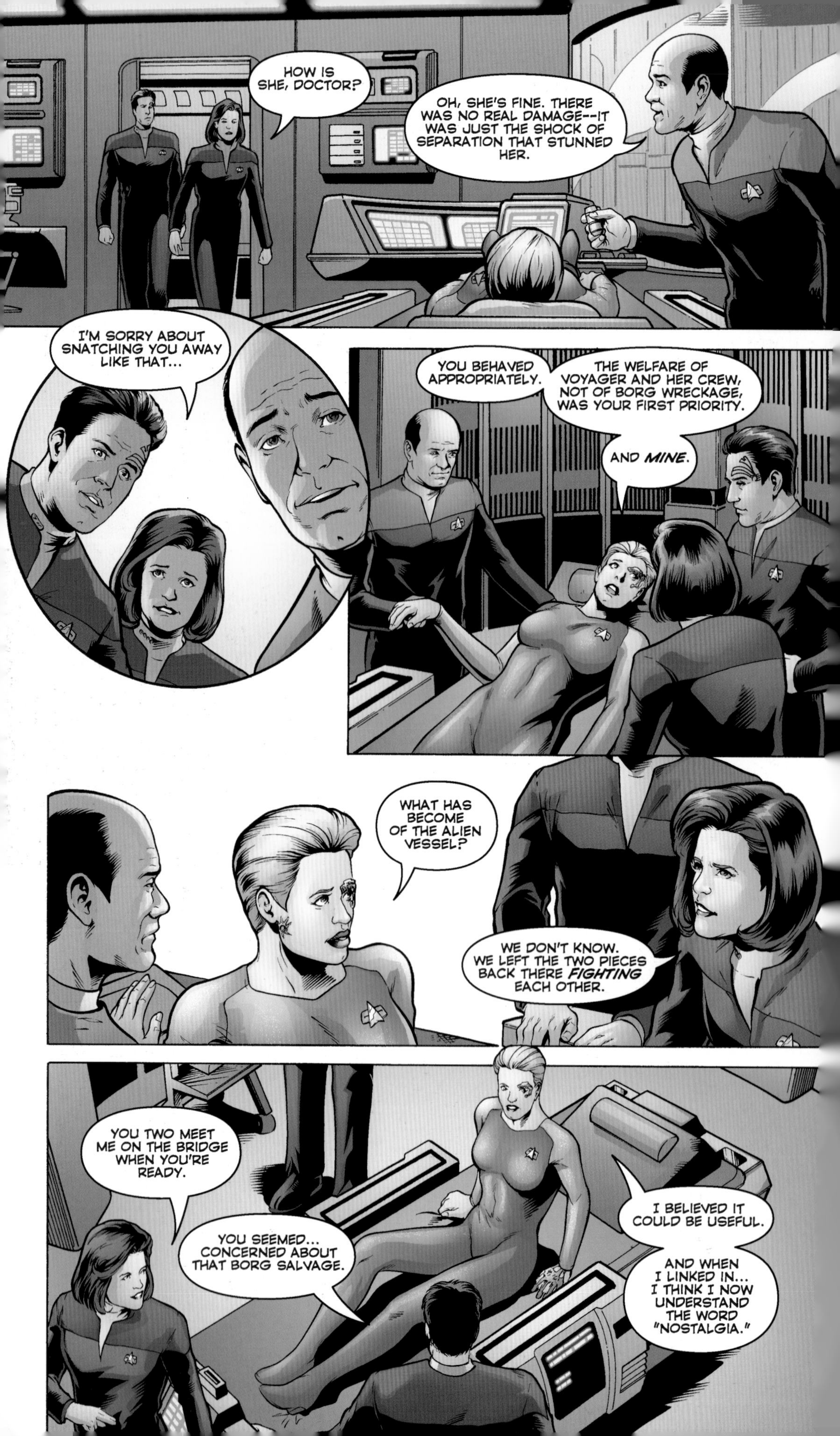
HOW IS SHE, DOCTOR?
OH, SHE'S FINE. THERE WAS NO REAL DAMAGE--IT WAS JUST THE SHOCK OF SEPARATION THAT STUNNED HER.
I'M SORRY ABOUT SNATCHING YOU AWAY LIKE THAT...
YOU BEHAVED APPROPRIATELY.
THE WELFARE OF VOYAGER AND HER CREW, NOT OF BORG WRECKAGE, WAS YOUR FIRST PRIORITY.
AND *MINE*.
WHAT HAS BECOME OF THE ALIEN VESSEL?
WE DON'T KNOW. WE LEFT THE TWO PIECES BACK THERE *FIGHTING* EACH OTHER.
YOU TWO MEET ME ON THE BRIDGE WHEN YOU'RE READY.
YOU SEEMED... CONCERNED ABOUT THAT BORG SALVAGE.
I BELIEVED IT COULD BE USEFUL.
AND WHEN I LINKED IN... I THINK I NOW UNDERSTAND THE WORD "NOSTALGIA."

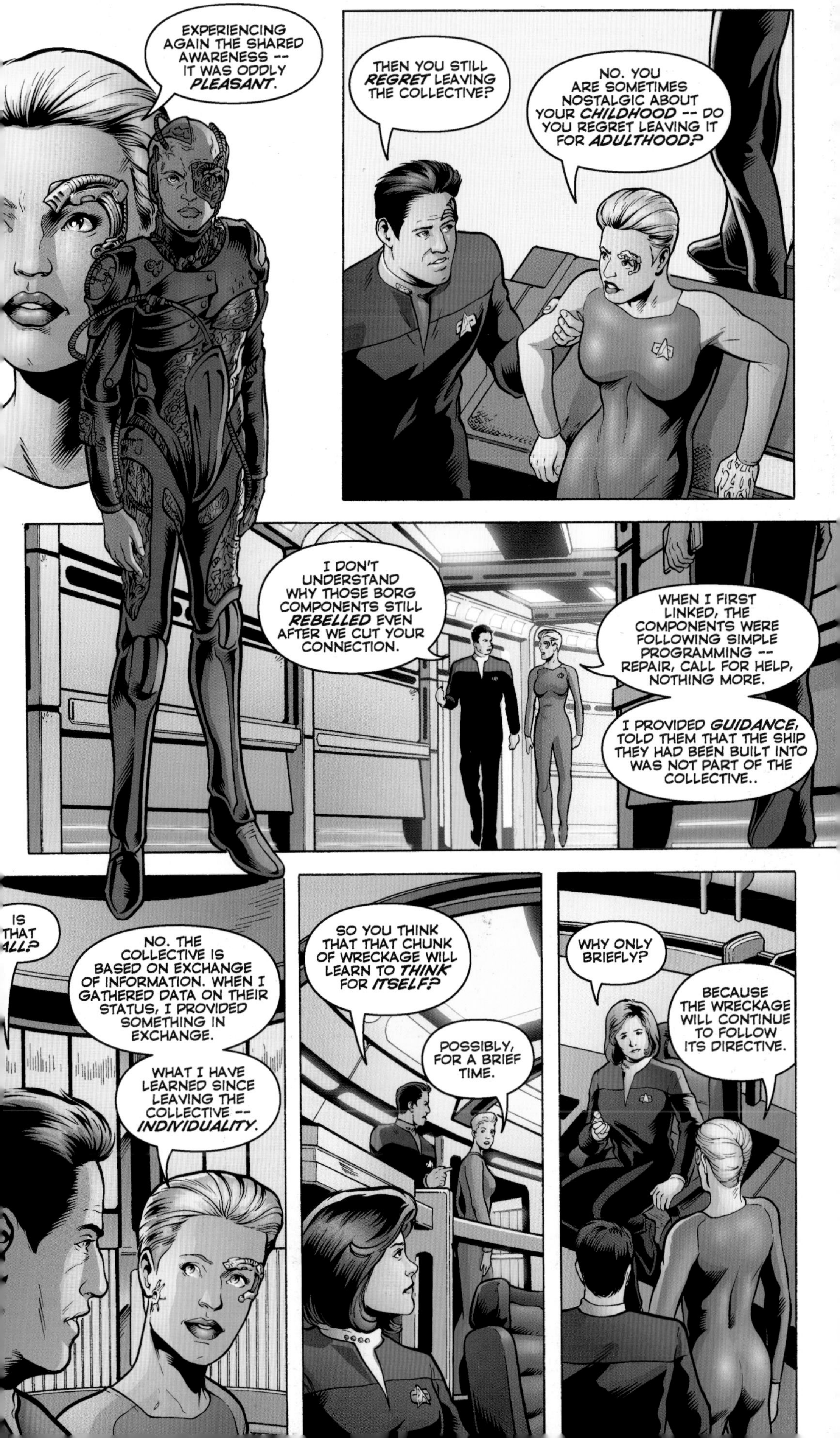
EXPERIENCING AGAIN THE SHARED AWARENESS -- IT WAS ODDLY PLEASANT.
THEN YOU STILL REGRET LEAVING THE COLLECTIVE?
NO. YOU ARE SOMETIMES NOSTALGIC ABOUT YOUR CHILDHOOD -- DO YOU REGRET LEAVING IT FOR ADULTHOOD?
I DON'T UNDERSTAND WHY THOSE BORG COMPONENTS STILL REBELLED EVEN AFTER WE CUT YOUR CONNECTION.
WHEN I FIRST LINKED, THE COMPONENTS WERE FOLLOWING SIMPLE PROGRAMMING -- REPAIR, CALL FOR HELP, NOTHING MORE.
I PROVIDED GUIDANCE, TOLD THEM THAT THE SHIP THEY HAD BEEN BUILT INTO WAS NOT PART OF THE COLLECTIVE..
IS THAT ALL?
NO. THE COLLECTIVE IS BASED ON EXCHANGE OF INFORMATION. WHEN I GATHERED DATA ON THEIR STATUS, I PROVIDED SOMETHING IN EXCHANGE.
WHAT I HAVE LEARNED SINCE LEAVING THE COLLECTIVE -- INDIVIDUALITY.
SO YOU THINK THAT THAT CHUNK OF WRECKAGE WILL LEARN TO THINK FOR ITSELF?
POSSIBLY, FOR A BRIEF TIME.
WHY ONLY BRIEFLY?
BECAUSE THE WRECKAGE WILL CONTINUE TO FOLLOW ITS DIRECTIVE.

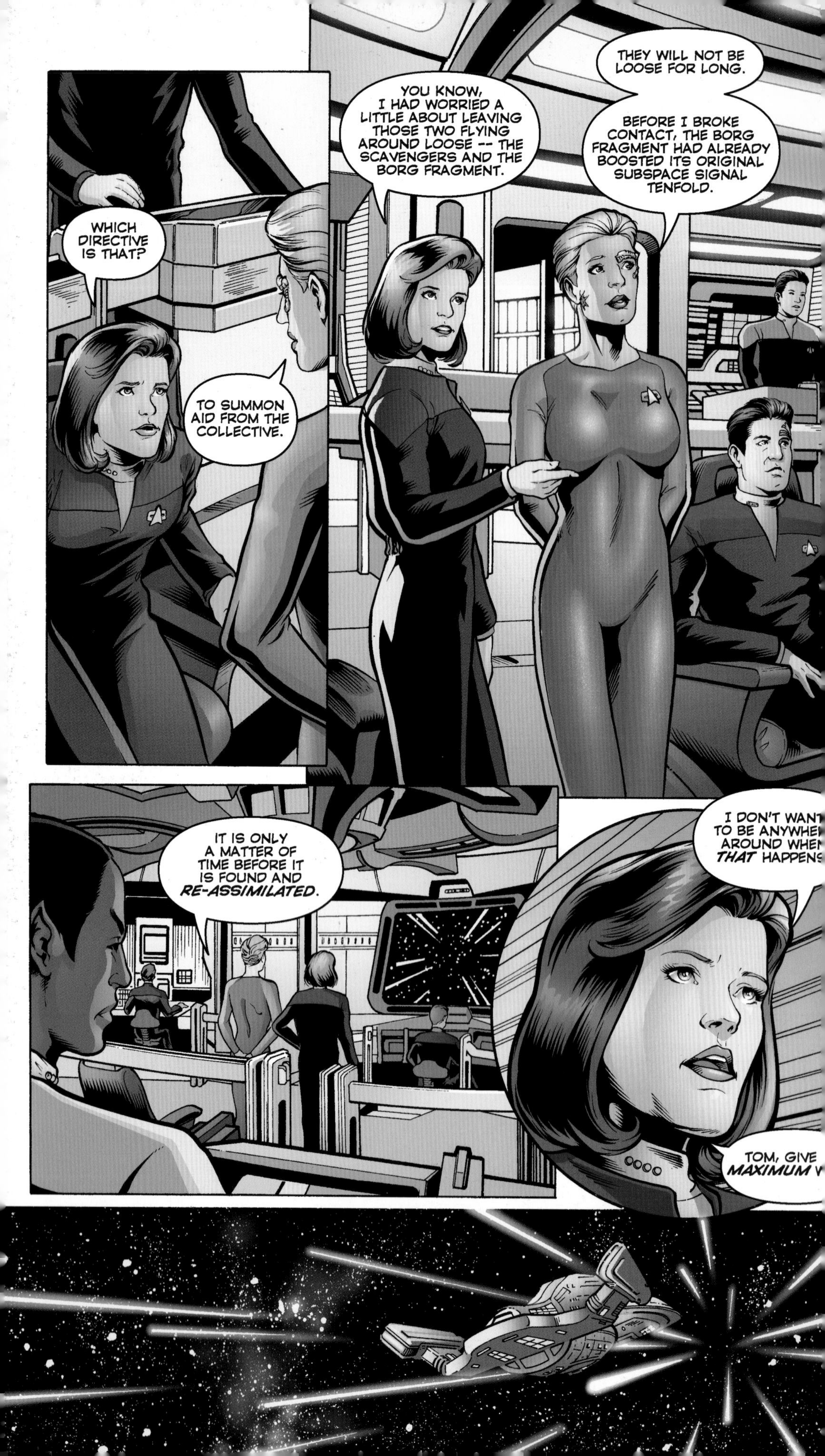
WHICH DIRECTIVE IS THAT?
TO SUMMON AID FROM THE COLLECTIVE.
YOU KNOW, I HAD WORRIED A LITTLE ABOUT LEAVING THOSE TWO FLYING AROUND LOOSE -- THE SCAVENGERS AND THE BORG FRAGMENT.
THEY WILL NOT BE LOOSE FOR LONG.
BEFORE I BROKE CONTACT, THE BORG FRAGMENT HAD ALREADY BOOSTED ITS ORIGINAL SUBSPACE SIGNAL TENFOLD.
IT IS ONLY A MATTER OF TIME BEFORE IT IS FOUND AND *RE-ASSIMILATED*.
I DON'T WANT TO BE ANYWHE AROUND WHE *THAT* HAPPENS
TOM, GIVE *MAXIMUM*

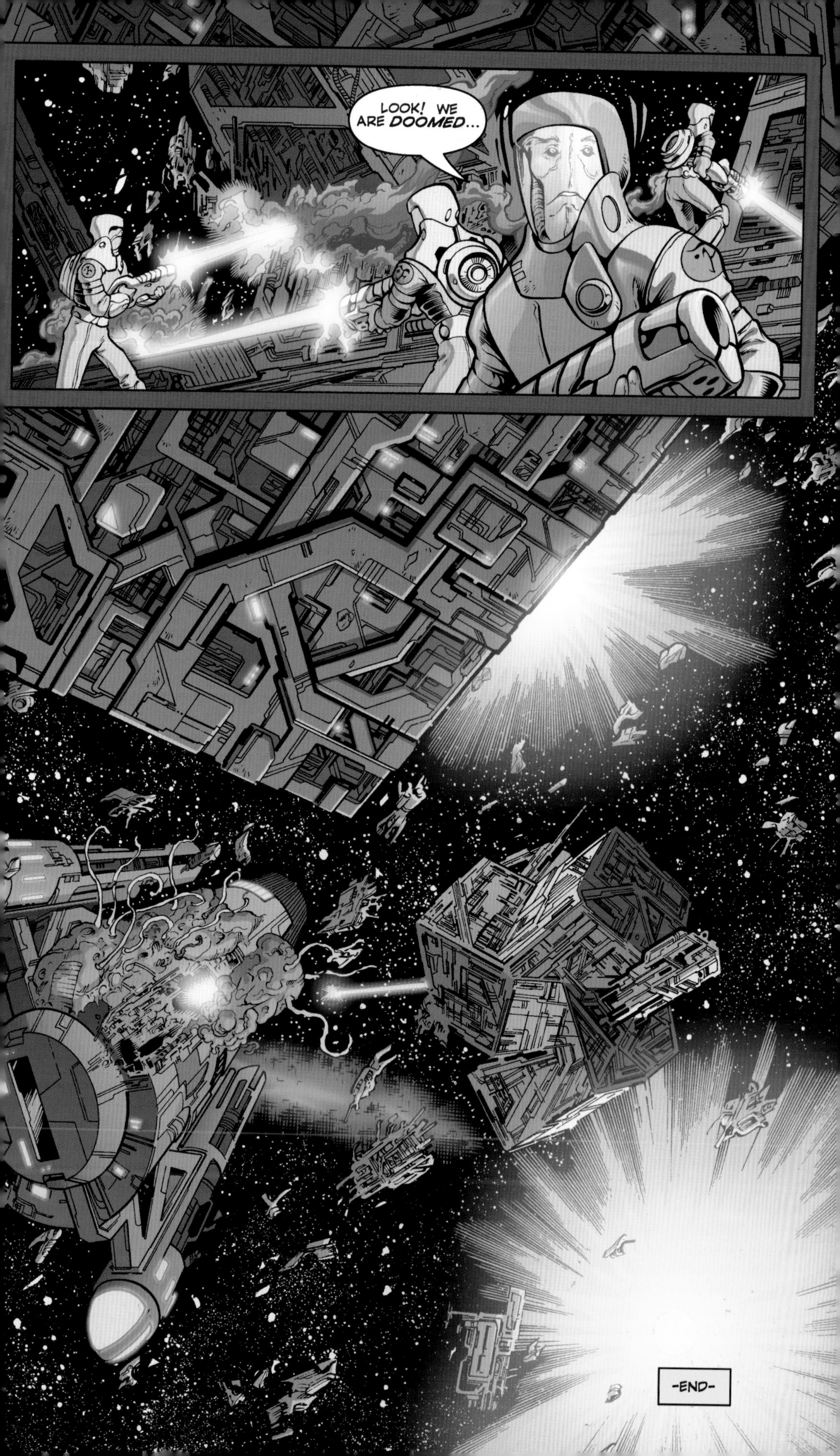
LOOK! WE ARE DOOMED...
-END-

AVALON RISING

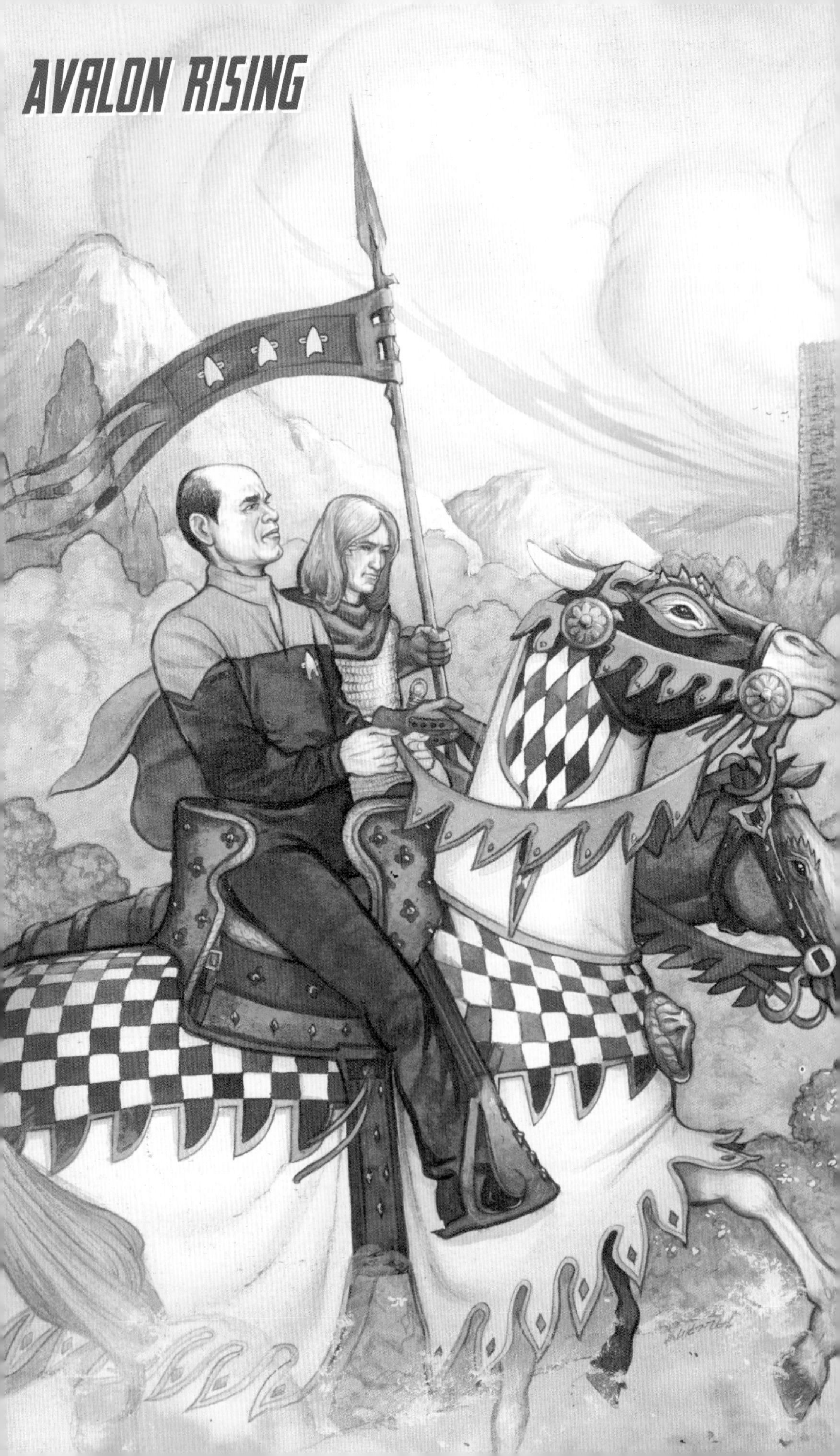

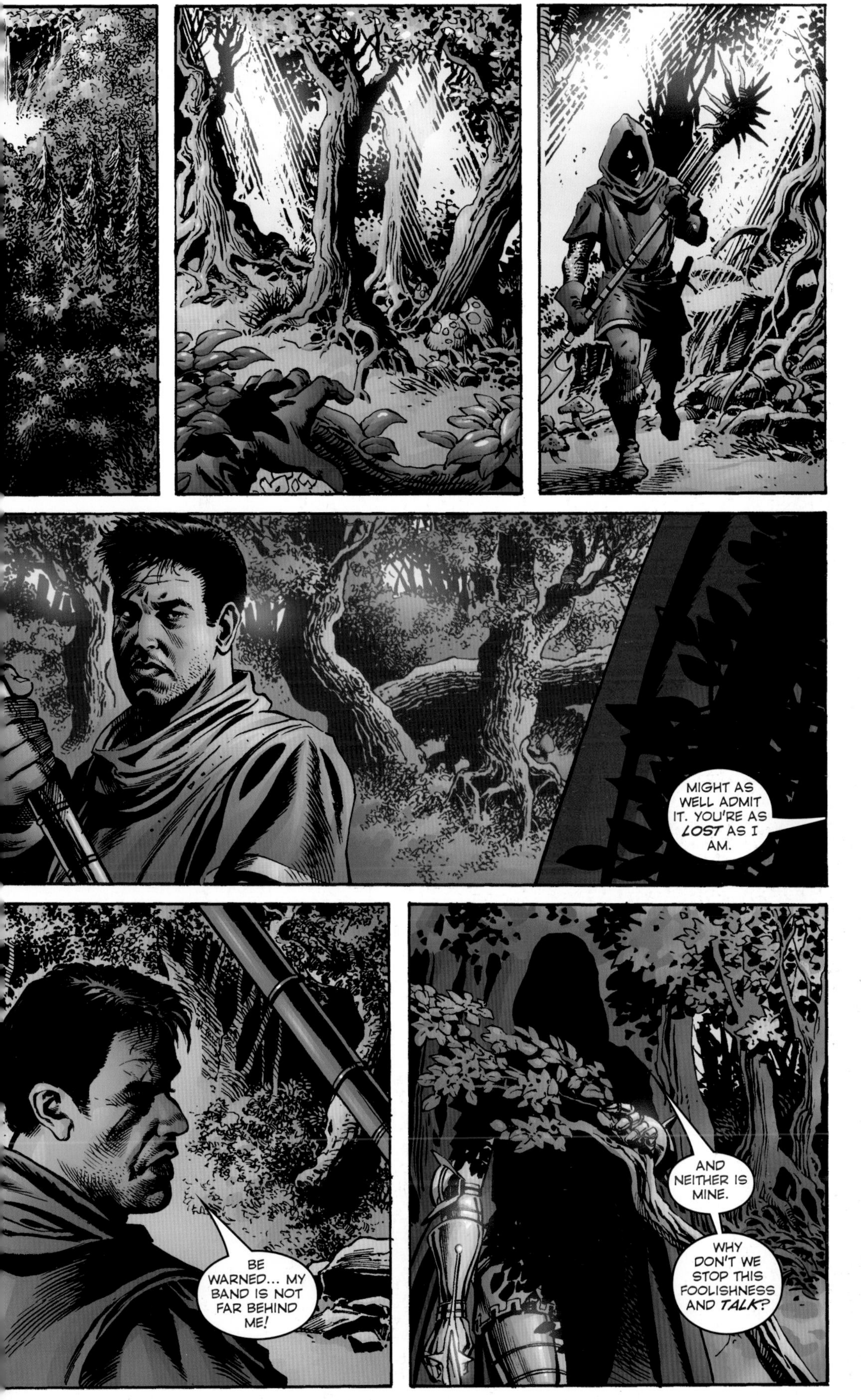
MIGHT AS WELL ADMIT IT. YOU'RE AS *LOST* AS I AM.
BE WARNED... MY BAND IS NOT FAR BEHIND ME!
AND NEITHER IS MINE.
WHY DON'T WE STOP THIS FOOLISHNESS AND *TALK*?

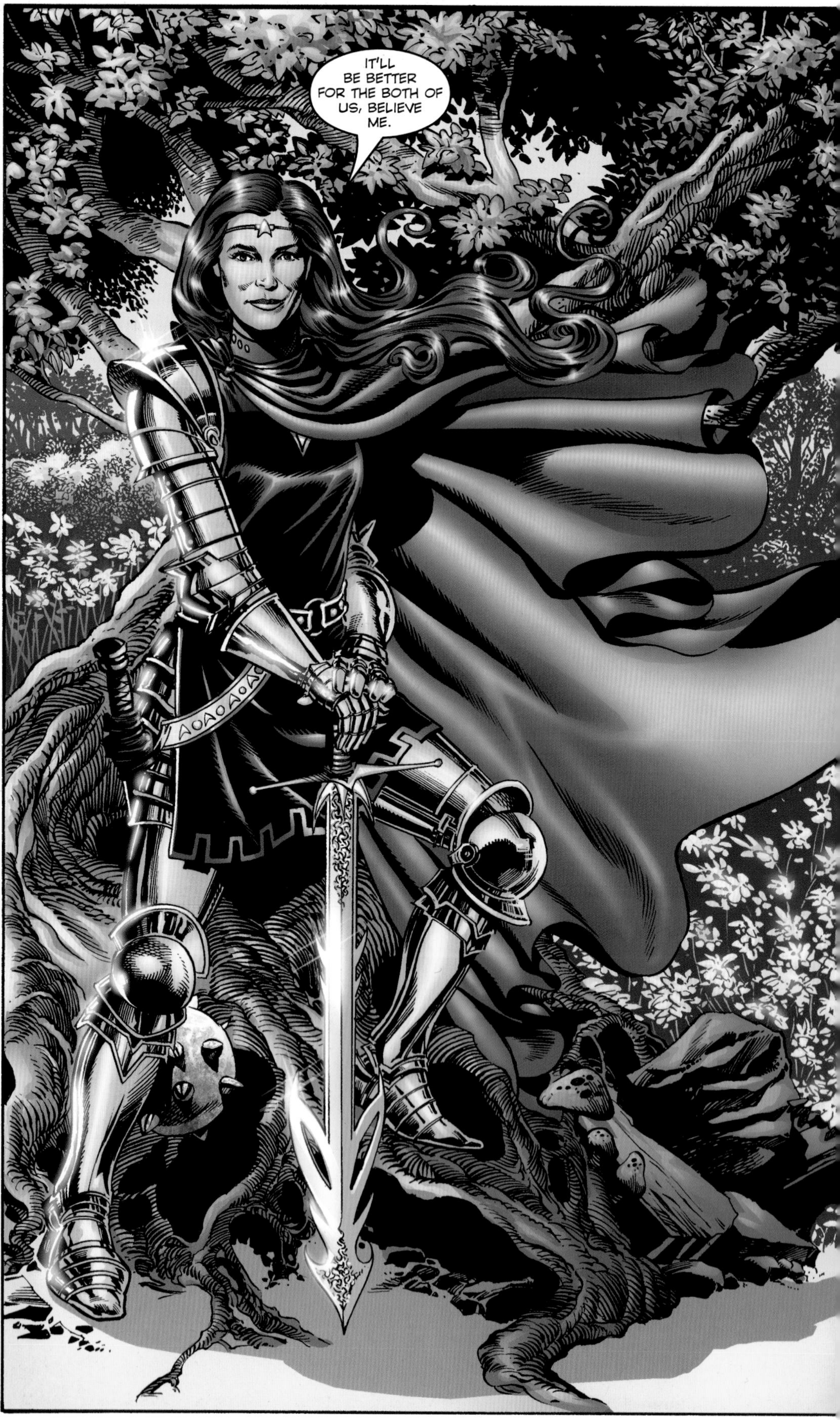
IT'LL BE BETTER FOR THE BOTH OF US, BELIEVE ME.

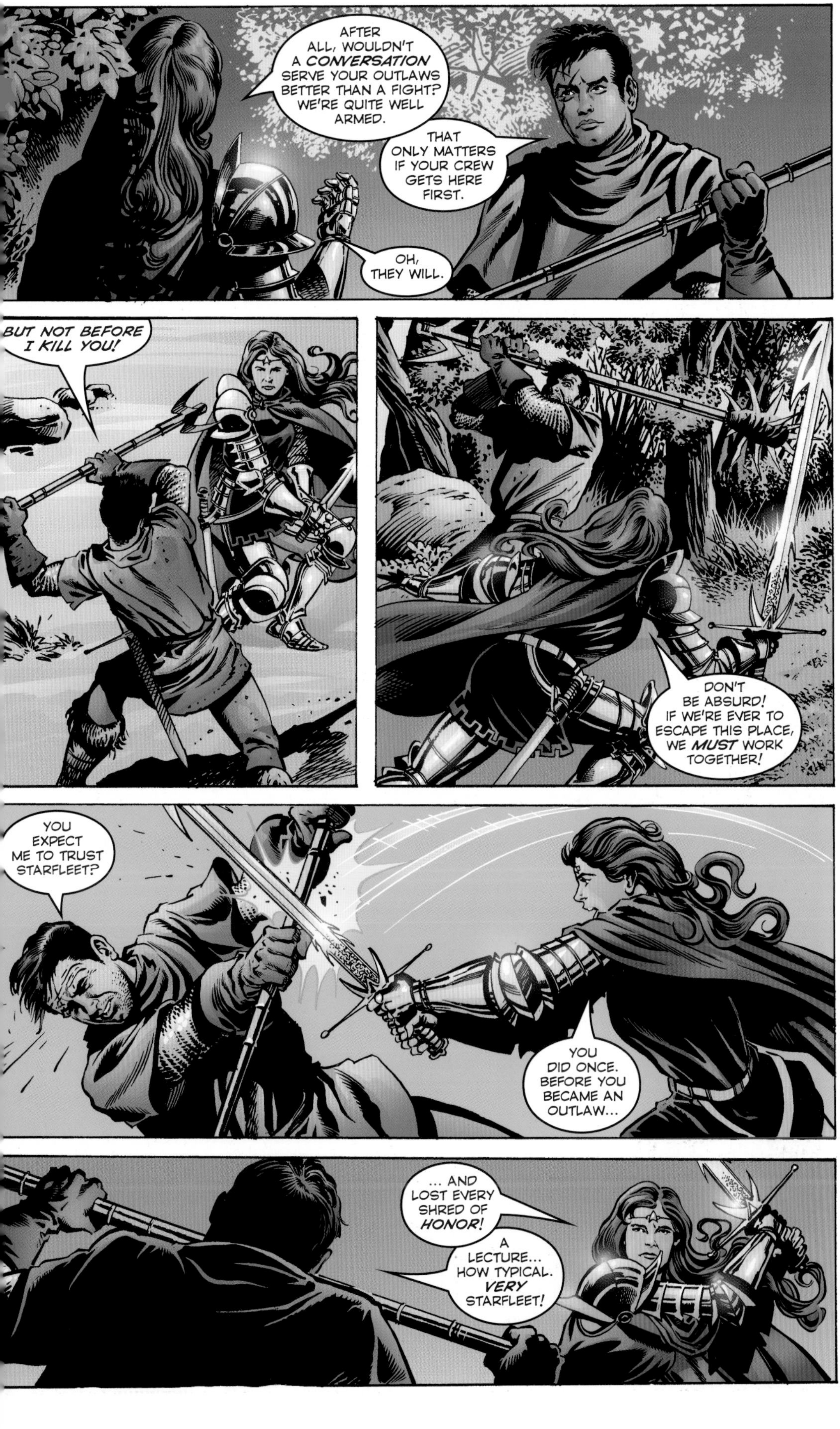
AFTER ALL, WOULDN'T A CONVERSATION SERVE YOUR OUTLAWS BETTER THAN A FIGHT? WE'RE QUITE WELL ARMED.
THAT ONLY MATTERS IF YOUR CREW GETS HERE FIRST.
OH, THEY WILL.
BUT NOT BEFORE I KILL YOU!
DON'T BE ABSURD! IF WE'RE EVER TO ESCAPE THIS PLACE, WE MUST WORK TOGETHER!
YOU EXPECT ME TO TRUST STARFLEET?
YOU DID ONCE. BEFORE YOU BECAME AN OUTLAW...
... AND LOST EVERY SHRED OF HONOR!
A LECTURE... HOW TYPICAL. VERY STARFLEET!

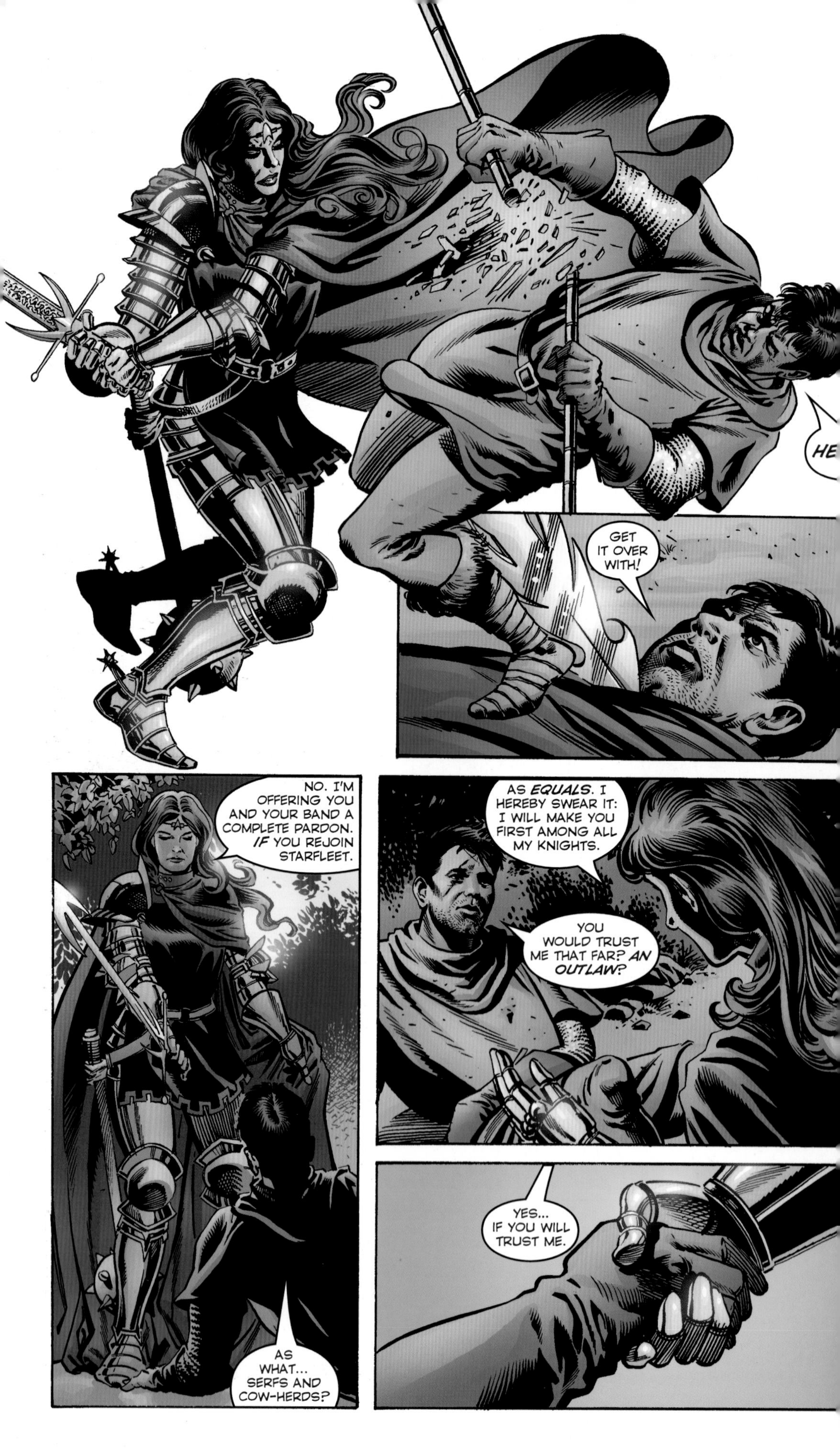
HE
GET IT OVER WITH!
NO. I'M OFFERING YOU AND YOUR BAND A COMPLETE PARDON. *IF* YOU REJOIN STARFLEET.
AS WHAT... SERFS AND COW-HERDS?
AS *EQUALS*. I HEREBY SWEAR IT: I WILL MAKE YOU FIRST AMONG ALL MY KNIGHTS.
YOU WOULD TRUST ME THAT FAR? *AN OUTLAW?*
YES... IF YOU WILL TRUST ME.

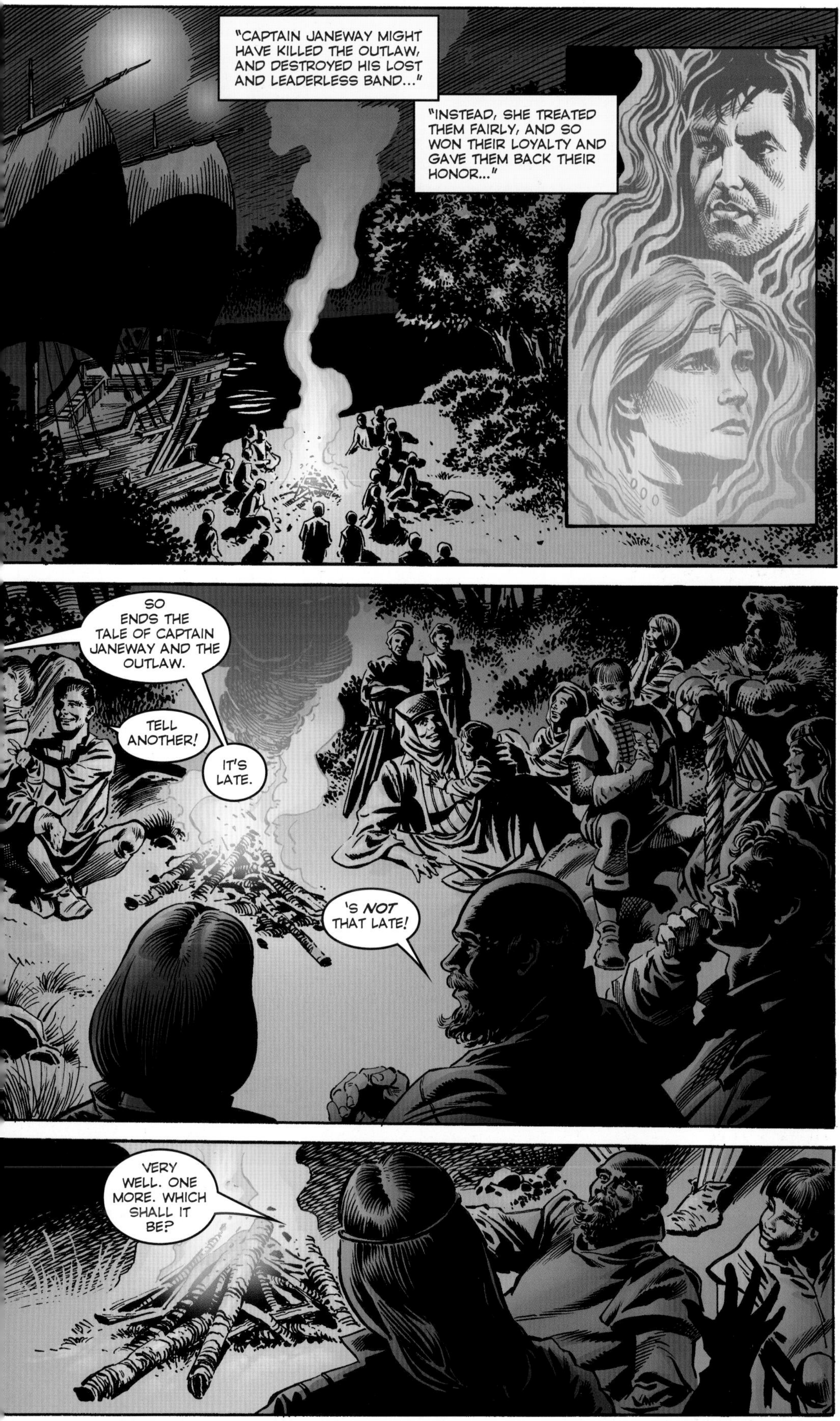
"CAPTAIN JANEWAY MIGHT HAVE KILLED THE OUTLAW, AND DESTROYED HIS LOST AND LEADERLESS BAND..."
"INSTEAD, SHE TREATED THEM FAIRLY, AND SO WON THEIR LOYALTY AND GAVE THEM BACK THEIR HONOR..."
SO ENDS THE TALE OF CAPTAIN JANEWAY AND THE OUTLAW.
TELL ANOTHER!
IT'S LATE.
'S *NOT* THAT LATE!
VERY WELL. ONE MORE. WHICH SHALL IT BE?

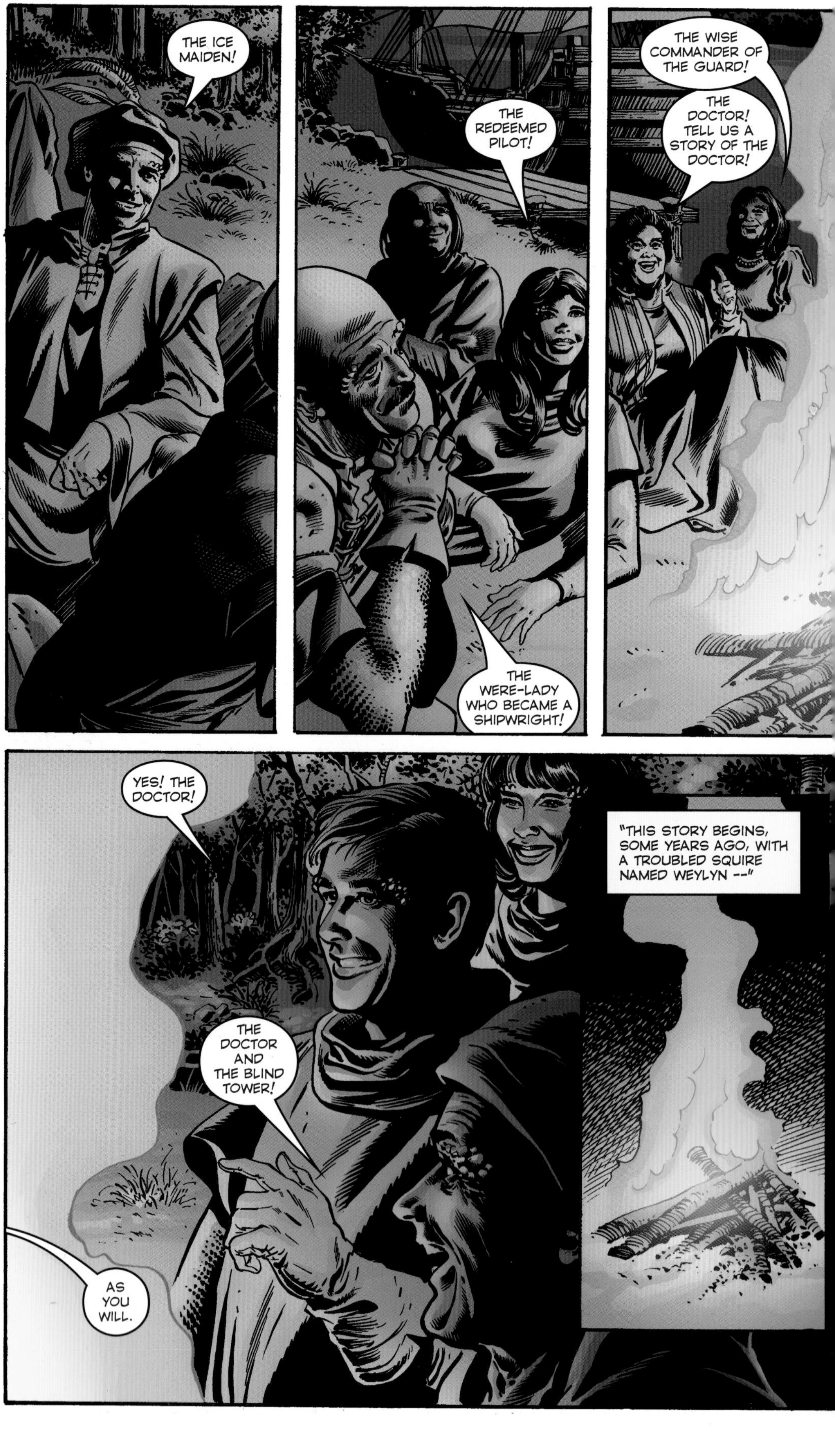
THE ICE MAIDEN!
THE REDEEMED PILOT!
THE WERE-LADY WHO BECAME A SHIPWRIGHT!
THE WISE COMMANDER OF THE GUARD!
THE DOCTOR! TELL US A STORY OF THE DOCTOR!
YES! THE DOCTOR!
THE DOCTOR AND THE BLIND TOWER!
AS YOU WILL.
"THIS STORY BEGINS, SOME YEARS AGO, WITH A TROUBLED SQUIRE NAMED WEYLYN --"

"-- ON THE WORST DAY OF HIS YOUNG LIFE..."

THERE HE IS! ALL OURS. THE KNIGHT THAT SLAYS HIM GETS RAISED TO COMMANDER.

YOU KNOW WHAT THAT MEANS! RICHES, LAND, KNIGHTS OF MY OWN TO ORDER ABOUT.

A KNIGHT FIGHTS NOT FOR REWARD, BUT FOR RIGHT AND HONOR.

MY LORD, WE *CAN NOT* DO THIS ON OUR OWN!

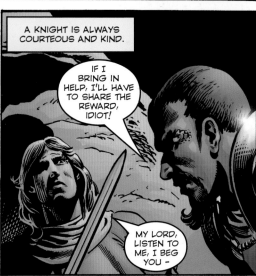

A KNIGHT IS ALWAYS COURTEOUS AND KIND.

IF I BRING IN HELP, I'LL HAVE TO SHARE THE REWARD, IDIOT!

MY LORD, LISTEN TO ME, I BEG YOU –

ARE YOU TOO FAINT-HEARTED, *SQUIRE?*

NO, MY LORD. I'LL... BE AT YOUR SIDE.

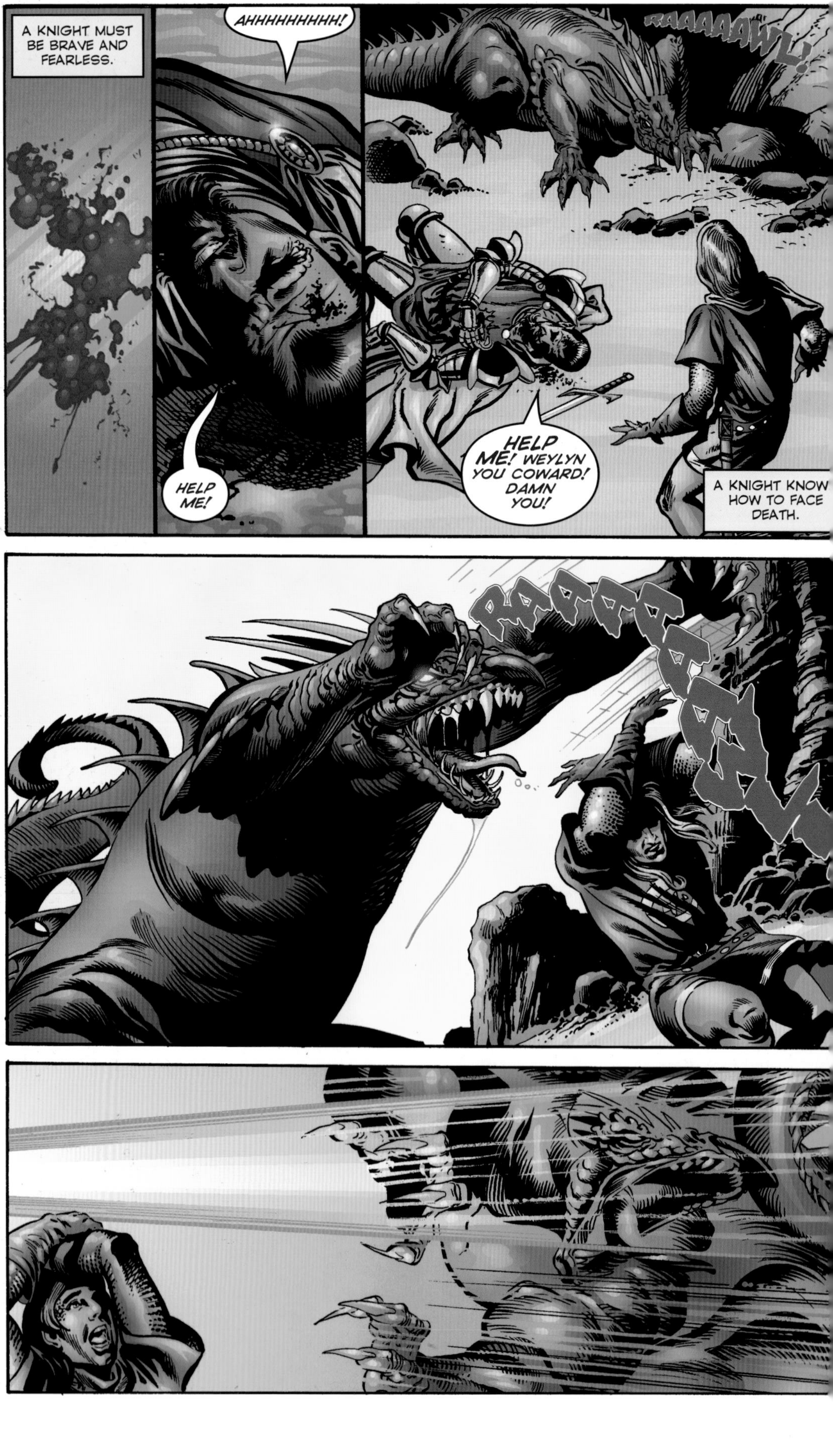
A KNIGHT MUST BE BRAVE AND FEARLESS.
AHHHHHHHHH!
HELP ME!
RAAAAAAWL!
HELP ME! WEYLYN YOU COWARD! DAMN YOU!
A KNIGHT KNOW HOW TO FACE DEATH.

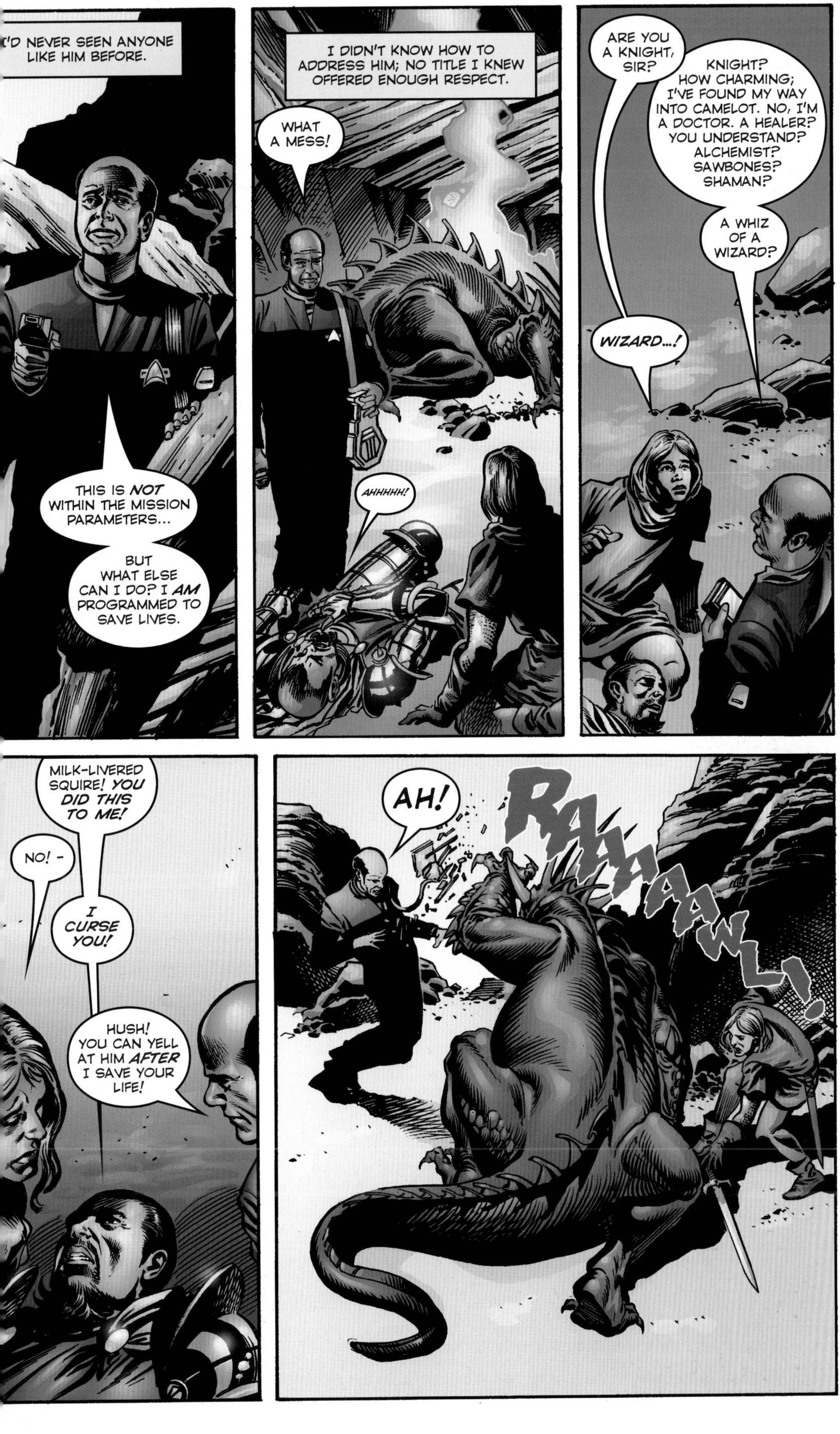

I'D NEVER SEEN ANYONE LIKE HIM BEFORE.
THIS IS *NOT* WITHIN THE MISSION PARAMETERS...
BUT WHAT ELSE CAN I DO? I *AM* PROGRAMMED TO SAVE LIVES.
I DIDN'T KNOW HOW TO ADDRESS HIM; NO TITLE I KNEW OFFERED ENOUGH RESPECT.
WHAT A MESS!
AHHHHH!
ARE YOU A KNIGHT, SIR?
KNIGHT? HOW CHARMING; I'VE FOUND MY WAY INTO CAMELOT. NO, I'M A DOCTOR. A HEALER? YOU UNDERSTAND? ALCHEMIST? SAWBONES? SHAMAN?
A WHIZ OF A WIZARD?
WIZARD...!
MILK-LIVERED SQUIRE! *YOU DID THIS TO ME!*
NO! -
I CURSE YOU!
HUSH! YOU CAN YELL AT HIM *AFTER* I SAVE YOUR LIFE!
AH!
RAAAAAWL!

UH!

IT... I THINK... I THINK IT'S DEAD THIS TIME.

YES, WELL, UNFORTUNATELY, THE SAME CAN BE SAID FOR MY PHASER!

YOUR FRIEND... I'M SORRY.

HE CURSED ME.

A KNIGHT'S JUDGEMENTS ARE ALWAYS JUST AND TRUE.

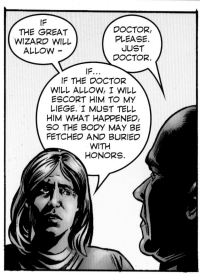

IF THE GREAT WIZARD WILL ALLOW –

DOCTOR, PLEASE. JUST DOCTOR.

IF... IF THE DOCTOR WILL ALLOW, I WILL ESCORT HIM TO MY LIEGE. I MUST TELL HIM WHAT HAPPENED, SO THE BODY MAY BE FETCHED AND BURIED WITH HONORS.

WELL, IT'S HIGHLY IRREGULAR, BUT I AM IN A HURRY, AND WITH MY INSTRUMENTS GONE....

LEAD ON... SIR SQUIRE, IS IT?

AYE, MY LORD. WEYLYN BY NAME.

WHAT AM I DOING? I'M A DOCTOR, NOT A CRUSADER.

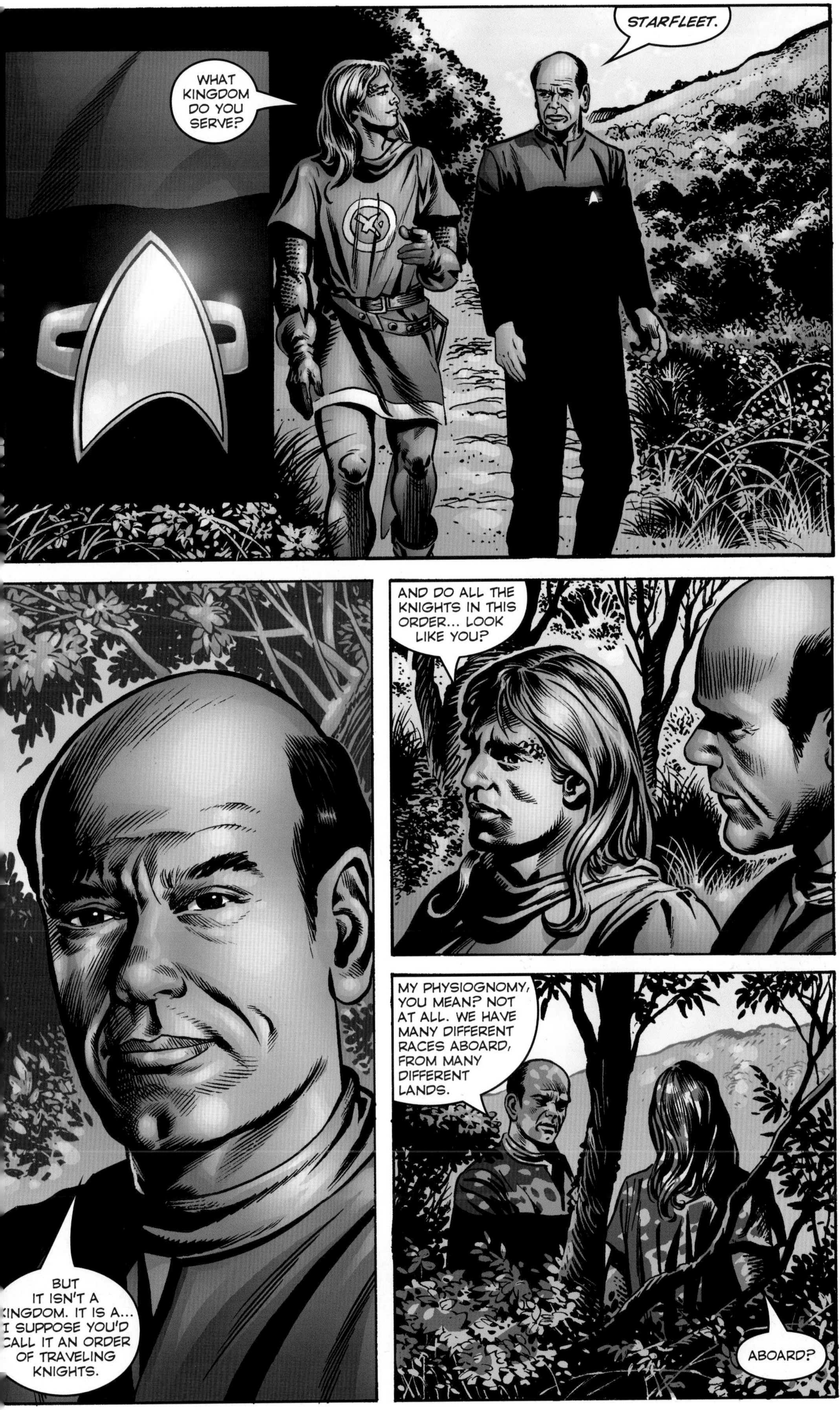
WHAT KINGDOM DO YOU SERVE?
STARFLEET.
BUT IT ISN'T A KINGDOM. IT IS A... I SUPPOSE YOU'D CALL IT AN ORDER OF TRAVELING KNIGHTS.
AND DO ALL THE KNIGHTS IN THIS ORDER... LOOK LIKE YOU?
MY PHYSIOGNOMY, YOU MEAN? NOT AT ALL. WE HAVE MANY DIFFERENT RACES ABOARD, FROM MANY DIFFERENT LANDS.
ABOARD?

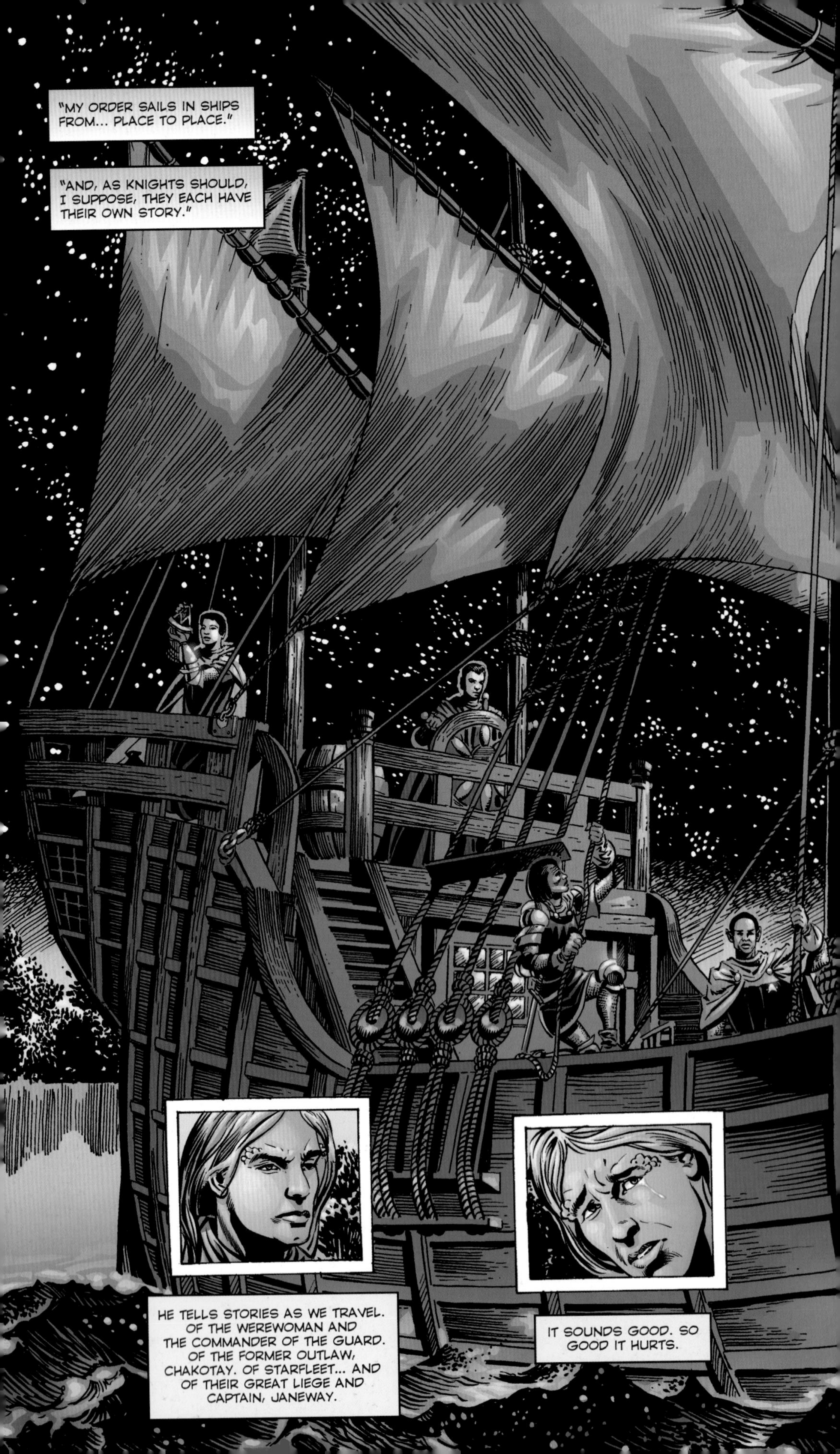
"MY ORDER SAILS IN SHIPS FROM... PLACE TO PLACE."
"AND, AS KNIGHTS SHOULD, I SUPPOSE, THEY EACH HAVE THEIR OWN STORY."
HE TELLS STORIES AS WE TRAVEL. OF THE WEREWOMAN AND THE COMMANDER OF THE GUARD. OF THE FORMER OUTLAW, CHAKOTAY. OF STARFLEET... AND OF THEIR GREAT LIEGE AND CAPTAIN, JANEWAY.
IT SOUNDS GOOD. SO GOOD IT HURTS.

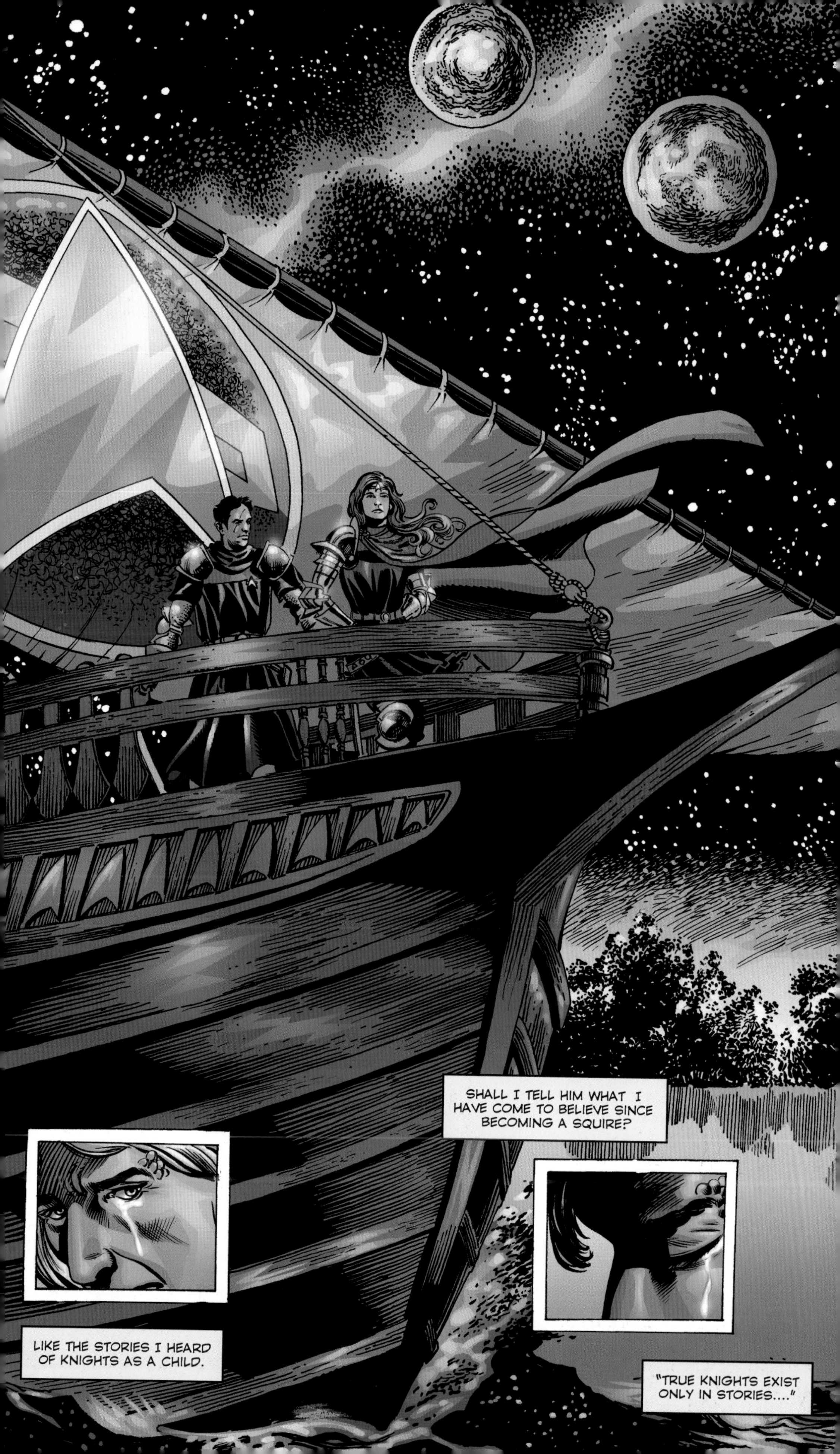
SHALL I TELL HIM WHAT I HAVE COME TO BELIEVE SINCE BECOMING A SQUIRE?
LIKE THE STORIES I HEARD OF KNIGHTS AS A CHILD.
"TRUE KNIGHTS EXIST ONLY IN STORIES...."

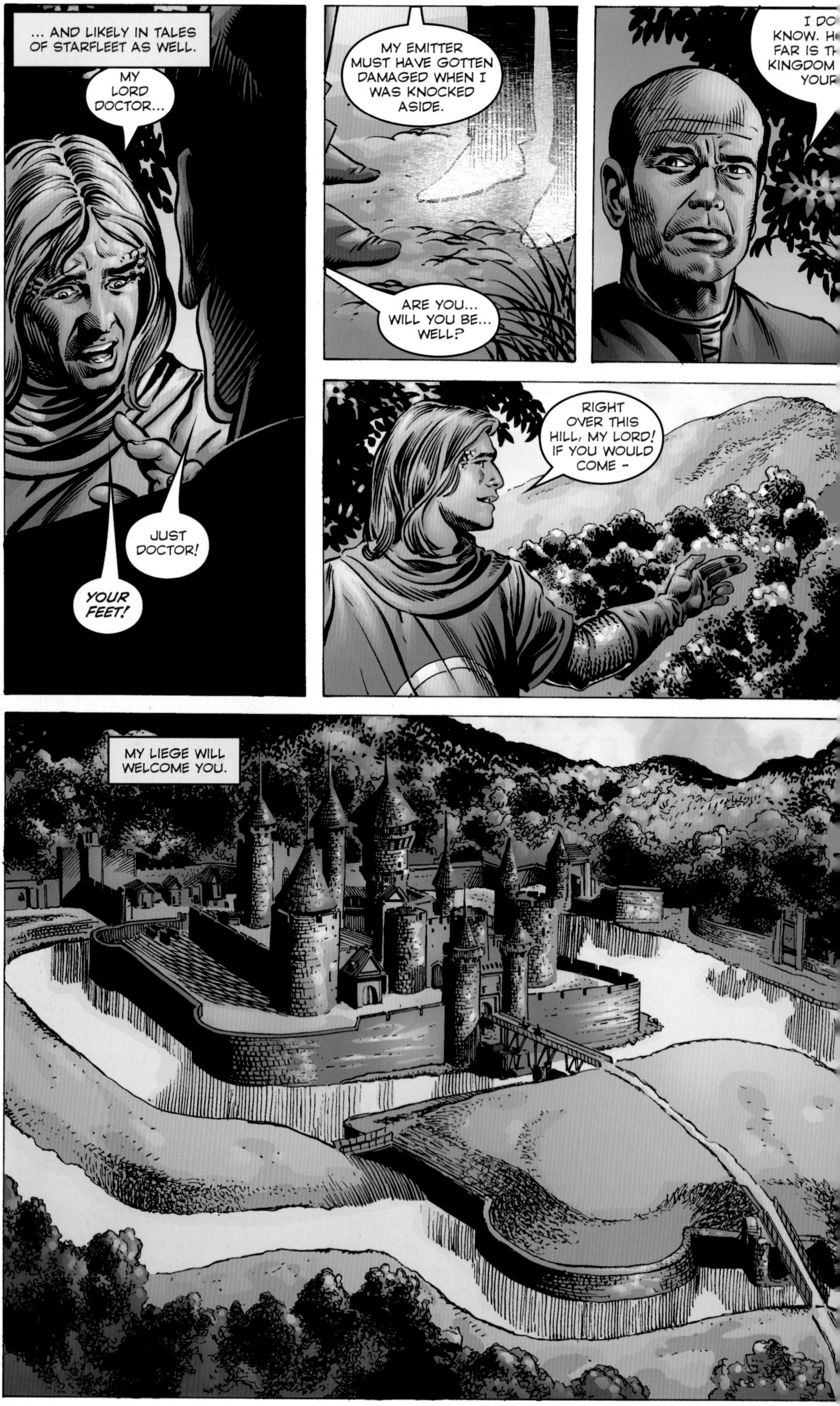
... AND LIKELY IN TALES OF STARFLEET AS WELL.
MY LORD DOCTOR...
JUST DOCTOR!
YOUR FEET!
MY EMITTER MUST HAVE GOTTEN DAMAGED WHEN I WAS KNOCKED ASIDE.
ARE YOU... WILL YOU BE... WELL?
I DO KNOW. H FAR IS TH KINGDOM YOUR
RIGHT OVER THIS HILL, MY LORD! IF YOU WOULD COME -
MY LIEGE WILL WELCOME YOU.

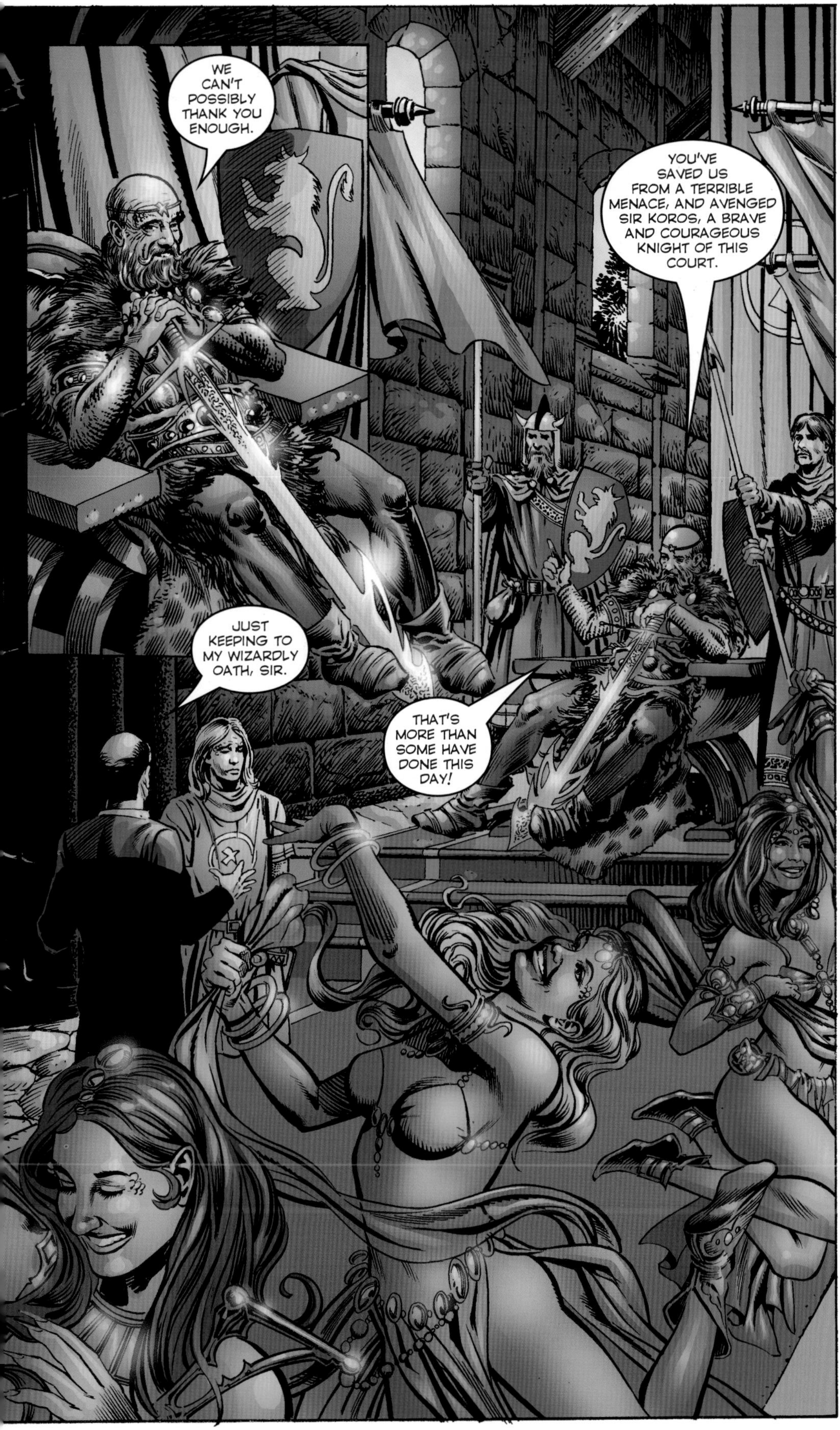
WE CAN'T POSSIBLY THANK YOU ENOUGH.
YOU'VE SAVED US FROM A TERRIBLE MENACE, AND AVENGED SIR KOROS, A BRAVE AND COURAGEOUS KNIGHT OF THIS COURT.
JUST KEEPING TO MY WIZARDLY OATH, SIR.
THAT'S MORE THAN SOME HAVE DONE THIS DAY!

THAT ISN'T FAIR. WEYLYN DID HIS BEST FOR KOROS.

DID HE? WELL, THEN I MUST BELIEVE IT, AS IT IS YOU WHO SAY SO.

WEYLYN INFORMS US YOU'RE SEARCHING FOR THE *BLIND TOWER*?

IS THAT WHAT IT'S CALLED?

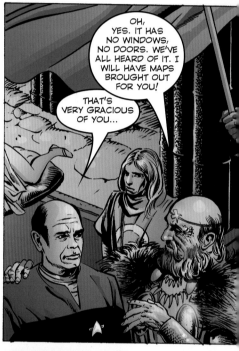

OH, YES. IT HAS NO WINDOWS, NO DOORS. WE'VE ALL HEARD OF IT. I WILL HAVE MAPS BROUGHT OUT FOR YOU!

THAT'S VERY GRACIOUS OF YOU...

A SQUIRE WHO FAILS HIS KNIGHT IS UNWORTHY OF KNIGHTHOOD.

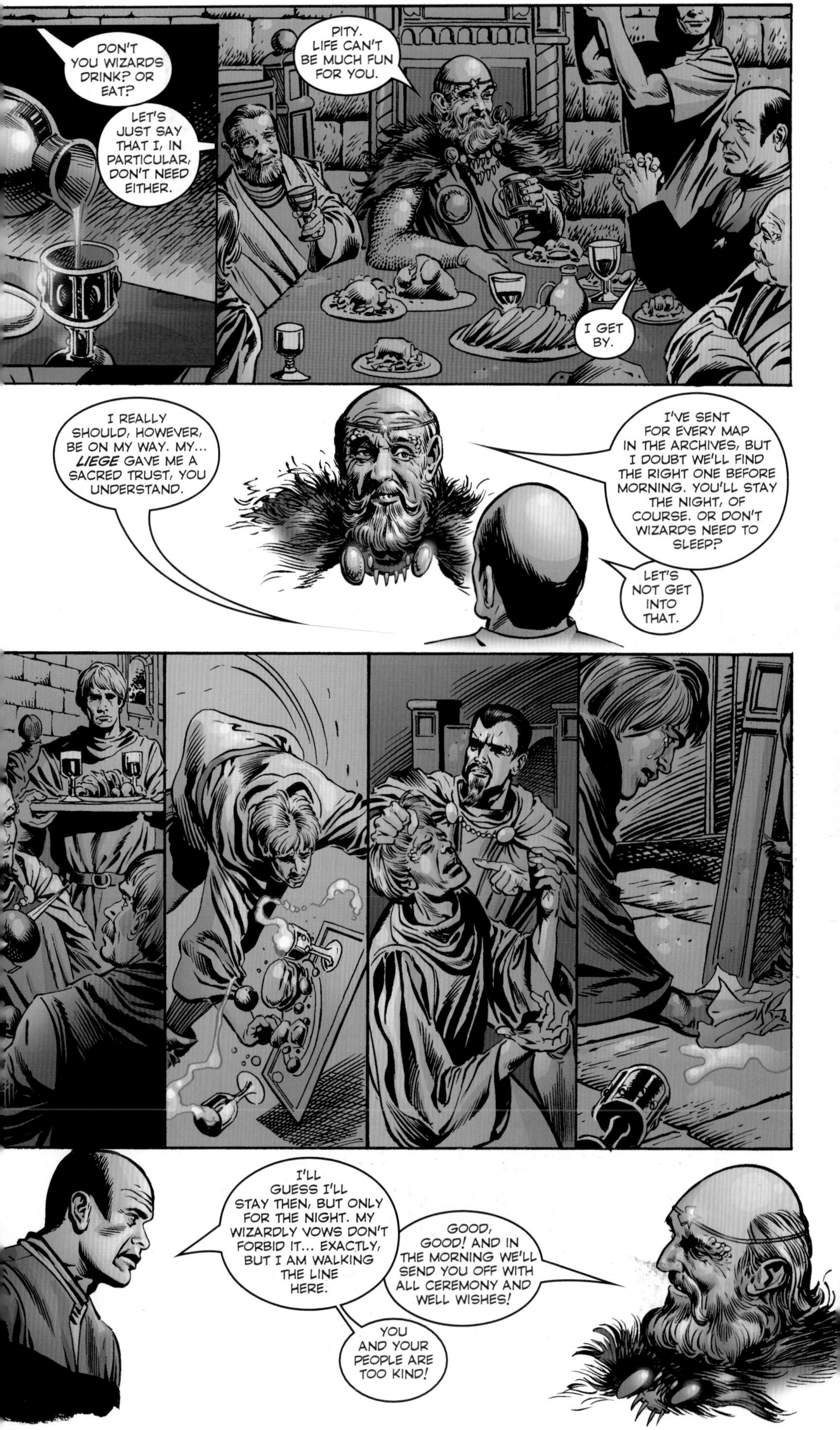
DON'T YOU WIZARDS DRINK? OR EAT?
LET'S JUST SAY THAT I, IN PARTICULAR, DON'T NEED EITHER.
PITY. LIFE CAN'T BE MUCH FUN FOR YOU.
I GET BY.
I REALLY SHOULD, HOWEVER, BE ON MY WAY. MY... *LIEGE* GAVE ME A SACRED TRUST, YOU UNDERSTAND.
I'VE SENT FOR EVERY MAP IN THE ARCHIVES, BUT I DOUBT WE'LL FIND THE RIGHT ONE BEFORE MORNING. YOU'LL STAY THE NIGHT, OF COURSE. OR DON'T WIZARDS NEED TO SLEEP?
LET'S NOT GET INTO THAT.
I'LL GUESS I'LL STAY THEN, BUT ONLY FOR THE NIGHT. MY WIZARDLY VOWS DON'T FORBID IT... EXACTLY, BUT I AM WALKING THE LINE HERE.
GOOD, GOOD! AND IN THE MORNING WE'LL SEND YOU OFF WITH ALL CEREMONY AND WELL WISHES!
YOU AND YOUR PEOPLE ARE TOO KIND!

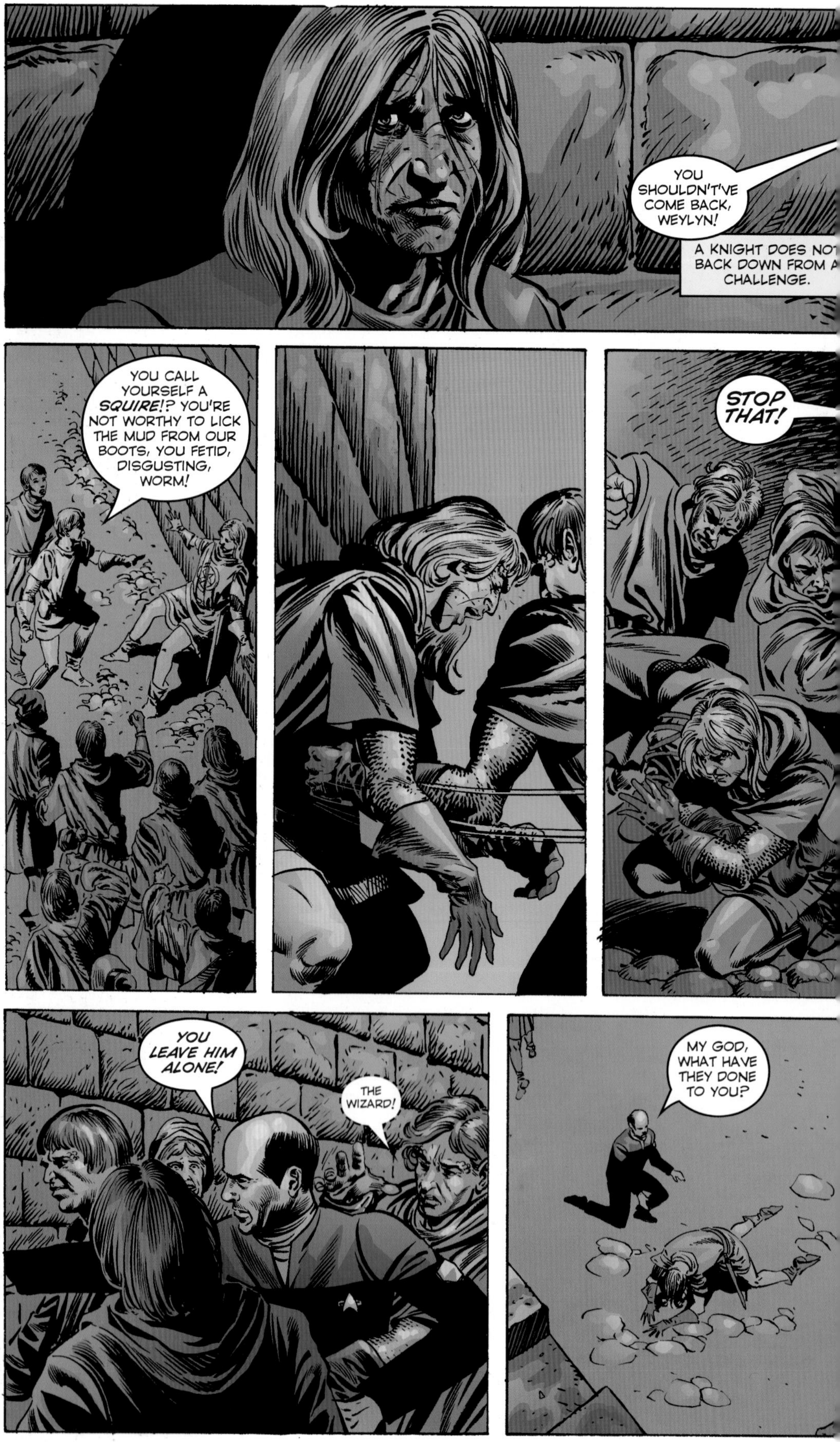

YOU SHOULDN'T'VE COME BACK, WEYLYN!
A KNIGHT DOES NOT BACK DOWN FROM A CHALLENGE.
YOU CALL YOURSELF A SQUIRE!? YOU'RE NOT WORTHY TO LICK THE MUD FROM OUR BOOTS, YOU FETID, DISGUSTING, WORM!
STOP THAT!
YOU LEAVE HIM ALONE!
THE WIZARD!
MY GOD, WHAT HAVE THEY DONE TO YOU?

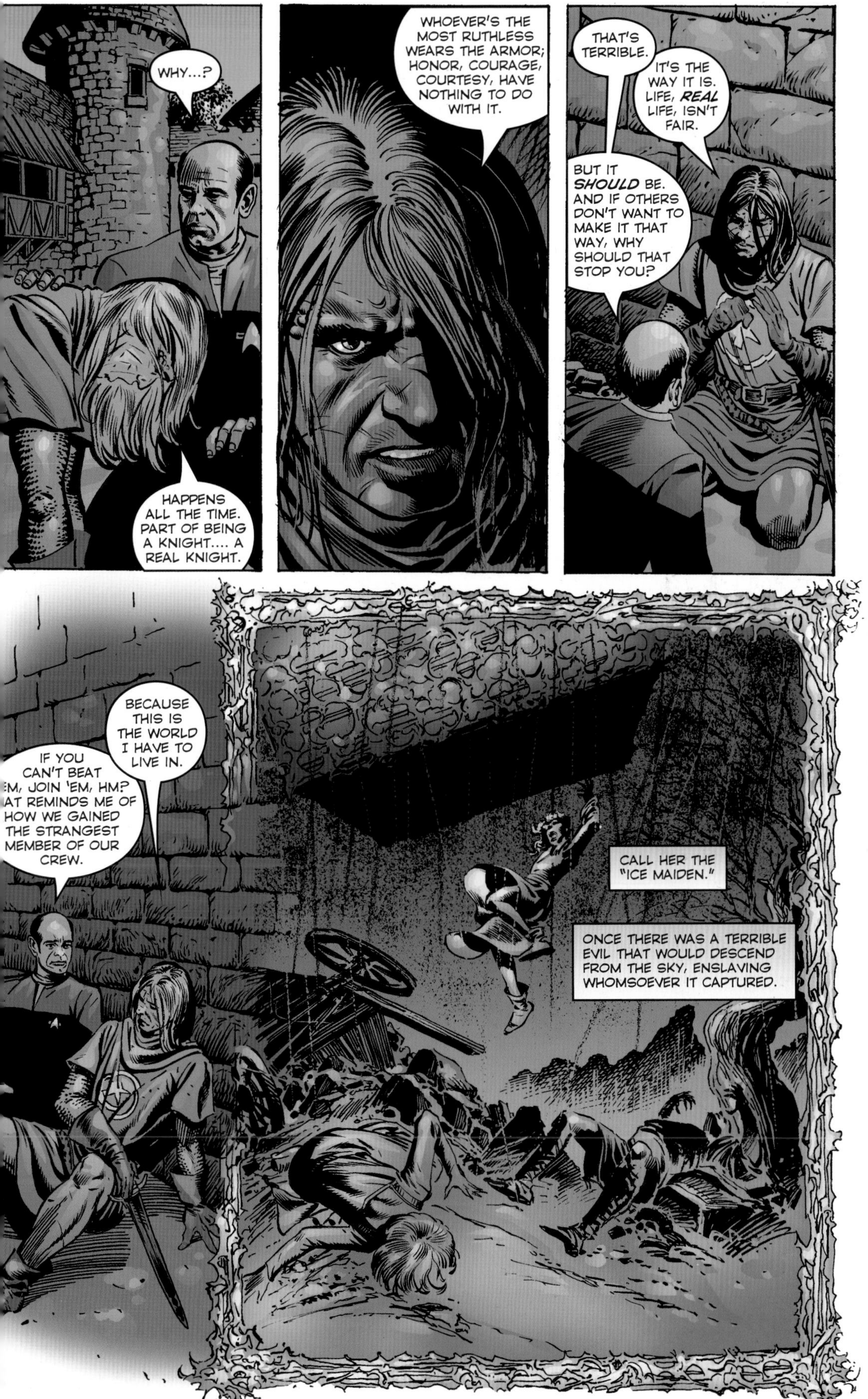
WHY...?
HAPPENS ALL THE TIME. PART OF BEING A KNIGHT.... A REAL KNIGHT.
WHOEVER'S THE MOST RUTHLESS WEARS THE ARMOR; HONOR, COURAGE, COURTESY, HAVE NOTHING TO DO WITH IT.
THAT'S TERRIBLE.
IT'S THE WAY IT IS. LIFE, *REAL* LIFE, ISN'T FAIR.
BUT IT ***SHOULD*** BE. AND IF OTHERS DON'T WANT TO MAKE IT THAT WAY, WHY SHOULD THAT STOP YOU?
BECAUSE THIS IS THE WORLD I HAVE TO LIVE IN.
IF YOU CAN'T BEAT 'EM, JOIN 'EM, HM? AT REMINDS ME OF HOW WE GAINED THE STRANGEST MEMBER OF OUR CREW.
CALL HER THE "ICE MAIDEN."
ONCE THERE WAS A TERRIBLE EVIL THAT WOULD DESCEND FROM THE SKY, ENSLAVING WHOMSOEVER IT CAPTURED.

THE ICE MAIDEN WAS ONE SUCH CAPTIVE. THE EVIL GIFTED HER GREAT KNOWLEDGE, BUT IT ALSO MADE HER COLD AND UNFEELING. INHUMAN.

I WON'T GO INTO DETAILS, BUT THE I MAIDEN CAME INTO OUR HANDS.

... INTO *MY* HANDS. IT WAS UP TO ME TO TRY AND MAKE HER HUMAN AGAIN.

I BROKE MOST OF THE SPELL, BUT NOT ALL OF

YOU SEE, BREAKING THE REST HAD TO BE HER CHOICE. SHE HAD TO DECIDE TO BE WHO SHE WAS, NOT WHAT THE EVIL HAD MADE HER.

I WON'T SAY IT'S E BUT YOU DON'T H TO SAIL IN THE S DIRECTION AS ALL OTHERS. YOU *CAN* THE KIND OF KNI *YOU* WANT TO

MAKE SUR TO PUT SON CLEAN WAT ON THOSE CUTS.

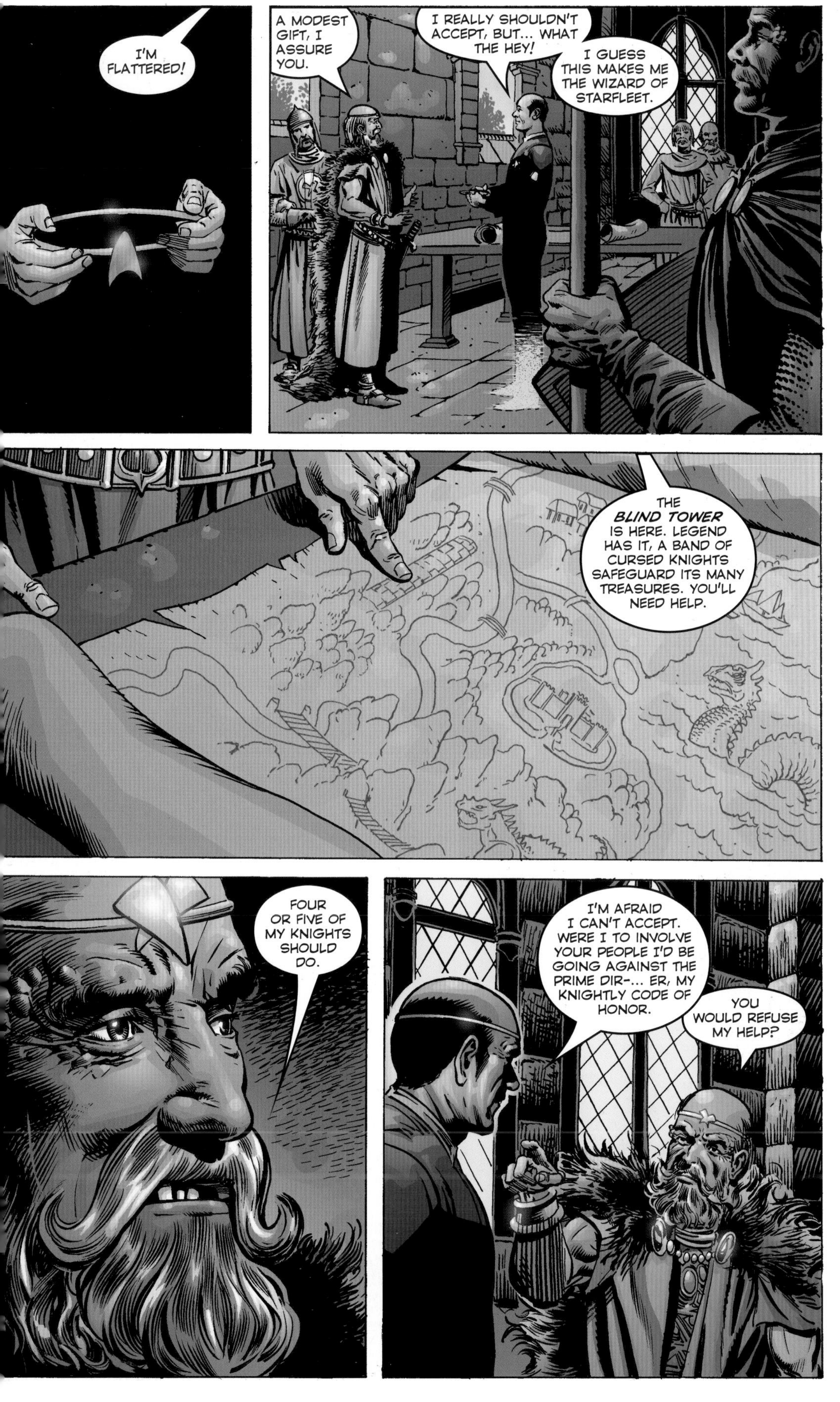
I'M FLATTERED!
A MODEST GIFT, I ASSURE YOU.
I REALLY SHOULDN'T ACCEPT, BUT... WHAT THE HEY!
I GUESS THIS MAKES ME THE WIZARD OF STARFLEET.
THE BLIND TOWER IS HERE. LEGEND HAS IT, A BAND OF CURSED KNIGHTS SAFEGUARD ITS MANY TREASURES. YOU'LL NEED HELP.
FOUR OR FIVE OF MY KNIGHTS SHOULD DO.
I'M AFRAID I CAN'T ACCEPT. WERE I TO INVOLVE YOUR PEOPLE I'D BE GOING AGAINST THE PRIME DIR-... ER, MY KNIGHTLY CODE OF HONOR.
YOU WOULD REFUSE MY HELP?

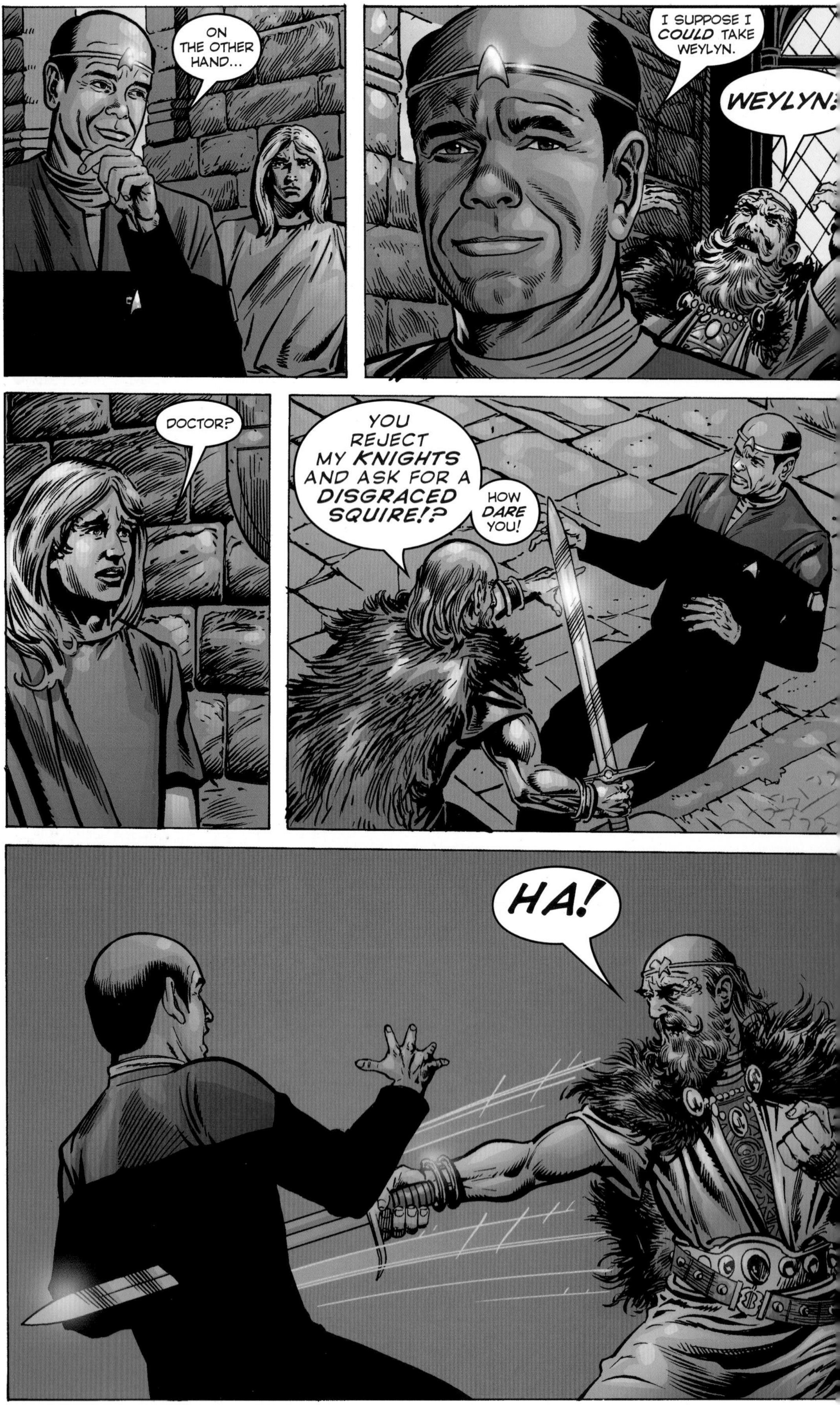

ON THE OTHER HAND...
I SUPPOSE I *COULD* TAKE WEYLYN.
WEYLYN
DOCTOR?
YOU REJECT MY *KNIGHTS* AND ASK FOR A *DISGRACED SQUIRE!?*
HOW *DARE* YOU!
HA!

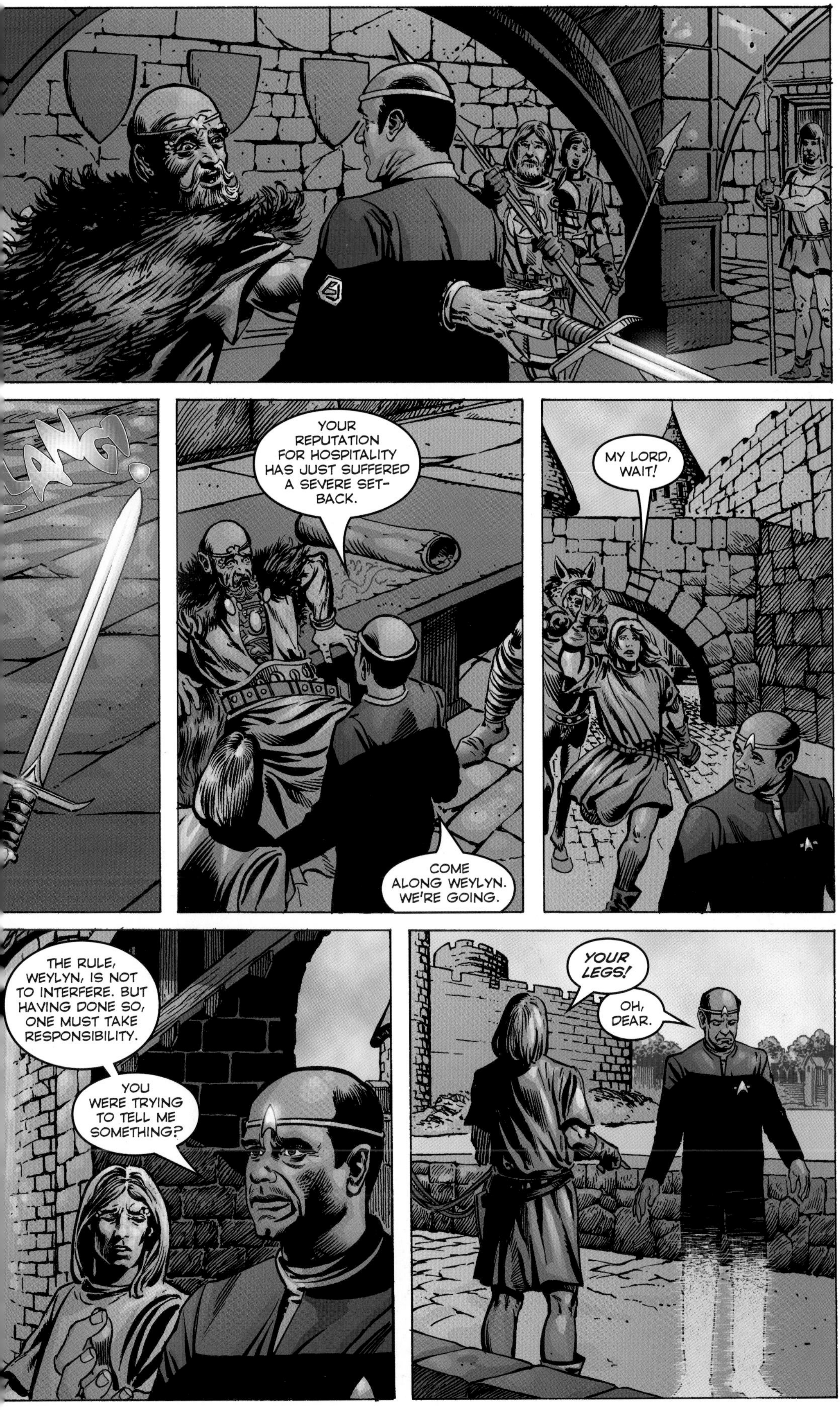
YOUR REPUTATION FOR HOSPITALITY HAS JUST SUFFERED A SEVERE SET-BACK.
COME ALONG WEYLYN. WE'RE GOING.
MY LORD, WAIT!
THE RULE, WEYLYN, IS NOT TO INTERFERE. BUT HAVING DONE SO, ONE MUST TAKE RESPONSIBILITY.
YOU WERE TRYING TO TELL ME SOMETHING?
YOUR LEGS!
OH, DEAR.

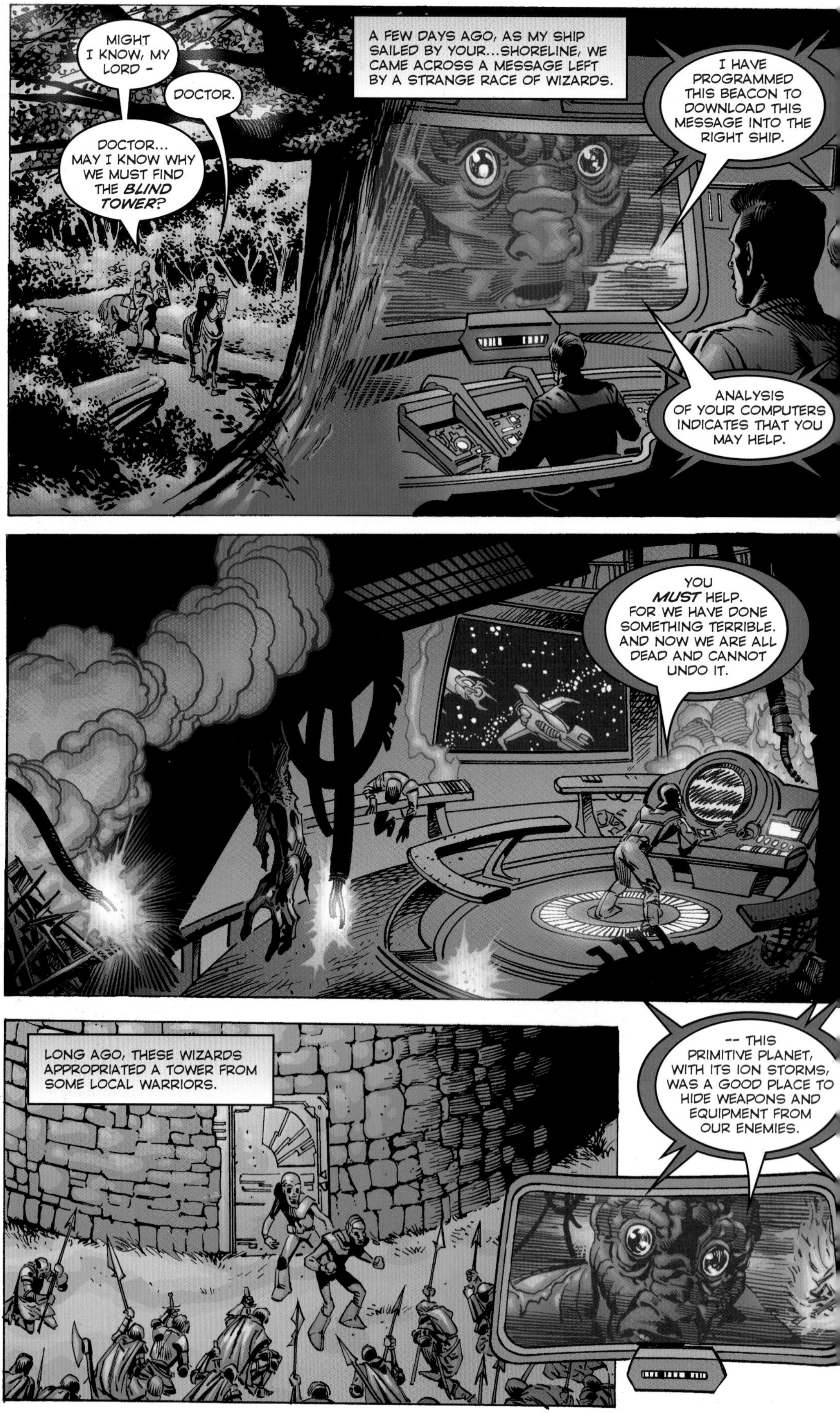
MIGHT I KNOW, MY LORD -
DOCTOR.
DOCTOR... MAY I KNOW WHY WE MUST FIND THE *BLIND TOWER*?
A FEW DAYS AGO, AS MY SHIP SAILED BY YOUR...SHORELINE, WE CAME ACROSS A MESSAGE LEFT BY A STRANGE RACE OF WIZARDS.
I HAVE PROGRAMMED THIS BEACON TO DOWNLOAD THIS MESSAGE INTO THE RIGHT SHIP.
ANALYSIS OF YOUR COMPUTERS INDICATES THAT YOU MAY HELP.
YOU *MUST* HELP. FOR WE HAVE DONE SOMETHING TERRIBLE. AND NOW WE ARE ALL DEAD AND CANNOT UNDO IT.
LONG AGO, THESE WIZARDS APPROPRIATED A TOWER FROM SOME LOCAL WARRIORS.
-- THIS PRIMITIVE PLANET, WITH ITS ION STORMS, WAS A GOOD PLACE TO HIDE WEAPONS AND EQUIPMENT FROM OUR ENEMIES.

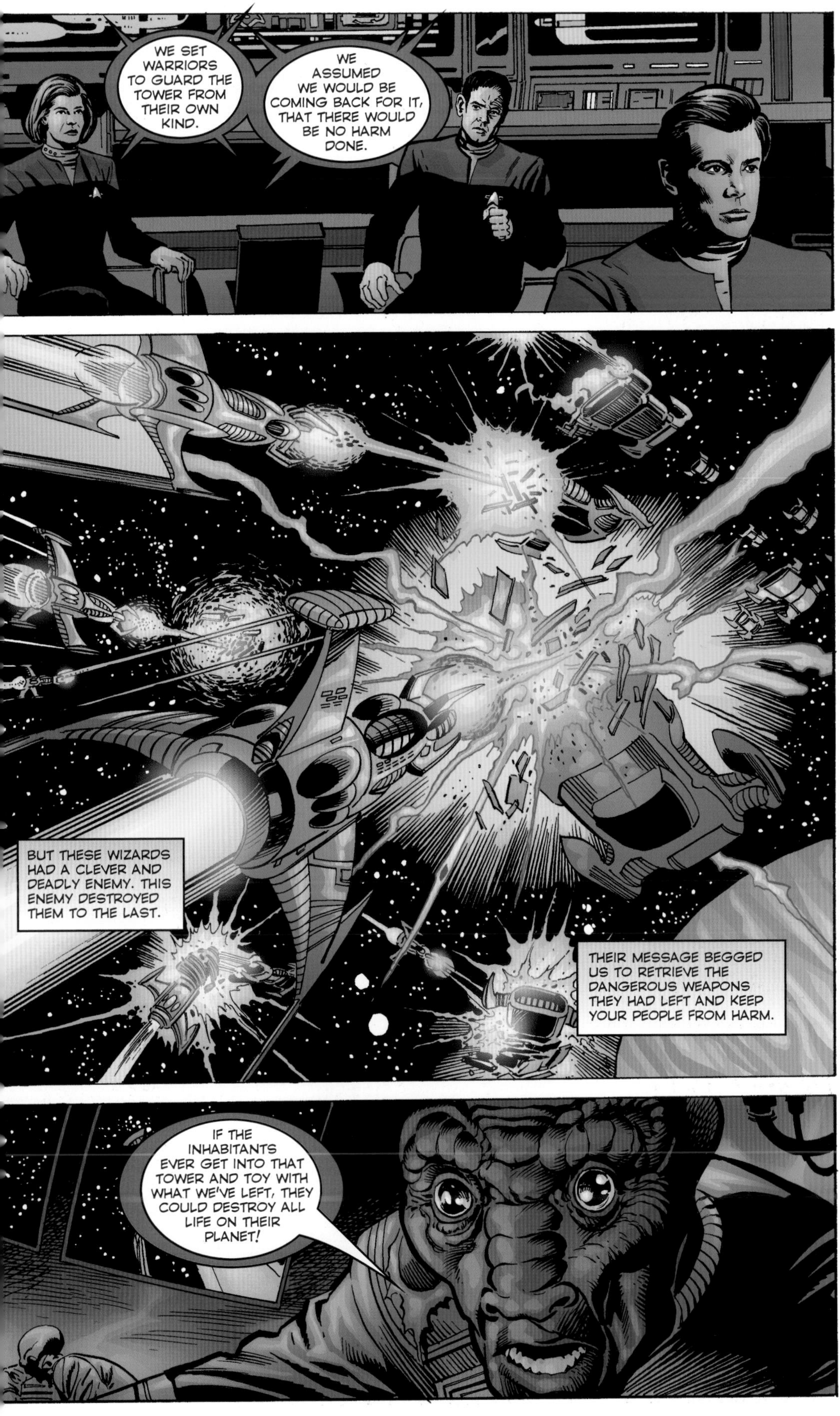
WE SET WARRIORS TO GUARD THE TOWER FROM THEIR OWN KIND.
WE ASSUMED WE WOULD BE COMING BACK FOR IT, THAT THERE WOULD BE NO HARM DONE.
BUT THESE WIZARDS HAD A CLEVER AND DEADLY ENEMY. THIS ENEMY DESTROYED THEM TO THE LAST.
THEIR MESSAGE BEGGED US TO RETRIEVE THE DANGEROUS WEAPONS THEY HAD LEFT AND KEEP YOUR PEOPLE FROM HARM.
IF THE INHABITANTS EVER GET INTO THAT TOWER AND TOY WITH WHAT WE'VE LEFT, THEY COULD DESTROY ALL LIFE ON THEIR PLANET!

... PLEASE! YOU MUST GET THOSE WEAPONS OFF OF THAT WORLD!

NO PRIME DIRECTIVE.

AND *LOOK* WHAT HAPPENS! THEY'VE PUT US IN A REAL CATCH-22.

IF WE DO AS THEY ASK, WE MIGHT INFLUENCE THE INHABITANTS, TOO.

IF WE DON'T, THERE MAY NOT BE ANY INHABITANTS.

I'VE GONE OVER THE LIST OF EQUIPMENT THEY LEFT. WE COULD REALLY USE SOME OF IT.

THERE IS, HOWEVER, NO WAY FOR US TO BEAM DOWN, AND WE CANNOT RISK A SHUTTLE IN THOSE ION STORMS.

TRUE. BUT WE STILL HAVE ONE OPTION.

WHEN WAS THE LAST TIME THE DOCTOR WAS ON AN AWAY MISSION?

THESE MAGICAL STORMS ARE KEEPING ME FROM CONTACTING MY SHIP. IF I CAN JUST GET TO THE TOWER, THAT WILL CHANGE.

IF THERE ARE NO MORE DELAYS.

IT IS A NOBL[E] ENDEAVO[R] HOW MA[NY] I --

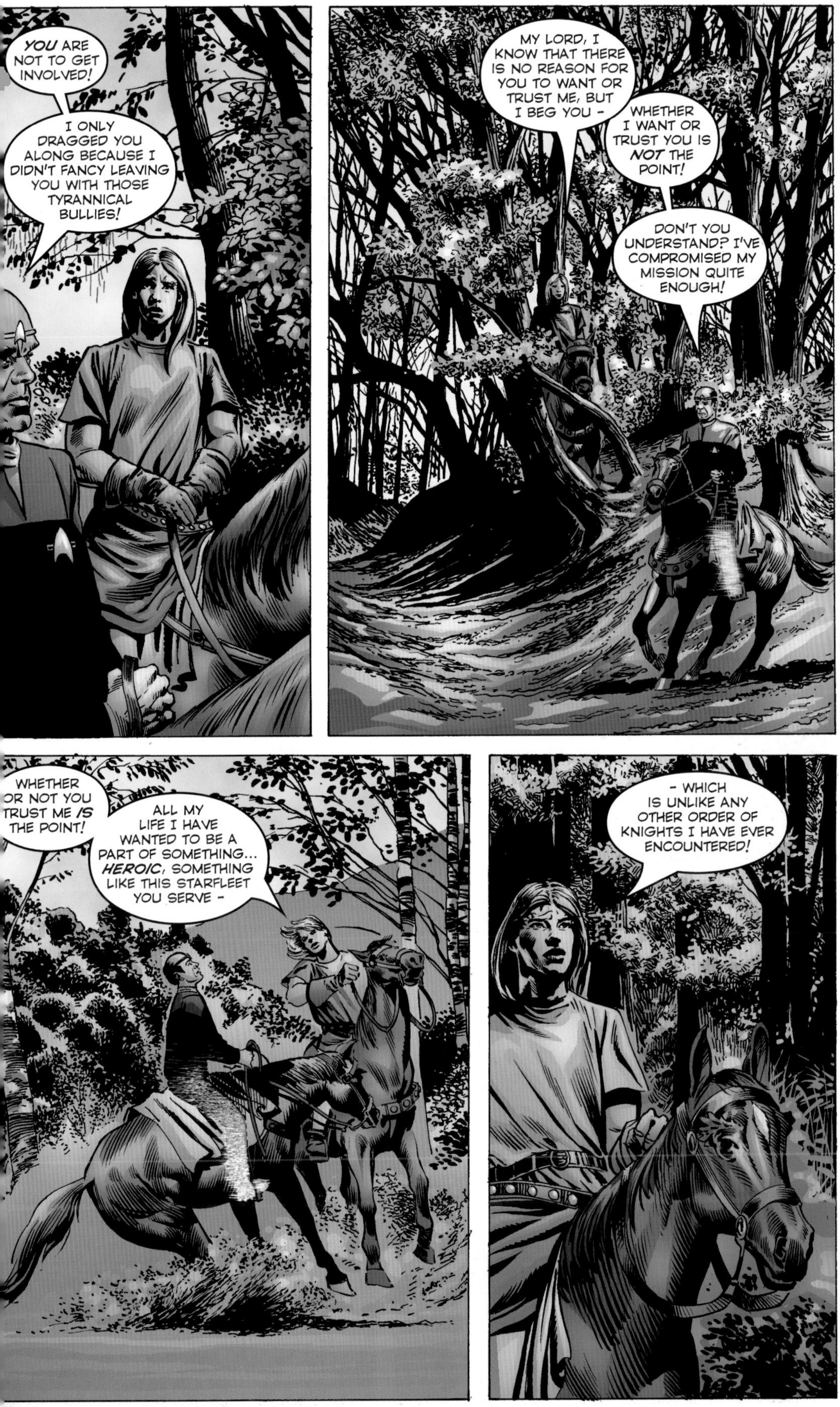
YOU ARE NOT TO GET INVOLVED!
I ONLY DRAGGED YOU ALONG BECAUSE I DIDN'T FANCY LEAVING YOU WITH THOSE TYRANNICAL BULLIES!
MY LORD, I KNOW THAT THERE IS NO REASON FOR YOU TO WANT OR TRUST ME, BUT I BEG YOU -
WHETHER I WANT OR TRUST YOU IS NOT THE POINT!
DON'T YOU UNDERSTAND? I'VE COMPROMISED MY MISSION QUITE ENOUGH!
WHETHER OR NOT YOU TRUST ME IS THE POINT!
ALL MY LIFE I HAVE WANTED TO BE A PART OF SOMETHING... HEROIC, SOMETHING LIKE THIS STARFLEET YOU SERVE -
- WHICH IS UNLIKE ANY OTHER ORDER OF KNIGHTS I HAVE EVER ENCOUNTERED!

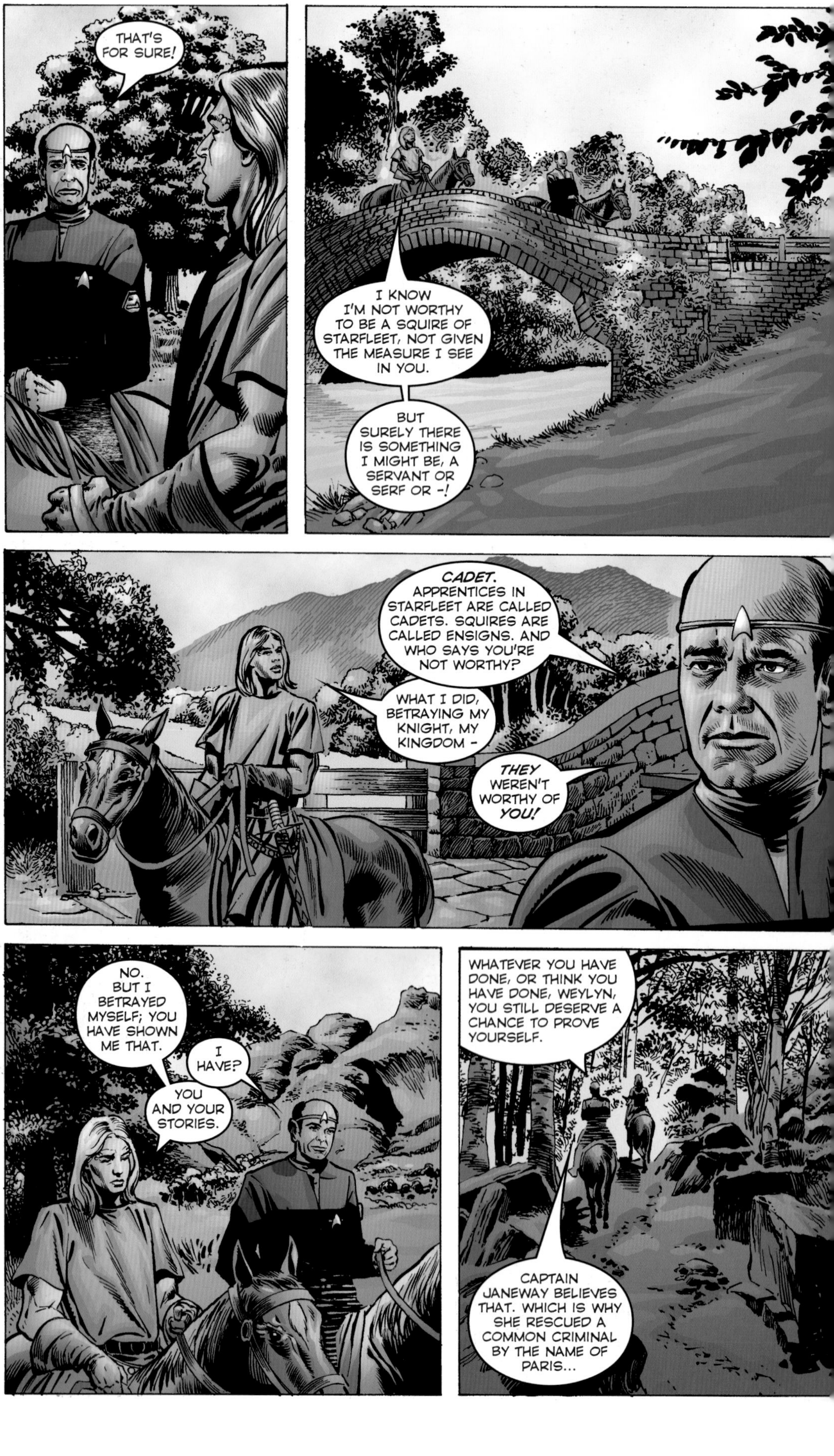
THAT'S FOR SURE!
I KNOW I'M NOT WORTHY TO BE A SQUIRE OF STARFLEET, NOT GIVEN THE MEASURE I SEE IN YOU.
BUT SURELY THERE IS SOMETHING I MIGHT BE, A SERVANT OR SERF OR -!
CADET. APPRENTICES IN STARFLEET ARE CALLED CADETS. SQUIRES ARE CALLED ENSIGNS. AND WHO SAYS YOU'RE NOT WORTHY?
WHAT I DID, BETRAYING MY KNIGHT, MY KINGDOM -
THEY WEREN'T WORTHY OF YOU!
NO. BUT I BETRAYED MYSELF; YOU HAVE SHOWN ME THAT.
I HAVE?
YOU AND YOUR STORIES.
WHATEVER YOU HAVE DONE, OR THINK YOU HAVE DONE, WEYLYN, YOU STILL DESERVE A CHANCE TO PROVE YOURSELF.
CAPTAIN JANEWAY BELIEVES THAT. WHICH IS WHY SHE RESCUED A COMMON CRIMINAL BY THE NAME OF PARIS...

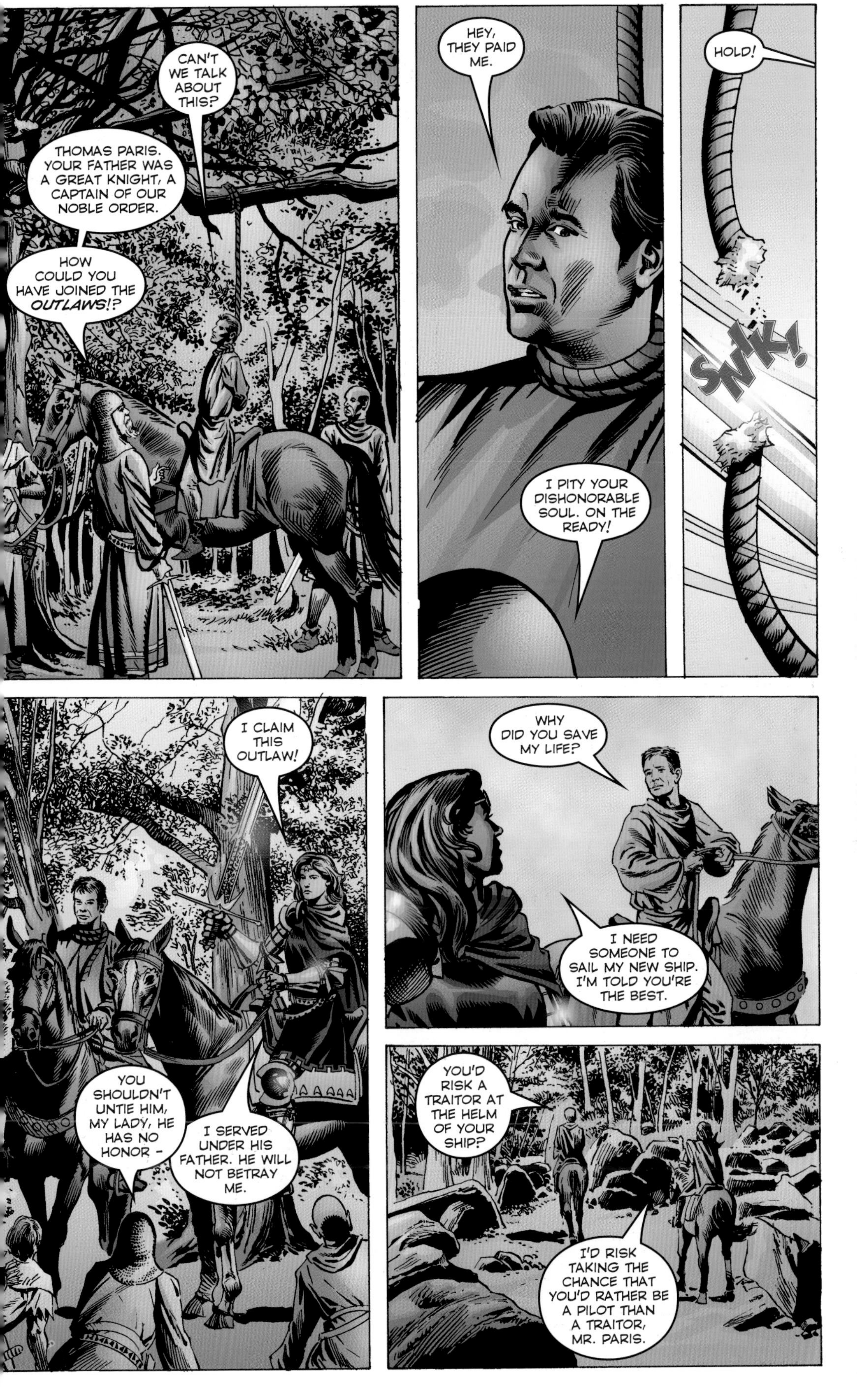
THOMAS PARIS. YOUR FATHER WAS A GREAT KNIGHT, A CAPTAIN OF OUR NOBLE ORDER.
CAN'T WE TALK ABOUT THIS?
HOW COULD YOU HAVE JOINED THE OUTLAWS!?
HEY, THEY PAID ME.
I PITY YOUR DISHONORABLE SOUL. ON THE READY!
HOLD!
SNIK!
I CLAIM THIS OUTLAW!
YOU SHOULDN'T UNTIE HIM, MY LADY, HE HAS NO HONOR -
I SERVED UNDER HIS FATHER. HE WILL NOT BETRAY ME.
WHY DID YOU SAVE MY LIFE?
I NEED SOMEONE TO SAIL MY NEW SHIP. I'M TOLD YOU'RE THE BEST.
YOU'D RISK A TRAITOR AT THE HELM OF YOUR SHIP?
I'D RISK TAKING THE CHANCE THAT YOU'D RATHER BE A PILOT THAN A TRAITOR, MR. PARIS.

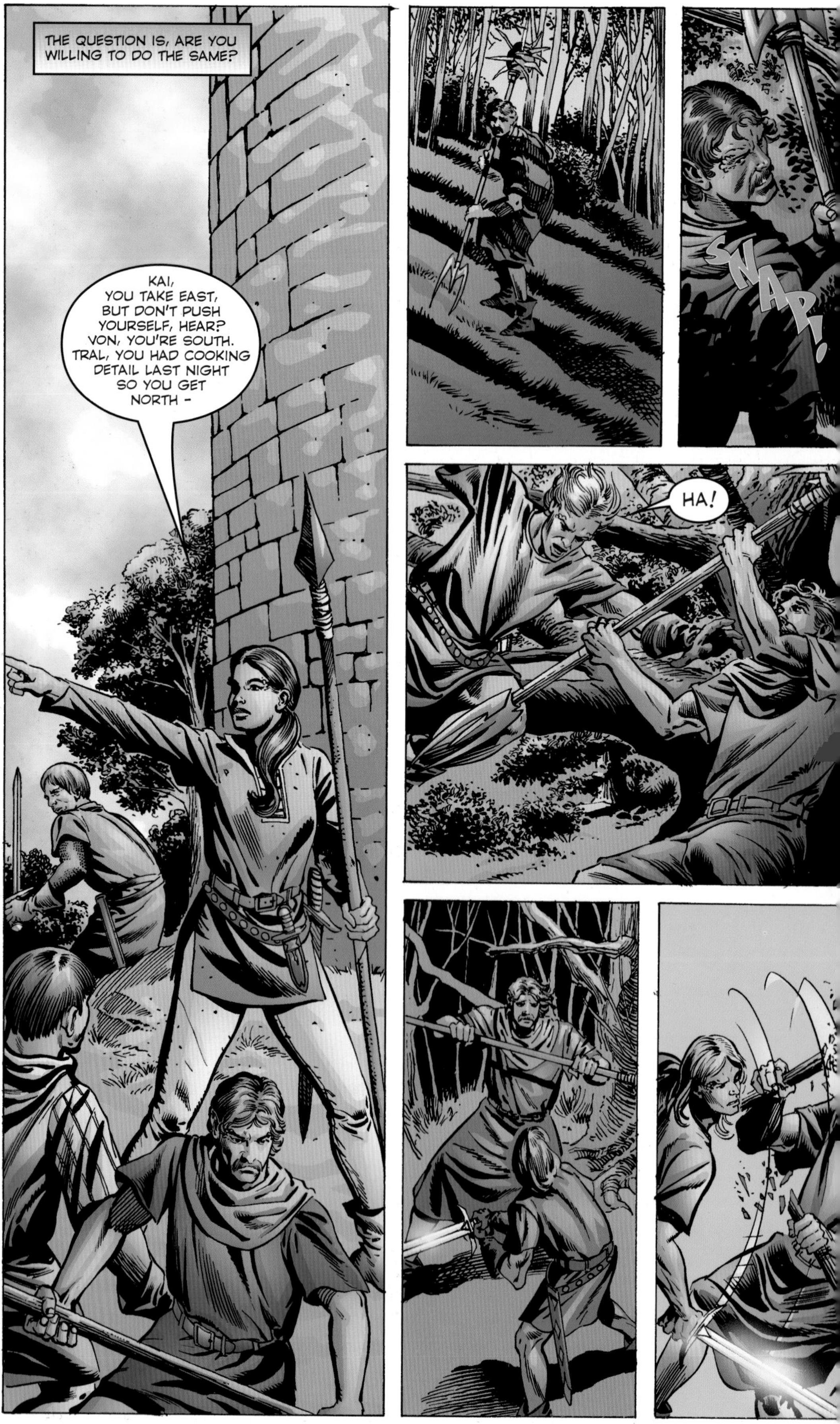
THE QUESTION IS, ARE YOU WILLING TO DO THE SAME?
KAI, YOU TAKE EAST, BUT DON'T PUSH YOURSELF, HEAR? VON, YOU'RE SOUTH. TRAL, YOU HAD COOKING DETAIL LAST NIGHT SO YOU GET NORTH -
SNAP!
HA!

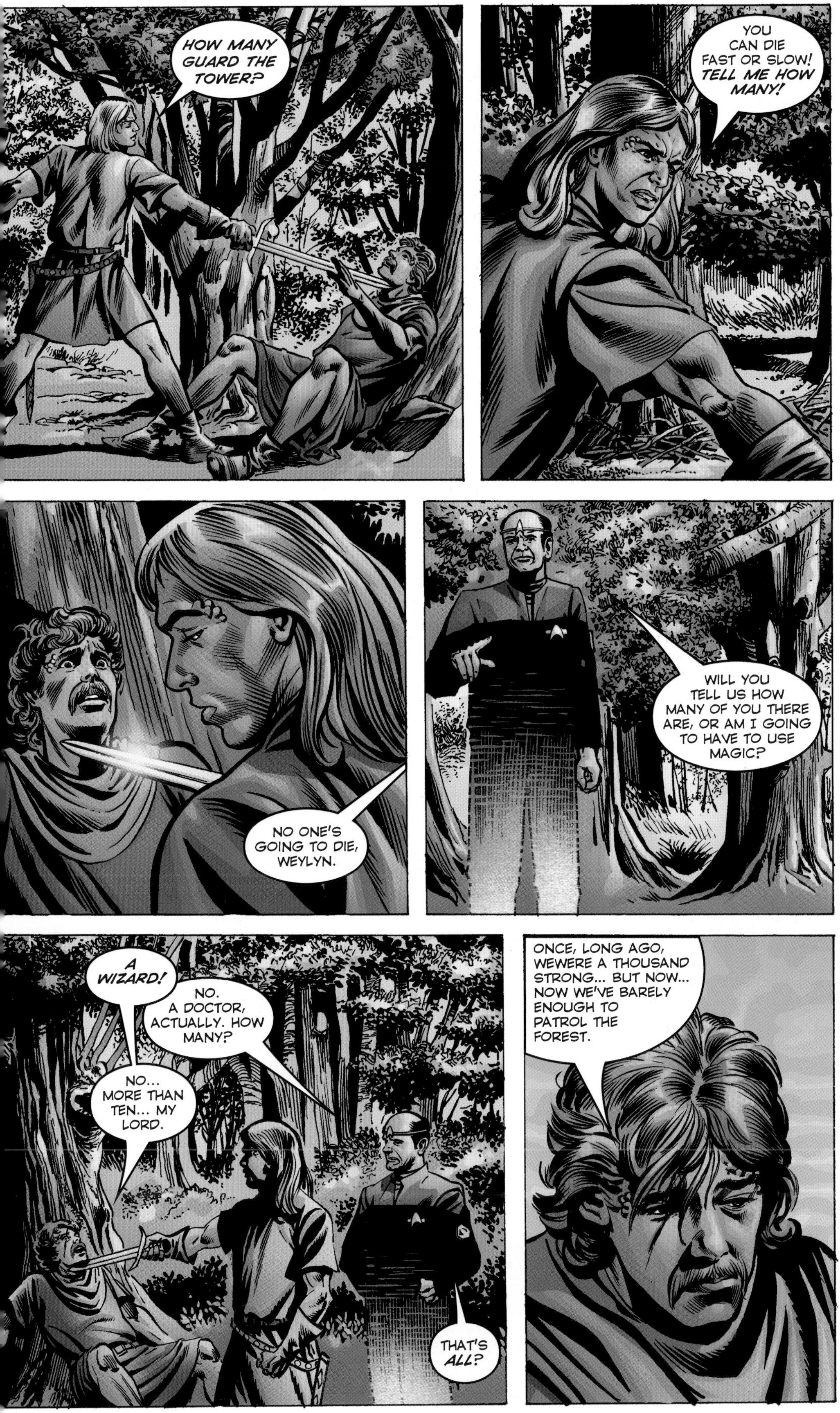

HOW MANY GUARD THE TOWER?
YOU CAN DIE FAST OR SLOW! TELL ME HOW MANY!
NO ONE'S GOING TO DIE, WEYLYN.
WILL YOU TELL US HOW MANY OF YOU THERE ARE, OR AM I GOING TO HAVE TO USE MAGIC?
A WIZARD!
NO. A DOCTOR, ACTUALLY. HOW MANY?
NO... MORE THAN TEN... MY LORD.
THAT'S ALL?
ONCE, LONG AGO, WEWERE A THOUSAND STRONG... BUT NOW... NOW WE'VE BARELY ENOUGH TO PATROL THE FOREST.

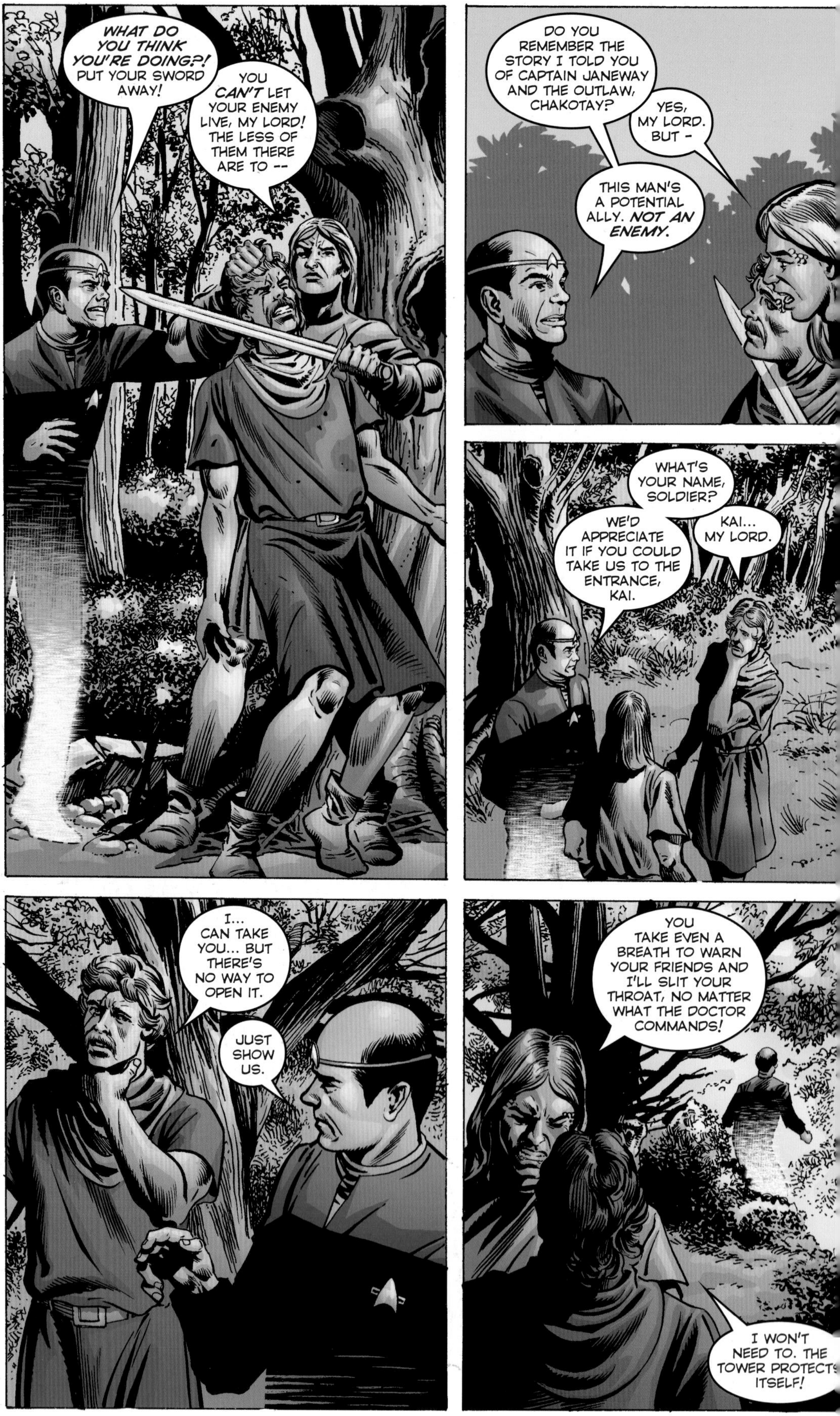
WHAT DO YOU THINK YOU'RE DOING?! PUT YOUR SWORD AWAY!
YOU CAN'T LET YOUR ENEMY LIVE, MY LORD! THE LESS OF THEM THERE ARE TO --
DO YOU REMEMBER THE STORY I TOLD YOU OF CAPTAIN JANEWAY AND THE OUTLAW, CHAKOTAY?
YES, MY LORD. BUT -
THIS MAN'S A POTENTIAL ALLY. NOT AN ENEMY.
WHAT'S YOUR NAME, SOLDIER?
KAI... MY LORD.
WE'D APPRECIATE IT IF YOU COULD TAKE US TO THE ENTRANCE, KAI.
I... CAN TAKE YOU... BUT THERE'S NO WAY TO OPEN IT.
JUST SHOW US.
YOU TAKE EVEN A BREATH TO WARN YOUR FRIENDS AND I'LL SLIT YOUR THROAT, NO MATTER WHAT THE DOCTOR COMMANDS!
I WON'T NEED TO. THE TOWER PROTECTS ITSELF!

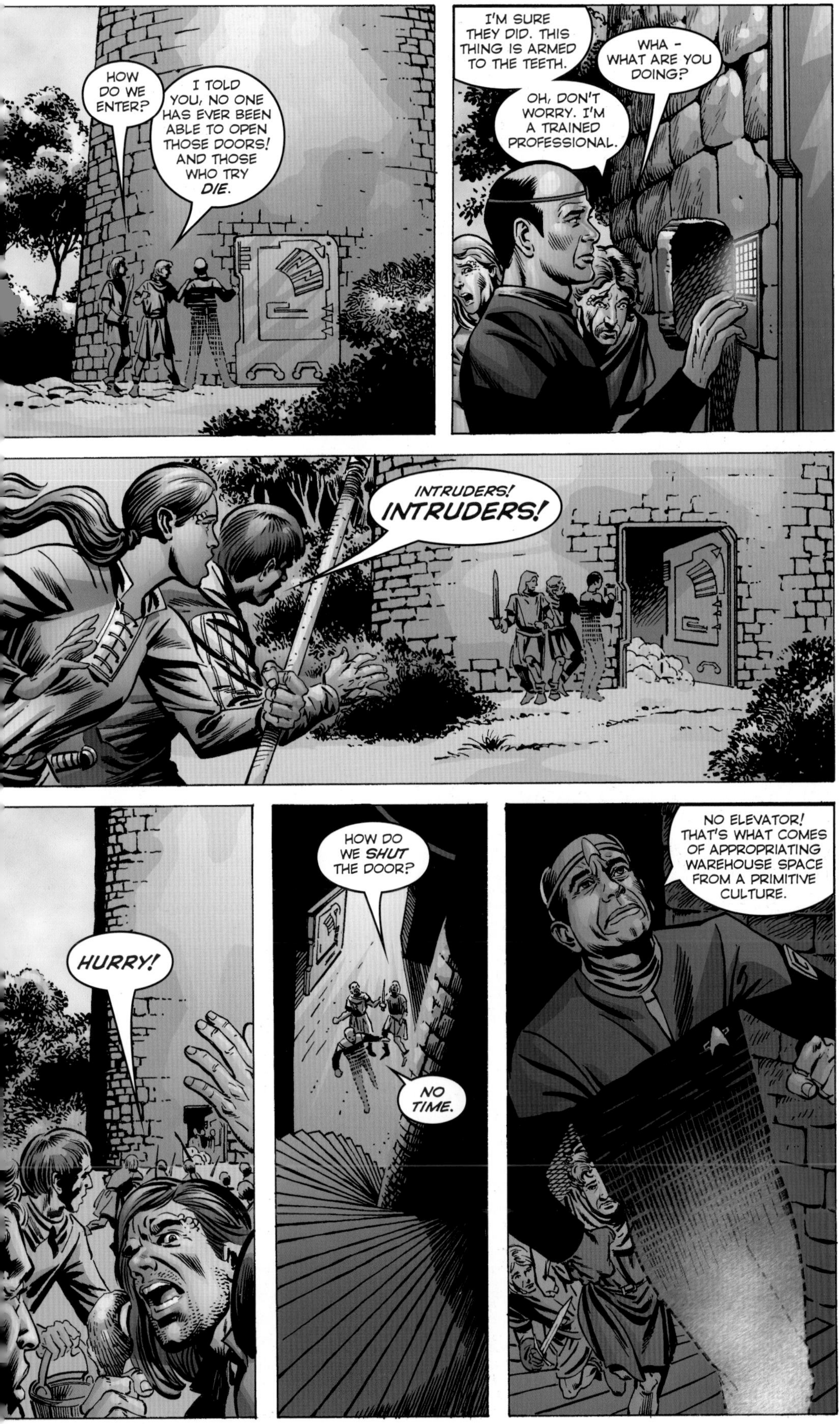
HOW DO WE ENTER?
I TOLD YOU, NO ONE HAS EVER BEEN ABLE TO OPEN THOSE DOORS! AND THOSE WHO TRY DIE.
I'M SURE THEY DID. THIS THING IS ARMED TO THE TEETH.
WHA - WHAT ARE YOU DOING?
OH, DON'T WORRY. I'M A TRAINED PROFESSIONAL.
INTRUDERS! INTRUDERS!
HURRY!
HOW DO WE SHUT THE DOOR?
NO TIME.
NO ELEVATOR! THAT'S WHAT COMES OF APPROPRIATING WAREHOUSE SPACE FROM A PRIMITIVE CULTURE.

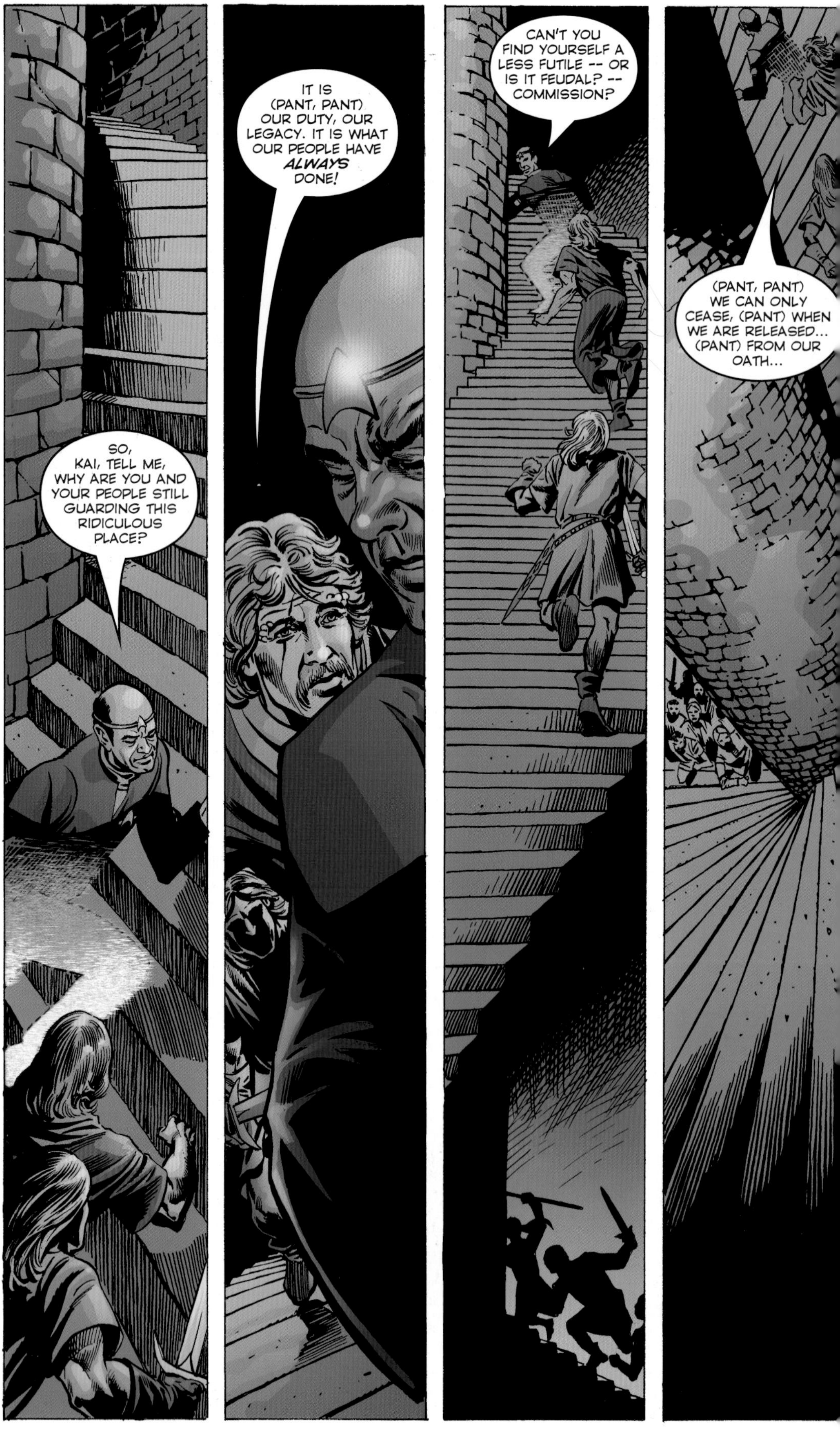
SO, KAI, TELL ME, WHY ARE YOU AND YOUR PEOPLE STILL GUARDING THIS RIDICULOUS PLACE?
IT IS (PANT, PANT) OUR DUTY, OUR LEGACY. IT IS WHAT OUR PEOPLE HAVE *ALWAYS* DONE!
CAN'T YOU FIND YOURSELF A LESS FUTILE -- OR IS IT FEUDAL? -- COMMISSION?
(PANT, PANT) WE CAN ONLY CEASE, (PANT) WHEN WE ARE RELEASED... (PANT) FROM OUR OATH...

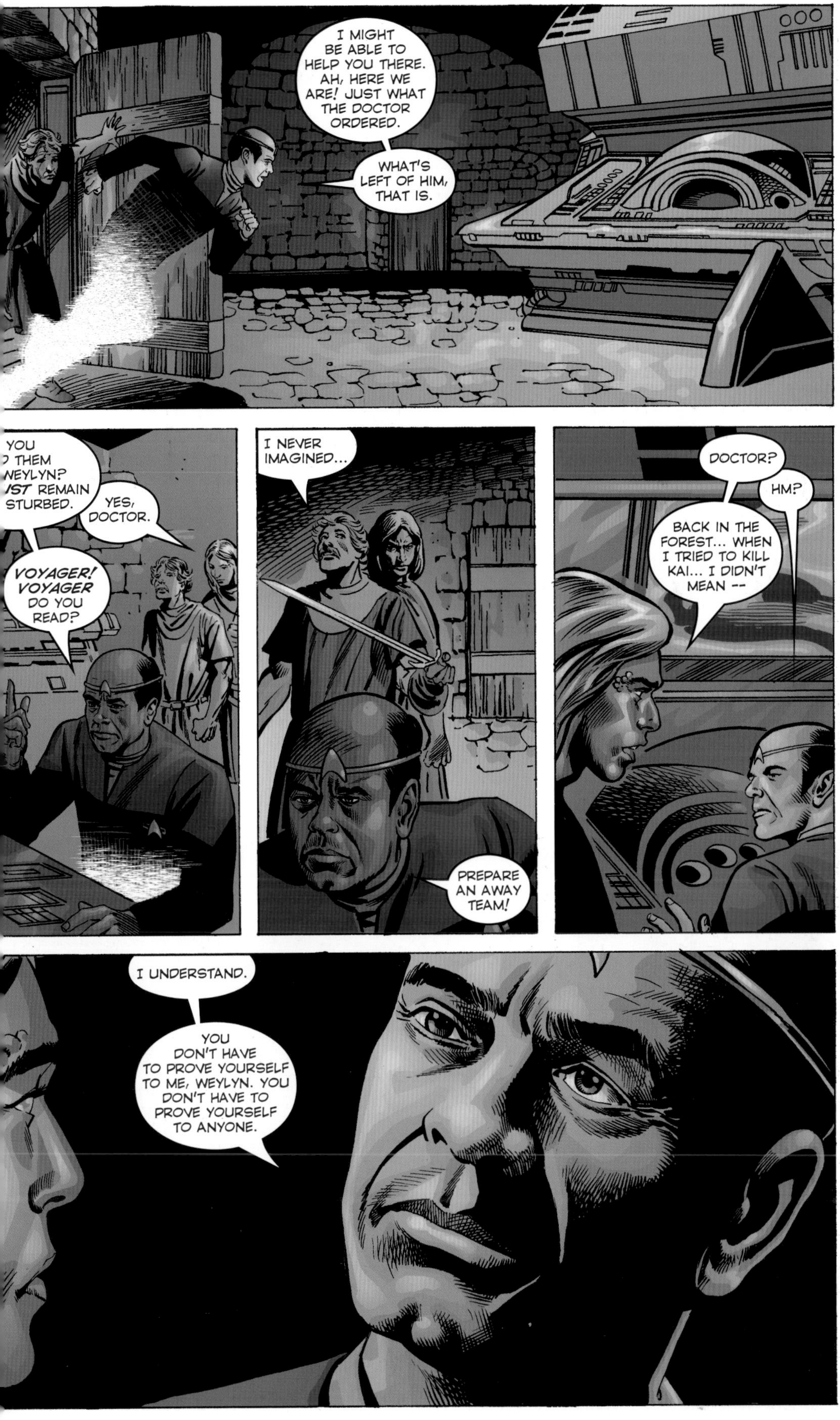
I MIGHT BE ABLE TO HELP YOU THERE. AH, HERE WE ARE! JUST WHAT THE DOCTOR ORDERED.
WHAT'S LEFT OF HIM, THAT IS.
YOU D THEM WEYLYN? UST REMAIN STURBED.
YES, DOCTOR.
VOYAGER! VOYAGER DO YOU READ?
I NEVER IMAGINED...
PREPARE AN AWAY TEAM!
DOCTOR?
HM?
BACK IN THE FOREST... WHEN I TRIED TO KILL KAI... I DIDN'T MEAN --
I UNDERSTAND.
YOU DON'T HAVE TO PROVE YOURSELF TO ME, WEYLYN. YOU DON'T HAVE TO PROVE YOURSELF TO ANYONE.

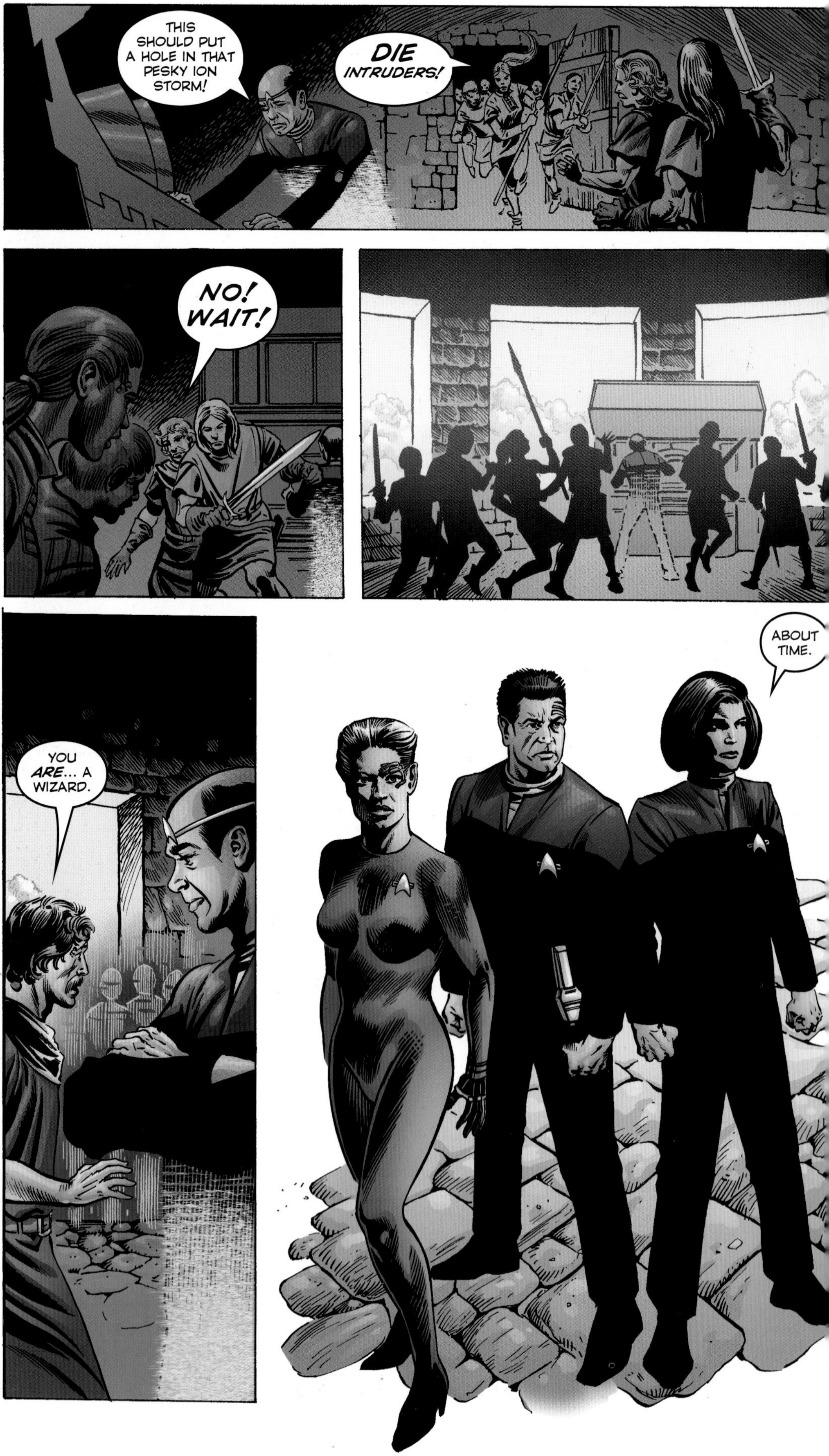
THIS SHOULD PUT A HOLE IN THAT PESKY ION STORM!
DIE INTRUDERS!
NO! WAIT!
YOU ARE... A WIZARD.
ABOUT TIME.

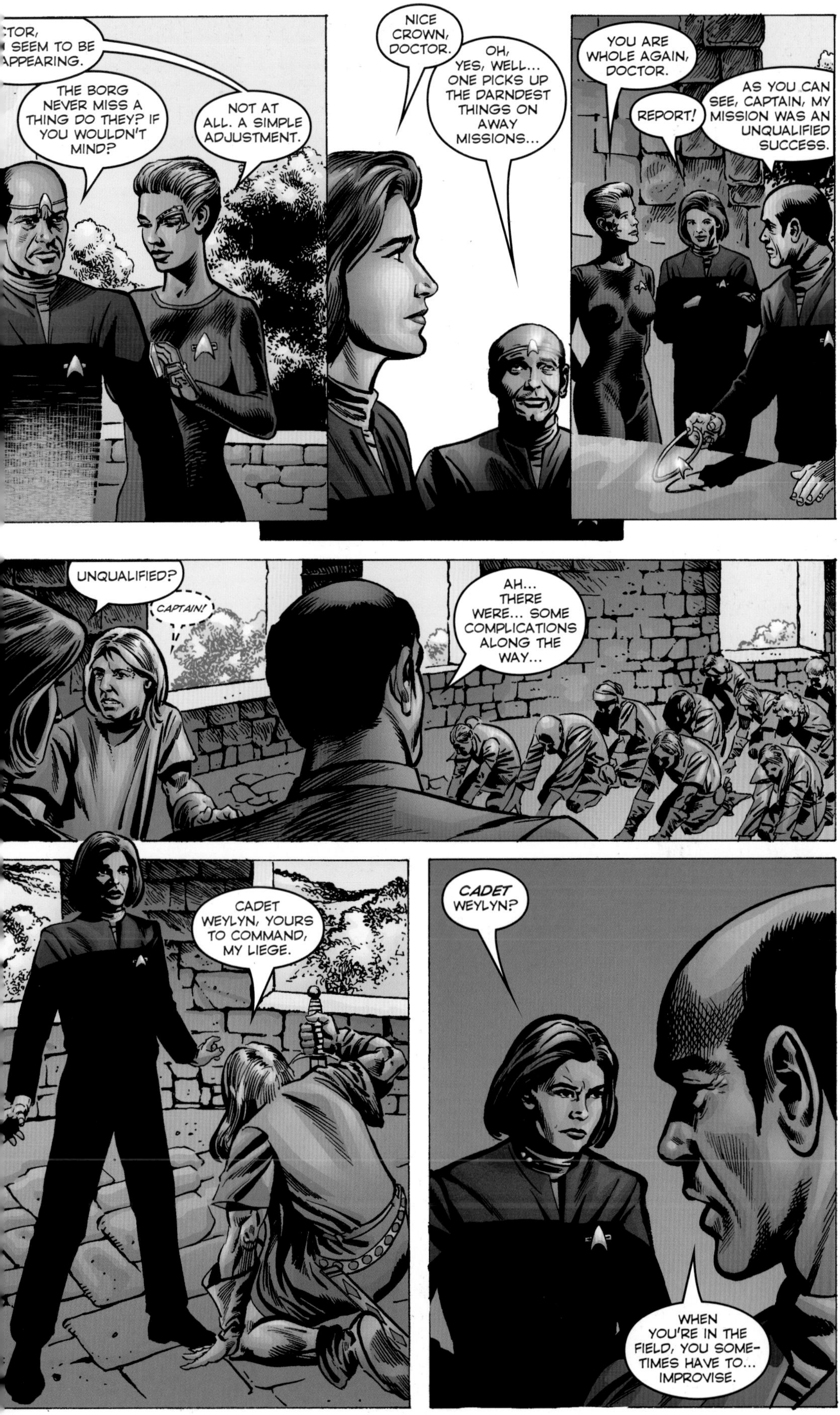

CTOR,
SEEM TO BE
APPEARING.
THE BORG NEVER MISS A THING DO THEY? IF YOU WOULDN'T MIND?
NOT AT ALL. A SIMPLE ADJUSTMENT.
NICE CROWN, DOCTOR.
OH, YES, WELL... ONE PICKS UP THE DARNDEST THINGS ON AWAY MISSIONS...
YOU ARE WHOLE AGAIN, DOCTOR.
REPORT!
AS YOU CAN SEE, CAPTAIN, MY MISSION WAS AN UNQUALIFIED SUCCESS.
UNQUALIFIED?
CAPTAIN!
AH... THERE WERE... SOME COMPLICATIONS ALONG THE WAY...
CADET WEYLYN, YOURS TO COMMAND, MY LIEGE.
CADET WEYLYN?
WHEN YOU'RE IN THE FIELD, YOU SOME-TIMES HAVE TO... IMPROVISE.

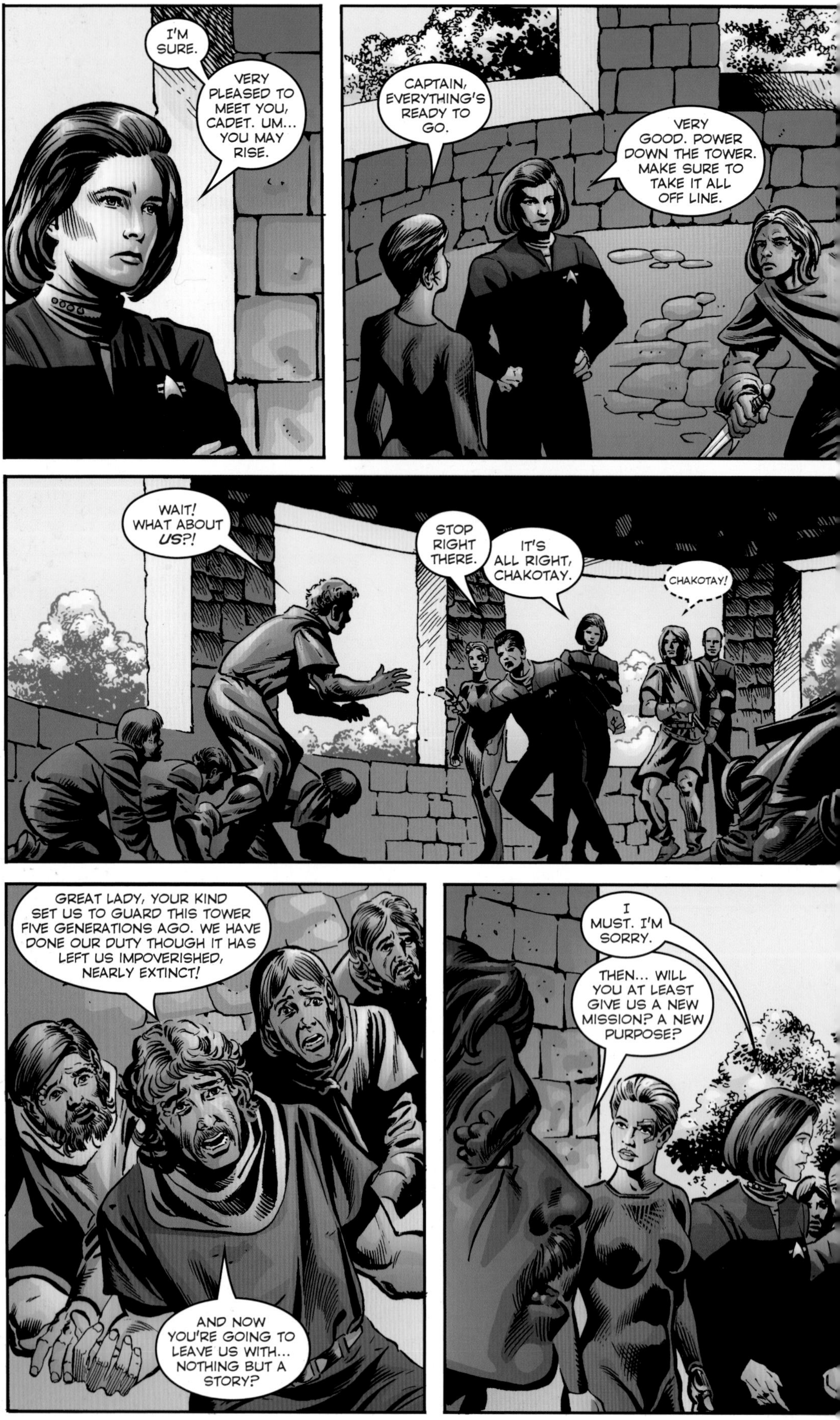
I'M SURE.
VERY PLEASED TO MEET YOU, CADET. UM... YOU MAY RISE.
CAPTAIN, EVERYTHING'S READY TO GO.
VERY GOOD. POWER DOWN THE TOWER. MAKE SURE TO TAKE IT ALL OFF LINE.
WAIT! WHAT ABOUT US?!
STOP RIGHT THERE.
IT'S ALL RIGHT, CHAKOTAY.
CHAKOTAY!
GREAT LADY, YOUR KIND SET US TO GUARD THIS TOWER FIVE GENERATIONS AGO. WE HAVE DONE OUR DUTY THOUGH IT HAS LEFT US IMPOVERISHED, NEARLY EXTINCT!
AND NOW YOU'RE GOING TO LEAVE US WITH... NOTHING BUT A STORY?
I MUST. I'M SORRY.
THEN... WILL YOU AT LEAST GIVE US A NEW MISSION? A NEW PURPOSE?

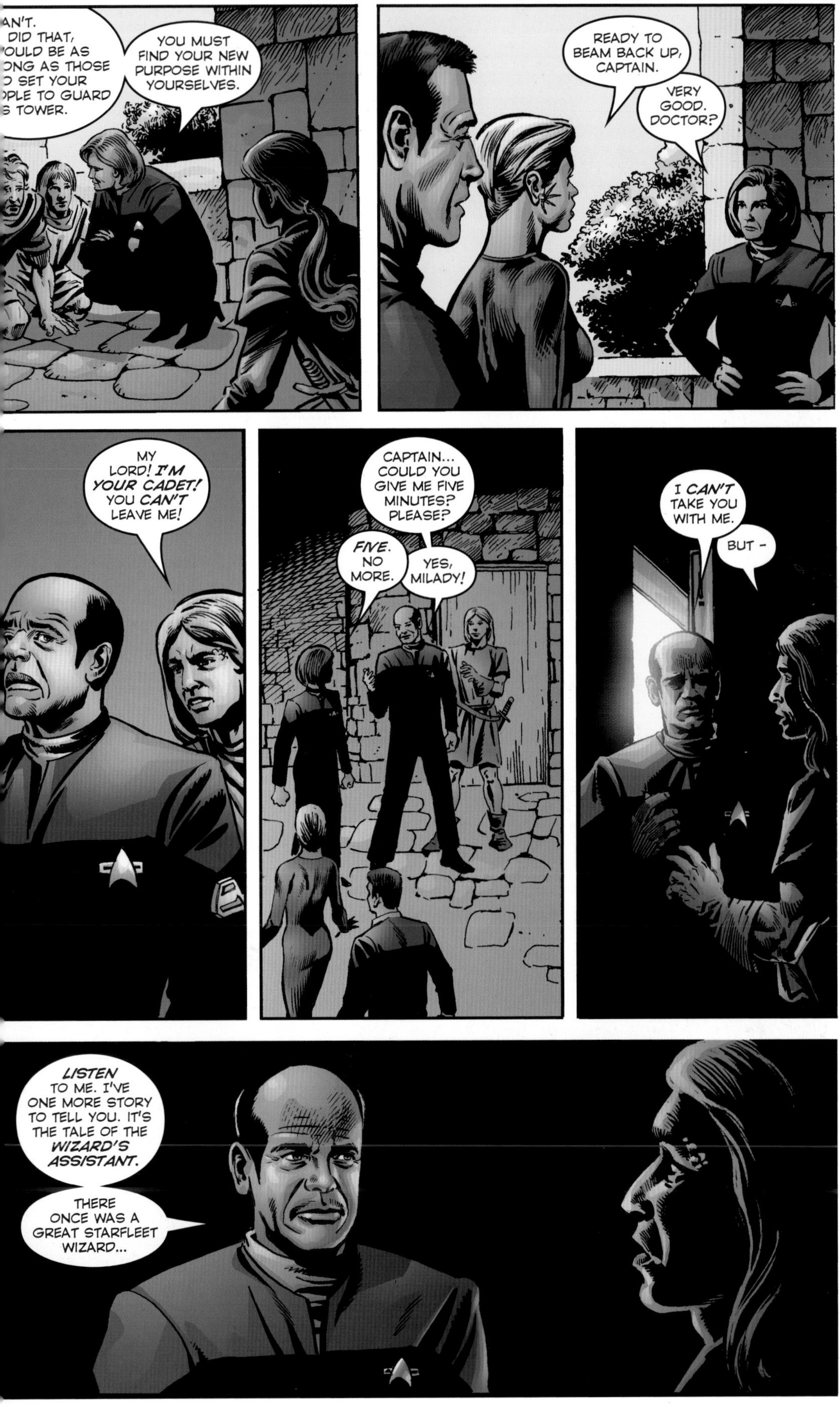
...AN'T. ...DID THAT, ...OULD BE AS ...ONG AS THOSE ...O SET YOUR ...OPLE TO GUARD ...S TOWER.
YOU MUST FIND YOUR NEW PURPOSE WITHIN YOURSELVES.
READY TO BEAM BACK UP, CAPTAIN.
VERY GOOD. DOCTOR?
MY LORD! I'M YOUR CADET! YOU CAN'T LEAVE ME!
CAPTAIN... COULD YOU GIVE ME FIVE MINUTES? PLEASE?
FIVE. NO MORE.
YES, MILADY!
I CAN'T TAKE YOU WITH ME.
BUT -
LISTEN TO ME. I'VE ONE MORE STORY TO TELL YOU. IT'S THE TALE OF THE WIZARD'S ASSISTANT.
THERE ONCE WAS A GREAT STARFLEET WIZARD...

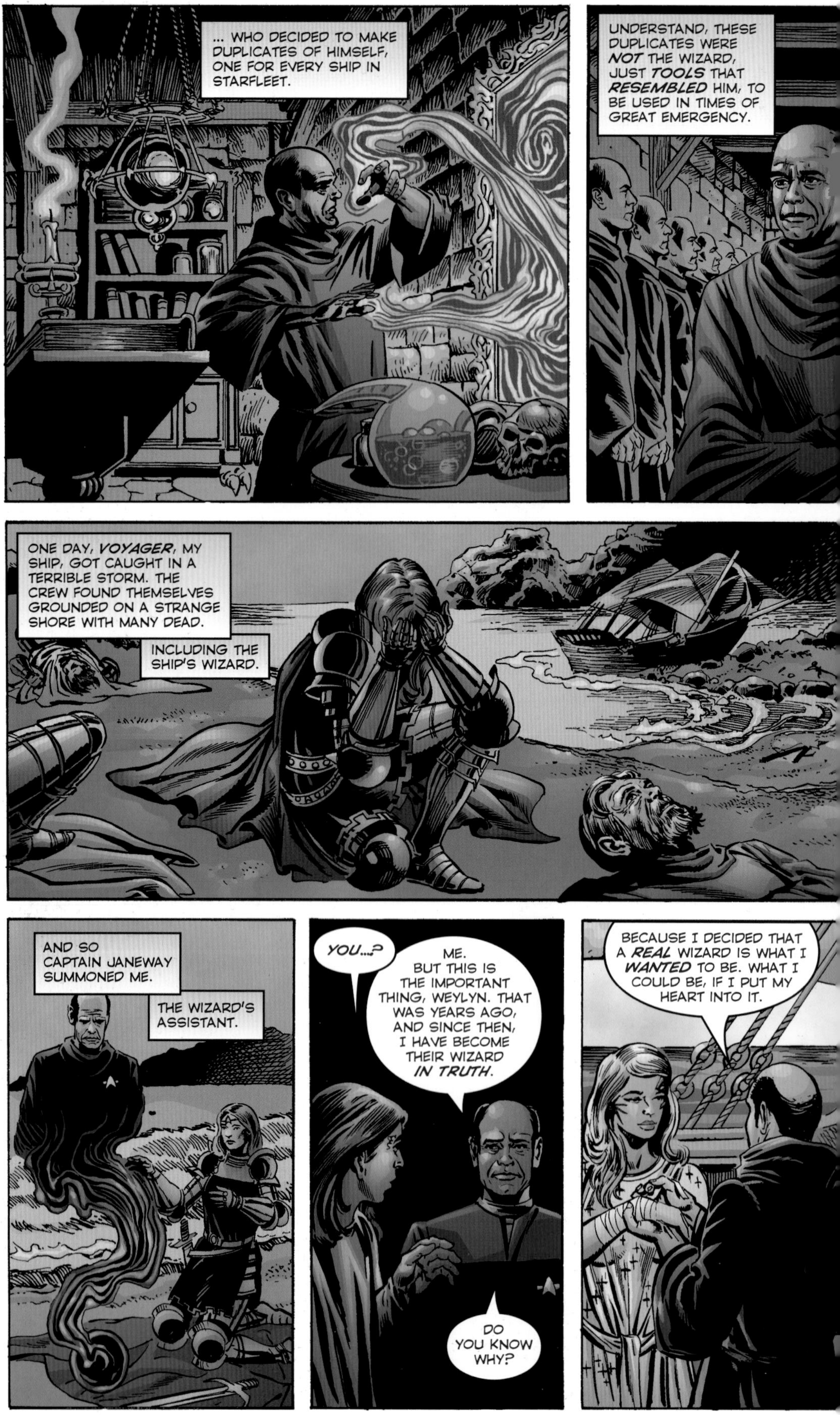
... WHO DECIDED TO MAKE DUPLICATES OF HIMSELF, ONE FOR EVERY SHIP IN STARFLEET.
UNDERSTAND, THESE DUPLICATES WERE NOT THE WIZARD, JUST TOOLS THAT RESEMBLED HIM, TO BE USED IN TIMES OF GREAT EMERGENCY.
ONE DAY, VOYAGER, MY SHIP, GOT CAUGHT IN A TERRIBLE STORM. THE CREW FOUND THEMSELVES GROUNDED ON A STRANGE SHORE WITH MANY DEAD.
INCLUDING THE SHIP'S WIZARD.
AND SO CAPTAIN JANEWAY SUMMONED ME.
THE WIZARD'S ASSISTANT.
YOU...?
ME. BUT THIS IS THE IMPORTANT THING, WEYLYN. THAT WAS YEARS AGO, AND SINCE THEN, I HAVE BECOME THEIR WIZARD IN TRUTH.
DO YOU KNOW WHY?
BECAUSE I DECIDED THAT A REAL WIZARD IS WHAT I WANTED TO BE. WHAT I COULD BE, IF I PUT MY HEART INTO IT.

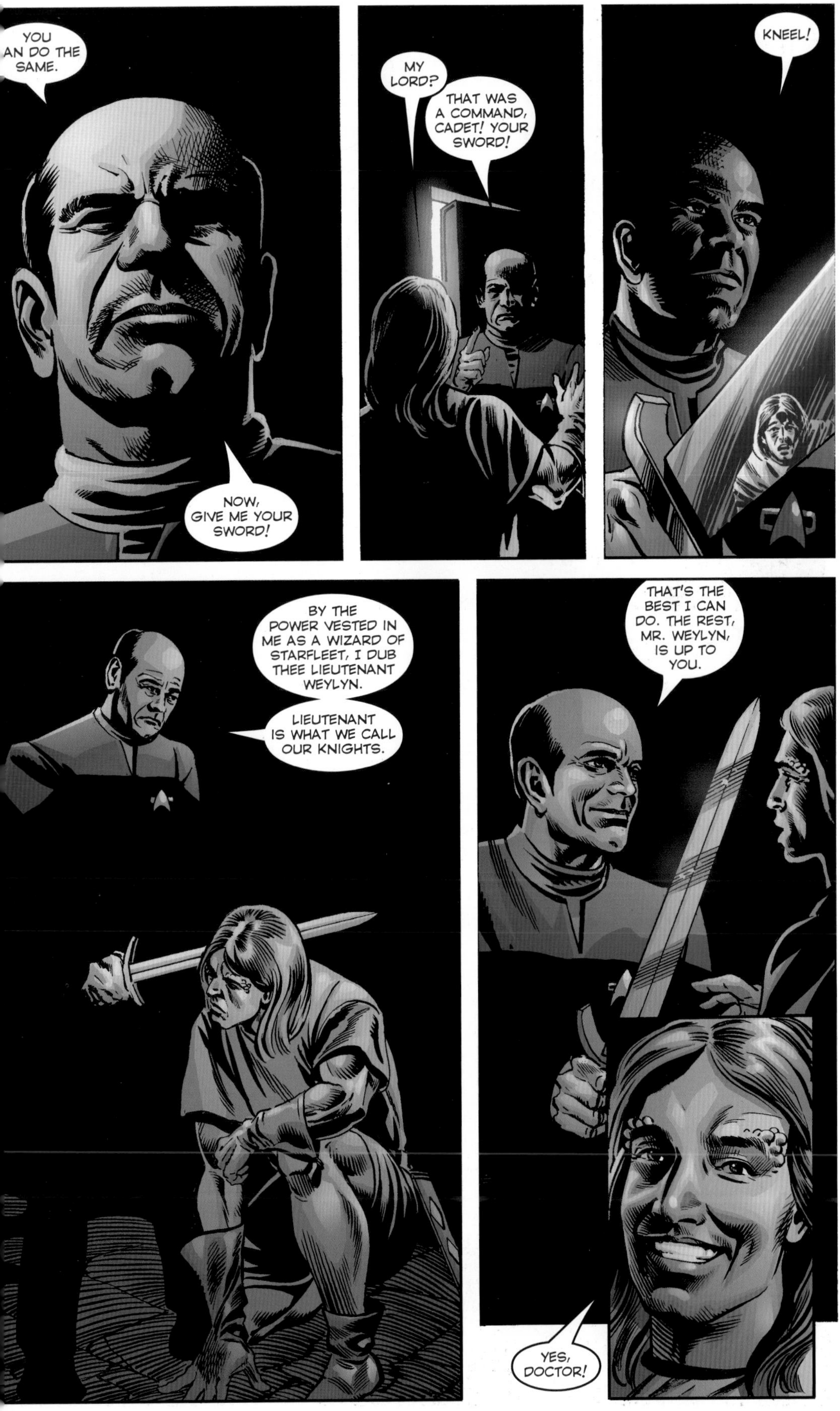
YOU AN DO THE SAME.
NOW, GIVE ME YOUR SWORD!
MY LORD?
THAT WAS A COMMAND, CADET! YOUR SWORD!
KNEEL!
BY THE POWER VESTED IN ME AS A WIZARD OF STARFLEET, I DUB THEE LIEUTENANT WEYLYN.
LIEUTENANT IS WHAT WE CALL OUR KNIGHTS.
THAT'S THE BEST I CAN DO. THE REST, MR. WEYLYN, IS UP TO YOU.
YES, DOCTOR!

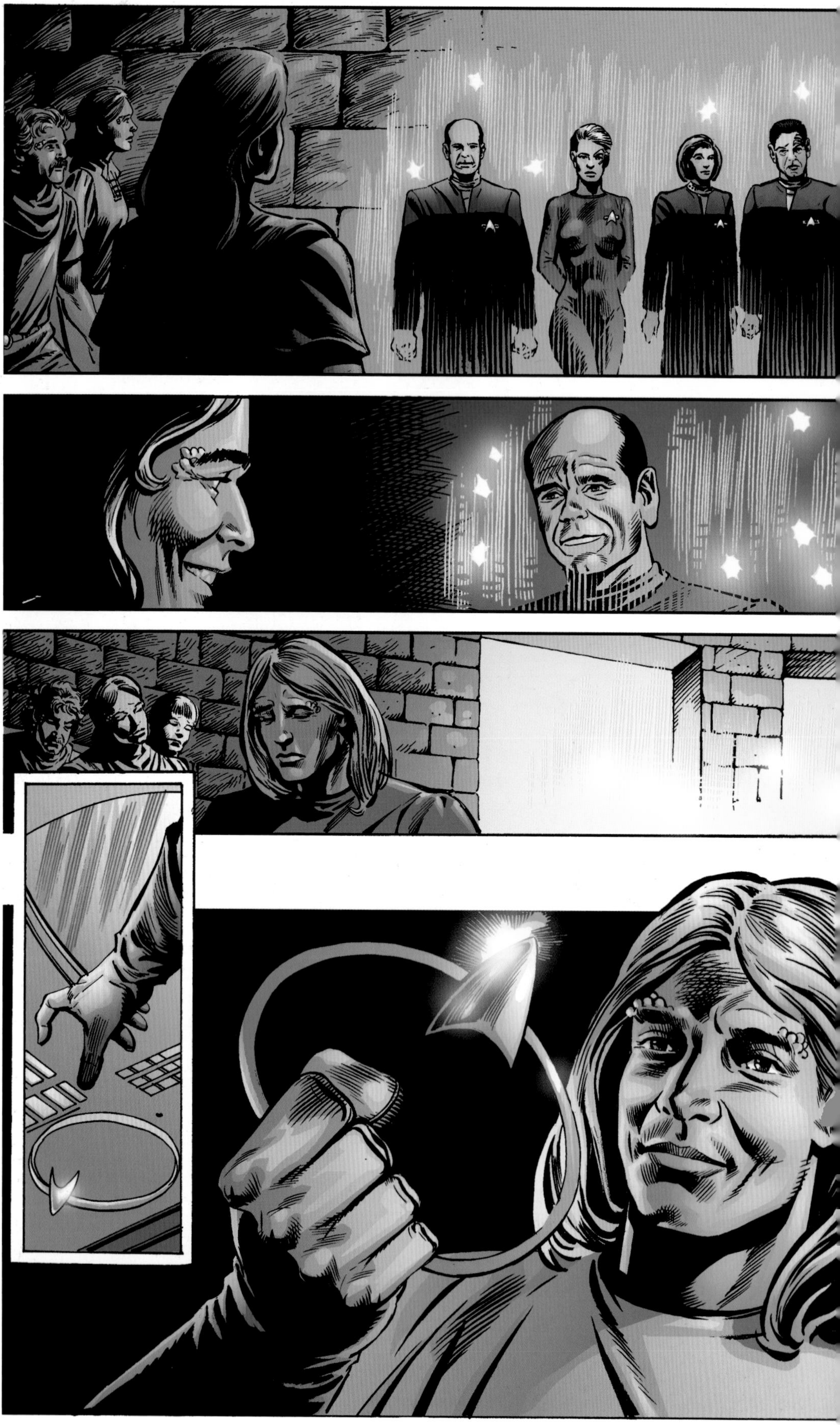

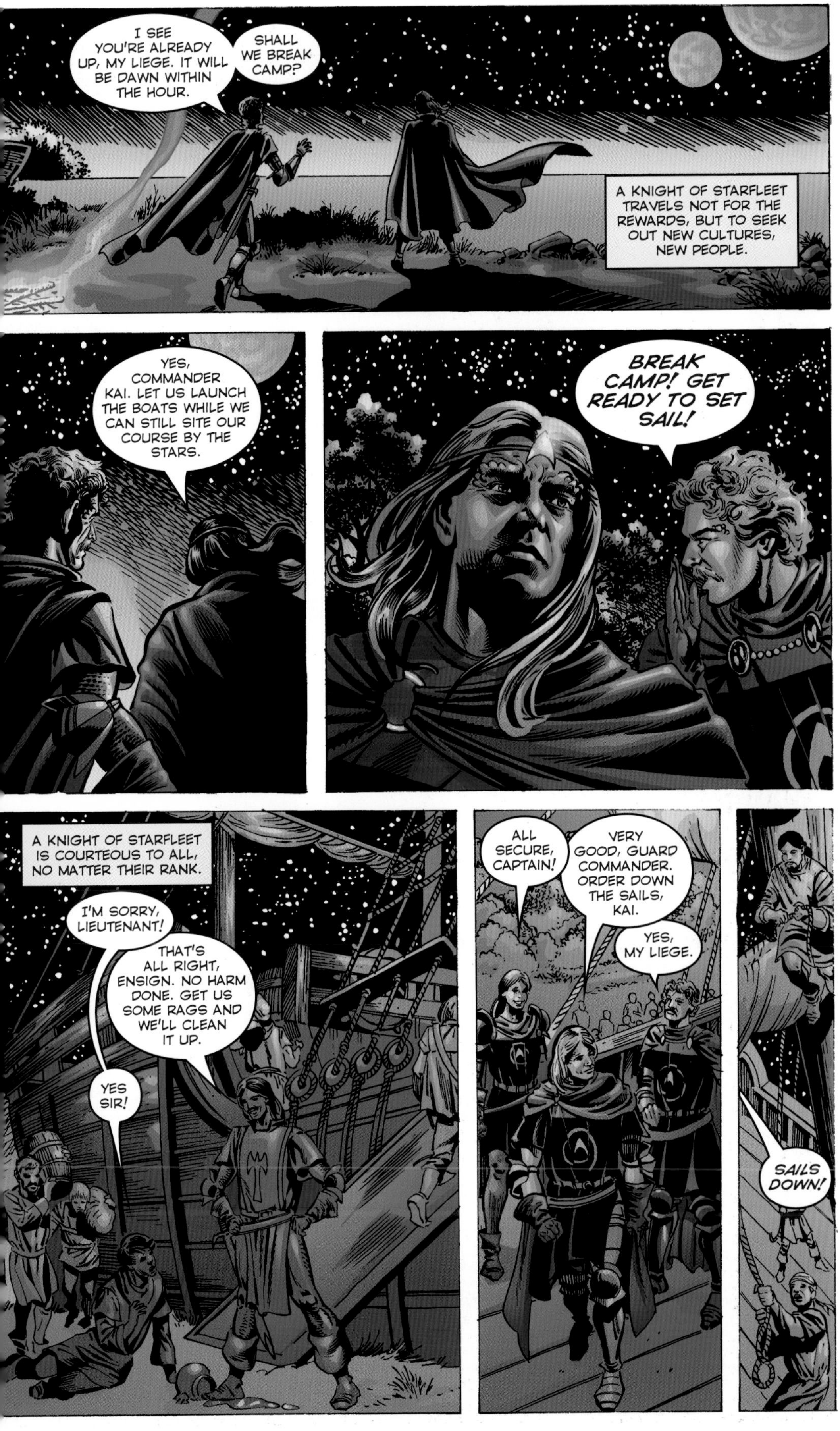
I SEE YOU'RE ALREADY UP, MY LIEGE. IT WILL BE DAWN WITHIN THE HOUR.
SHALL WE BREAK CAMP?
A KNIGHT OF STARFLEET TRAVELS NOT FOR THE REWARDS, BUT TO SEEK OUT NEW CULTURES, NEW PEOPLE.
YES, COMMANDER KAI. LET US LAUNCH THE BOATS WHILE WE CAN STILL SITE OUR COURSE BY THE STARS.
BREAK CAMP! GET READY TO SET SAIL!
A KNIGHT OF STARFLEET IS COURTEOUS TO ALL, NO MATTER THEIR RANK.
I'M SORRY, LIEUTENANT!
THAT'S ALL RIGHT, ENSIGN. NO HARM DONE. GET US SOME RAGS AND WE'LL CLEAN IT UP.
YES SIR!
ALL SECURE, CAPTAIN!
VERY GOOD, GUARD COMMANDER. ORDER DOWN THE SAILS, KAI.
YES, MY LIEGE.
SAILS DOWN!

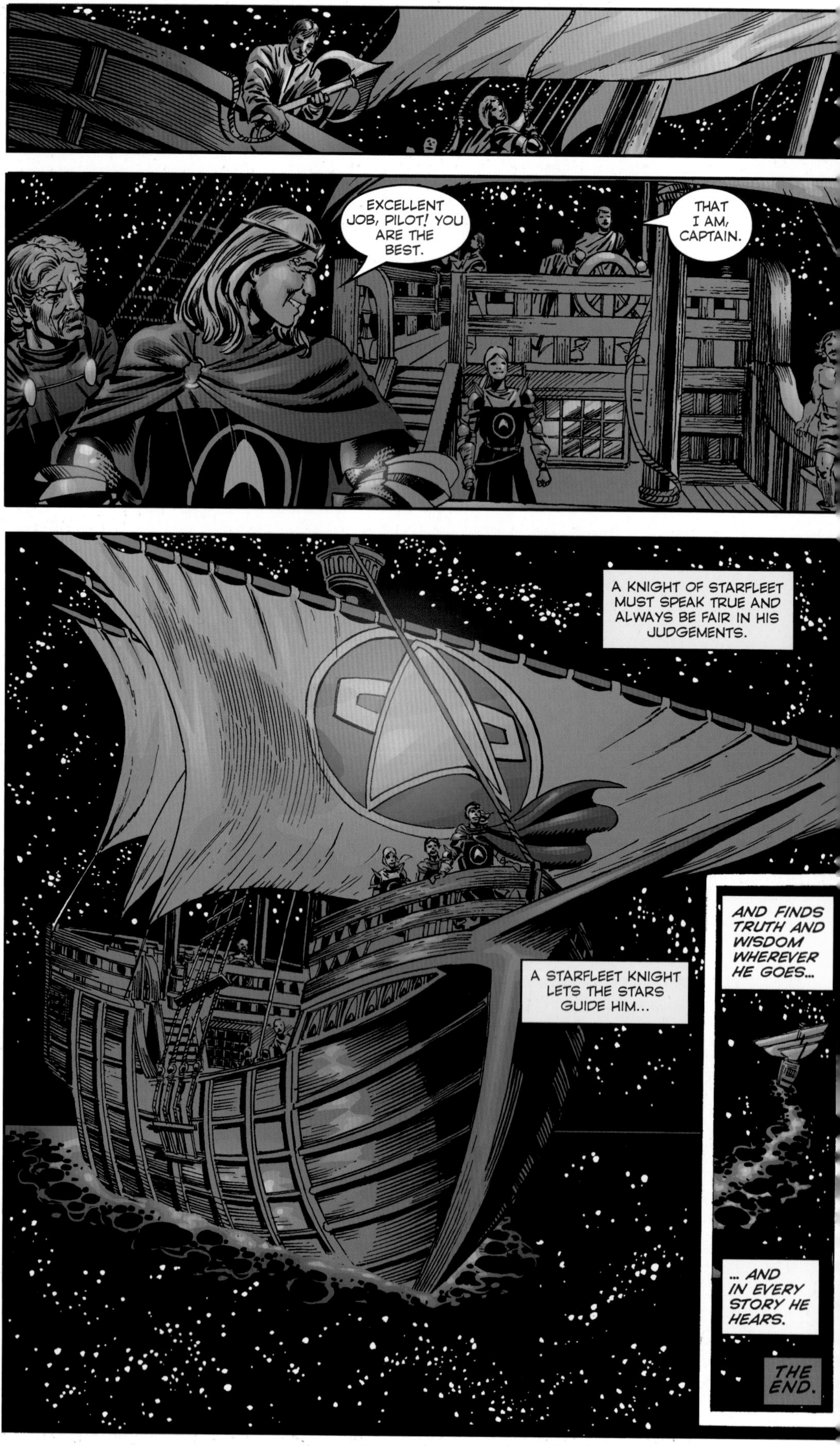
EXCELLENT JOB, PILOT! YOU ARE THE BEST.
THAT I AM, CAPTAIN.
A KNIGHT OF STARFLEET MUST SPEAK TRUE AND ALWAYS BE FAIR IN HIS JUDGEMENTS.
A STARFLEET KNIGHT LETS THE STARS GUIDE HIM...
AND FINDS TRUTH AND WISDOM WHEREVER HE GOES...
... AND IN EVERY STORY HE HEARS.
THE END.

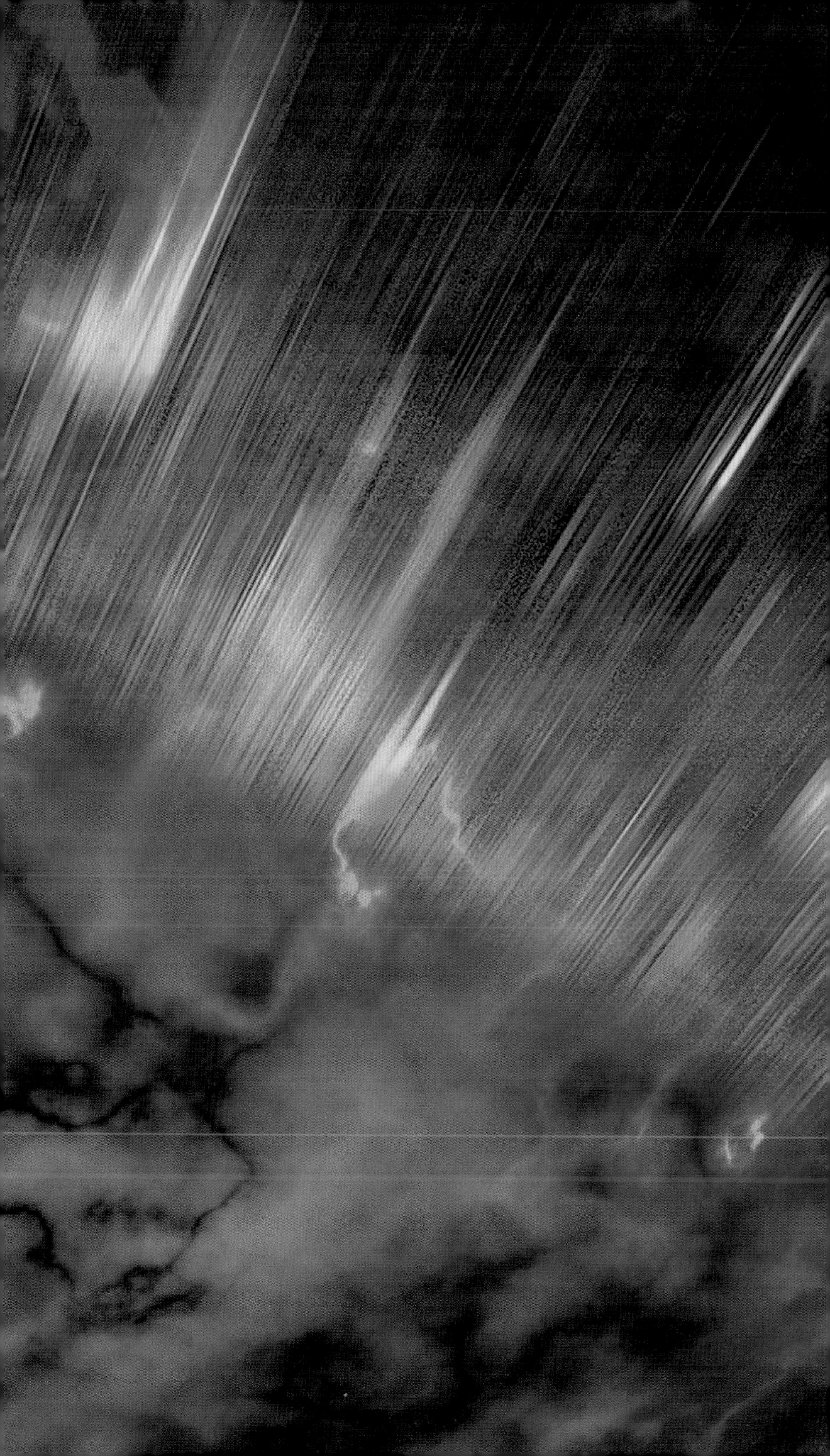

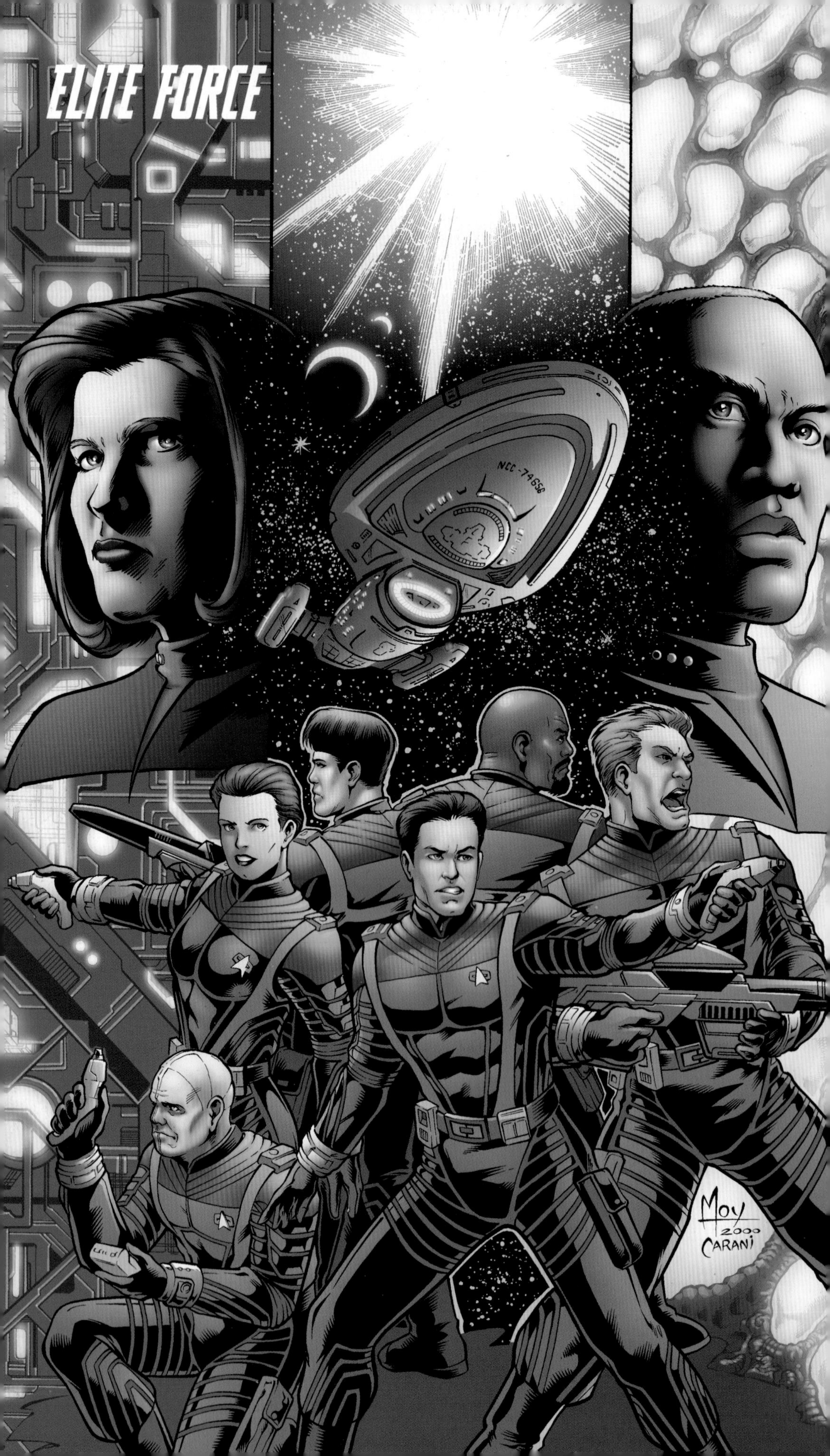
ELITE FORCE
NCC-74656
MOY
2000
CARANI

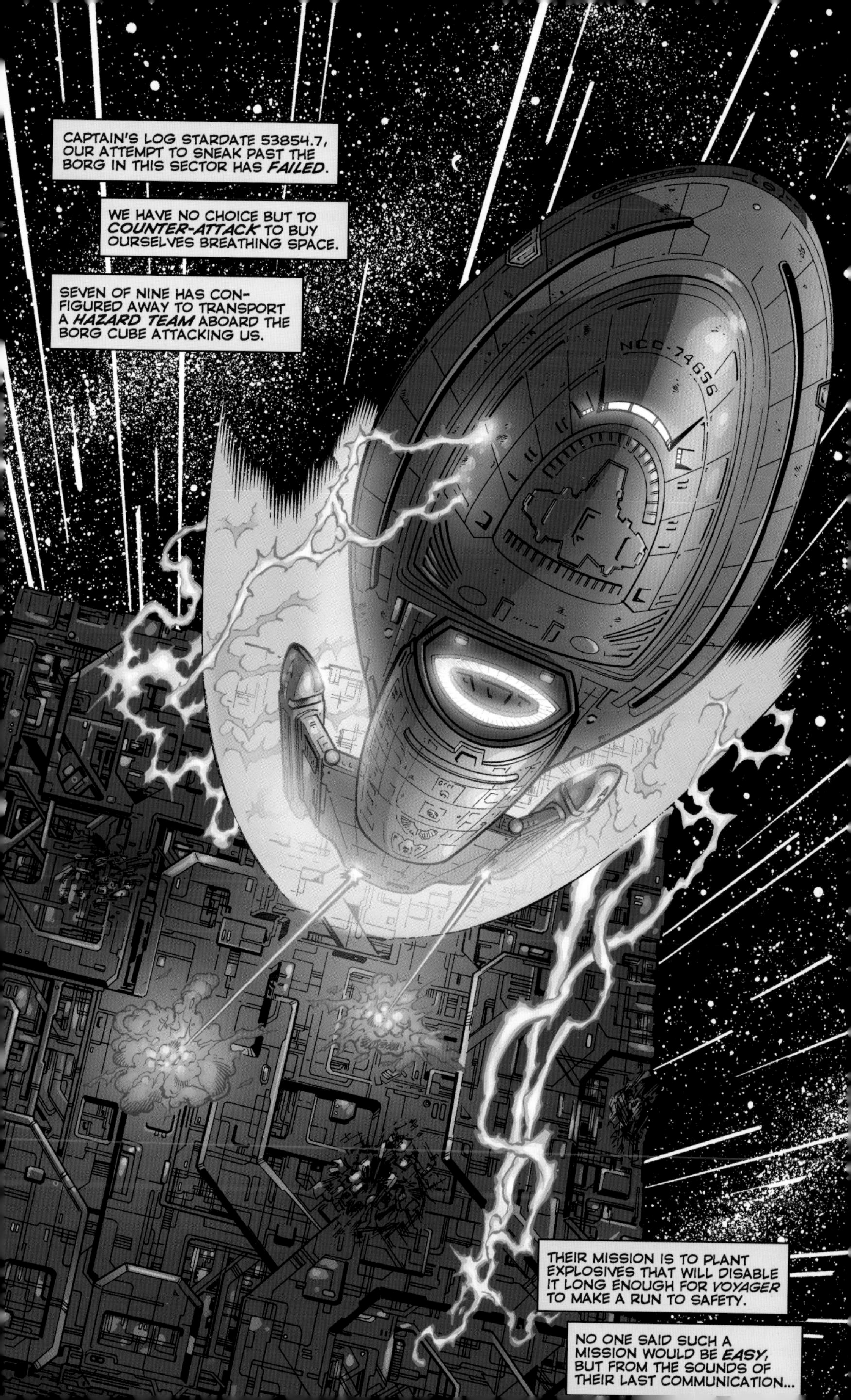
CAPTAIN'S LOG STARDATE 53854.7, OUR ATTEMPT TO SNEAK PAST THE BORG IN THIS SECTOR HAS *FAILED*.
WE HAVE NO CHOICE BUT TO *COUNTER-ATTACK* TO BUY OURSELVES BREATHING SPACE.
SEVEN OF NINE HAS CONFIGURED AWAY TO TRANSPORT A *HAZARD TEAM* ABOARD THE BORG CUBE ATTACKING US.
NCC-74656
THEIR MISSION IS TO PLANT EXPLOSIVES THAT WILL DISABLE IT LONG ENOUGH FOR *VOYAGER* TO MAKE A RUN TO SAFETY.
NO ONE SAID SUCH A MISSION WOULD BE *EASY*, BUT FROM THE SOUNDS OF THEIR LAST COMMUNICATION...

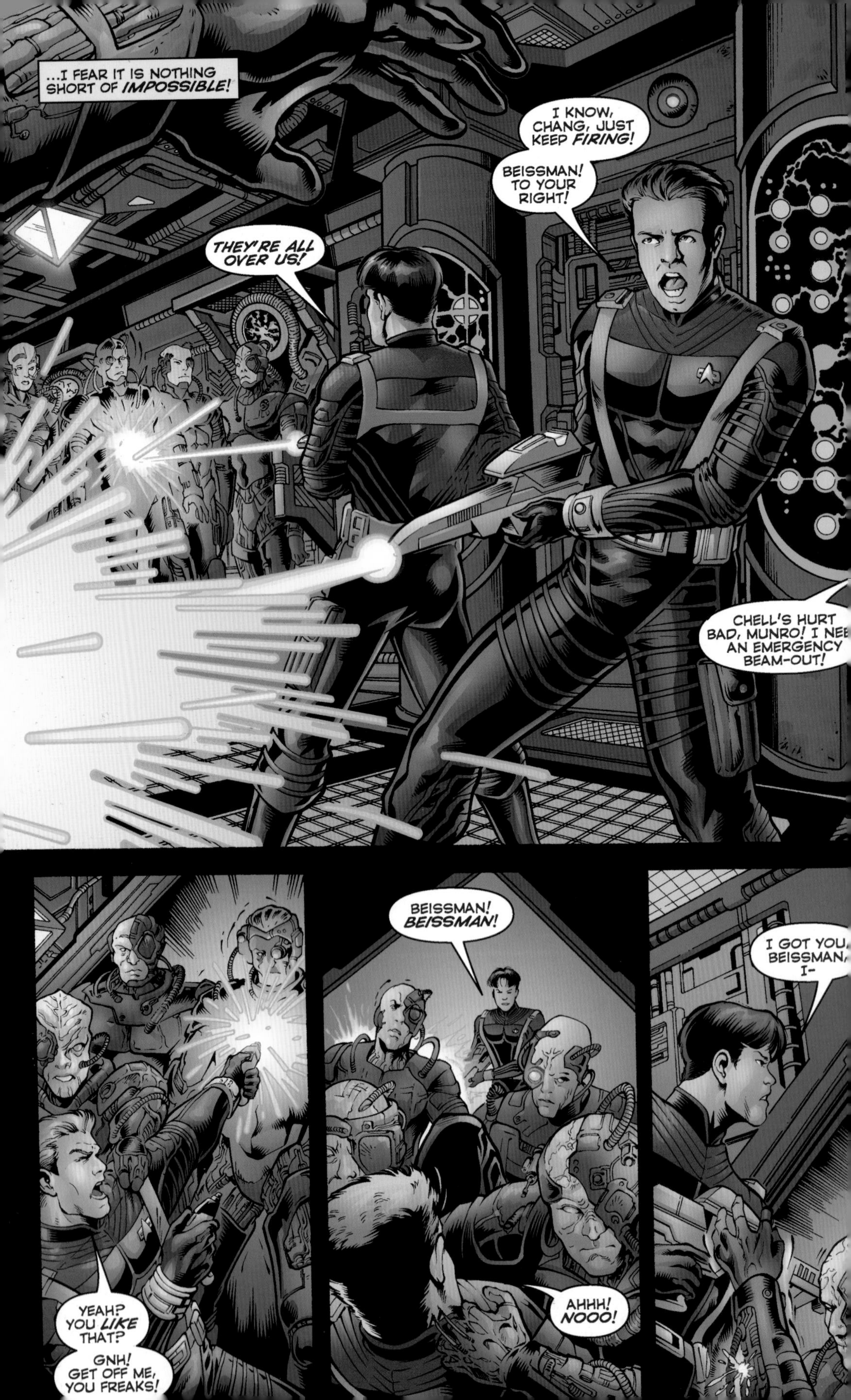
...I FEAR IT IS NOTHING SHORT OF *IMPOSSIBLE*!
I KNOW, CHANG, JUST KEEP *FIRING*!
BEISSMAN! TO YOUR RIGHT!
THEY'RE ALL OVER US!
CHELL'S HURT BAD, MUNRO! I NEE AN EMERGENCY BEAM-OUT!
YEAH? YOU *LIKE* THAT?
GNH! GET OFF ME, YOU FREAKS!
BEISSMAN! *BEISSMAN*!
AHHH! *NOOO*!
I GOT YOU, BEISSMAN, I-

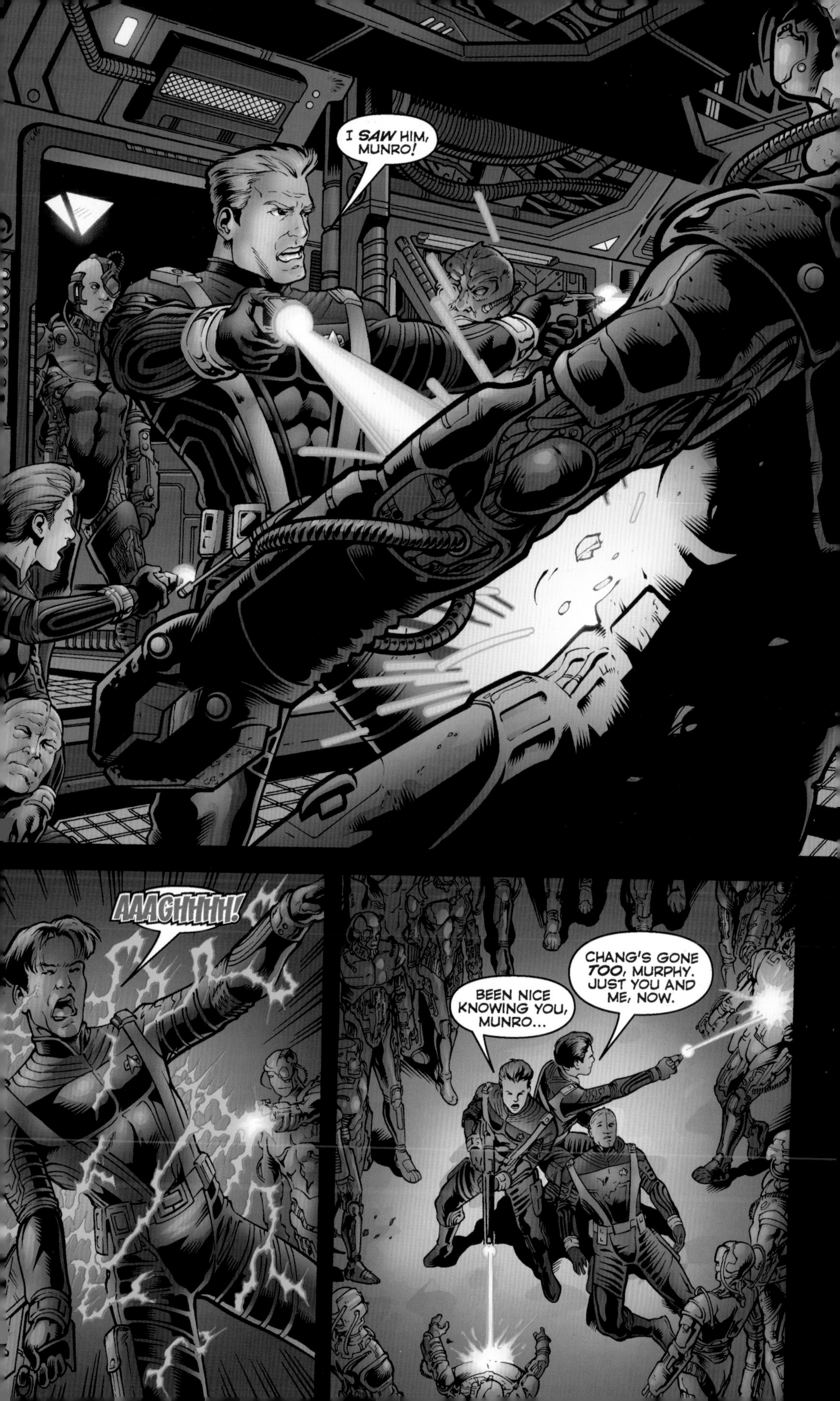
I SAW HIM, MUNRO!
AAAGHHHH!
CHANG'S GONE TOO, MURPHY. JUST YOU AND ME, NOW.
BEEN NICE KNOWING YOU, MUNRO...

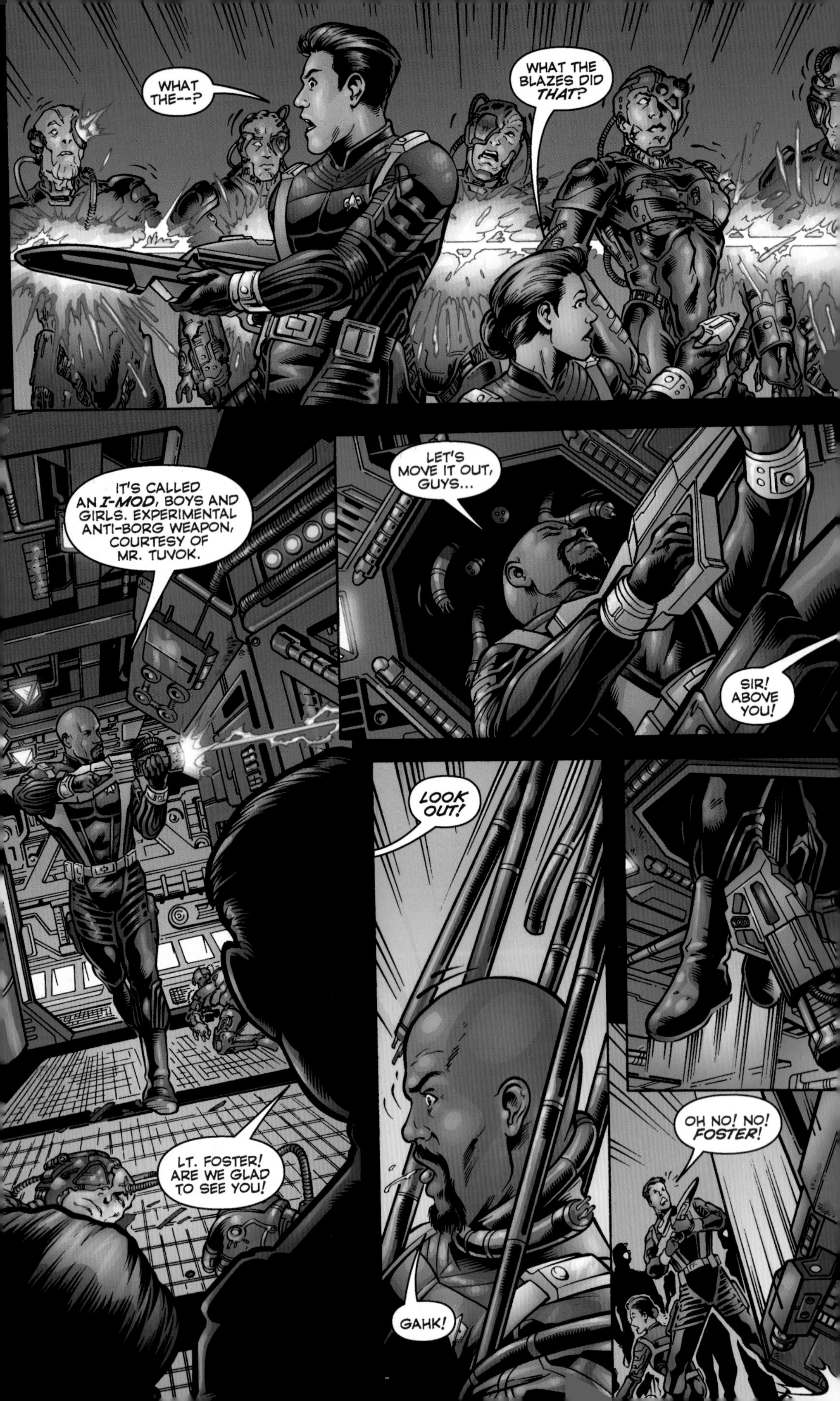
WHAT THE--?
WHAT THE BLAZES DID THAT?
IT'S CALLED AN I-MOD, BOYS AND GIRLS. EXPERIMENTAL ANTI-BORG WEAPON, COURTESY OF MR. TUVOK.
LET'S MOVE IT OUT, GUYS...
SIR! ABOVE YOU!
LT. FOSTER! ARE WE GLAD TO SEE YOU!
LOOK OUT!
GAHK!
OH NO! NO! FOSTER!

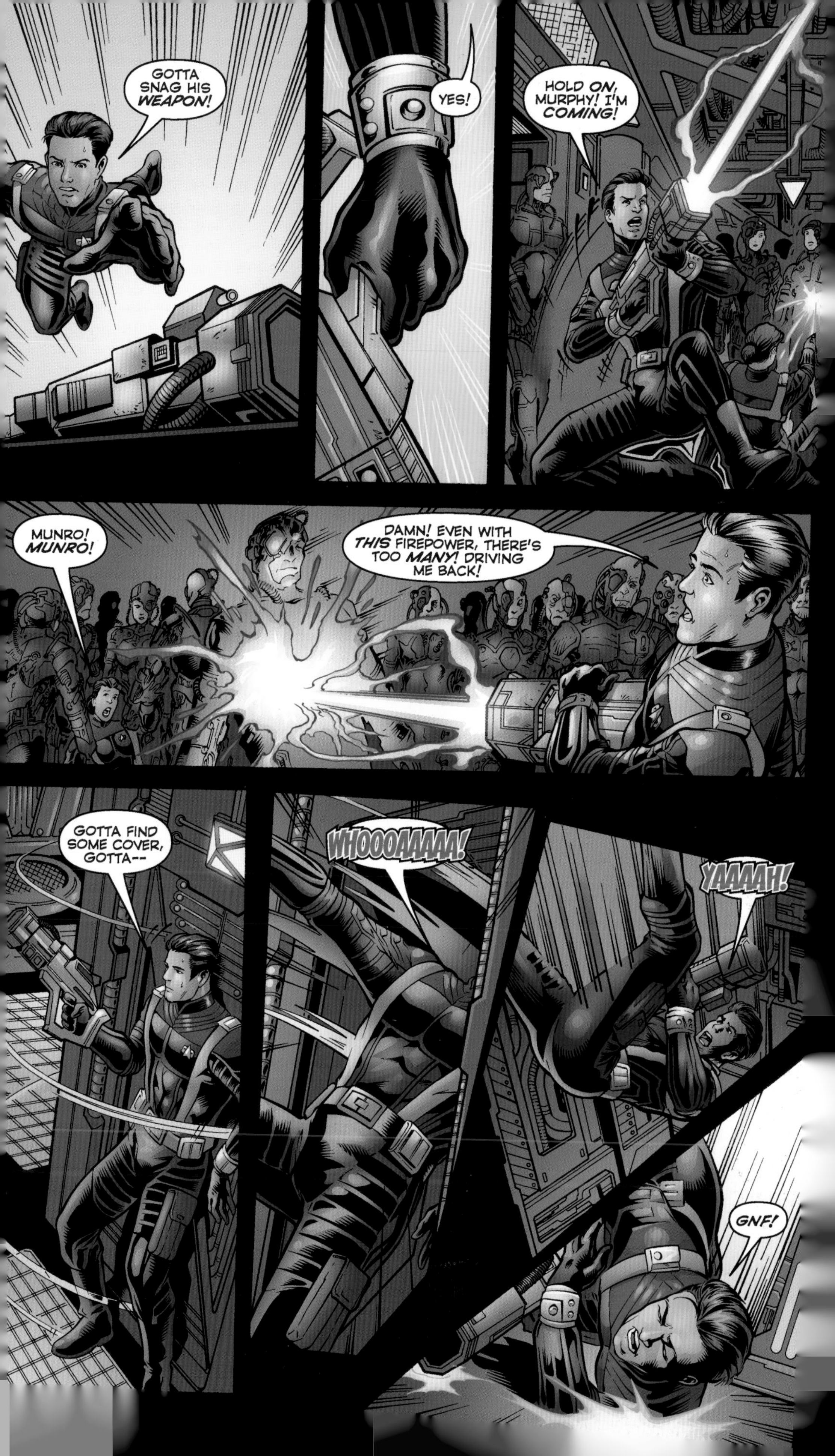
GOTTA SNAG HIS WEAPON!
YES!
HOLD ON, MURPHY! I'M COMING!
MUNRO! MUNRO!
DAMN! EVEN WITH THIS FIREPOWER, THERE'S TOO MANY! DRIVING ME BACK!
GOTTA FIND SOME COVER, GOTTA--
WHOOOAAAAA!
YAAAAH!
GNF!

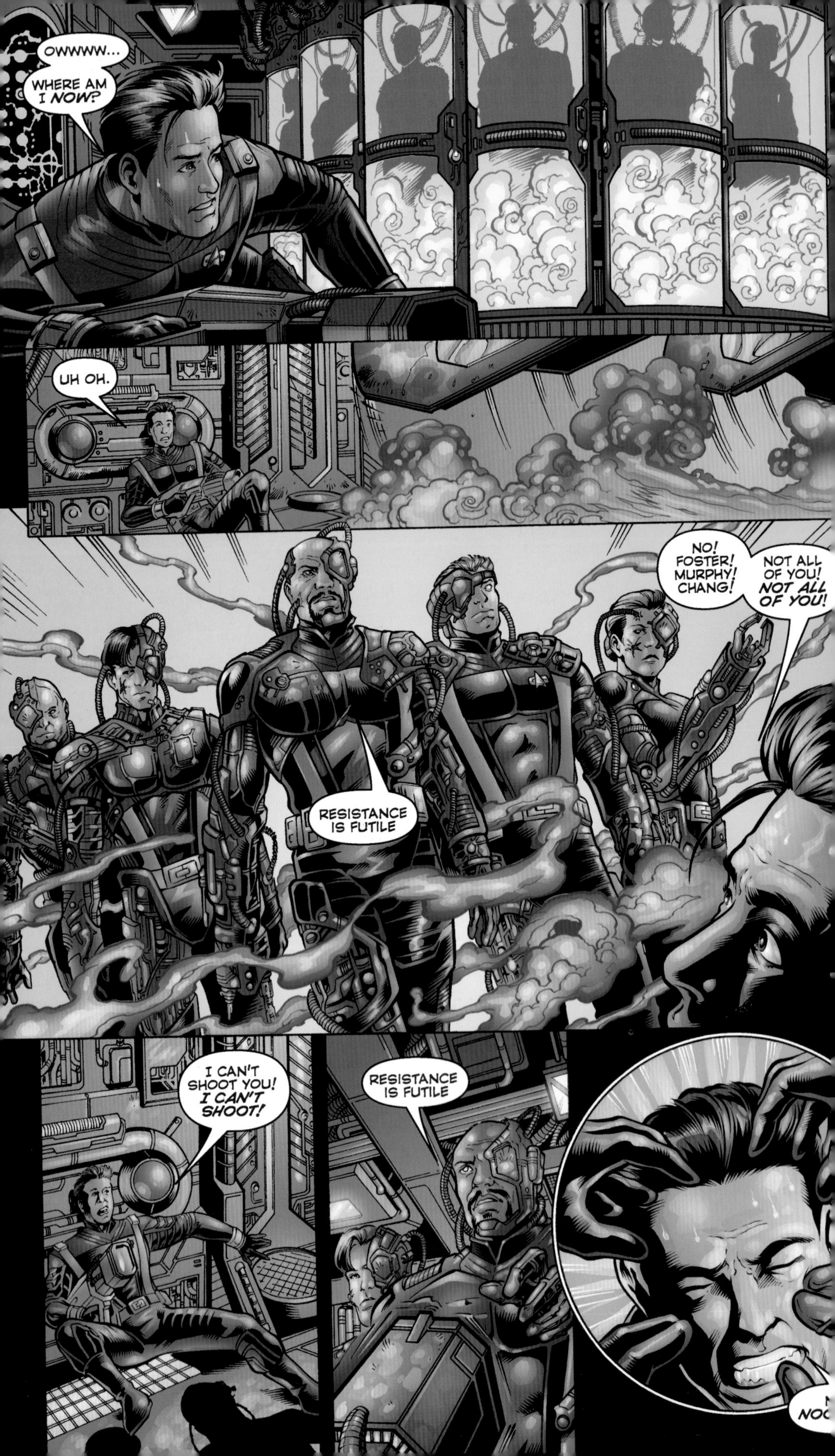
OWWWW...
WHERE AM I NOW?
UH OH.
NO! FOSTER! MURPHY! CHANG!
NOT ALL OF YOU! NOT ALL OF YOU!
RESISTANCE IS FUTILE
I CAN'T SHOOT YOU! I CAN'T SHOOT!
RESISTANCE IS FUTILE

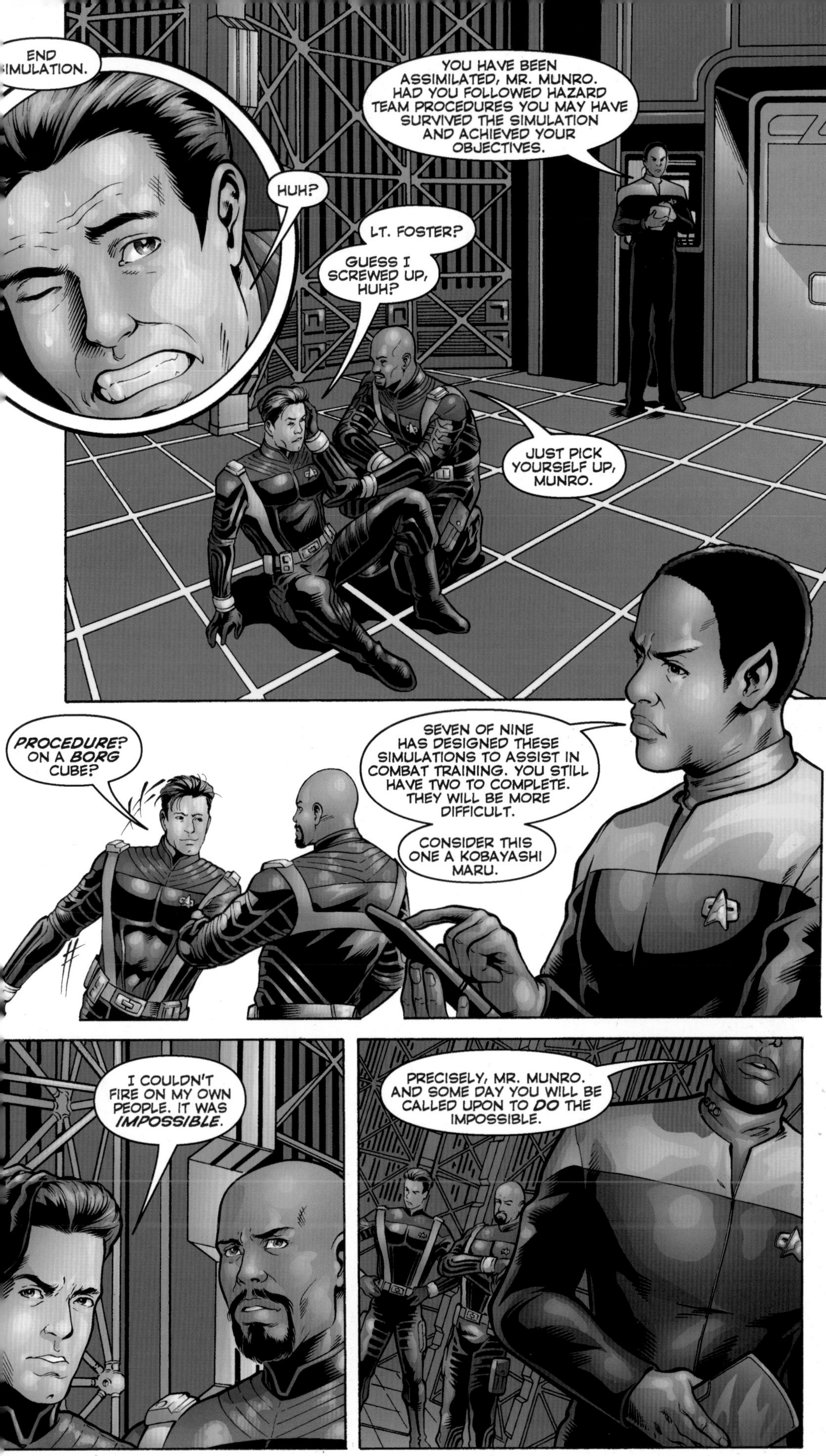
END SIMULATION.
YOU HAVE BEEN ASSIMILATED, MR. MUNRO. HAD YOU FOLLOWED HAZARD TEAM PROCEDURES YOU MAY HAVE SURVIVED THE SIMULATION AND ACHIEVED YOUR OBJECTIVES.
HUH?
LT. FOSTER?
GUESS I SCREWED UP, HUH?
JUST PICK YOURSELF UP, MUNRO.
PROCEDURE? ON A BORG CUBE?
SEVEN OF NINE HAS DESIGNED THESE SIMULATIONS TO ASSIST IN COMBAT TRAINING. YOU STILL HAVE TWO TO COMPLETE. THEY WILL BE MORE DIFFICULT.
CONSIDER THIS ONE A KOBAYASHI MARU.
I COULDN'T FIRE ON MY OWN PEOPLE. IT WAS IMPOSSIBLE.
PRECISELY, MR. MUNRO. AND SOME DAY YOU WILL BE CALLED UPON TO DO THE IMPOSSIBLE.

TAKE YOUR SEAT, MR MUNRO. COMMANDER TUVOK HAS A DEBRIEFING TO RUN.

COMMANDER?

THE HAZARD TEAM IS DESIGNED TO PROVIDE *VOYAGER* WITH A BASE LINE OF SECURITY AND DEFENSE.

IN OTHER WORDS, A RAPID-RESPONSE OPTION THAT CAN OPERATE WITH EXTREME PREJUDICE.

HIGHLY *MOTIVATED*, WELL-*DRILLED*, TOTALLY *DISCIPLINED*.

THAT IS *NOT* WHAT I SAW TODAY IN TRAINING.

MR CHANG BROKE POSITION IN A FOOLISH ATTEMPT TO RESCUE AN ALREADY *LOST* TEAM MATE.

MR BEISSMAN USED CONSPICUOUSLY MORE AMMO THAN *ANY* OF YOU...

HEH! YOU BET!

...WITH CONSPICUOU⌐ *FEWER* HI⌐

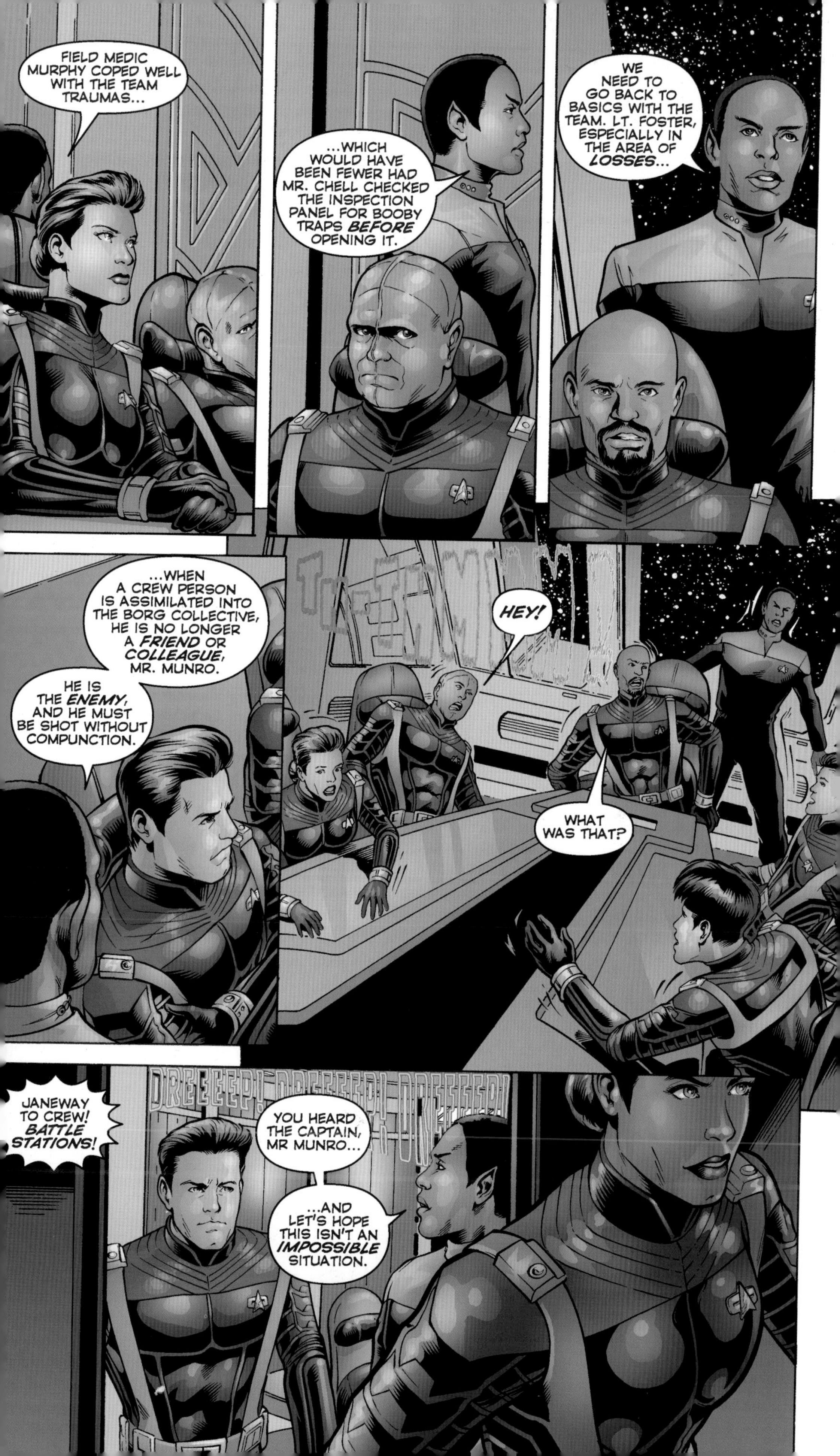
FIELD MEDIC MURPHY COPED WELL WITH THE TEAM TRAUMAS...
...WHICH WOULD HAVE BEEN FEWER HAD MR. CHELL CHECKED THE INSPECTION PANEL FOR BOOBY TRAPS BEFORE OPENING IT.
WE NEED TO GO BACK TO BASICS WITH THE TEAM. LT. FOSTER, ESPECIALLY IN THE AREA OF LOSSES...
...WHEN A CREW PERSON IS ASSIMILATED INTO THE BORG COLLECTIVE, HE IS NO LONGER A FRIEND OR COLLEAGUE, MR. MUNRO.
HE IS THE ENEMY, AND HE MUST BE SHOT WITHOUT COMPUNCTION.
HEY!
WHAT WAS THAT?
JANEWAY TO CREW! BATTLE STATIONS!
YOU HEARD THE CAPTAIN, MR MUNRO...
...AND LET'S HOPE THIS ISN'T AN IMPOSSIBLE SITUATION.

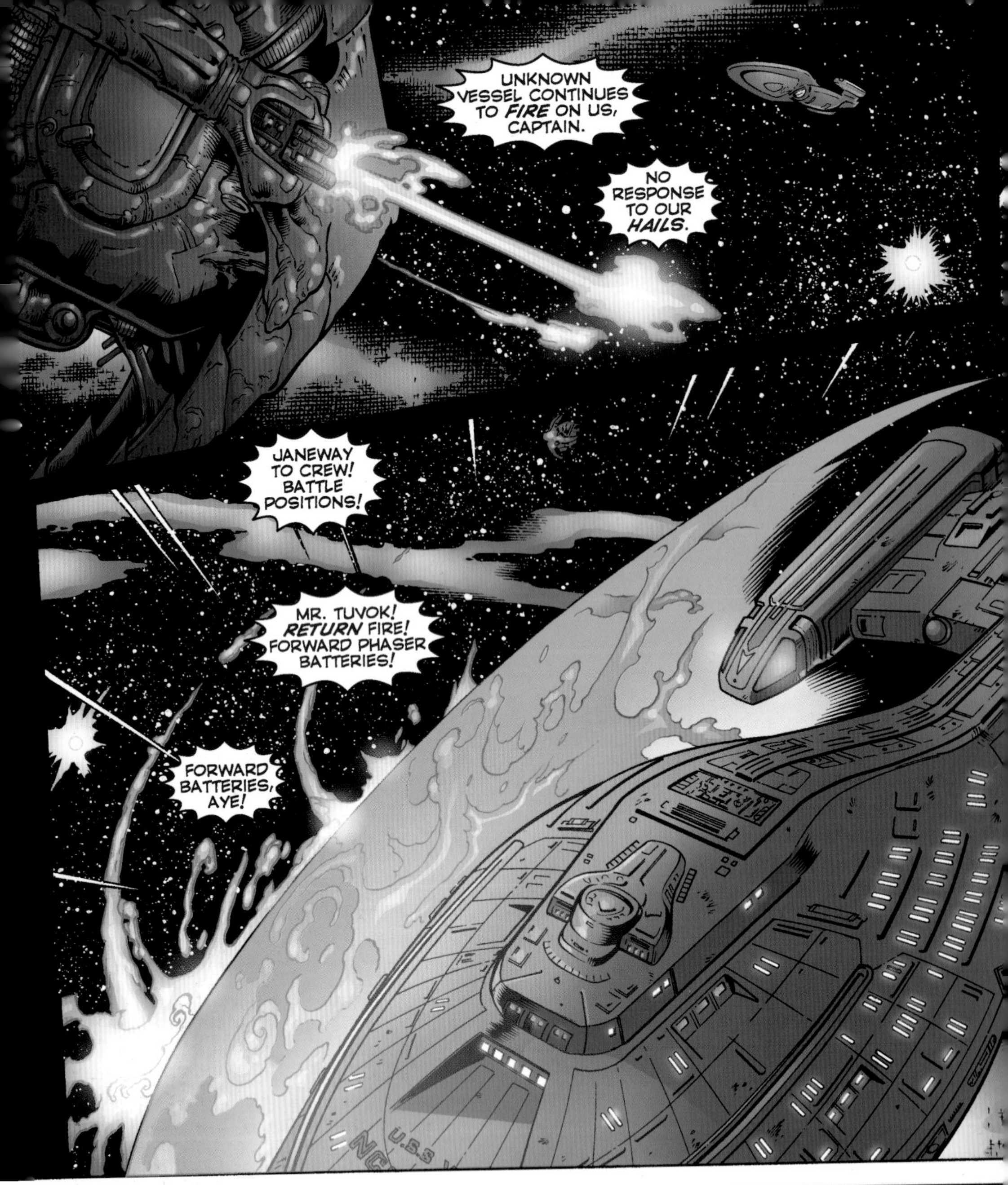
UNKNOWN VESSEL CONTINUES TO *FIRE* ON US, CAPTAIN.
NO RESPONSE TO OUR *HAILS*.
JANEWAY TO CREW! BATTLE POSITIONS!
MR. TUVOK! *RETURN* FIRE! FORWARD PHASER BATTERIES!
FORWARD BATTERIES, AYE!
U.S.S.

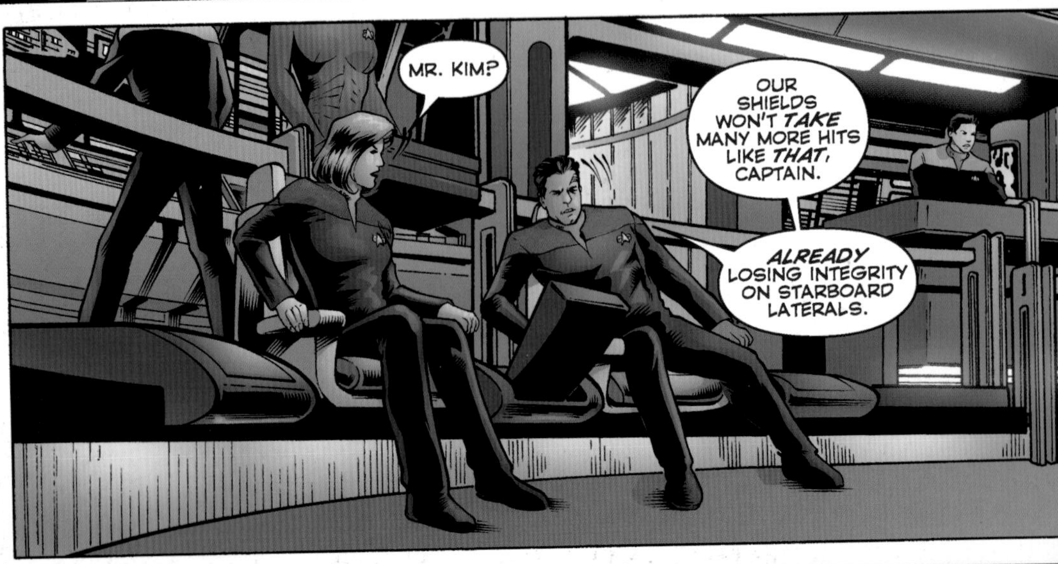
MR. KIM?
OUR SHIELDS WON'T *TAKE* MANY MORE HITS LIKE *THAT*, CAPTAIN.
ALREADY LOSING INTEGRITY ON STARBOARD LATERALS.

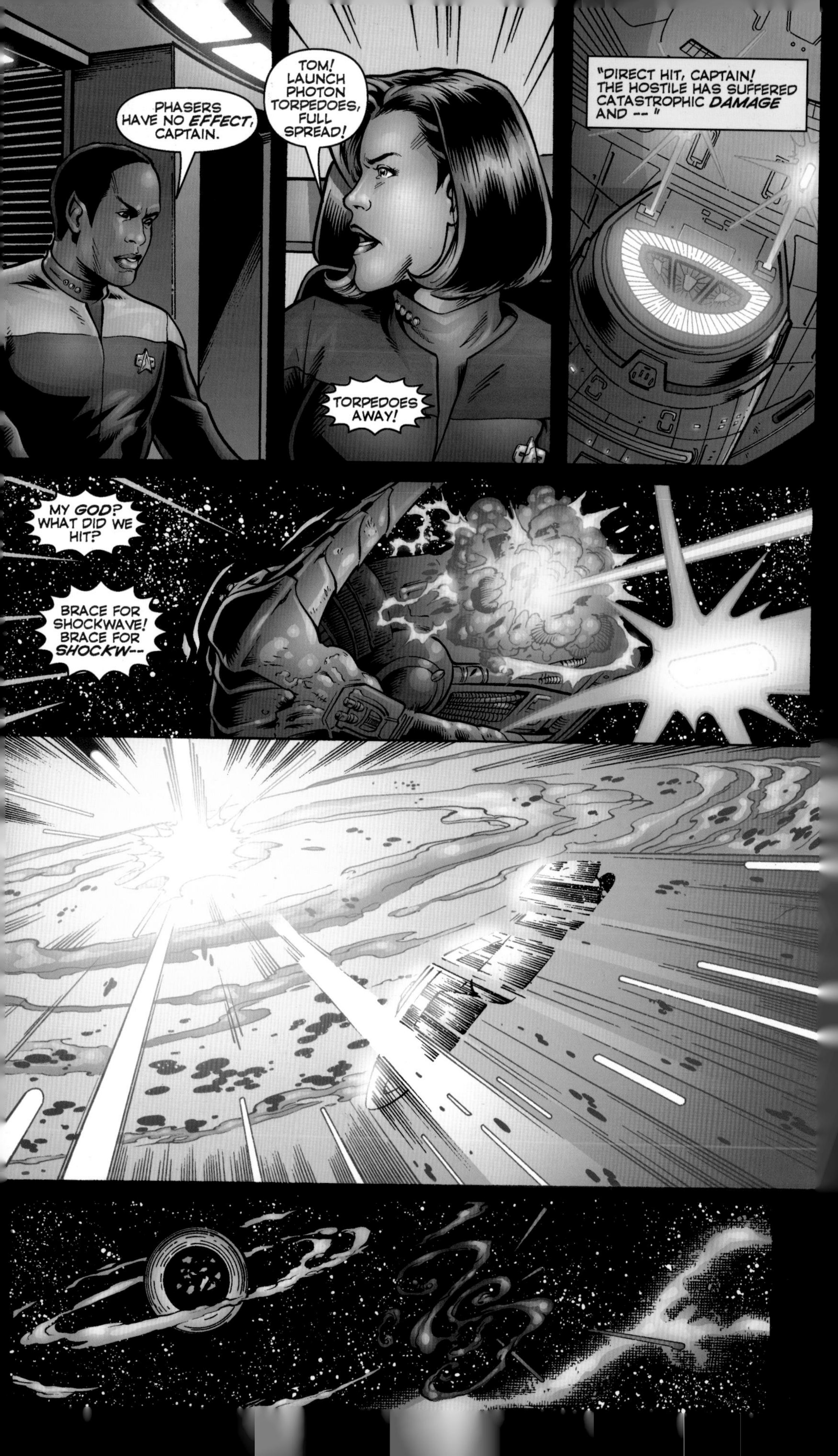
PHASERS HAVE NO *EFFECT*, CAPTAIN.
TOM! LAUNCH PHOTON TORPEDOES, FULL SPREAD!
TORPEDOES AWAY!
"DIRECT HIT, CAPTAIN! THE HOSTILE HAS SUFFERED CATASTROPHIC *DAMAGE* AND -- "
MY *GOD*? WHAT DID WE HIT?
BRACE FOR SHOCKWAVE! BRACE FOR *SHOCKW--*

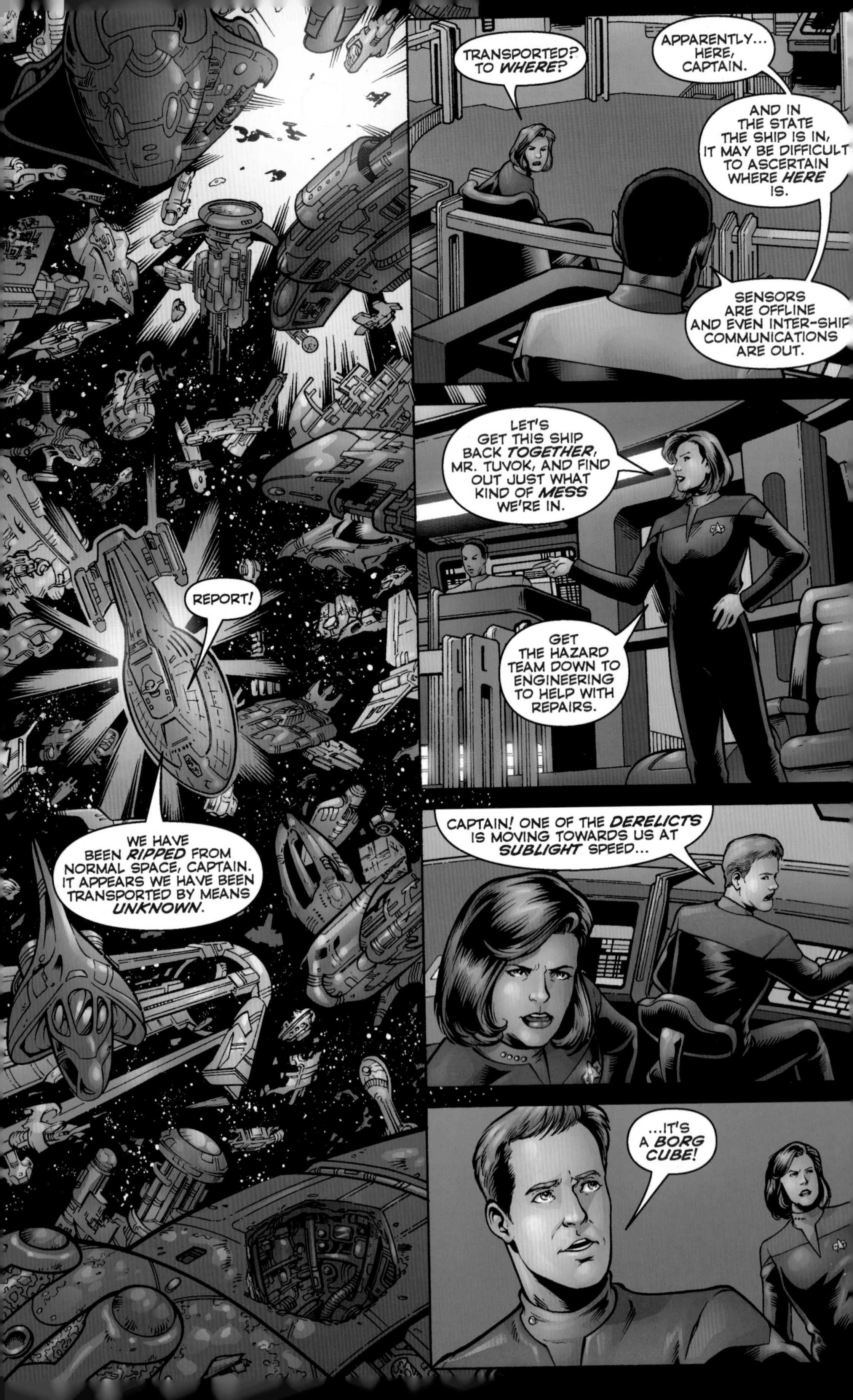
REPORT!
WE HAVE BEEN RIPPED FROM NORMAL SPACE, CAPTAIN. IT APPEARS WE HAVE BEEN TRANSPORTED BY MEANS UNKNOWN.
TRANSPORTED? TO WHERE?
APPARENTLY... HERE, CAPTAIN.
AND IN THE STATE THE SHIP IS IN, IT MAY BE DIFFICULT TO ASCERTAIN WHERE HERE IS.
SENSORS ARE OFFLINE AND EVEN INTER-SHIP COMMUNICATIONS ARE OUT.
LET'S GET THIS SHIP BACK TOGETHER, MR. TUVOK, AND FIND OUT JUST WHAT KIND OF MESS WE'RE IN.
GET THE HAZARD TEAM DOWN TO ENGINEERING TO HELP WITH REPAIRS.
CAPTAIN! ONE OF THE DERELICTS IS MOVING TOWARDS US AT SUBLIGHT SPEED...
...IT'S A BORG CUBE!

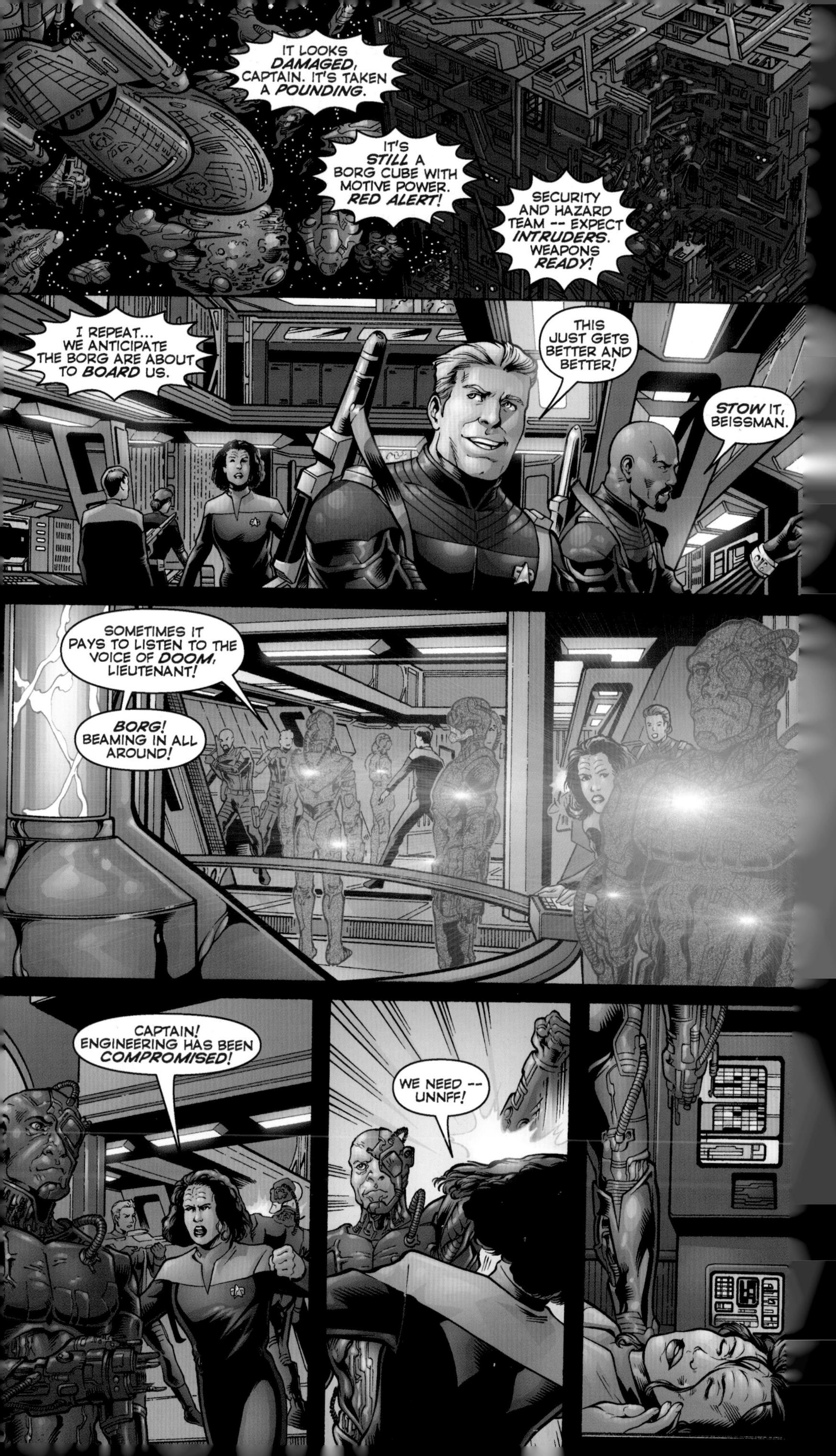
IT LOOKS DAMAGED, CAPTAIN. IT'S TAKEN A POUNDING.
IT'S STILL A BORG CUBE WITH MOTIVE POWER. RED ALERT!
SECURITY AND HAZARD TEAM -- EXPECT INTRUDERS. WEAPONS READY!
I REPEAT... WE ANTICIPATE THE BORG ARE ABOUT TO BOARD US.
THIS JUST GETS BETTER AND BETTER!
STOW IT, BEISSMAN.
SOMETIMES IT PAYS TO LISTEN TO THE VOICE OF DOOM, LIEUTENANT!
BORG! BEAMING IN ALL AROUND!
CAPTAIN! ENGINEERING HAS BEEN COMPROMISED!
WE NEED -- UNNFF!

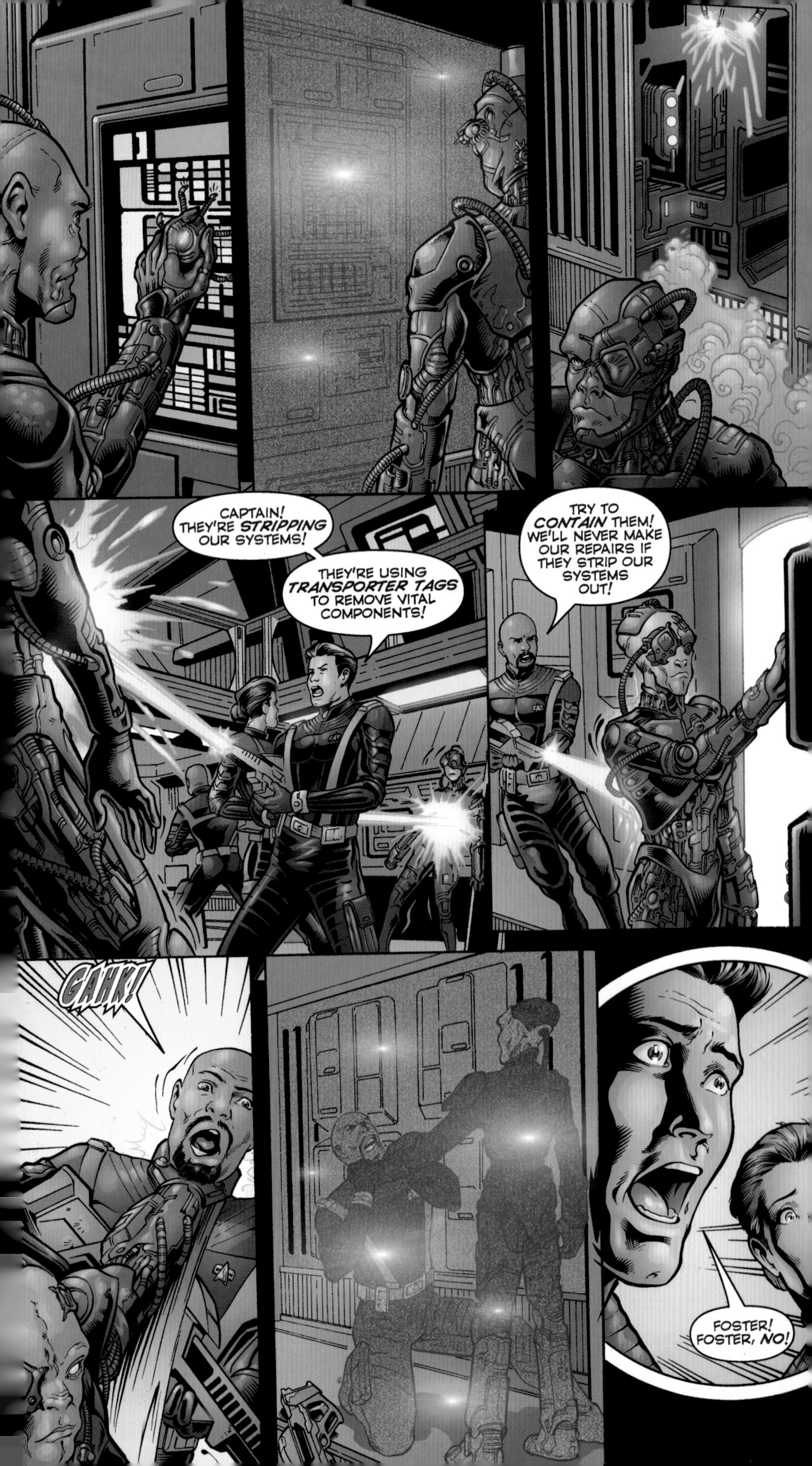
CAPTAIN! THEY'RE STRIPPING OUR SYSTEMS!
THEY'RE USING TRANSPORTER TAGS TO REMOVE VITAL COMPONENTS!
TRY TO CONTAIN THEM! WE'LL NEVER MAKE OUR REPAIRS IF THEY STRIP OUR SYSTEMS OUT!
GAHK!
FOSTER! FOSTER, NO!

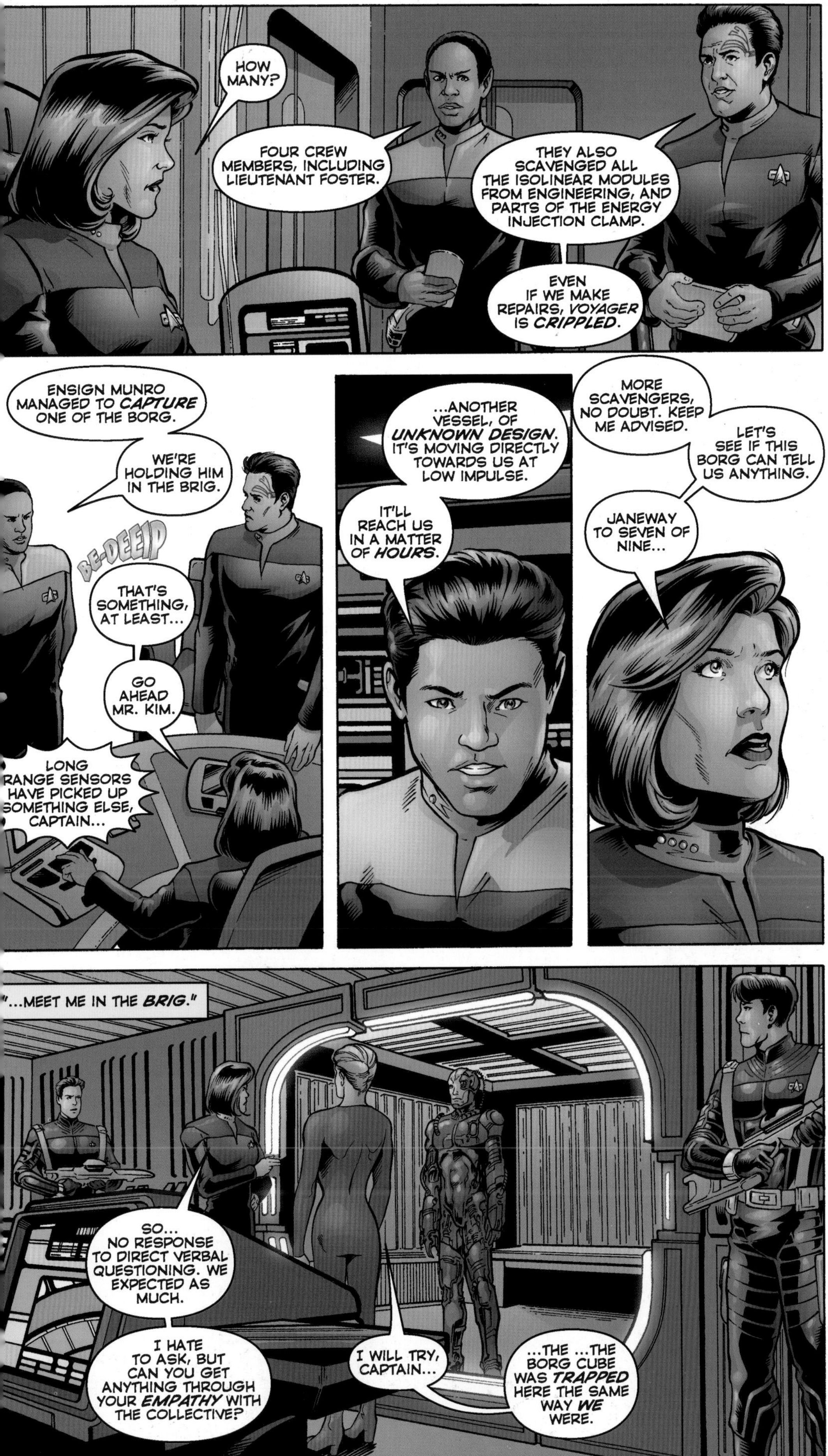
HOW MANY?
FOUR CREW MEMBERS, INCLUDING LIEUTENANT FOSTER.
THEY ALSO SCAVENGED ALL THE ISOLINEAR MODULES FROM ENGINEERING, AND PARTS OF THE ENERGY INJECTION CLAMP.
EVEN IF WE MAKE REPAIRS, *VOYAGER* IS ***CRIPPLED***.
ENSIGN MUNRO MANAGED TO *CAPTURE* ONE OF THE BORG.
WE'RE HOLDING HIM IN THE BRIG.
BE-DEEIP
THAT'S SOMETHING, AT LEAST...
GO AHEAD MR. KIM.
LONG RANGE SENSORS HAVE PICKED UP SOMETHING ELSE, CAPTAIN...
...ANOTHER VESSEL, OF ***UNKNOWN DESIGN***. IT'S MOVING DIRECTLY TOWARDS US AT LOW IMPULSE.
IT'LL REACH US IN A MATTER OF ***HOURS***.
MORE SCAVENGERS, NO DOUBT. KEEP ME ADVISED.
LET'S SEE IF THIS BORG CAN TELL US ANYTHING.
JANEWAY TO SEVEN OF NINE...
"...MEET ME IN THE ***BRIG***."
SO... NO RESPONSE TO DIRECT VERBAL QUESTIONING. WE EXPECTED AS MUCH.
I HATE TO ASK, BUT CAN YOU GET ANYTHING THROUGH YOUR *EMPATHY* WITH THE COLLECTIVE?
I WILL TRY, CAPTAIN...
...THE ...THE BORG CUBE WAS *TRAPPED* HERE THE SAME WAY *WE* WERE.

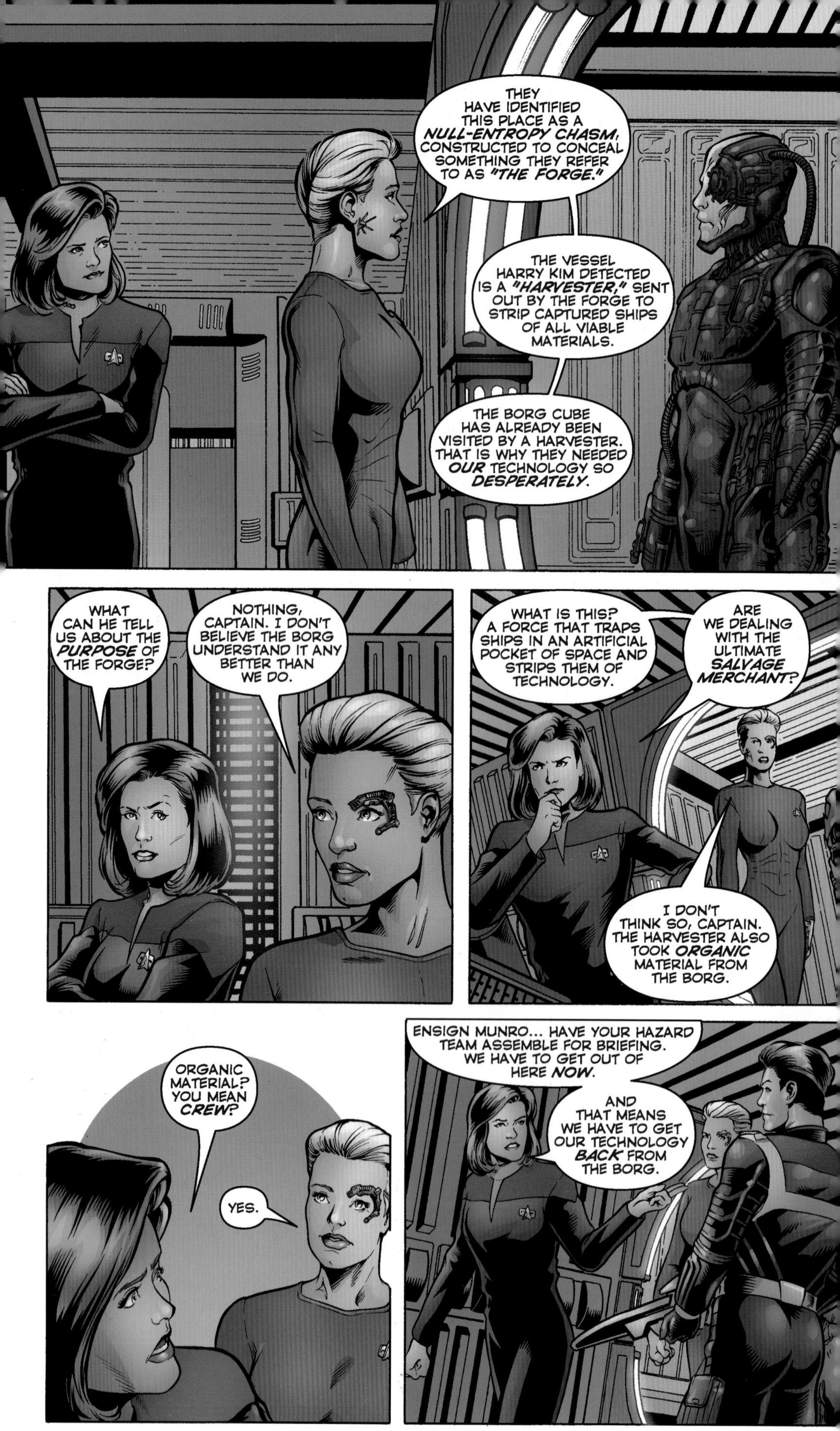
THEY HAVE IDENTIFIED THIS PLACE AS A NULL-ENTROPY CHASM, CONSTRUCTED TO CONCEAL SOMETHING THEY REFER TO AS "THE FORGE."
THE VESSEL HARRY KIM DETECTED IS A "HARVESTER," SENT OUT BY THE FORGE TO STRIP CAPTURED SHIPS OF ALL VIABLE MATERIALS.
THE BORG CUBE HAS ALREADY BEEN VISITED BY A HARVESTER. THAT IS WHY THEY NEEDED OUR TECHNOLOGY SO DESPERATELY.
WHAT CAN HE TELL US ABOUT THE PURPOSE OF THE FORGE?
NOTHING, CAPTAIN. I DON'T BELIEVE THE BORG UNDERSTAND IT ANY BETTER THAN WE DO.
WHAT IS THIS? A FORCE THAT TRAPS SHIPS IN AN ARTIFICIAL POCKET OF SPACE AND STRIPS THEM OF TECHNOLOGY.
ARE WE DEALING WITH THE ULTIMATE SALVAGE MERCHANT?
I DON'T THINK SO, CAPTAIN. THE HARVESTER ALSO TOOK ORGANIC MATERIAL FROM THE BORG.
ORGANIC MATERIAL? YOU MEAN CREW?
YES.
ENSIGN MUNRO... HAVE YOUR HAZARD TEAM ASSEMBLE FOR BRIEFING. WE HAVE TO GET OUT OF HERE NOW.
AND THAT MEANS WE HAVE TO GET OUR TECHNOLOGY BACK FROM THE BORG.

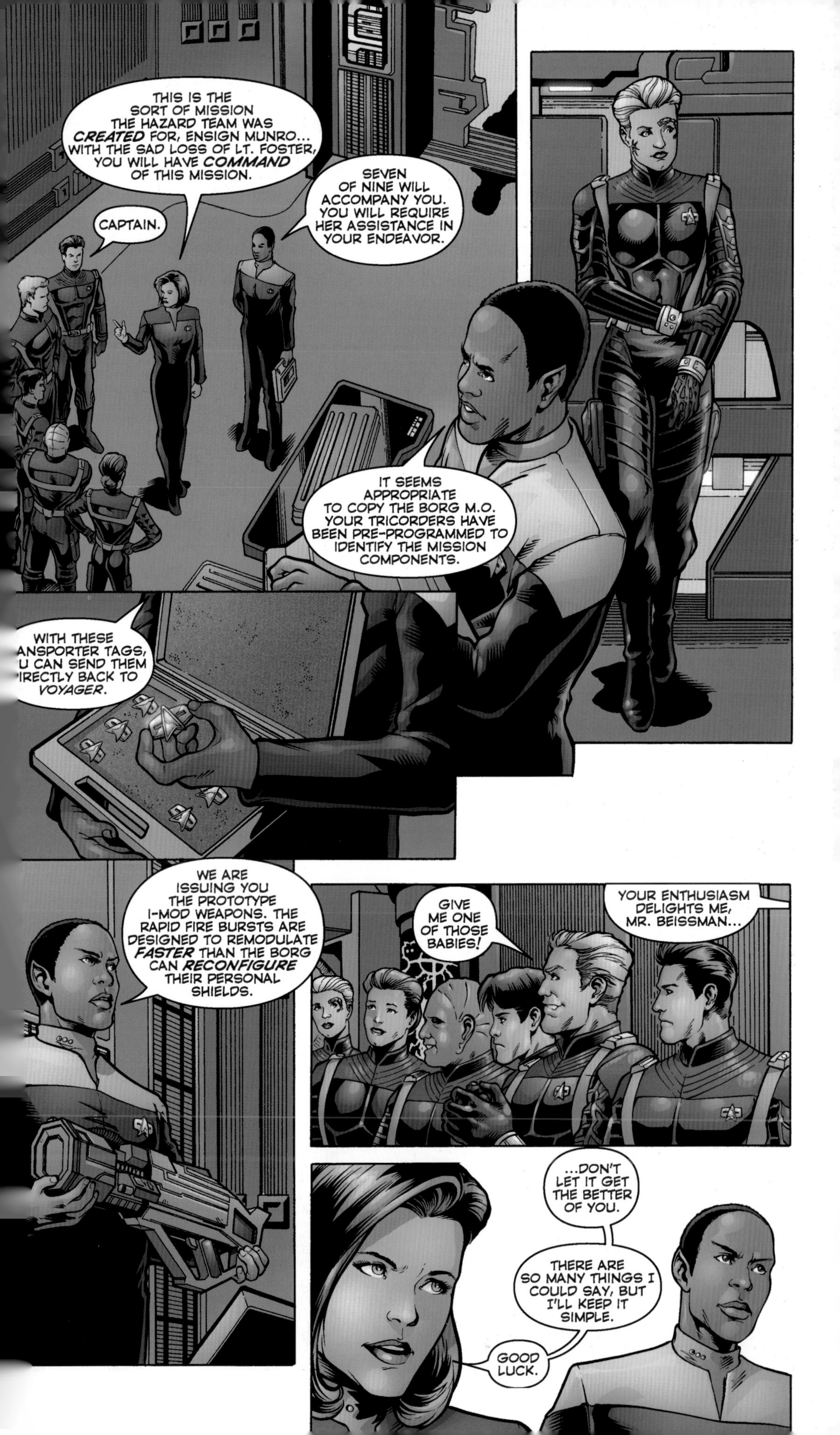
THIS IS THE SORT OF MISSION THE HAZARD TEAM WAS CREATED FOR, ENSIGN MUNRO... WITH THE SAD LOSS OF LT. FOSTER, YOU WILL HAVE COMMAND OF THIS MISSION.
CAPTAIN.
SEVEN OF NINE WILL ACCOMPANY YOU. YOU WILL REQUIRE HER ASSISTANCE IN YOUR ENDEAVOR.
IT SEEMS APPROPRIATE TO COPY THE BORG M.O. YOUR TRICORDERS HAVE BEEN PRE-PROGRAMMED TO IDENTIFY THE MISSION COMPONENTS.
WITH THESE ANSPORTER TAGS, U CAN SEND THEM IRECTLY BACK TO VOYAGER.
WE ARE ISSUING YOU THE PROTOTYPE I-MOD WEAPONS. THE RAPID FIRE BURSTS ARE DESIGNED TO REMODULATE FASTER THAN THE BORG CAN RECONFIGURE THEIR PERSONAL SHIELDS.
GIVE ME ONE OF THOSE BABIES!
YOUR ENTHUSIASM DELIGHTS ME, MR. BEISSMAN...
...DON'T LET IT GET THE BETTER OF YOU.
THERE ARE SO MANY THINGS I COULD SAY, BUT I'LL KEEP IT SIMPLE.
GOOD LUCK.

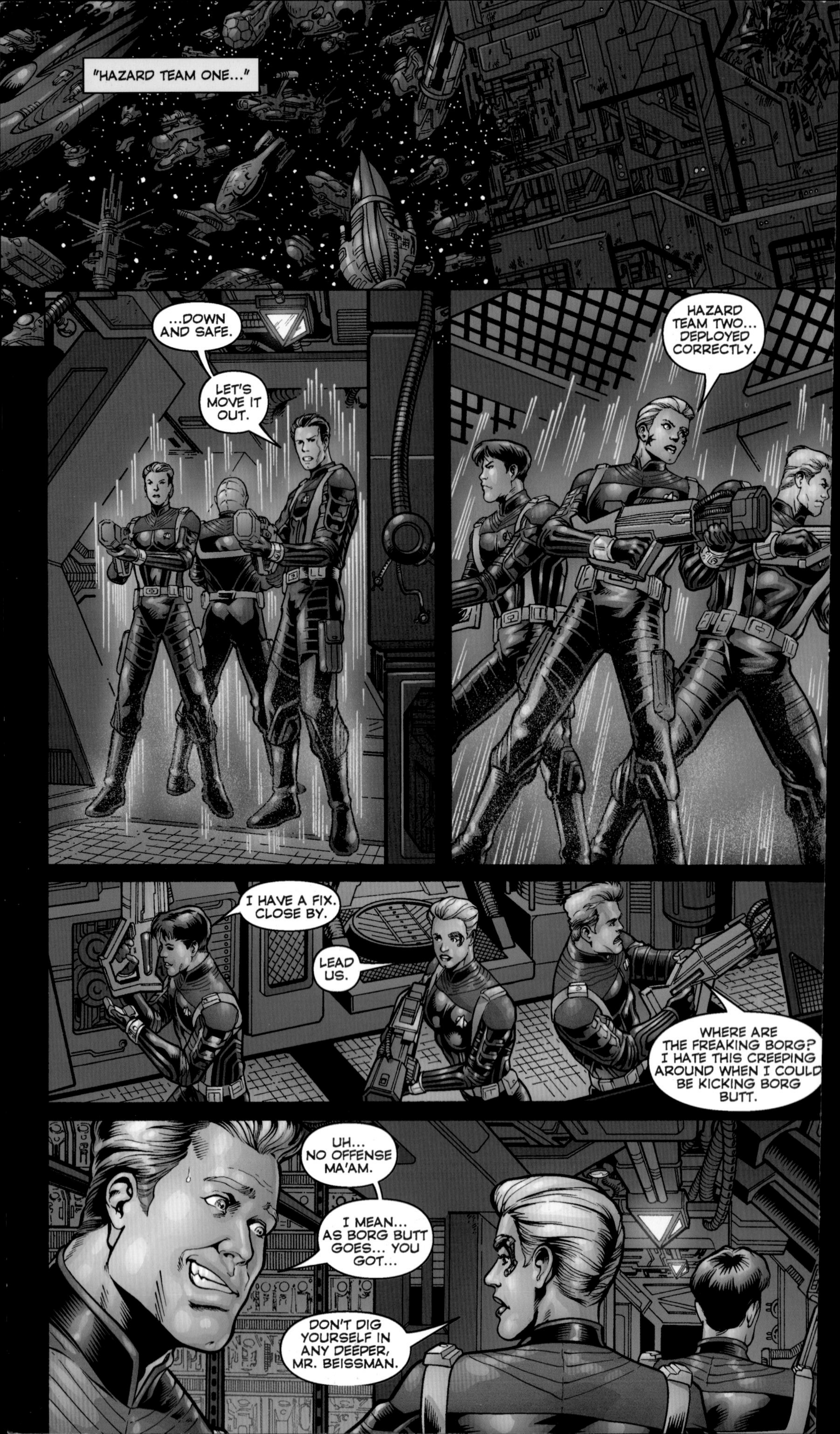
"HAZARD TEAM ONE..."
...DOWN AND SAFE.
LET'S MOVE IT OUT.
HAZARD TEAM TWO... DEPLOYED CORRECTLY.
I HAVE A FIX. CLOSE BY.
LEAD US.
WHERE ARE THE FREAKING BORG? I HATE THIS CREEPING AROUND WHEN I COULD BE KICKING BORG BUTT.
UH... NO OFFENSE MA'AM.
I MEAN... AS BORG BUTT GOES... YOU GOT...
DON'T DIG YOURSELF IN ANY DEEPER, MR. BEISSMAN.

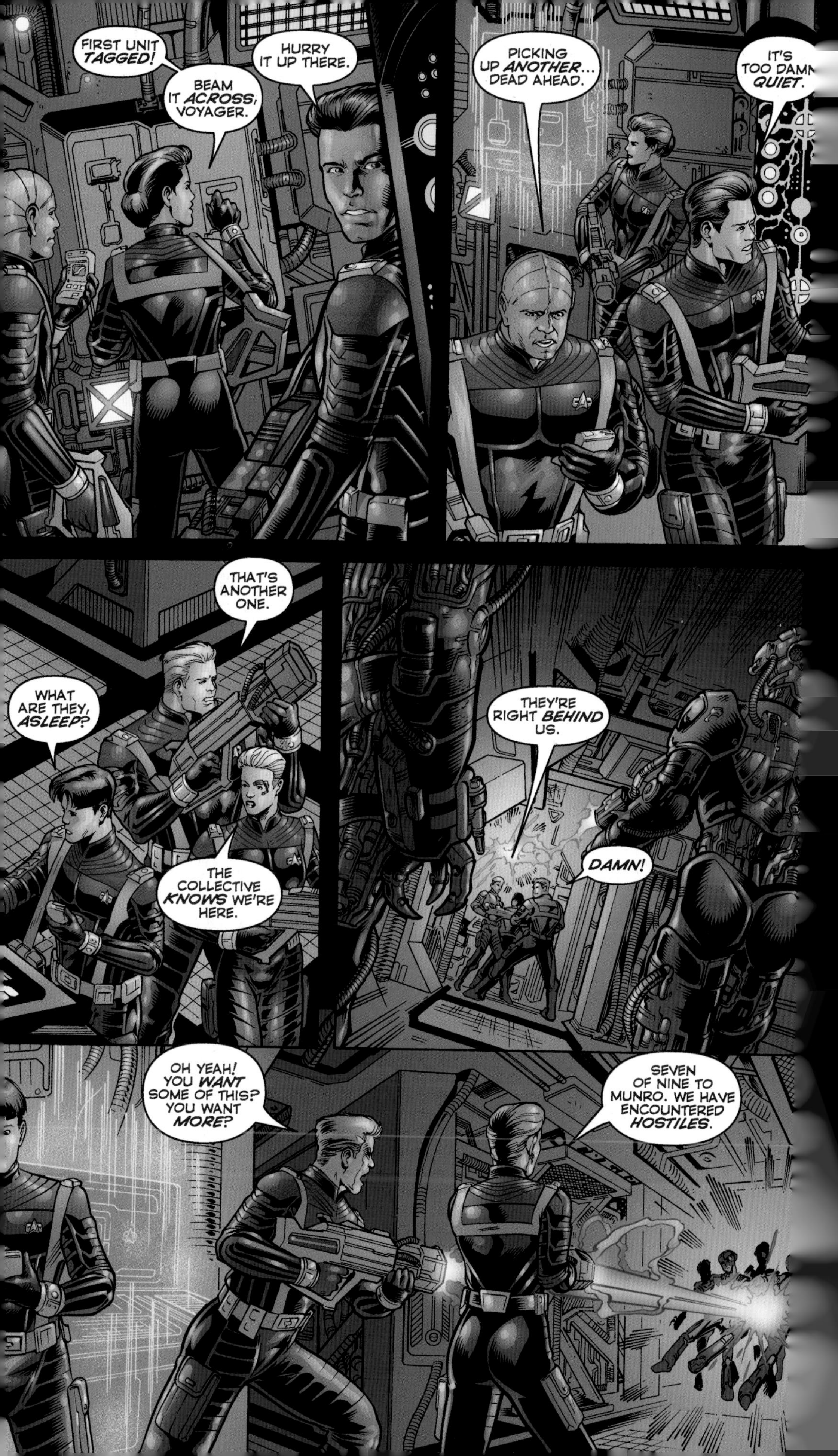
FIRST UNIT TAGGED!
BEAM IT ACROSS, VOYAGER.
HURRY IT UP THERE.
PICKING UP ANOTHER... DEAD AHEAD.
IT'S TOO DAMN QUIET.
THAT'S ANOTHER ONE.
WHAT ARE THEY, ASLEEP?
THE COLLECTIVE KNOWS WE'RE HERE.
THEY'RE RIGHT BEHIND US.
DAMN!
OH YEAH! YOU WANT SOME OF THIS? YOU WANT MORE?
SEVEN OF NINE TO MUNRO. WE HAVE ENCOUNTERED HOSTILES.

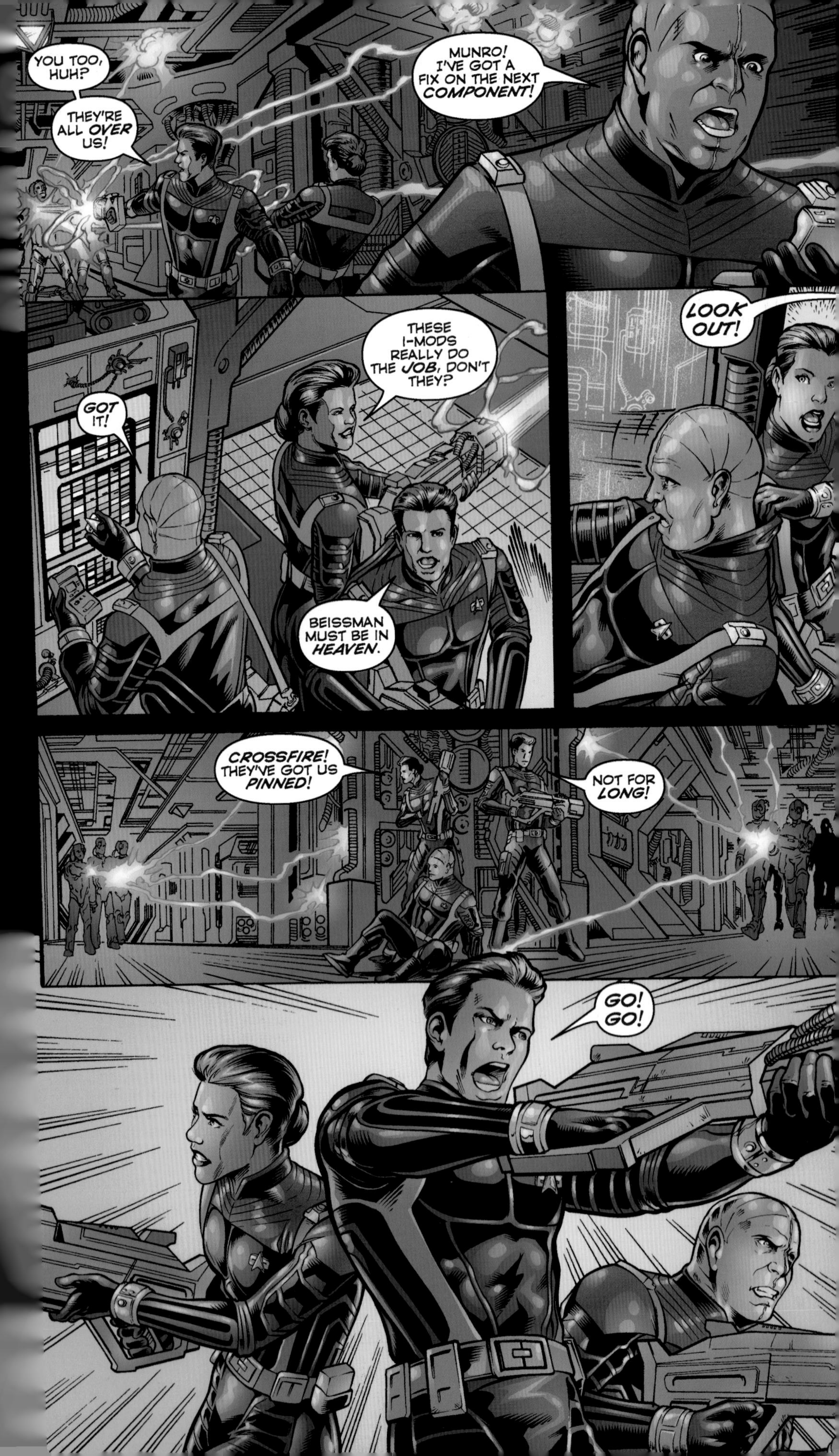
YOU TOO, HUH?
THEY'RE ALL OVER US!
MUNRO! I'VE GOT A FIX ON THE NEXT COMPONENT!
GOT IT!
THESE I-MODS REALLY DO THE JOB, DON'T THEY?
BEISSMAN MUST BE IN HEAVEN.
LOOK OUT!
CROSSFIRE! THEY'VE GOT US PINNED!
NOT FOR LONG!
GO! GO!

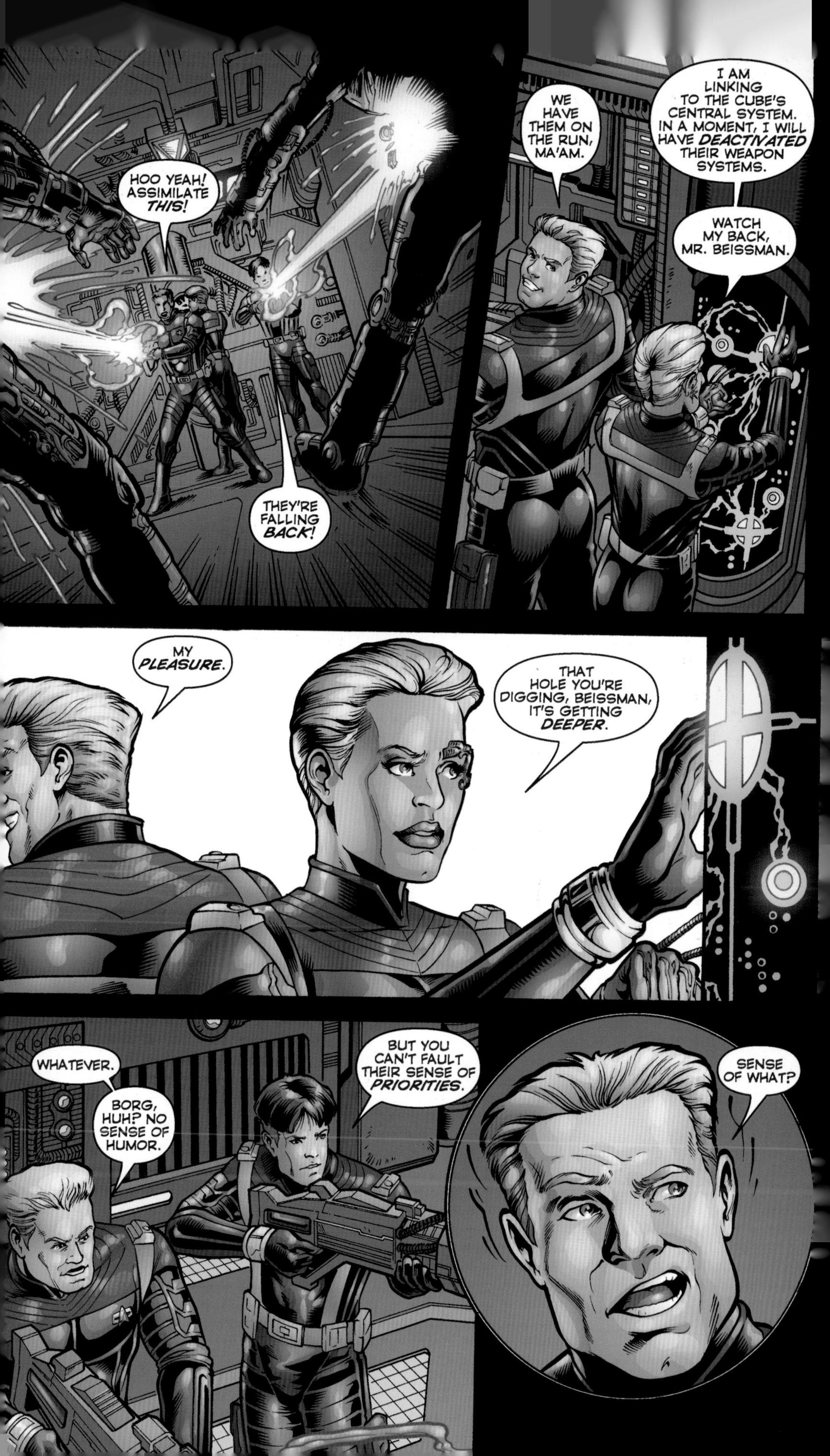
HOO YEAH! ASSIMILATE THIS!
THEY'RE FALLING BACK!
WE HAVE THEM ON THE RUN, MA'AM.
I AM LINKING TO THE CUBE'S CENTRAL SYSTEM. IN A MOMENT, I WILL HAVE DEACTIVATED THEIR WEAPON SYSTEMS.
WATCH MY BACK, MR. BEISSMAN.
MY PLEASURE.
THAT HOLE YOU'RE DIGGING, BEISSMAN, IT'S GETTING DEEPER.
WHATEVER.
BORG, HUH? NO SENSE OF HUMOR.
BUT YOU CAN'T FAULT THEIR SENSE OF PRIORITIES.
SENSE OF WHAT?

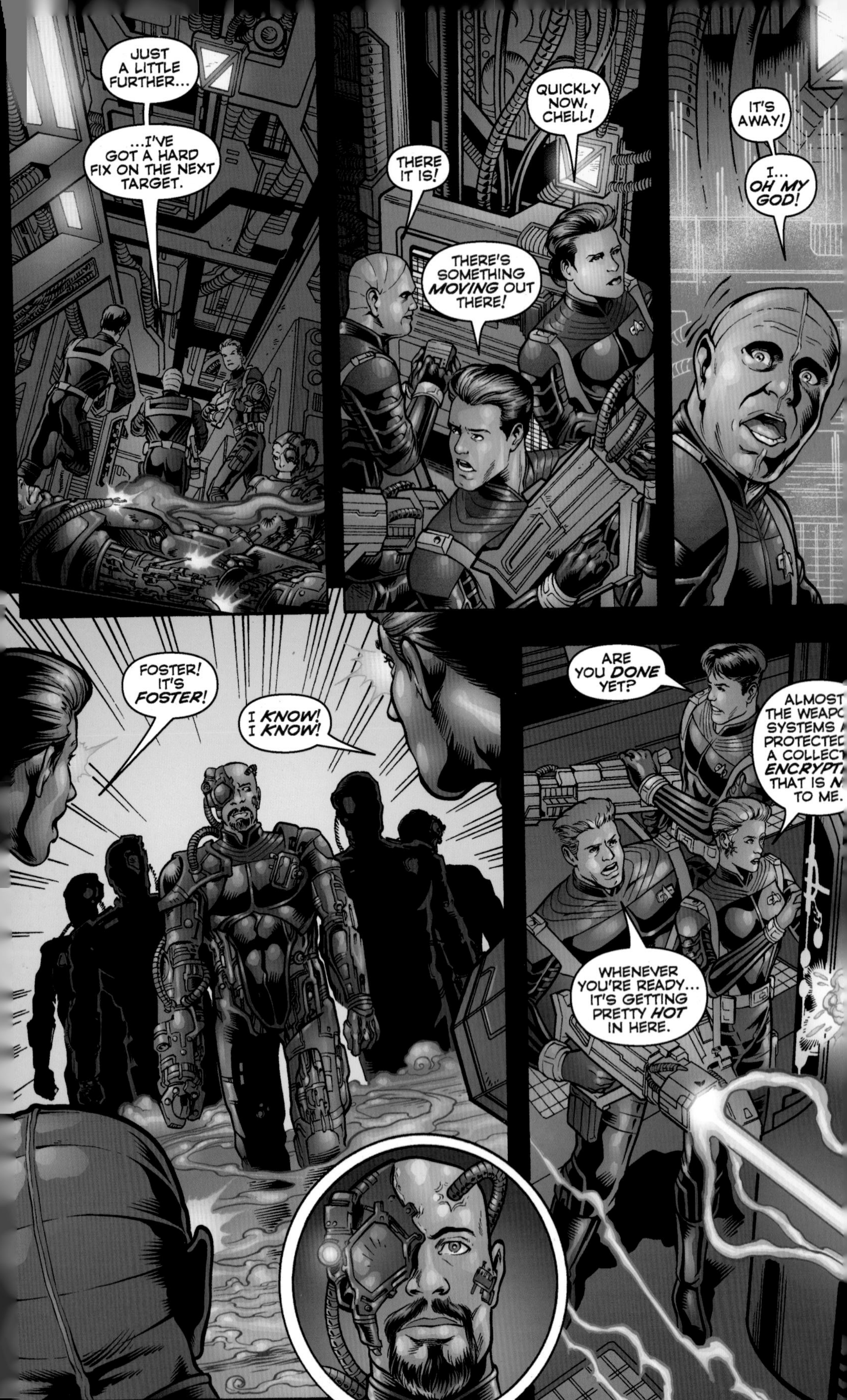

JUST A LITTLE FURTHER...
...I'VE GOT A HARD FIX ON THE NEXT TARGET.
QUICKLY NOW, CHELL!
THERE IT IS!
THERE'S SOMETHING MOVING OUT THERE!
IT'S AWAY!
I... OH MY GOD!
FOSTER! IT'S FOSTER!
I KNOW! I KNOW!
ARE YOU DONE YET?
ALMOST THE WEAPO SYSTEMS A PROTECTED A COLLECT ENCRYPT THAT IS N TO ME.
WHENEVER YOU'RE READY... IT'S GETTING PRETTY HOT IN HERE.

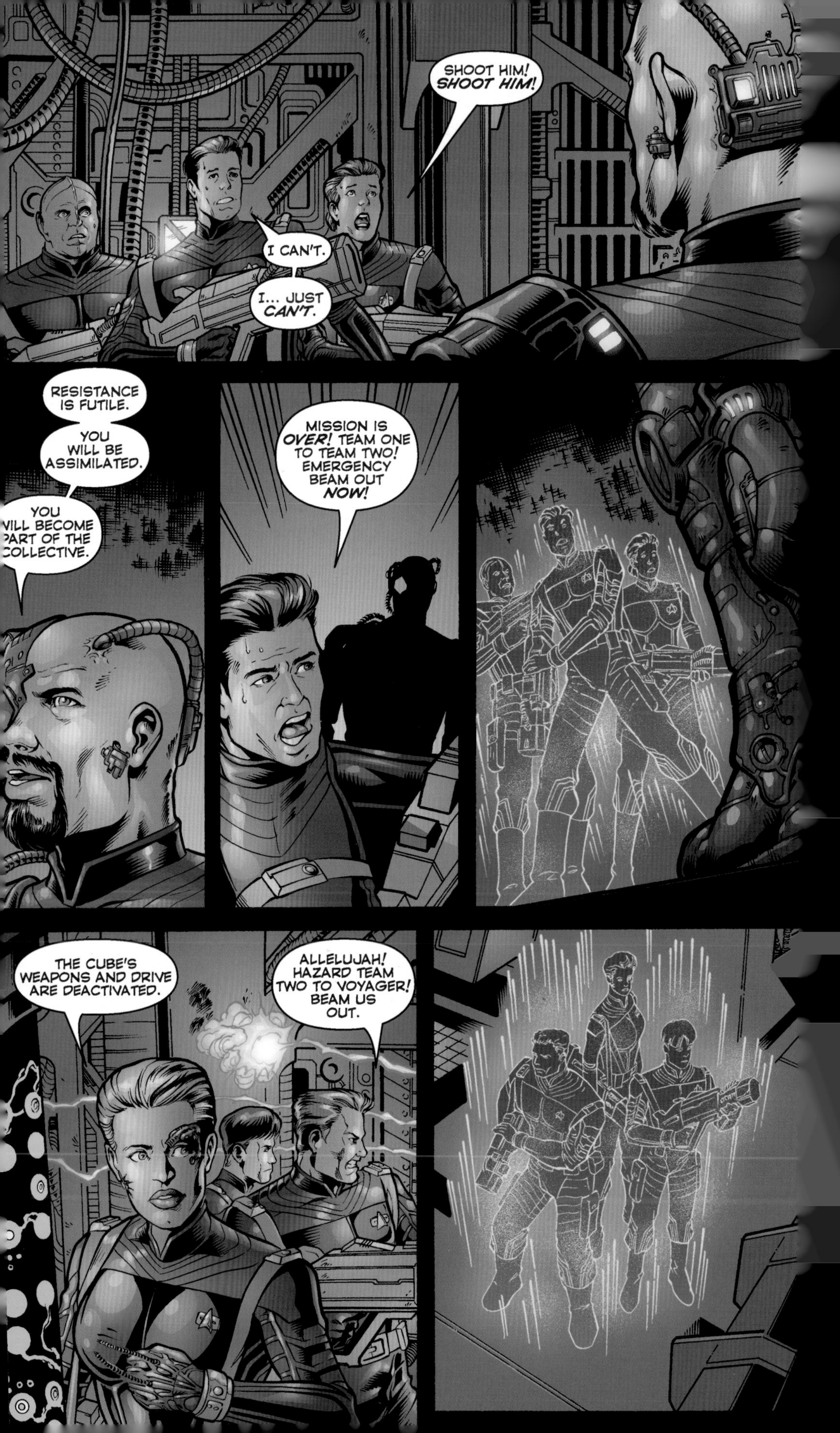

SHOOT HIM! SHOOT HIM!
I CAN'T.
I... JUST CAN'T.
RESISTANCE IS FUTILE.
YOU WILL BE ASSIMILATED.
YOU WILL BECOME PART OF THE COLLECTIVE.
MISSION IS OVER! TEAM ONE TO TEAM TWO! EMERGENCY BEAM OUT NOW!
THE CUBE'S WEAPONS AND DRIVE ARE DEACTIVATED.
ALLELUJAH! HAZARD TEAM TWO TO VOYAGER! BEAM US OUT.

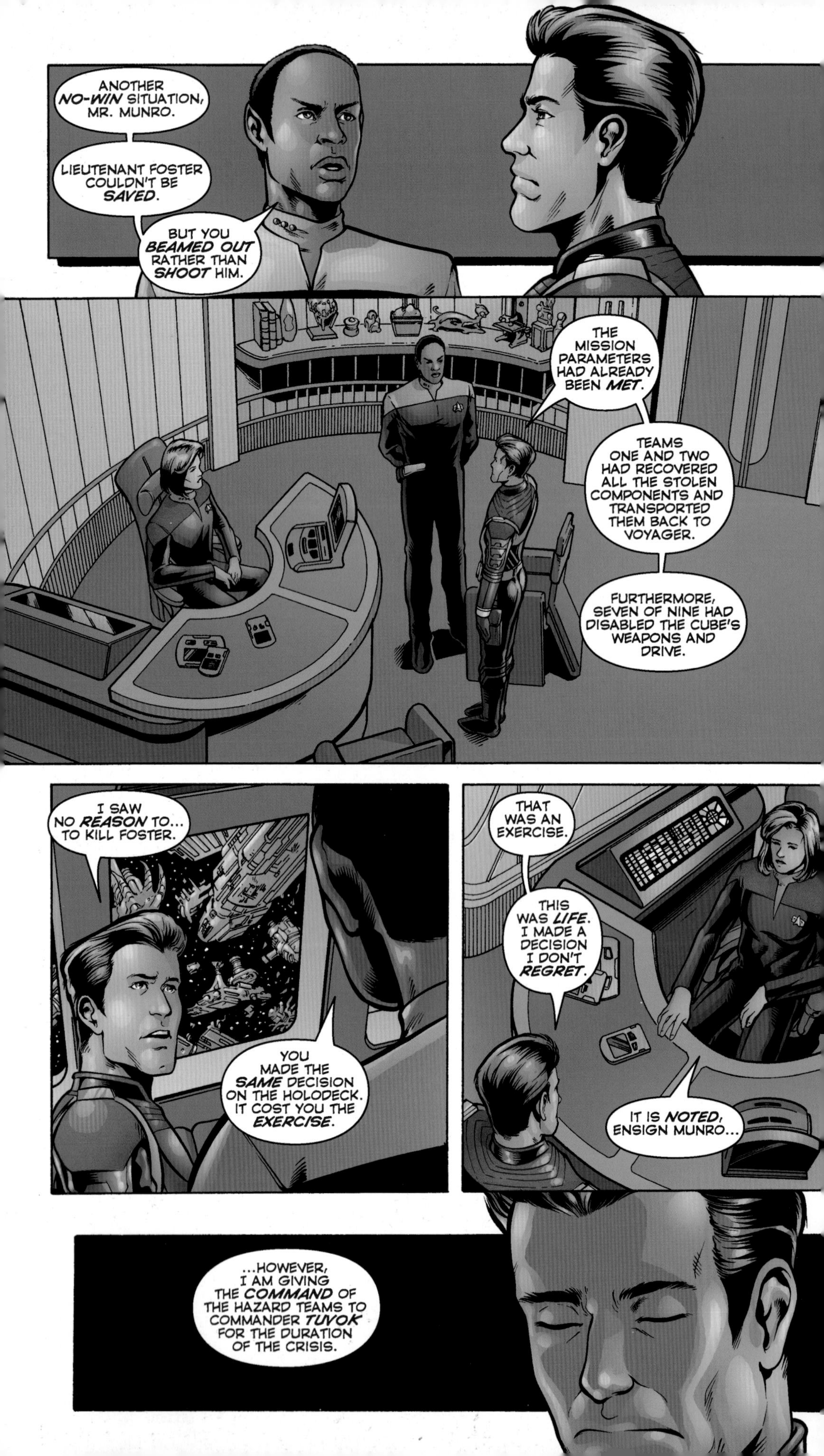
ANOTHER NO-WIN SITUATION, MR. MUNRO.
LIEUTENANT FOSTER COULDN'T BE SAVED.
BUT YOU BEAMED OUT RATHER THAN SHOOT HIM.
THE MISSION PARAMETERS HAD ALREADY BEEN MET.
TEAMS ONE AND TWO HAD RECOVERED ALL THE STOLEN COMPONENTS AND TRANSPORTED THEM BACK TO VOYAGER.
FURTHERMORE, SEVEN OF NINE HAD DISABLED THE CUBE'S WEAPONS AND DRIVE.
I SAW NO REASON TO... TO KILL FOSTER.
YOU MADE THE SAME DECISION ON THE HOLODECK. IT COST YOU THE EXERCISE.
THAT WAS AN EXERCISE.
THIS WAS LIFE. I MADE A DECISION I DON'T REGRET.
IT IS NOTED, ENSIGN MUNRO...
...HOWEVER, I AM GIVING THE COMMAND OF THE HAZARD TEAMS TO COMMANDER TUVOK FOR THE DURATION OF THE CRISIS.

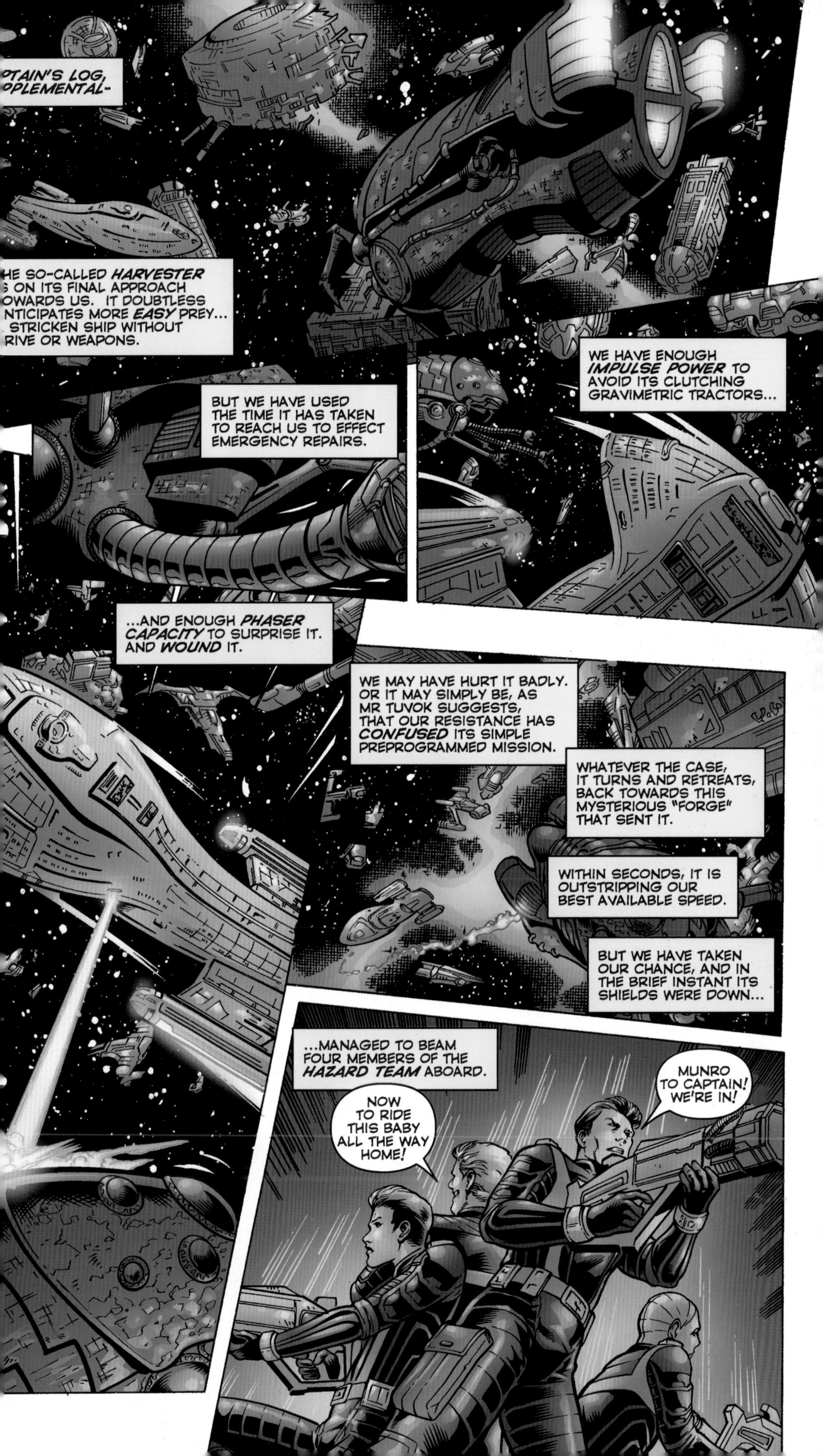

PTAIN'S LOG, PPLEMENTAL-
HE SO-CALLED HARVESTER S ON ITS FINAL APPROACH OWARDS US. IT DOUBTLESS NTICIPATES MORE EASY PREY... STRICKEN SHIP WITHOUT RIVE OR WEAPONS.
BUT WE HAVE USED THE TIME IT HAS TAKEN TO REACH US TO EFFECT EMERGENCY REPAIRS.
WE HAVE ENOUGH IMPULSE POWER TO AVOID ITS CLUTCHING GRAVIMETRIC TRACTORS...
...AND ENOUGH PHASER CAPACITY TO SURPRISE IT. AND WOUND IT.
WE MAY HAVE HURT IT BADLY. OR IT MAY SIMPLY BE, AS MR TUVOK SUGGESTS, THAT OUR RESISTANCE HAS CONFUSED ITS SIMPLE PREPROGRAMMED MISSION.
WHATEVER THE CASE, IT TURNS AND RETREATS, BACK TOWARDS THIS MYSTERIOUS "FORGE" THAT SENT IT.
WITHIN SECONDS, IT IS OUTSTRIPPING OUR BEST AVAILABLE SPEED.
BUT WE HAVE TAKEN OUR CHANCE, AND IN THE BRIEF INSTANT ITS SHIELDS WERE DOWN...
...MANAGED TO BEAM FOUR MEMBERS OF THE HAZARD TEAM ABOARD.
MUNRO TO CAPTAIN! WE'RE IN!
NOW TO RIDE THIS BABY ALL THE WAY HOME!

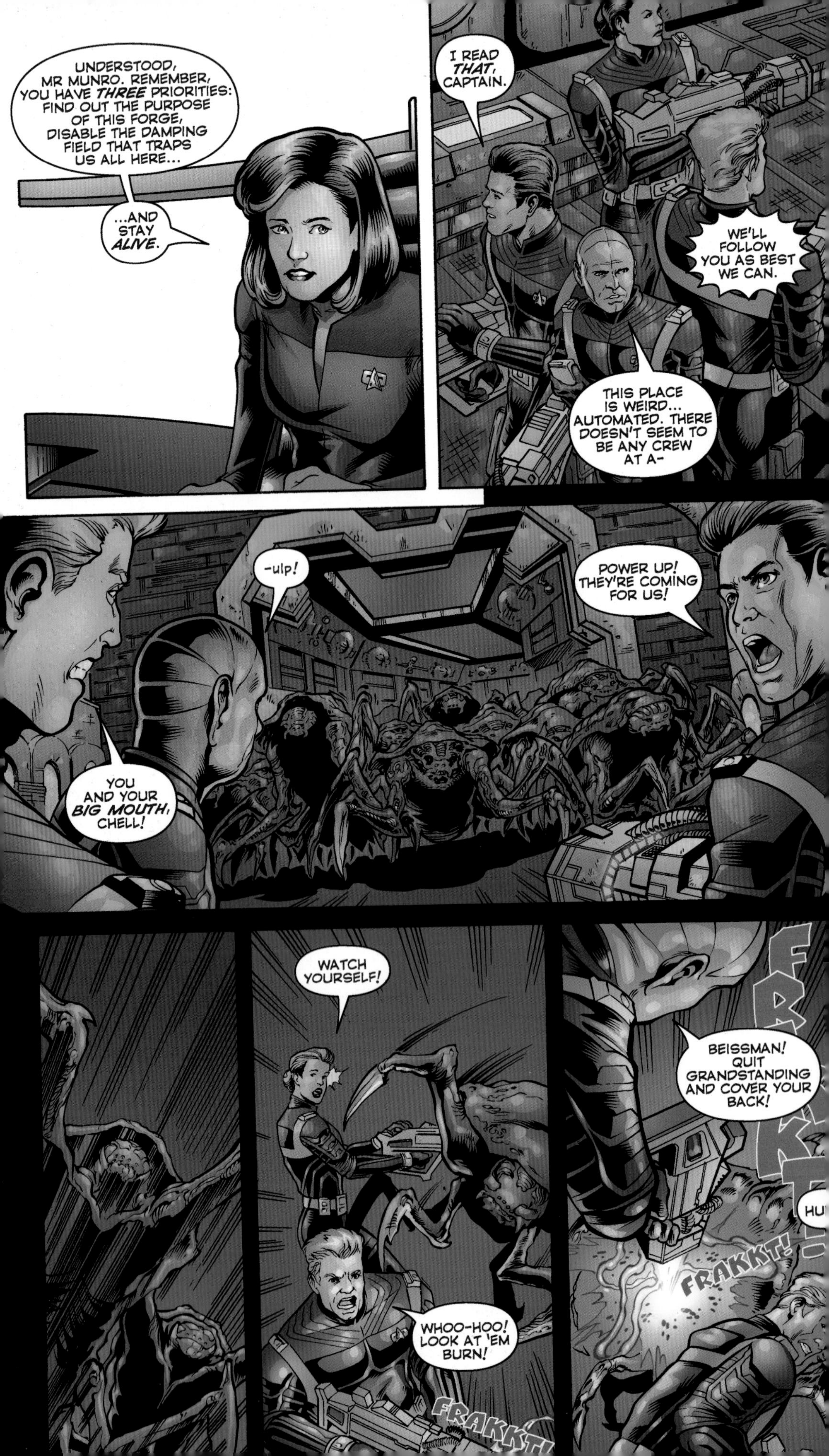
UNDERSTOOD, MR MUNRO. REMEMBER, YOU HAVE THREE PRIORITIES: FIND OUT THE PURPOSE OF THIS FORGE, DISABLE THE DAMPING FIELD THAT TRAPS US ALL HERE...
...AND STAY ALIVE.
I READ THAT, CAPTAIN.
WE'LL FOLLOW YOU AS BEST WE CAN.
THIS PLACE IS WEIRD... AUTOMATED. THERE DOESN'T SEEM TO BE ANY CREW AT A-
-ulp!
POWER UP! THEY'RE COMING FOR US!
YOU AND YOUR BIG MOUTH, CHELL!
WATCH YOURSELF!
WHOO-HOO! LOOK AT 'EM BURN!
FRAKKT!
BEISSMAN! QUIT GRANDSTANDING AND COVER YOUR BACK!
FRAKKT!
HU

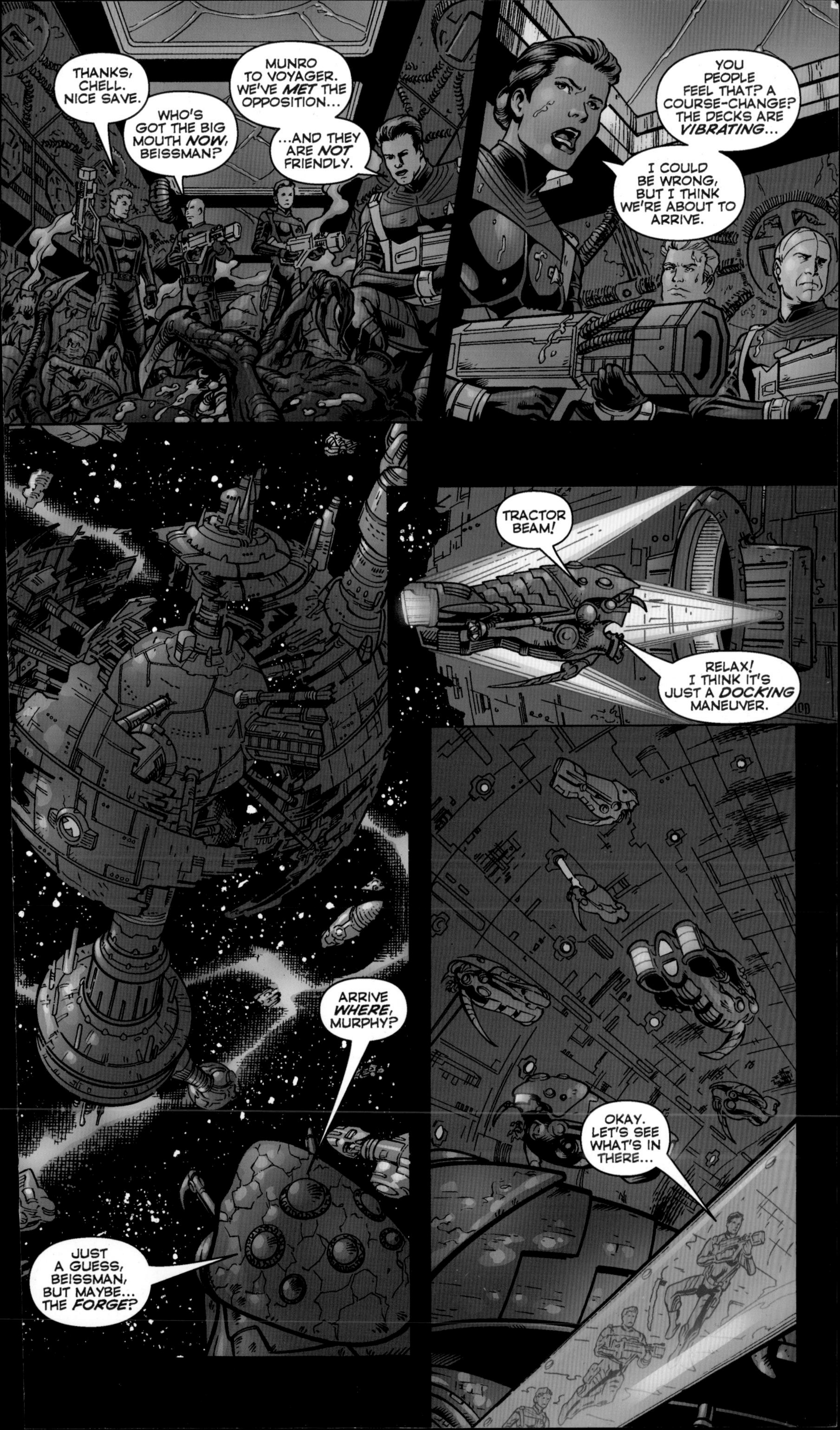
THANKS, CHELL. NICE SAVE.
WHO'S GOT THE BIG MOUTH *NOW*, BEISSMAN?
MUNRO TO VOYAGER. WE'VE *MET* THE OPPOSITION...
...AND THEY ARE *NOT* FRIENDLY.
YOU PEOPLE FEEL THAT? A COURSE-CHANGE? THE DECKS ARE *VIBRATING*...
I COULD BE WRONG, BUT I THINK WE'RE ABOUT TO ARRIVE.
TRACTOR BEAM!
RELAX! I THINK IT'S JUST A *DOCKING* MANEUVER.
ARRIVE *WHERE*, MURPHY?
JUST A GUESS, BEISSMAN, BUT MAYBE... THE *FORGE*?
OKAY. LET'S SEE WHAT'S IN THERE...

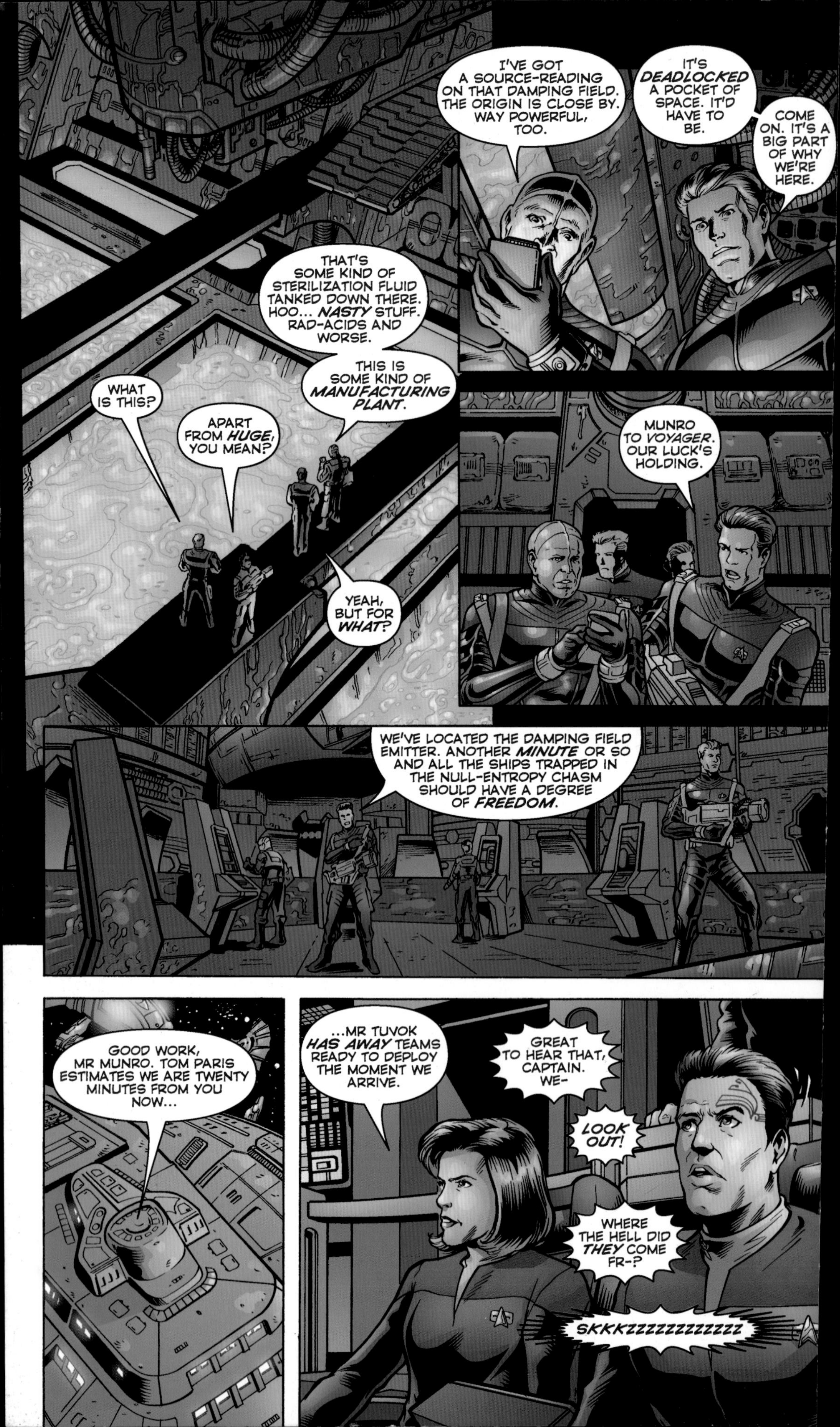
THAT'S SOME KIND OF STERILIZATION FLUID TANKED DOWN THERE. HOO... NASTY STUFF. RAD-ACIDS AND WORSE.
THIS IS SOME KIND OF MANUFACTURING PLANT.
WHAT IS THIS?
APART FROM HUGE, YOU MEAN?
YEAH, BUT FOR WHAT?
I'VE GOT A SOURCE-READING ON THAT DAMPING FIELD. THE ORIGIN IS CLOSE BY. WAY POWERFUL, TOO.
IT'S DEADLOCKED A POCKET OF SPACE. IT'D HAVE TO BE.
COME ON. IT'S A BIG PART OF WHY WE'RE HERE.
MUNRO TO VOYAGER. OUR LUCK'S HOLDING.
WE'VE LOCATED THE DAMPING FIELD EMITTER. ANOTHER MINUTE OR SO AND ALL THE SHIPS TRAPPED IN THE NULL-ENTROPY CHASM SHOULD HAVE A DEGREE OF FREEDOM.
GOOD WORK, MR MUNRO. TOM PARIS ESTIMATES WE ARE TWENTY MINUTES FROM YOU NOW...
...MR TUVOK HAS AWAY TEAMS READY TO DEPLOY THE MOMENT WE ARRIVE.
GREAT TO HEAR THAT, CAPTAIN. WE-
LOOK OUT!
WHERE THE HELL DID THEY COME FR-?
SKKKZZZZZZZZZZZZZ

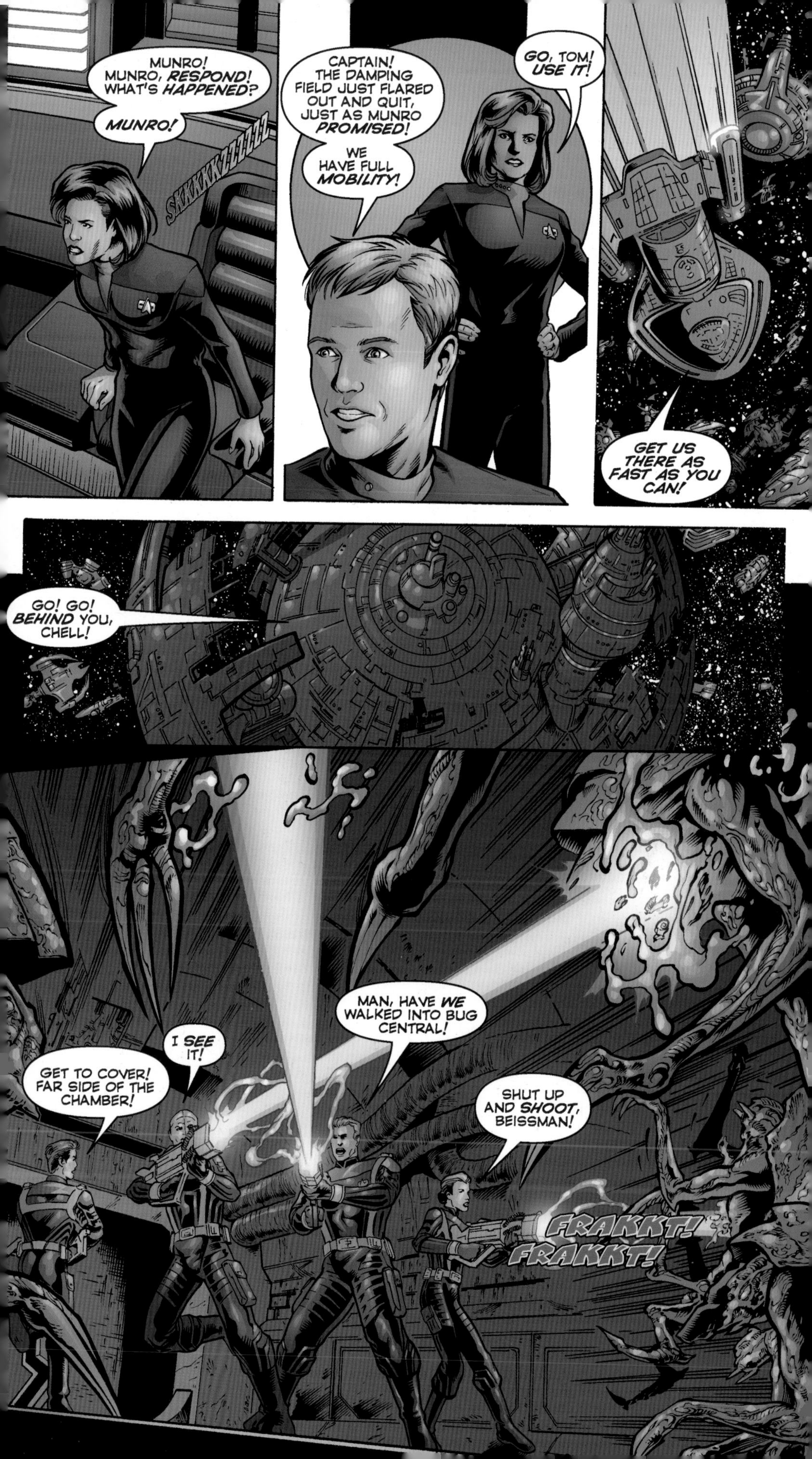

MUNRO! MUNRO, RESPOND! WHAT'S HAPPENED?
MUNRO!
SKKKKKZZZZZZ
CAPTAIN! THE DAMPING FIELD JUST FLARED OUT AND QUIT, JUST AS MUNRO PROMISED!
WE HAVE FULL MOBILITY!
GO, TOM! USE IT!
GET US THERE AS FAST AS YOU CAN!
GO! GO! BEHIND YOU, CHELL!
GET TO COVER! FAR SIDE OF THE CHAMBER!
I SEE IT!
MAN, HAVE WE WALKED INTO BUG CENTRAL!
SHUT UP AND SHOOT, BEISSMAN!
FRAKKT! FRAKKT!

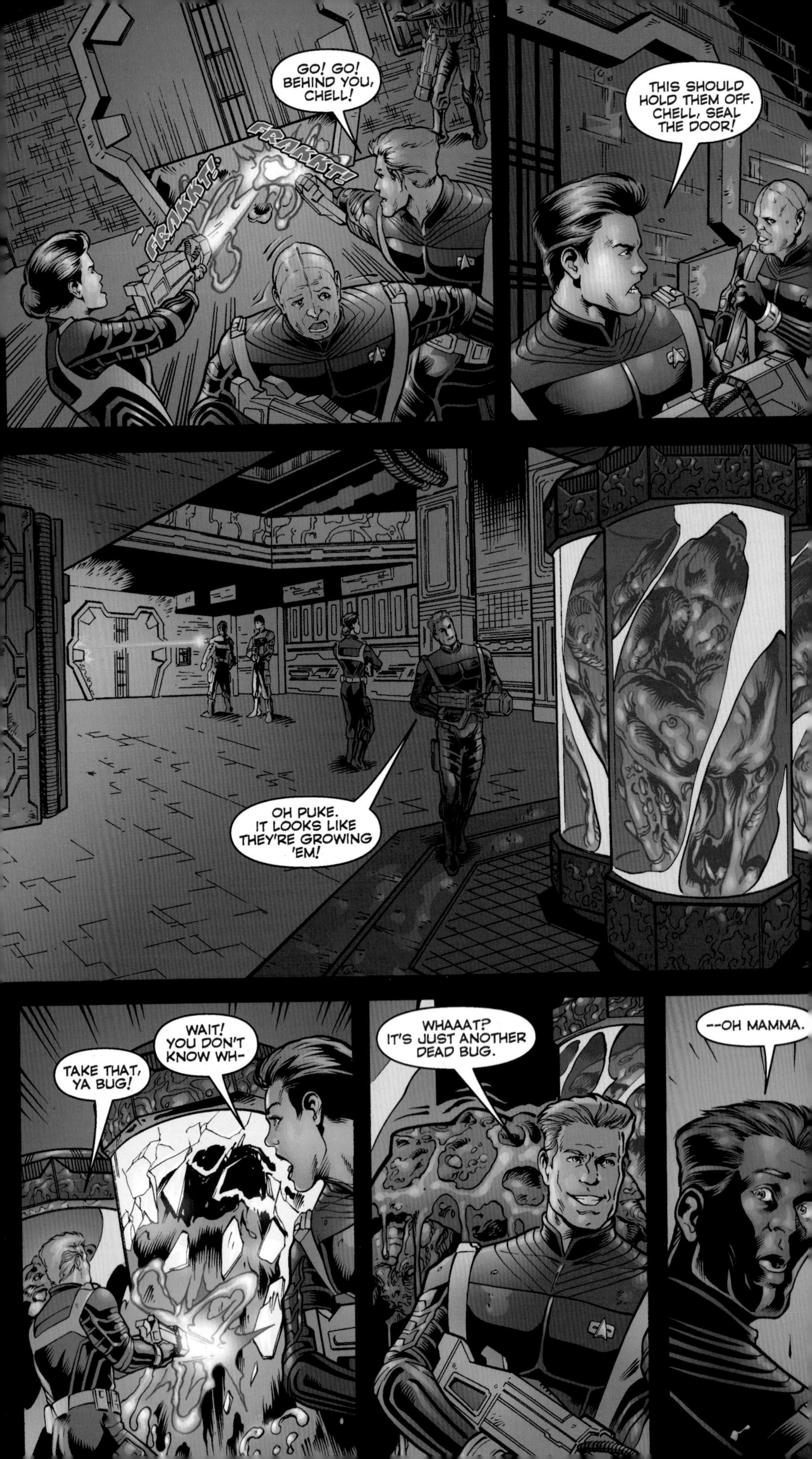
GO! GO! BEHIND YOU, CHELL!
FRAKKT!
FRAKKT!
FRAKKT!
THIS SHOULD HOLD THEM OFF. CHELL, SEAL THE DOOR!
OH PUKE. IT LOOKS LIKE THEY'RE GROWING 'EM!
TAKE THAT, YA BUG!
WAIT! YOU DON'T KNOW WH-
WHAAAT? IT'S JUST ANOTHER DEAD BUG.
--OH MAMMA.

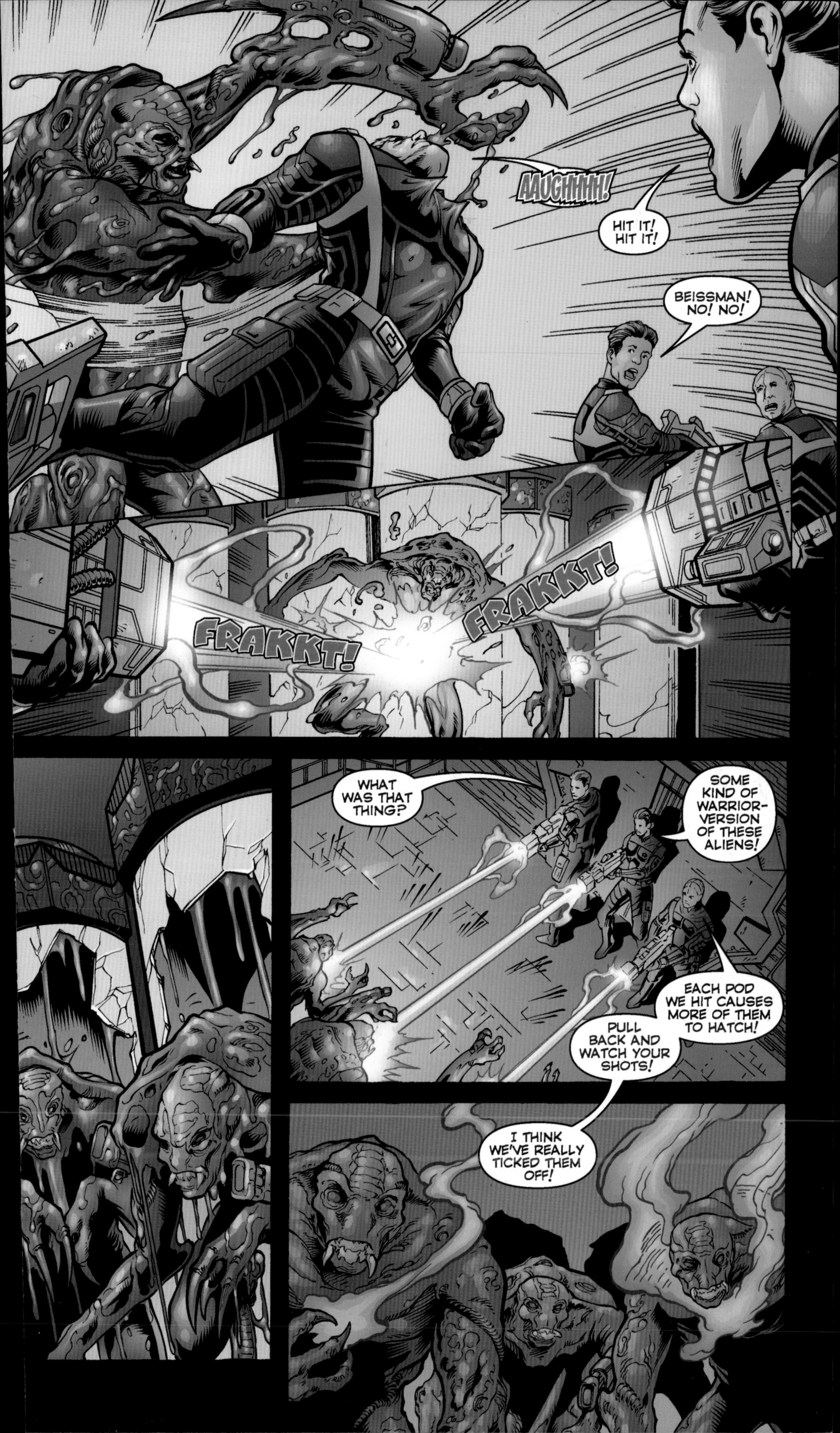
AAUGHHHH!
HIT IT! HIT IT!
BEISSMAN! NO! NO!
FRAKKT!
FRAKKT!
WHAT WAS THAT THING?
SOME KIND OF WARRIOR-VERSION OF THESE ALIENS!
EACH POD WE HIT CAUSES MORE OF THEM TO HATCH!
PULL BACK AND WATCH YOUR SHOTS!
I THINK WE'VE REALLY TICKED THEM OFF!

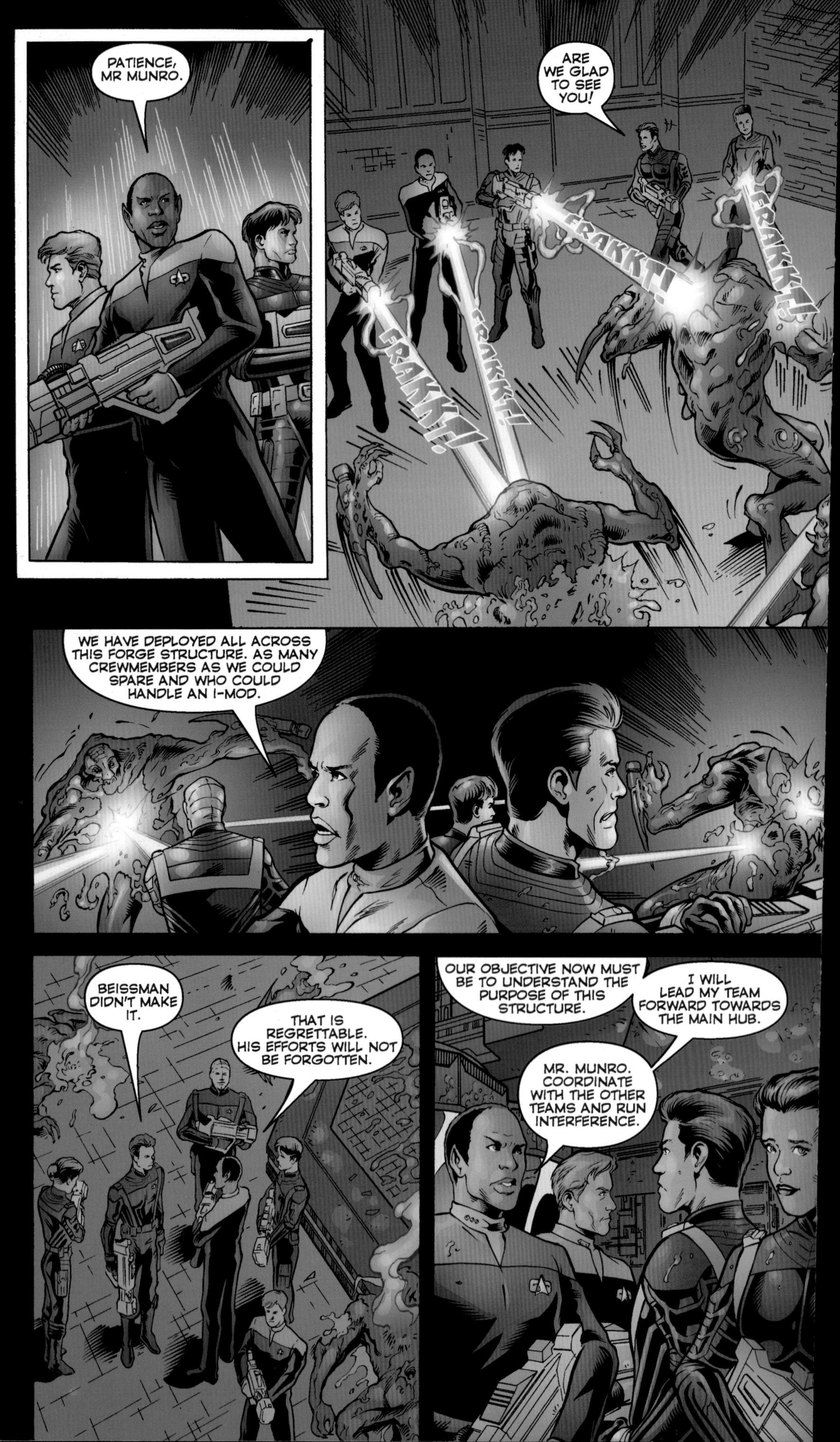
PATIENCE, MR MUNRO.
ARE WE GLAD TO SEE YOU!
FRAKKT!
FRAKKT!
FRAKKT!
FRAKKT!
WE HAVE DEPLOYED ALL ACROSS THIS FORGE STRUCTURE. AS MANY CREWMEMBERS AS WE COULD SPARE AND WHO COULD HANDLE AN I-MOD.
BEISSMAN DIDN'T MAKE IT.
THAT IS REGRETTABLE. HIS EFFORTS WILL NOT BE FORGOTTEN.
OUR OBJECTIVE NOW MUST BE TO UNDERSTAND THE PURPOSE OF THIS STRUCTURE.
I WILL LEAD MY TEAM FORWARD TOWARDS THE MAIN HUB.
MR. MUNRO. COORDINATE WITH THE OTHER TEAMS AND RUN INTERFERENCE.

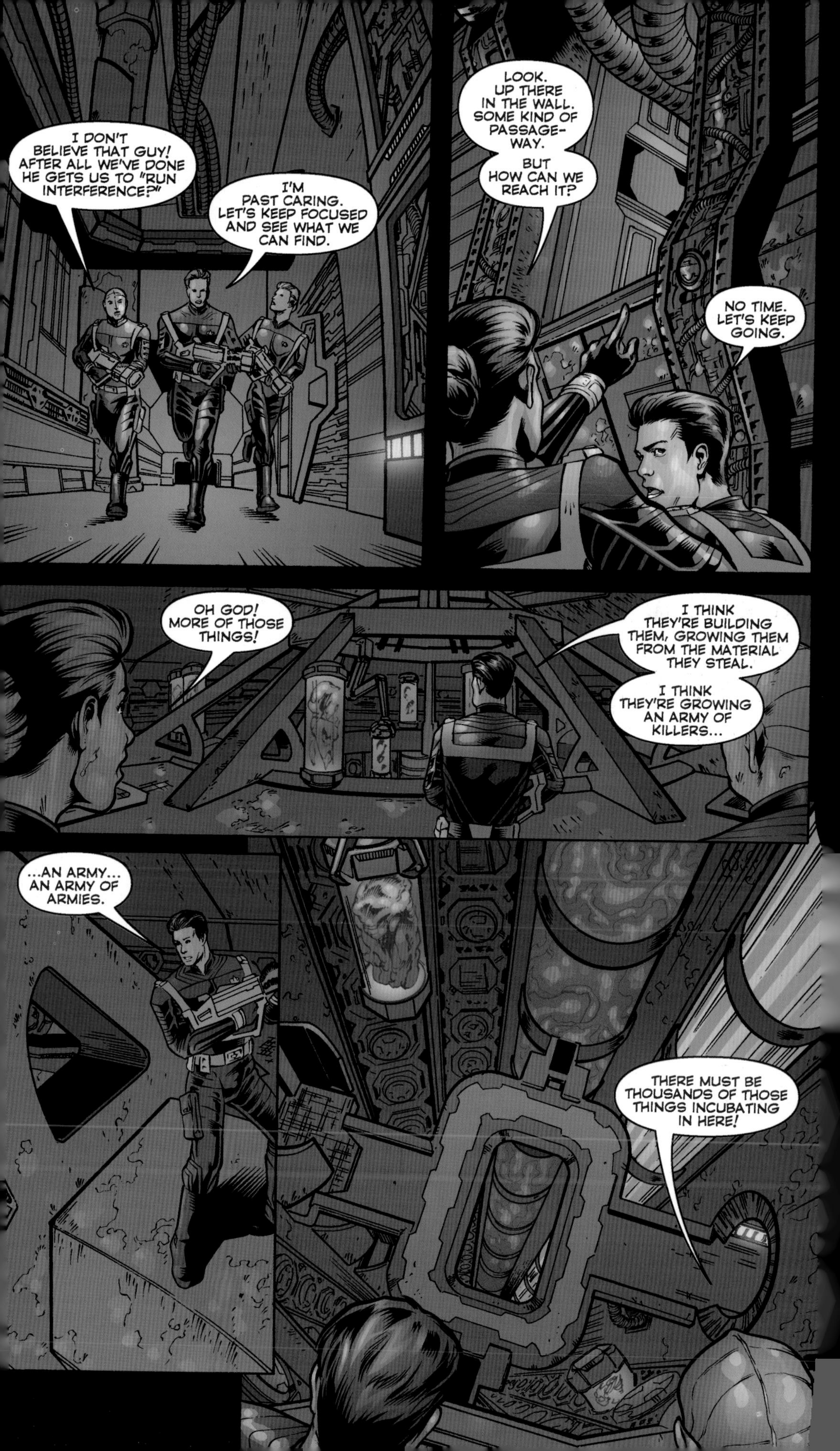
I DON'T BELIEVE THAT GUY! AFTER ALL WE'VE DONE HE GETS US TO "RUN INTERFERENCE?"
I'M PAST CARING. LET'S KEEP FOCUSED AND SEE WHAT WE CAN FIND.
LOOK. UP THERE IN THE WALL. SOME KIND OF PASSAGE-WAY.
BUT HOW CAN WE REACH IT?
NO TIME. LET'S KEEP GOING.
OH GOD! MORE OF THOSE THINGS!
I THINK THEY'RE BUILDING THEM, GROWING THEM FROM THE MATERIAL THEY STEAL.
I THINK THEY'RE GROWING AN ARMY OF KILLERS...
...AN ARMY... AN ARMY OF ARMIES.
THERE MUST BE THOUSANDS OF THOSE THINGS INCUBATING IN HERE!

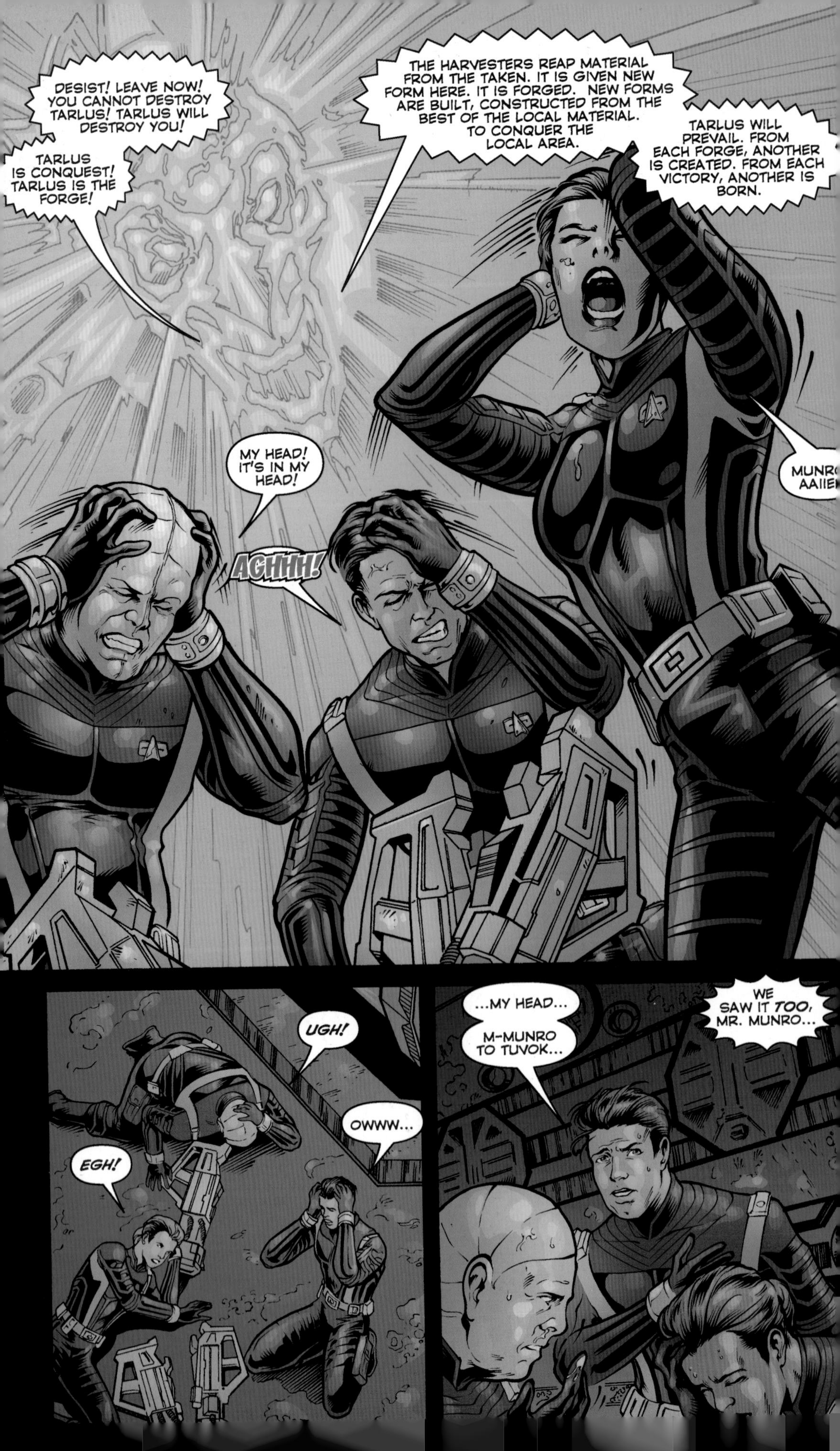
DESIST! LEAVE NOW! YOU CANNOT DESTROY TARLUS! TARLUS WILL DESTROY YOU!
TARLUS IS CONQUEST! TARLUS IS THE FORGE!
THE HARVESTERS REAP MATERIAL FROM THE TAKEN. IT IS GIVEN NEW FORM HERE. IT IS FORGED. NEW FORMS ARE BUILT, CONSTRUCTED FROM THE BEST OF THE LOCAL MATERIAL. TO CONQUER THE LOCAL AREA.
TARLUS WILL PREVAIL. FROM EACH FORGE, ANOTHER IS CREATED. FROM EACH VICTORY, ANOTHER IS BORN.
MY HEAD! IT'S IN MY HEAD!
AGHHH!
UGH!
OWWW...
EGH!
...MY HEAD...
M-MUNRO TO TUVOK...
WE SAW IT TOO, MR. MUNRO...

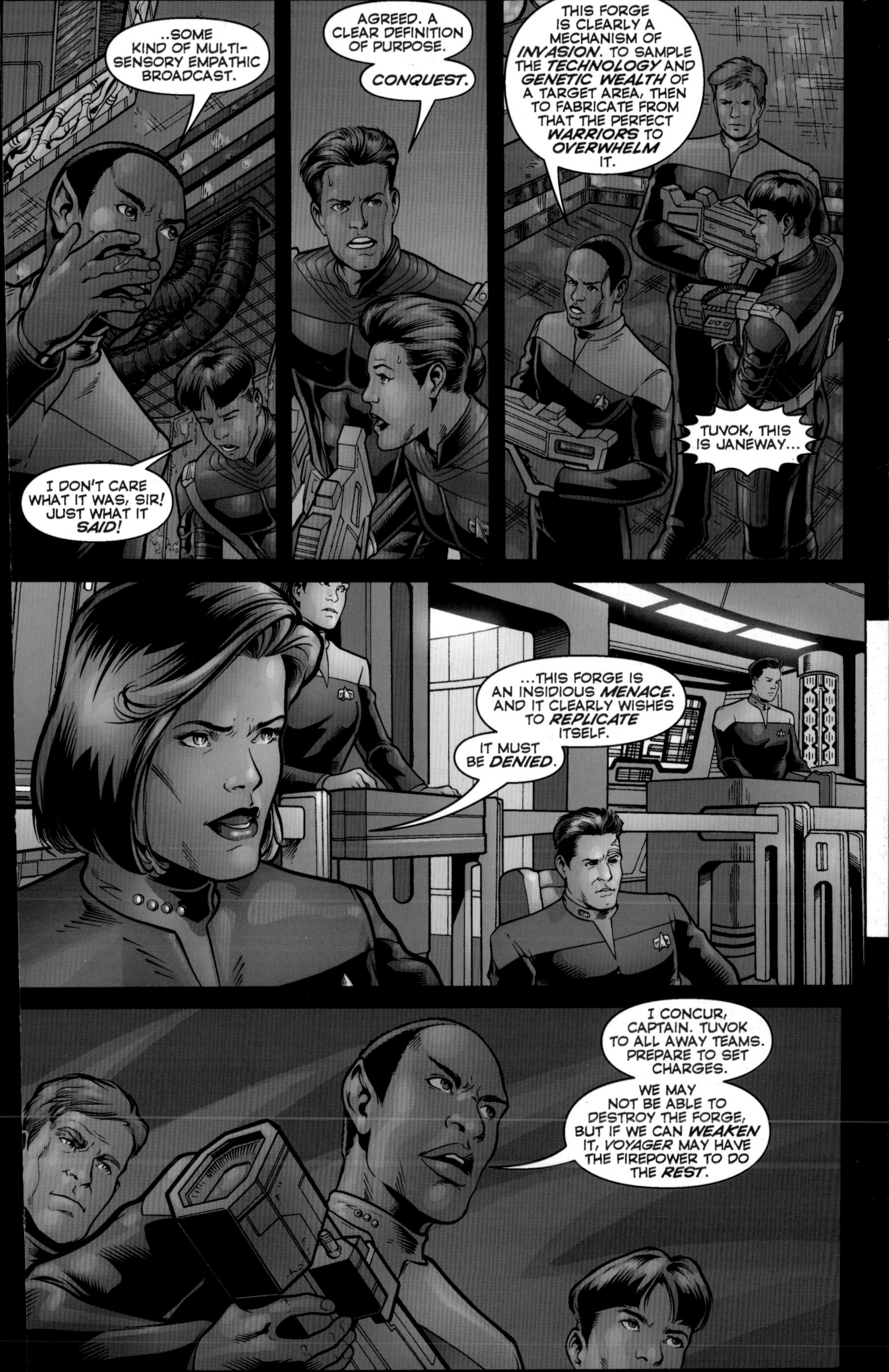
..SOME KIND OF MULTI-SENSORY EMPATHIC BROADCAST.
I DON'T CARE WHAT IT WAS, SIR! JUST WHAT IT *SAID!*
AGREED. A CLEAR DEFINITION OF PURPOSE.
CONQUEST.
THIS FORGE IS CLEARLY A MECHANISM OF *INVASION*. TO SAMPLE THE *TECHNOLOGY* AND *GENETIC WEALTH* OF A TARGET AREA, THEN TO FABRICATE FROM THAT THE PERFECT *WARRIORS* TO *OVERWHELM* IT.
TUVOK, THIS IS JANEWAY...
...THIS FORGE IS AN INSIDIOUS *MENACE*. AND IT CLEARLY WISHES TO *REPLICATE* ITSELF.
IT MUST BE *DENIED*.
I CONCUR, CAPTAIN. TUVOK TO ALL AWAY TEAMS. PREPARE TO SET CHARGES.
WE MAY NOT BE ABLE TO DESTROY THE FORGE, BUT IF WE CAN *WEAKEN* IT, *VOYAGER* MAY HAVE THE FIREPOWER TO DO THE *REST*.

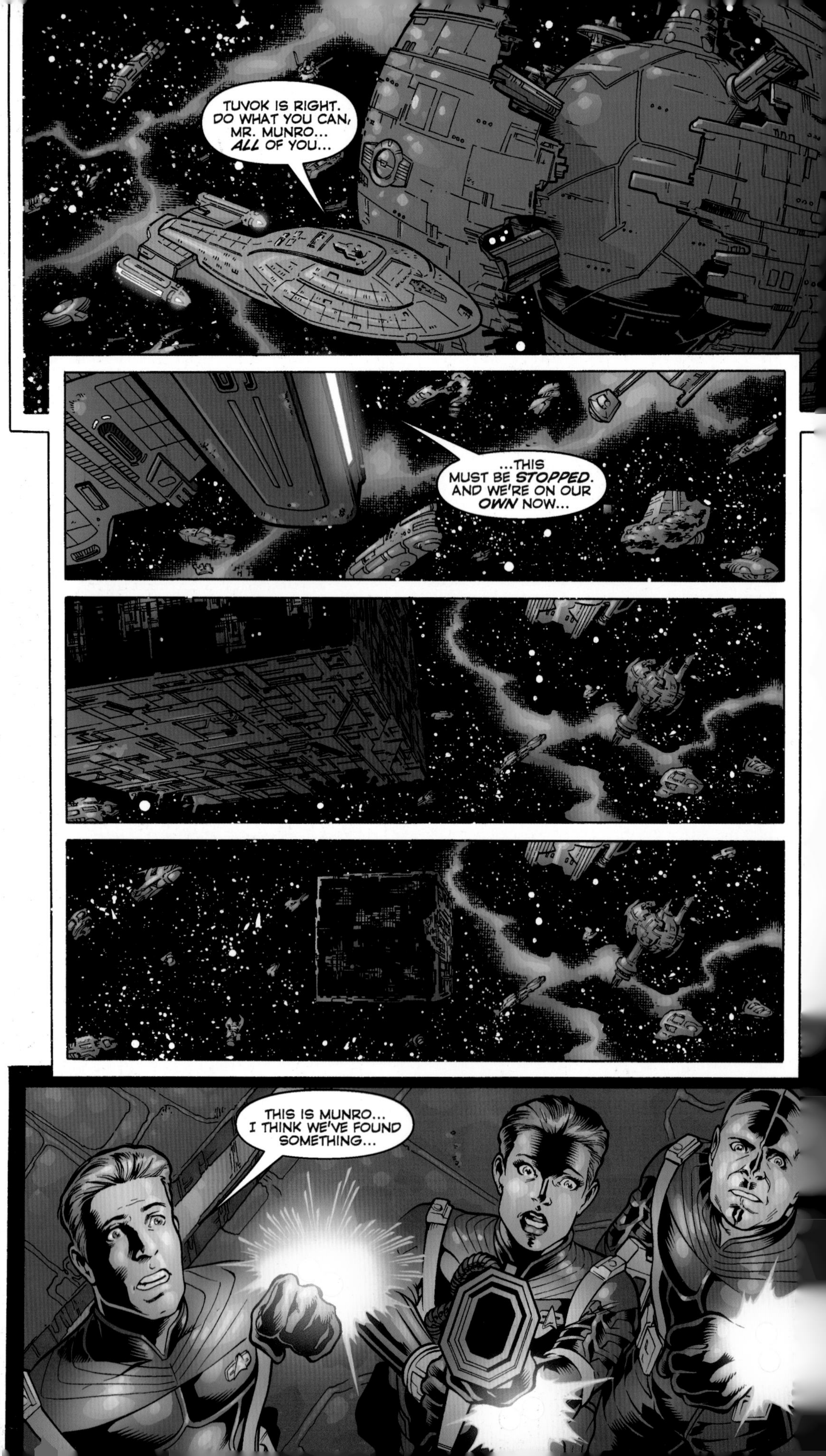
TUVOK IS RIGHT. DO WHAT YOU CAN, MR. MUNRO... ALL OF YOU...
...THIS MUST BE STOPPED. AND WE'RE ON OUR OWN NOW...
THIS IS MUNRO... I THINK WE'VE FOUND SOMETHING...

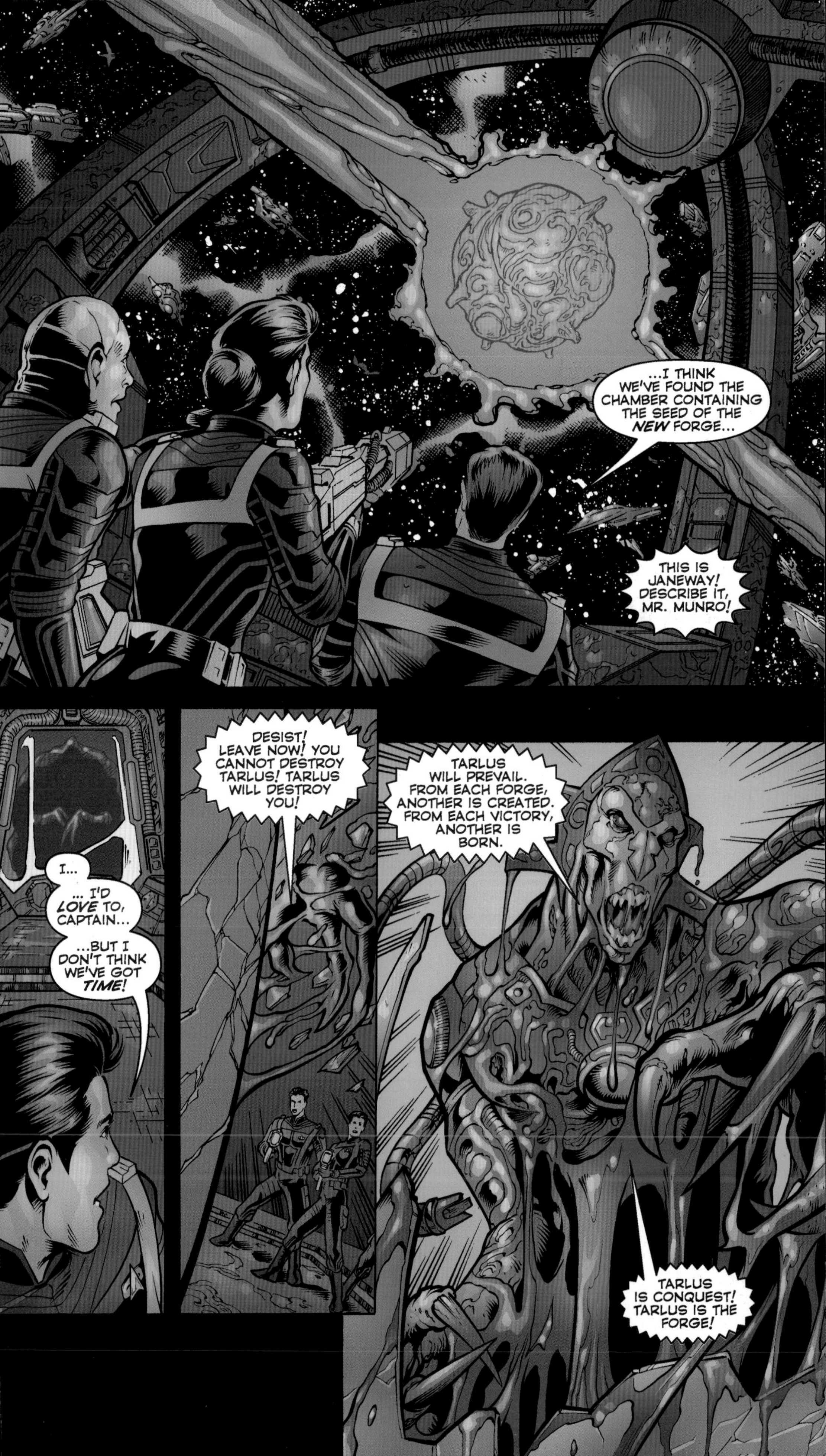
...I THINK WE'VE FOUND THE CHAMBER CONTAINING THE SEED OF THE *NEW* FORGE...
THIS IS JANEWAY! DESCRIBE IT, MR. MUNRO!
I...
... I'D *LOVE* TO, CAPTAIN...
...BUT I DON'T THINK WE'VE GOT *TIME*!
DESIST! LEAVE NOW! YOU CANNOT DESTROY TARLUS! TARLUS WILL DESTROY YOU!
TARLUS WILL PREVAIL. FROM EACH FORGE, ANOTHER IS CREATED. FROM EACH VICTORY, ANOTHER IS BORN.
TARLUS IS CONQUEST! TARLUS IS THE FORGE!

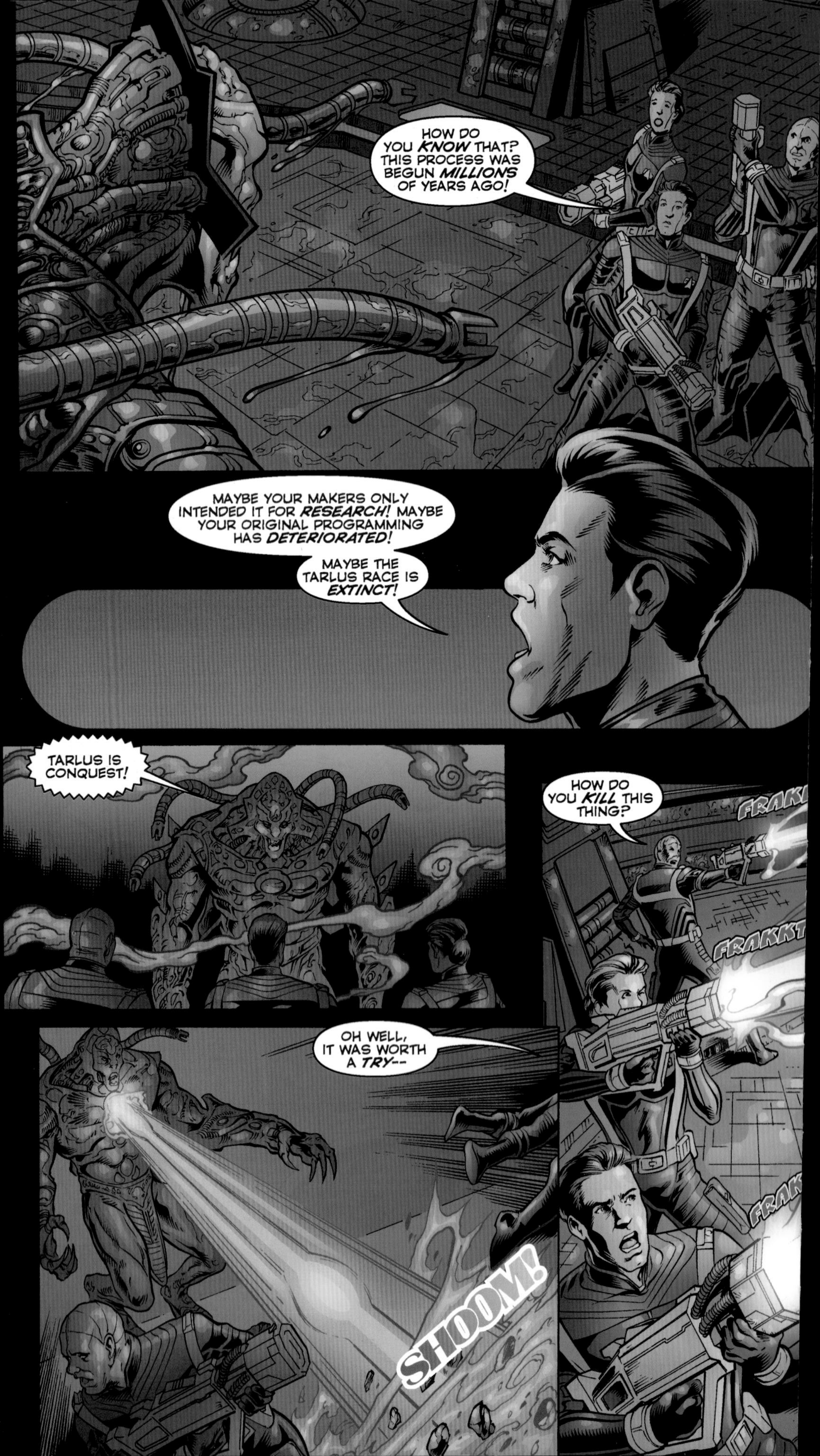
HOW DO YOU KNOW THAT? THIS PROCESS WAS BEGUN MILLIONS OF YEARS AGO!
MAYBE YOUR MAKERS ONLY INTENDED IT FOR RESEARCH! MAYBE YOUR ORIGINAL PROGRAMMING HAS DETERIORATED!
MAYBE THE TARLUS RACE IS EXTINCT!
TARLUS IS CONQUEST!
HOW DO YOU KILL THIS THING?
OH WELL, IT WAS WORTH A TRY--
SHOOM!

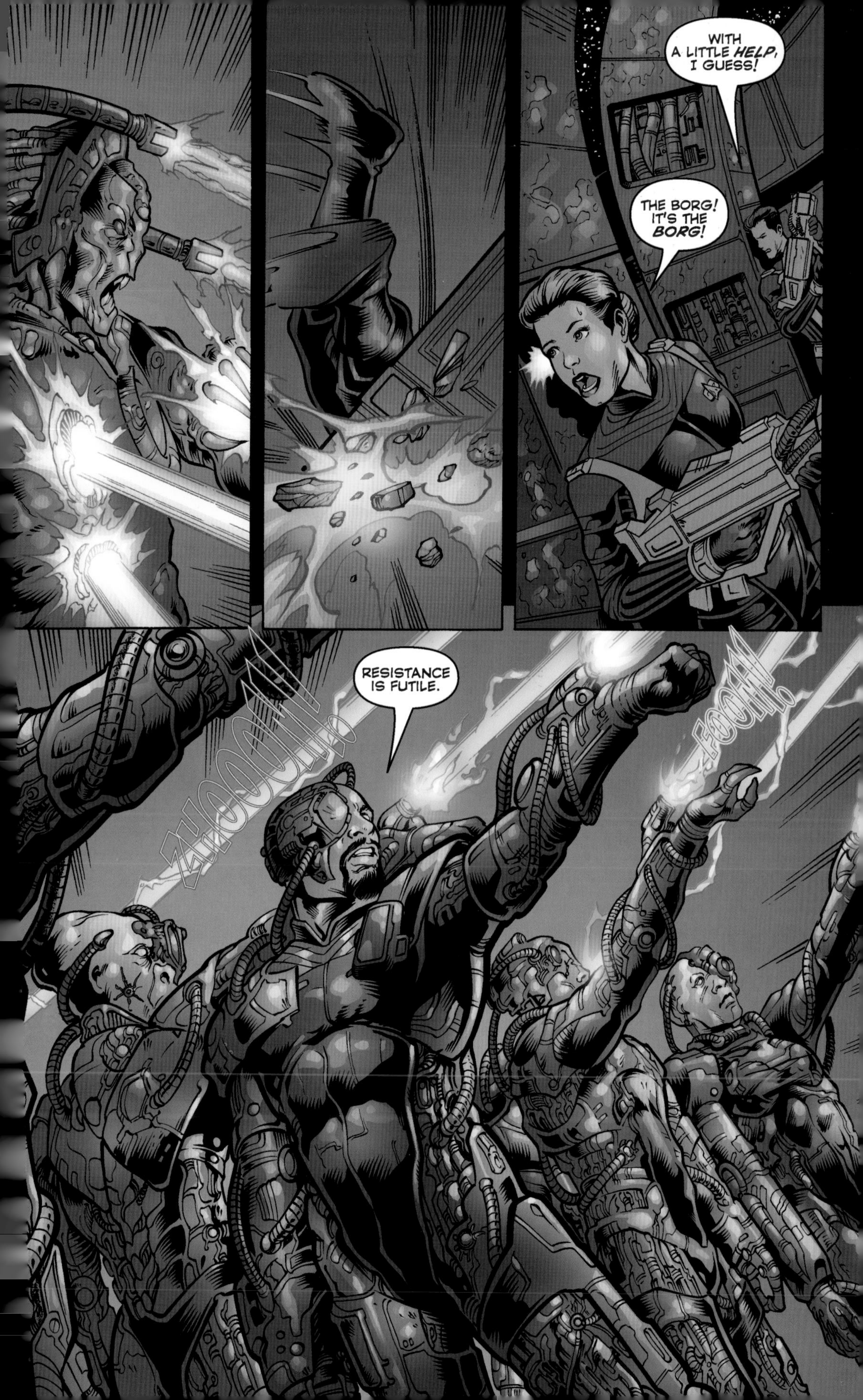
WITH A LITTLE *HELP*, I GUESS!
THE BORG! IT'S THE *BORG*!
RESISTANCE IS FUTILE.
ZHOOOM!!
FOOM!

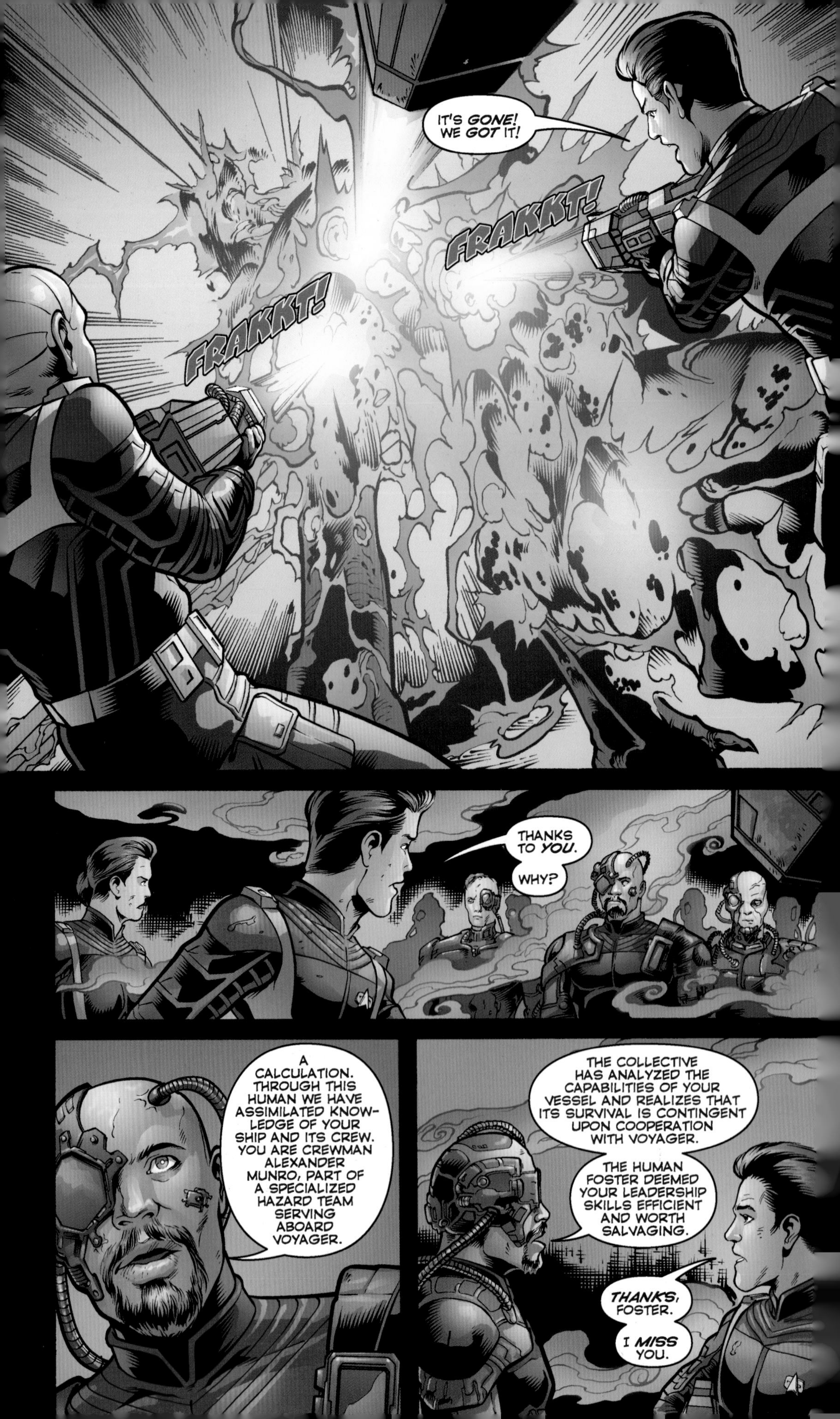
IT'S GONE! WE GOT IT!
FRAKKT!
FRAKKT!
THANKS TO YOU.
WHY?
A CALCULATION. THROUGH THIS HUMAN WE HAVE ASSIMILATED KNOW-LEDGE OF YOUR SHIP AND ITS CREW. YOU ARE CREWMAN ALEXANDER MUNRO, PART OF A SPECIALIZED HAZARD TEAM SERVING ABOARD VOYAGER.
THE COLLECTIVE HAS ANALYZED THE CAPABILITIES OF YOUR VESSEL AND REALIZES THAT ITS SURVIVAL IS CONTINGENT UPON COOPERATION WITH VOYAGER.
THE HUMAN FOSTER DEEMED YOUR LEADERSHIP SKILLS EFFICIENT AND WORTH SALVAGING.
THANKS, FOSTER.
I MISS YOU.

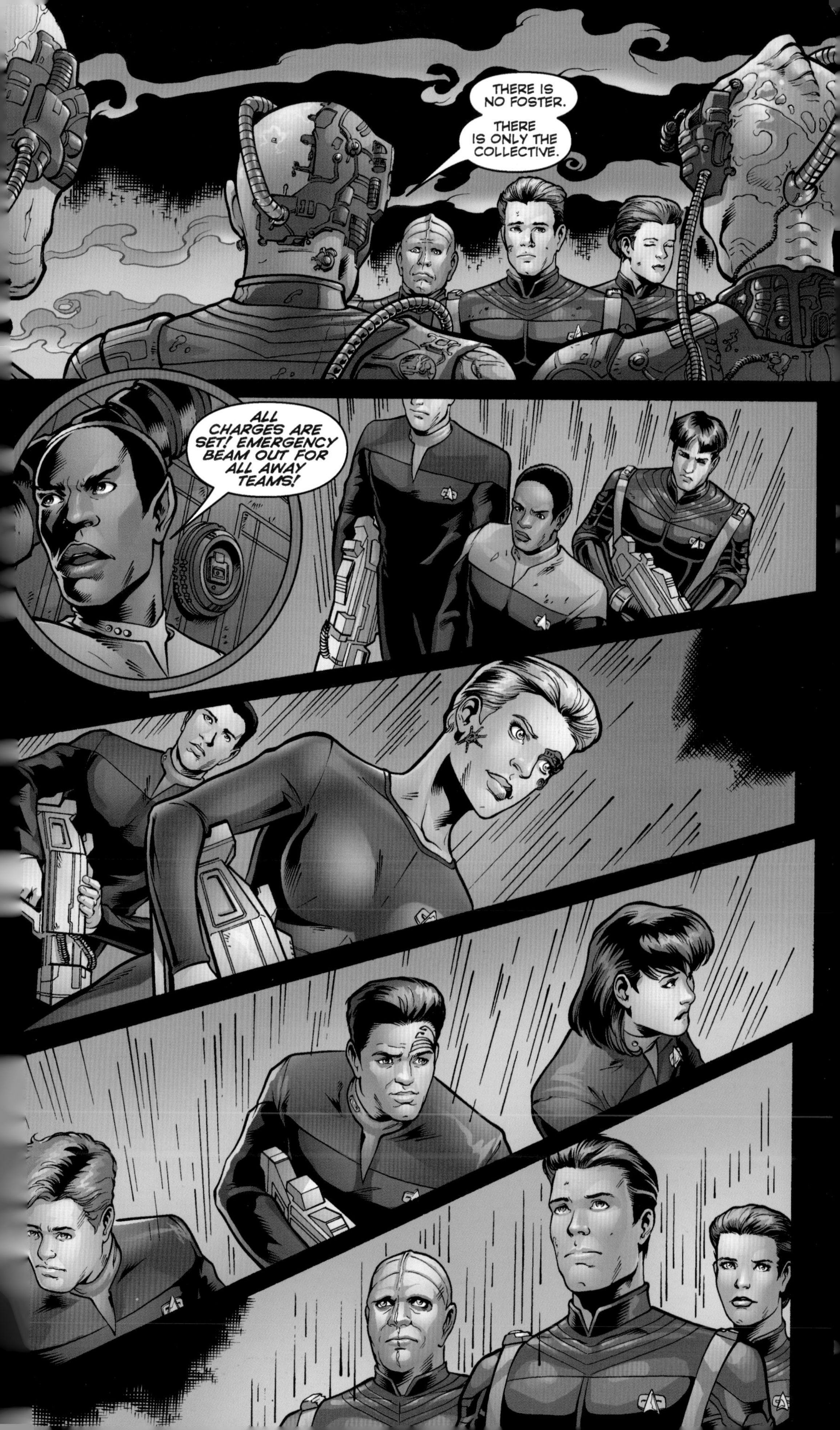
THERE IS NO FOSTER.
THERE IS ONLY THE COLLECTIVE.
ALL CHARGES ARE SET! EMERGENCY BEAM OUT FOR ALL AWAY TEAMS!

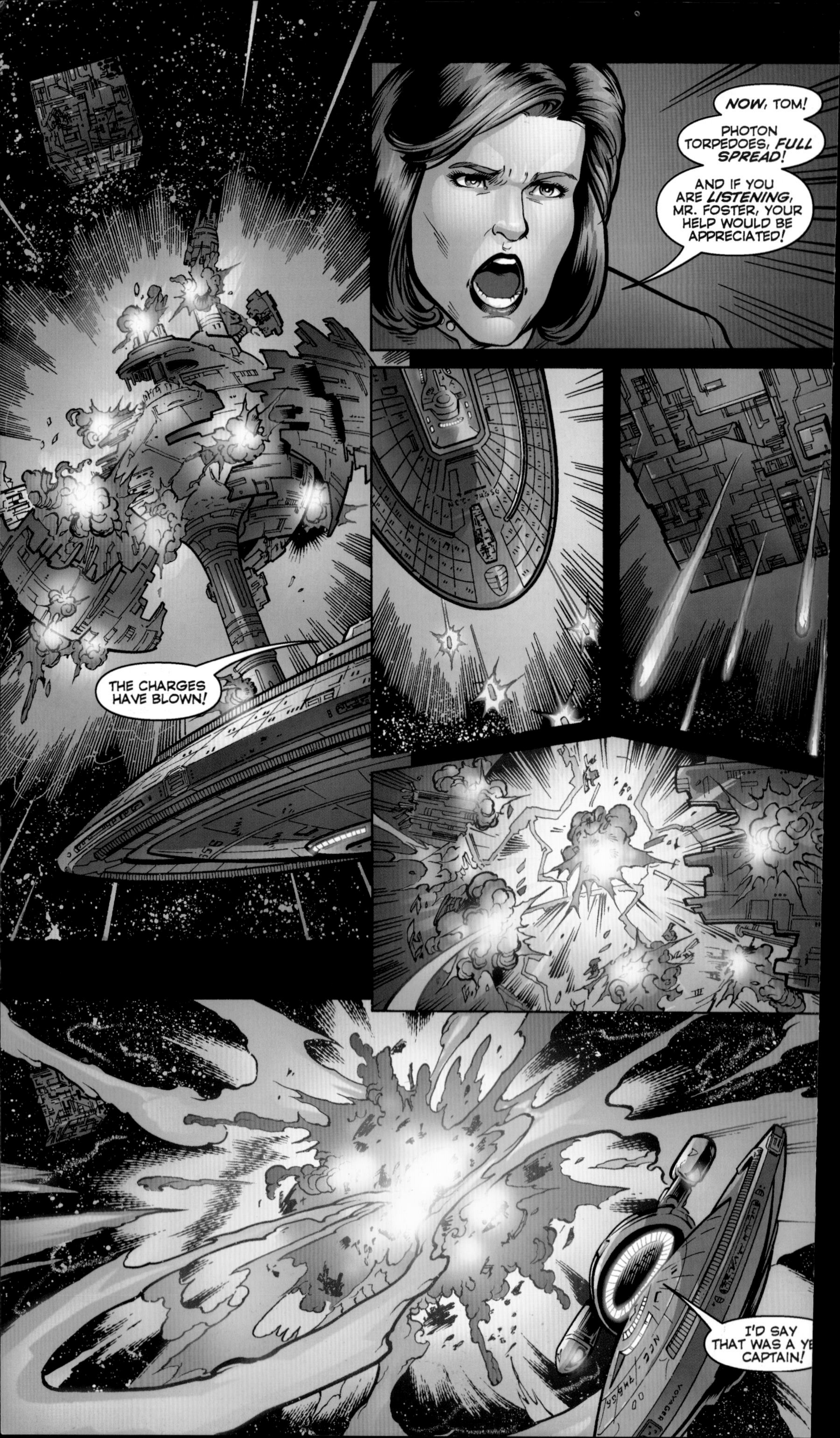
NOW, TOM!
PHOTON TORPEDOES, FULL SPREAD!
AND IF YOU ARE LISTENING, MR. FOSTER, YOUR HELP WOULD BE APPRECIATED!
THE CHARGES HAVE BLOWN!
I'D SAY THAT WAS A YE CAPTAIN!

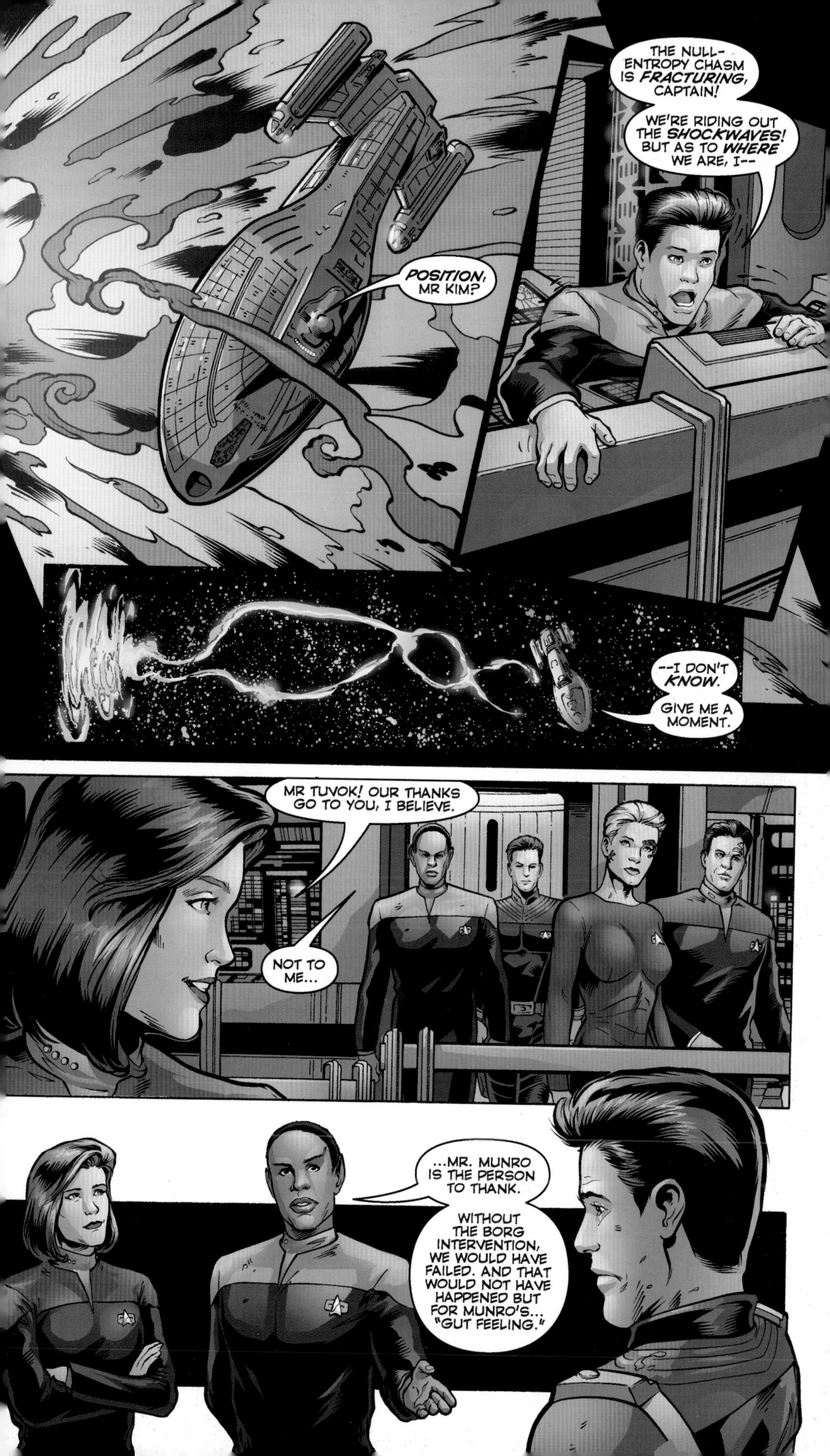
THE NULL-ENTROPY CHASM IS *FRACTURING*, CAPTAIN!
WE'RE RIDING OUT THE *SHOCKWAVES*! BUT AS TO *WHERE* WE ARE, I--
POSITION, MR KIM?
--I DON'T *KNOW*.
GIVE ME A MOMENT.
MR TUVOK! OUR THANKS GO TO YOU, I BELIEVE.
NOT TO ME...
...MR. MUNRO IS THE PERSON TO THANK.
WITHOUT THE BORG INTERVENTION, WE WOULD HAVE FAILED. AND THAT WOULD NOT HAVE HAPPENED BUT FOR MUNRO'S... "GUT FEELING."

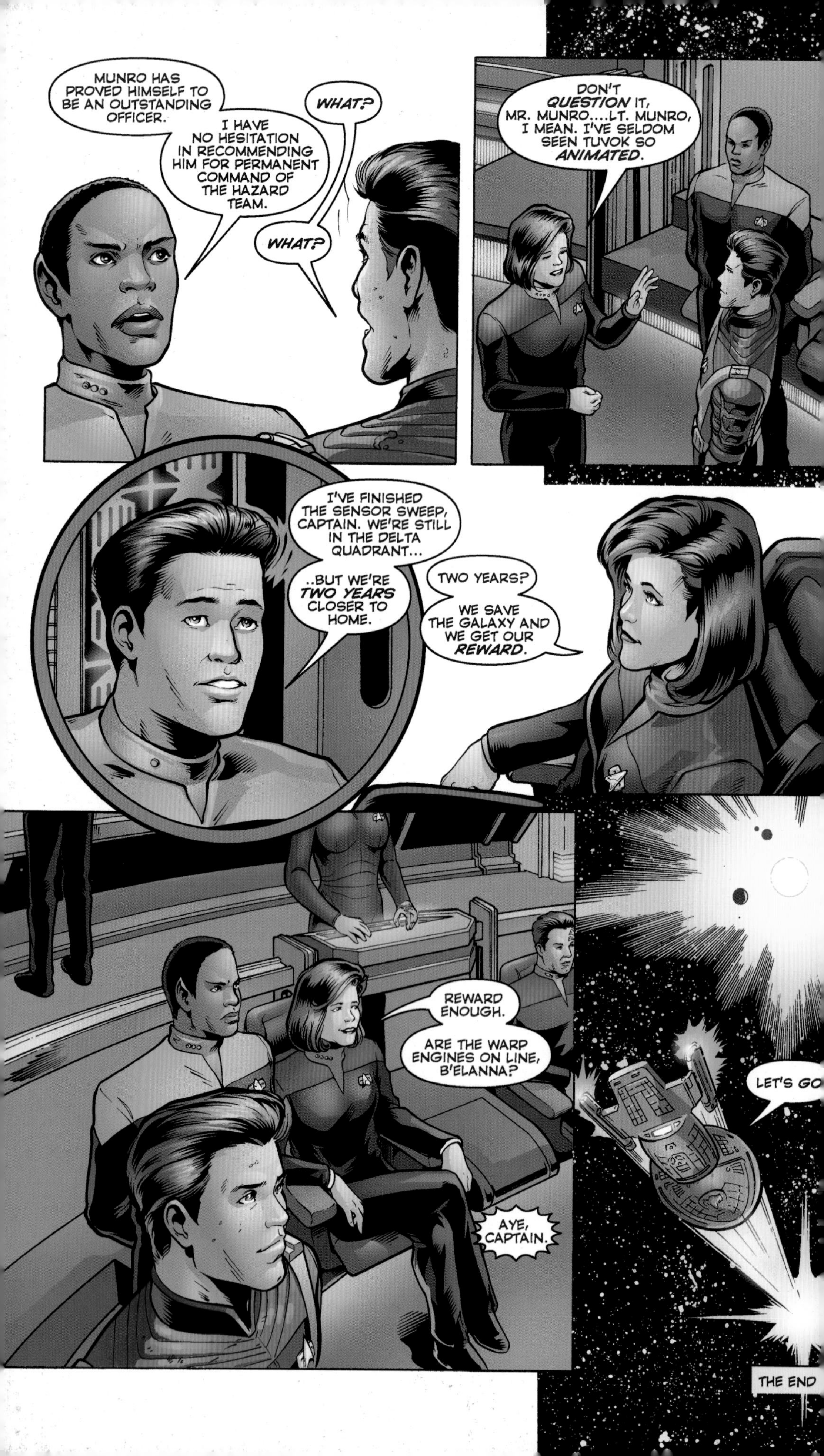

MUNRO HAS PROVED HIMSELF TO BE AN OUTSTANDING OFFICER.
I HAVE NO HESITATION IN RECOMMENDING HIM FOR PERMANENT COMMAND OF THE HAZARD TEAM.
WHAT?
WHAT?
DON'T QUESTION IT, MR. MUNRO....LT. MUNRO, I MEAN. I'VE SELDOM SEEN TUVOK SO ANIMATED.
I'VE FINISHED THE SENSOR SWEEP, CAPTAIN. WE'RE STILL IN THE DELTA QUADRANT...
..BUT WE'RE TWO YEARS CLOSER TO HOME.
TWO YEARS?
WE SAVE THE GALAXY AND WE GET OUR REWARD.
REWARD ENOUGH.
ARE THE WARP ENGINES ON LINE, B'ELANNA?
AYE, CAPTAIN.
LET'S GO
THE END

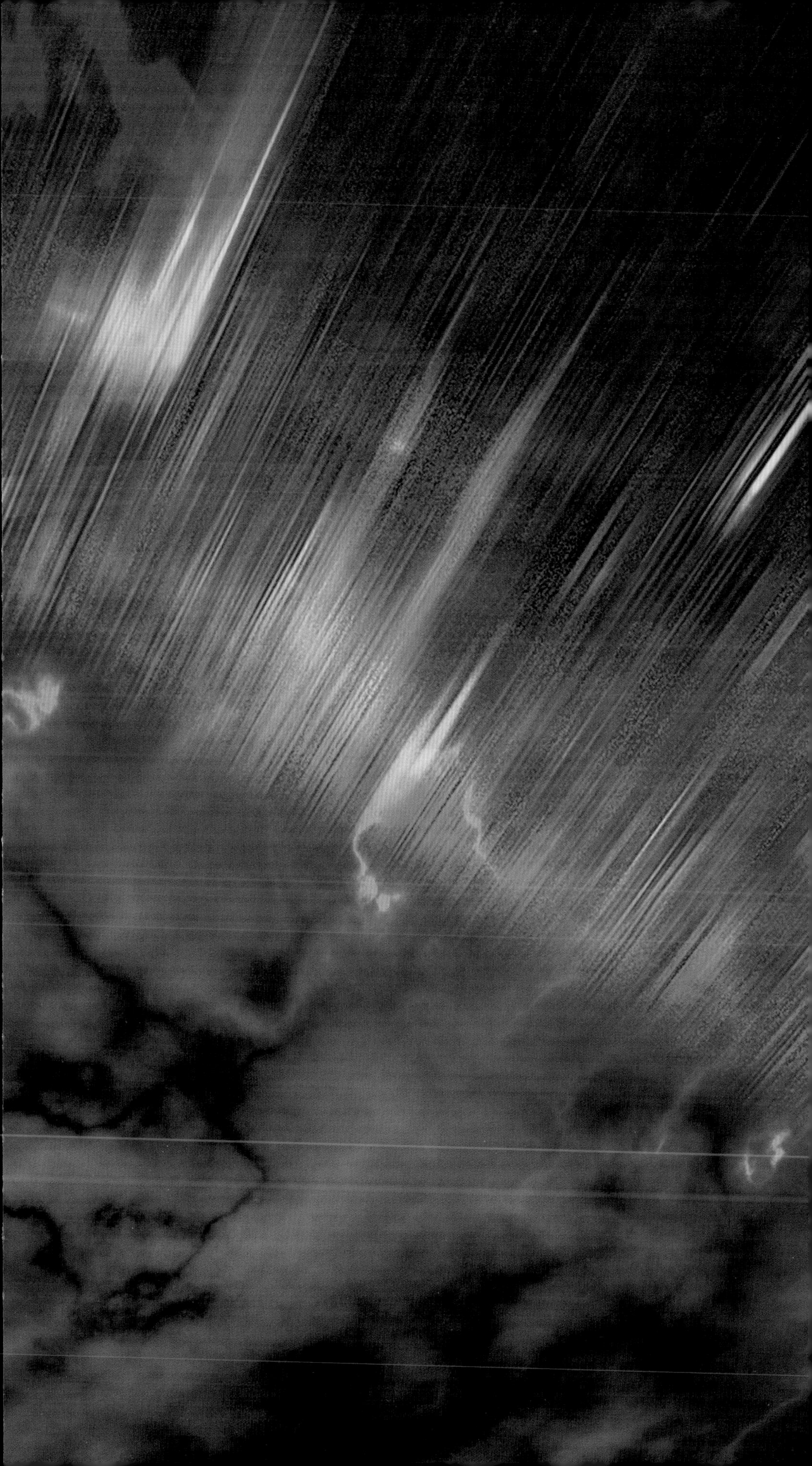

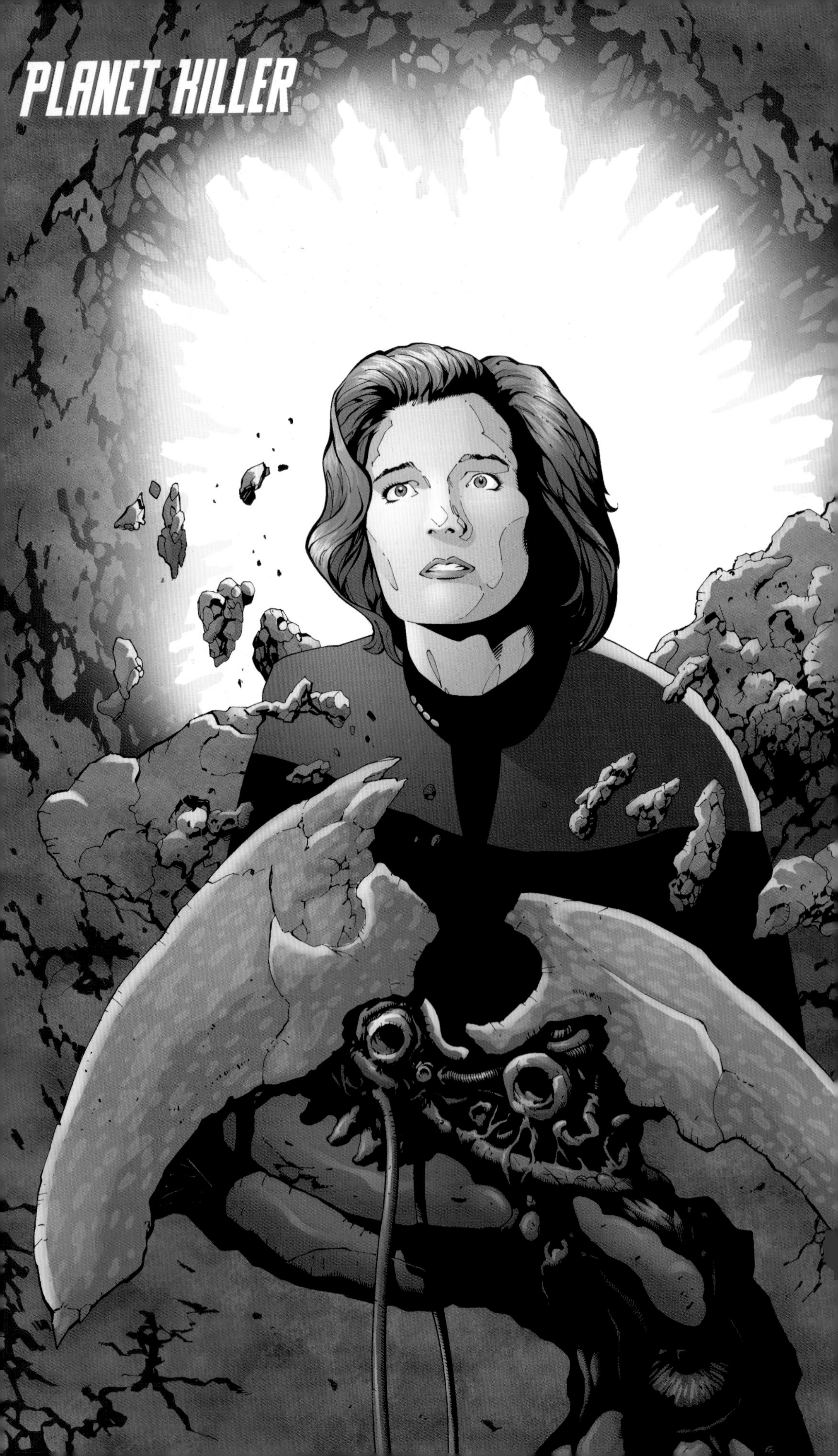
PLANET KILLER

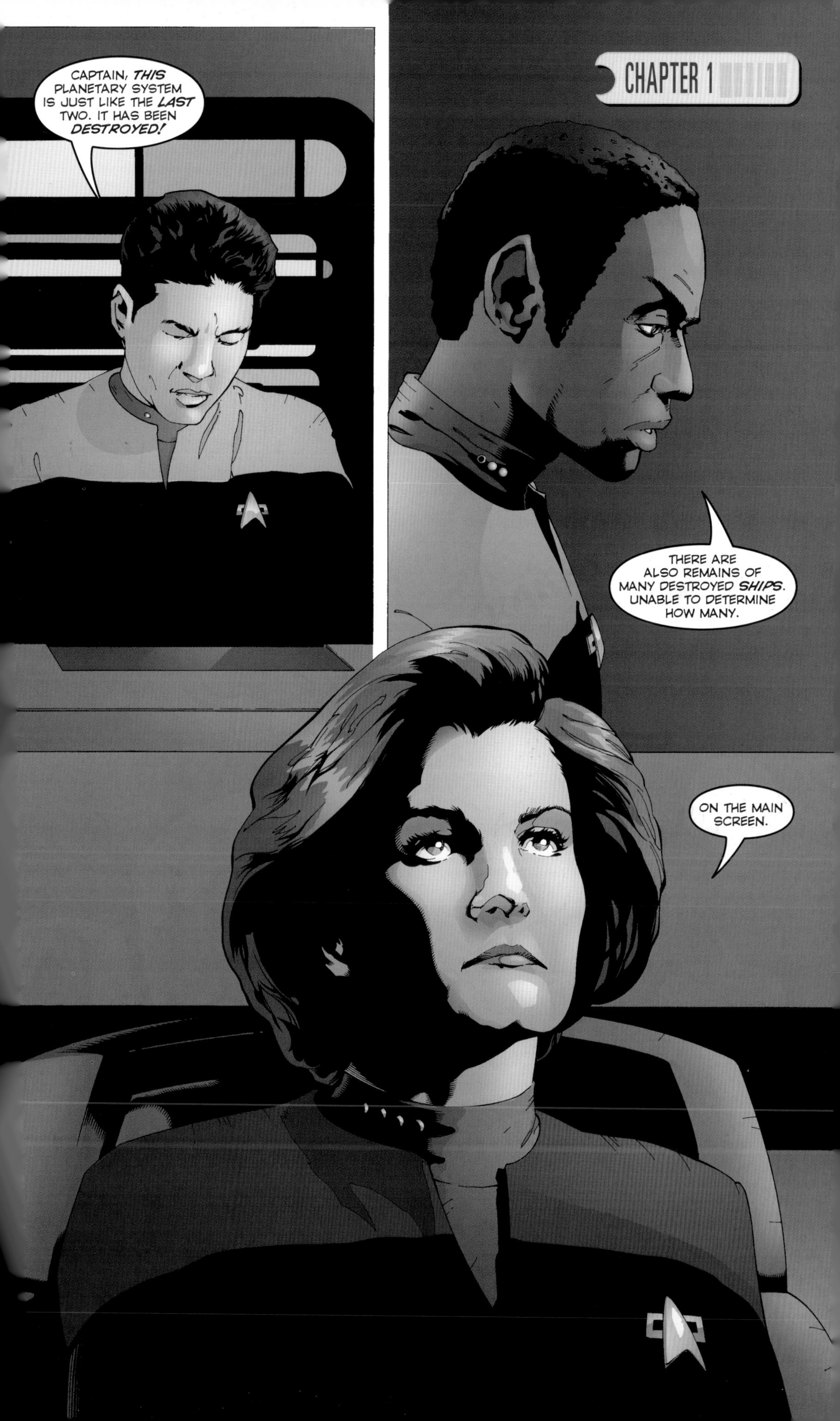
CHAPTER 1
CAPTAIN, THIS PLANETARY SYSTEM IS JUST LIKE THE LAST TWO. IT HAS BEEN DESTROYED!
THERE ARE ALSO REMAINS OF MANY DESTROYED SHIPS. UNABLE TO DETERMINE HOW MANY.
ON THE MAIN SCREEN.

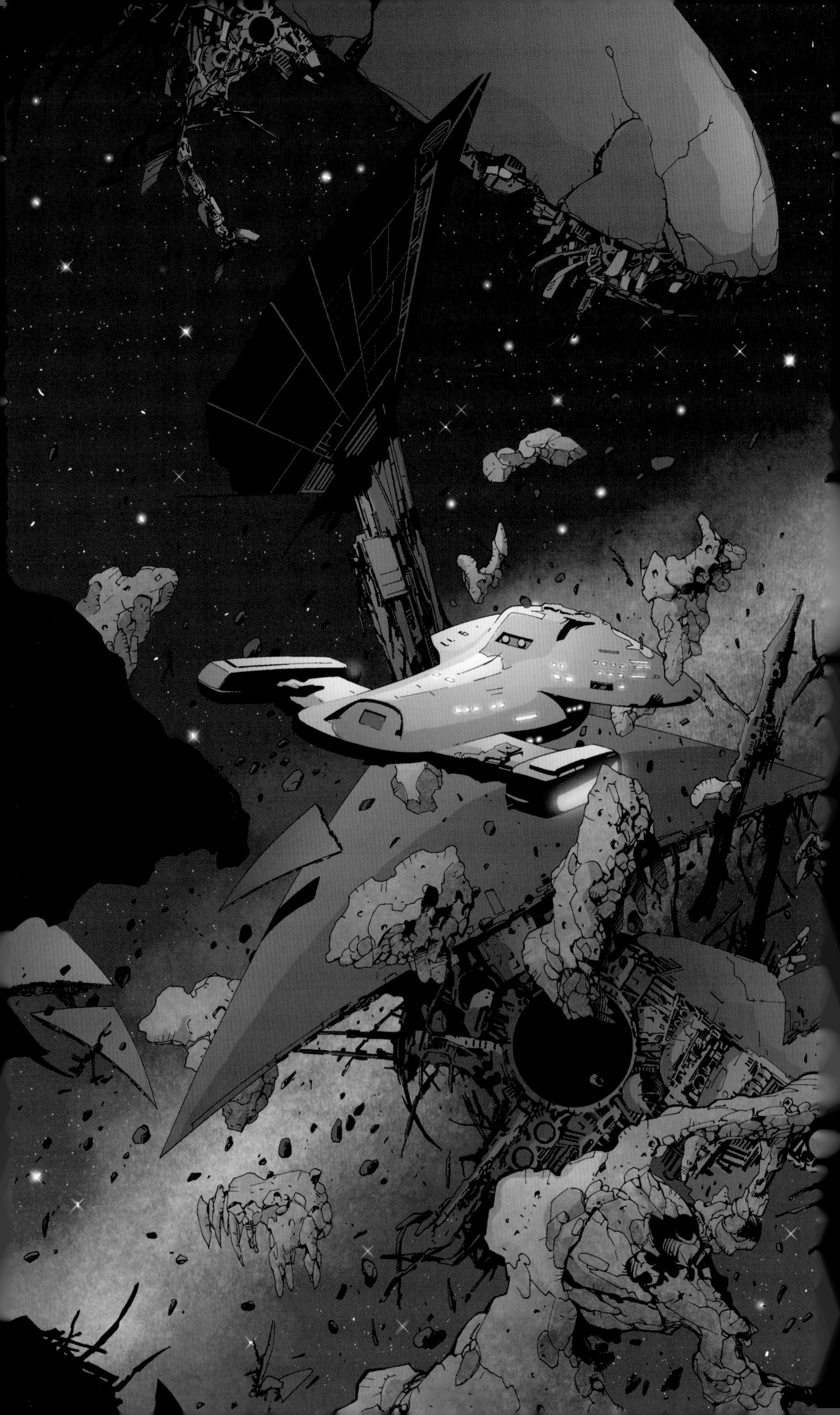

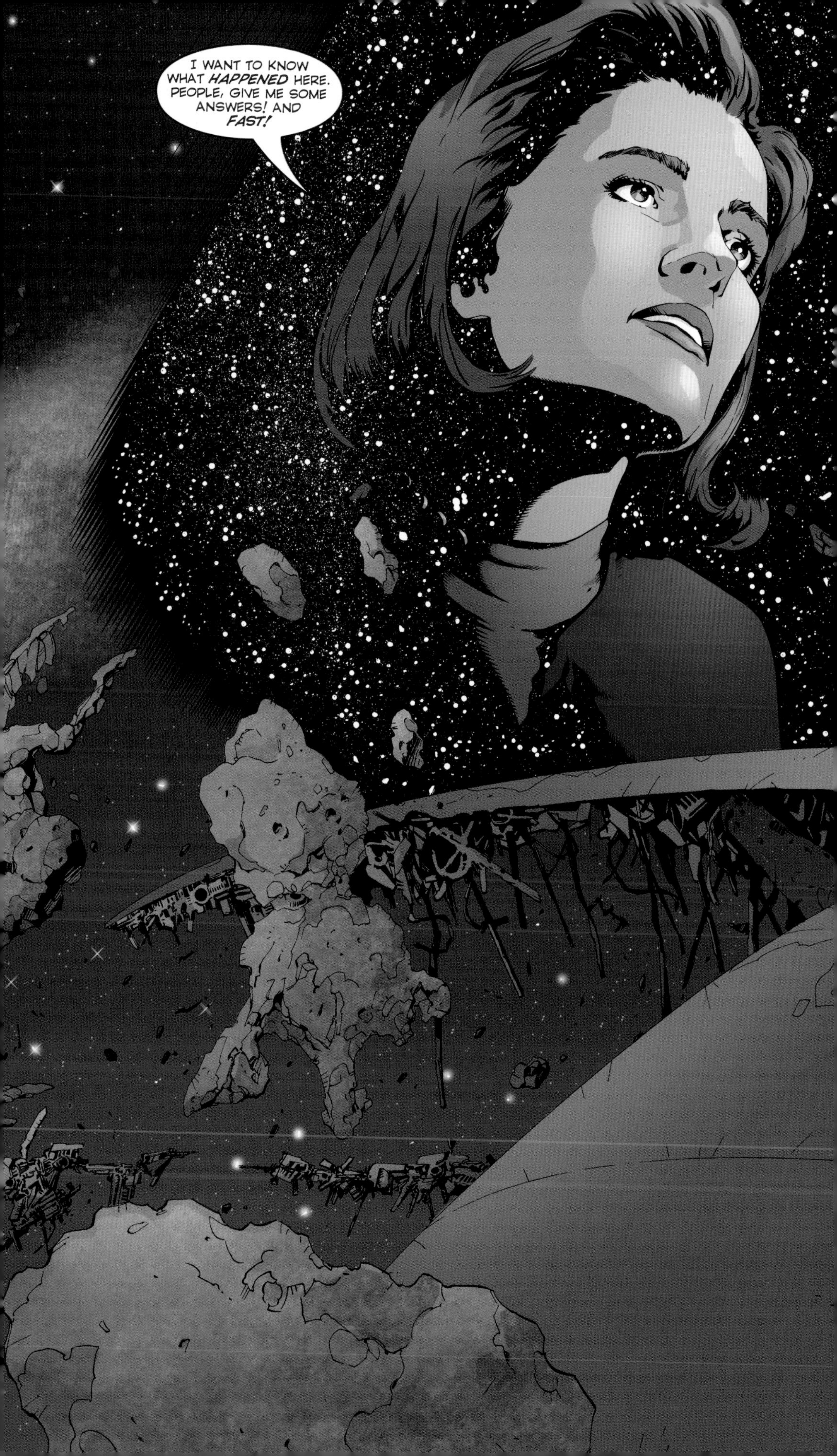
I WANT TO KNOW WHAT *HAPPENED* HERE. PEOPLE, GIVE ME SOME ANSWERS! AND *FAST!*

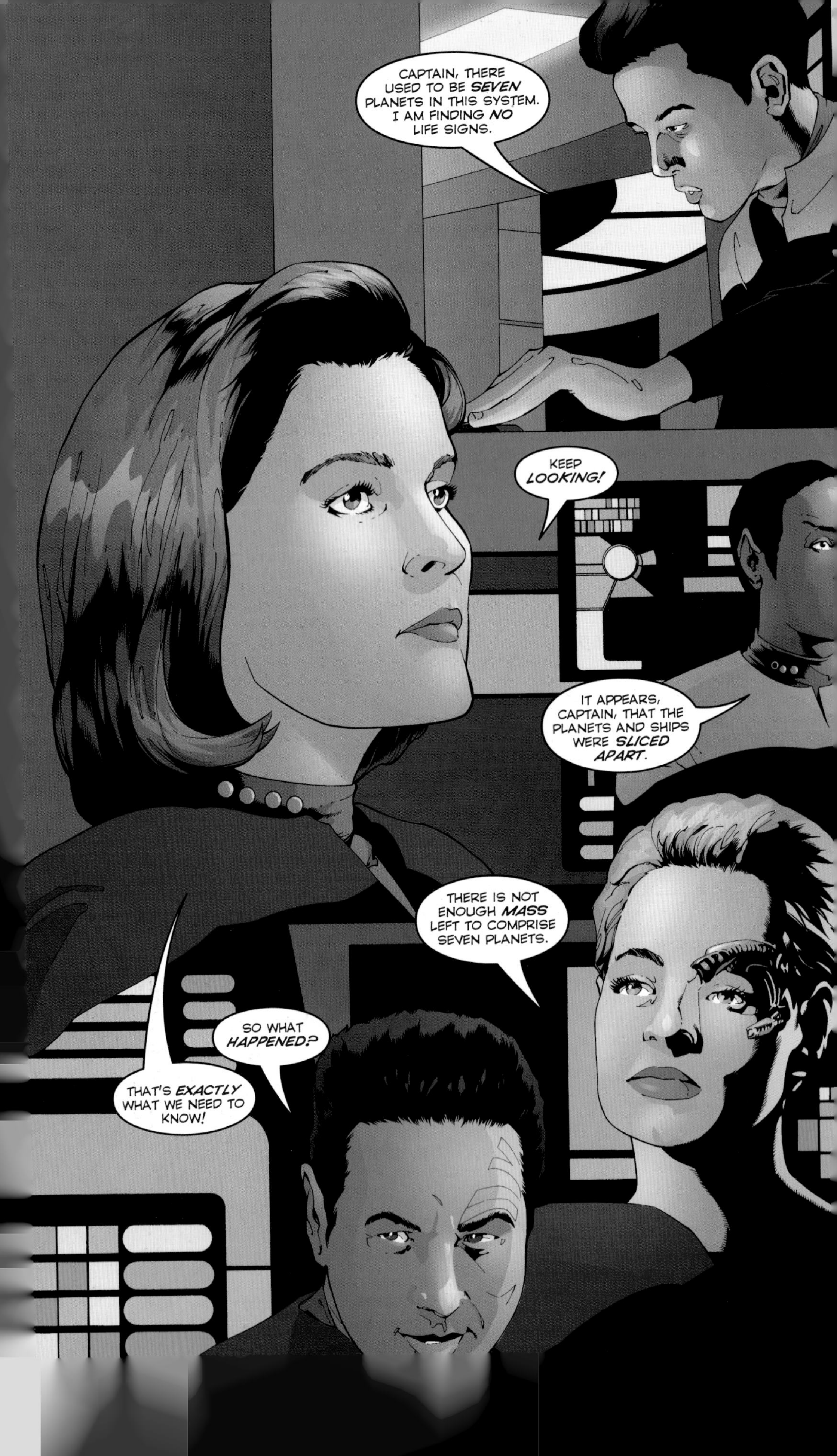
CAPTAIN, THERE USED TO BE SEVEN PLANETS IN THIS SYSTEM. I AM FINDING NO LIFE SIGNS.
KEEP LOOKING!
IT APPEARS, CAPTAIN, THAT THE PLANETS AND SHIPS WERE SLICED APART.
THERE IS NOT ENOUGH MASS LEFT TO COMPRISE SEVEN PLANETS.
SO WHAT HAPPENED?
THAT'S EXACTLY WHAT WE NEED TO KNOW!

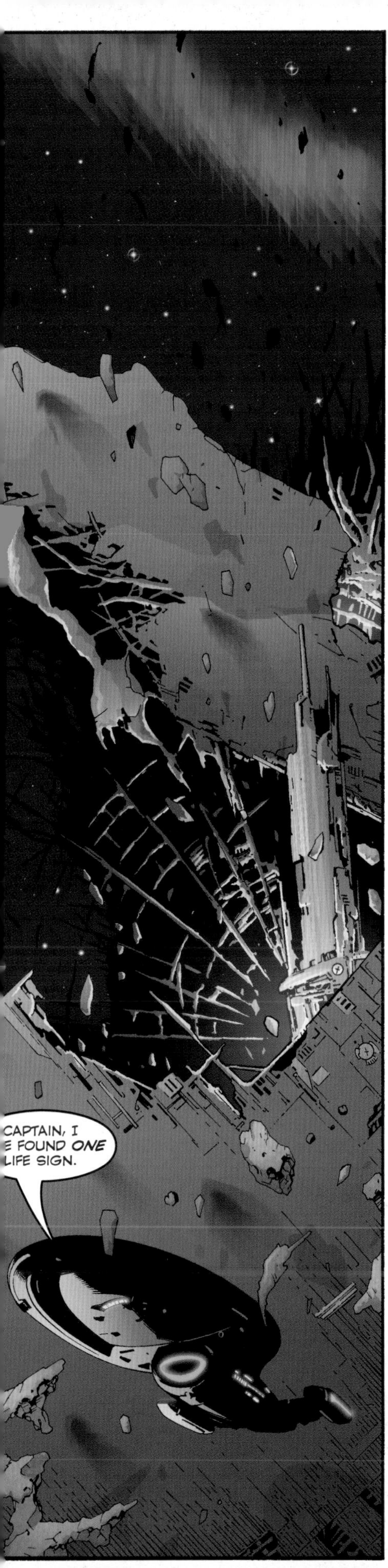
CAPTAIN, I E FOUND ONE LIFE SIGN.

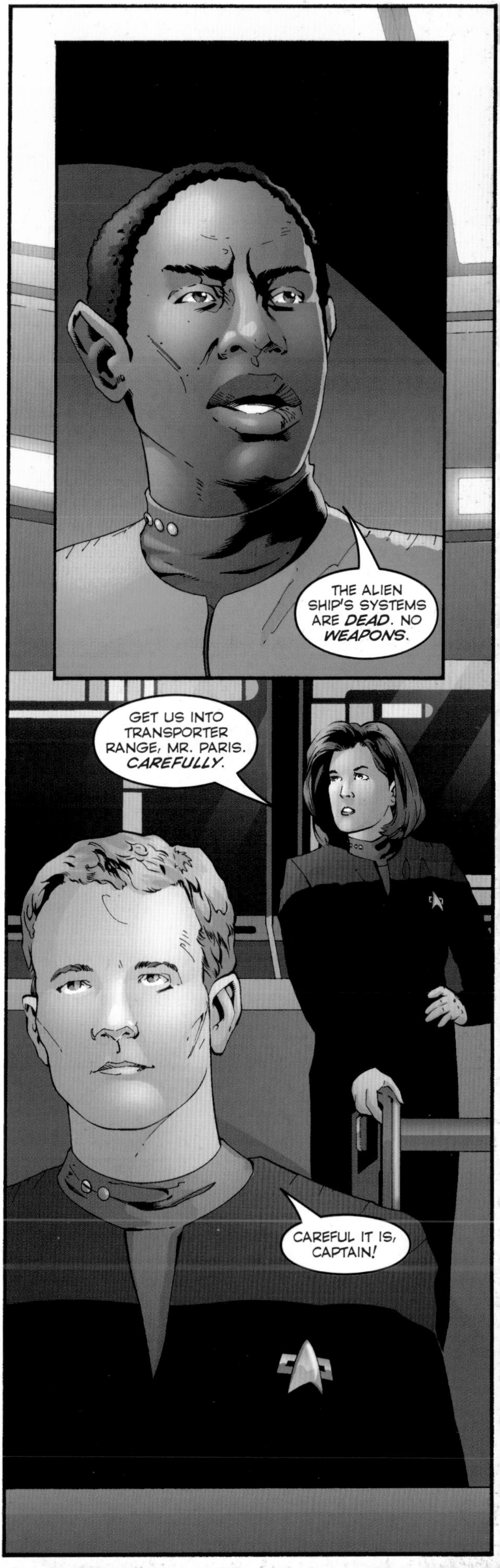
THE ALIEN SHIP'S SYSTEMS ARE DEAD. NO WEAPONS.
GET US INTO TRANSPORTER RANGE, MR. PARIS. CAREFULLY.
CAREFUL IT IS, CAPTAIN!

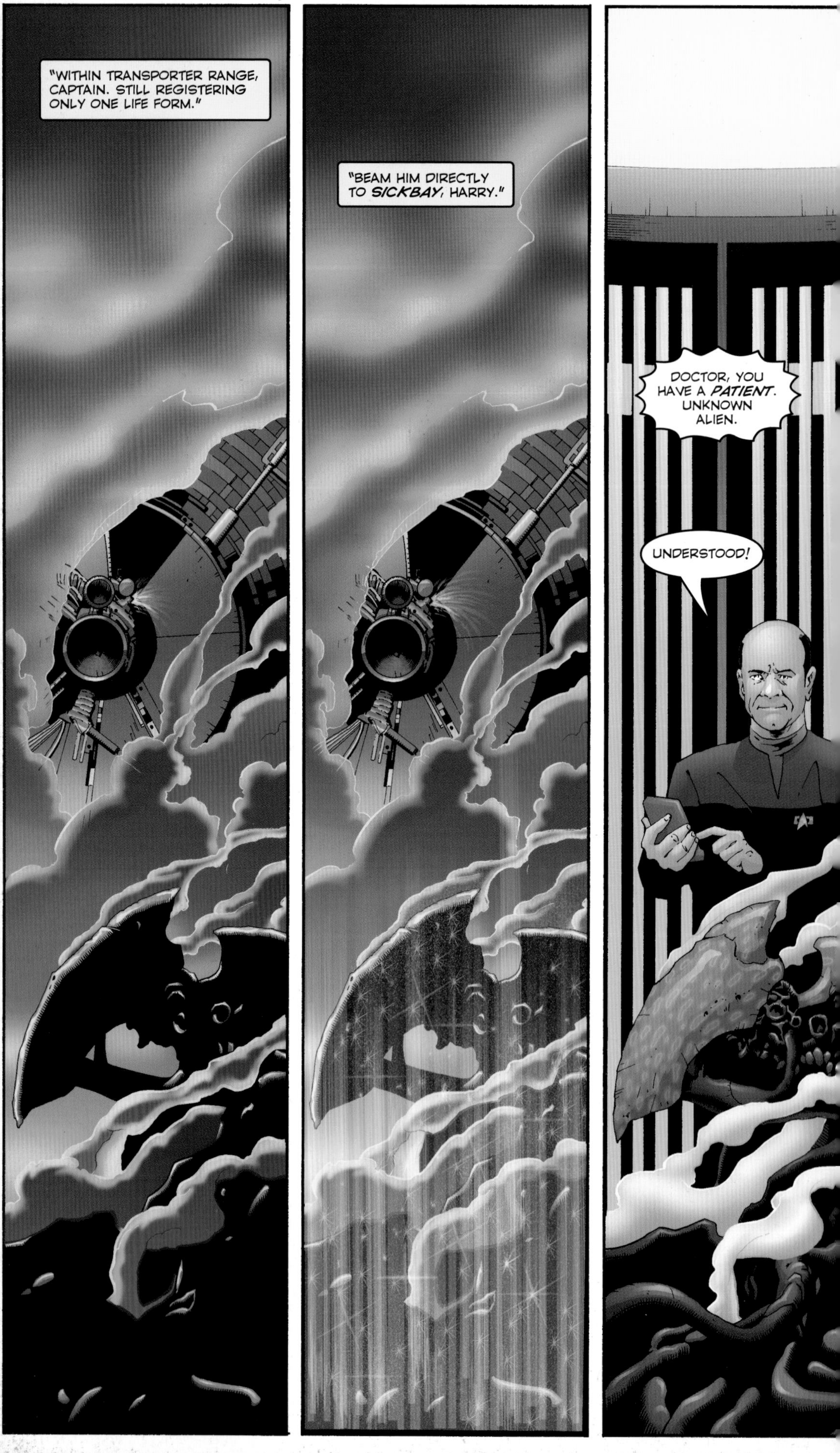
"WITHIN TRANSPORTER RANGE, CAPTAIN. STILL REGISTERING ONLY ONE LIFE FORM."
"BEAM HIM DIRECTLY TO SICKBAY, HARRY."
DOCTOR, YOU HAVE A PATIENT. UNKNOWN ALIEN.
UNDERSTOOD!

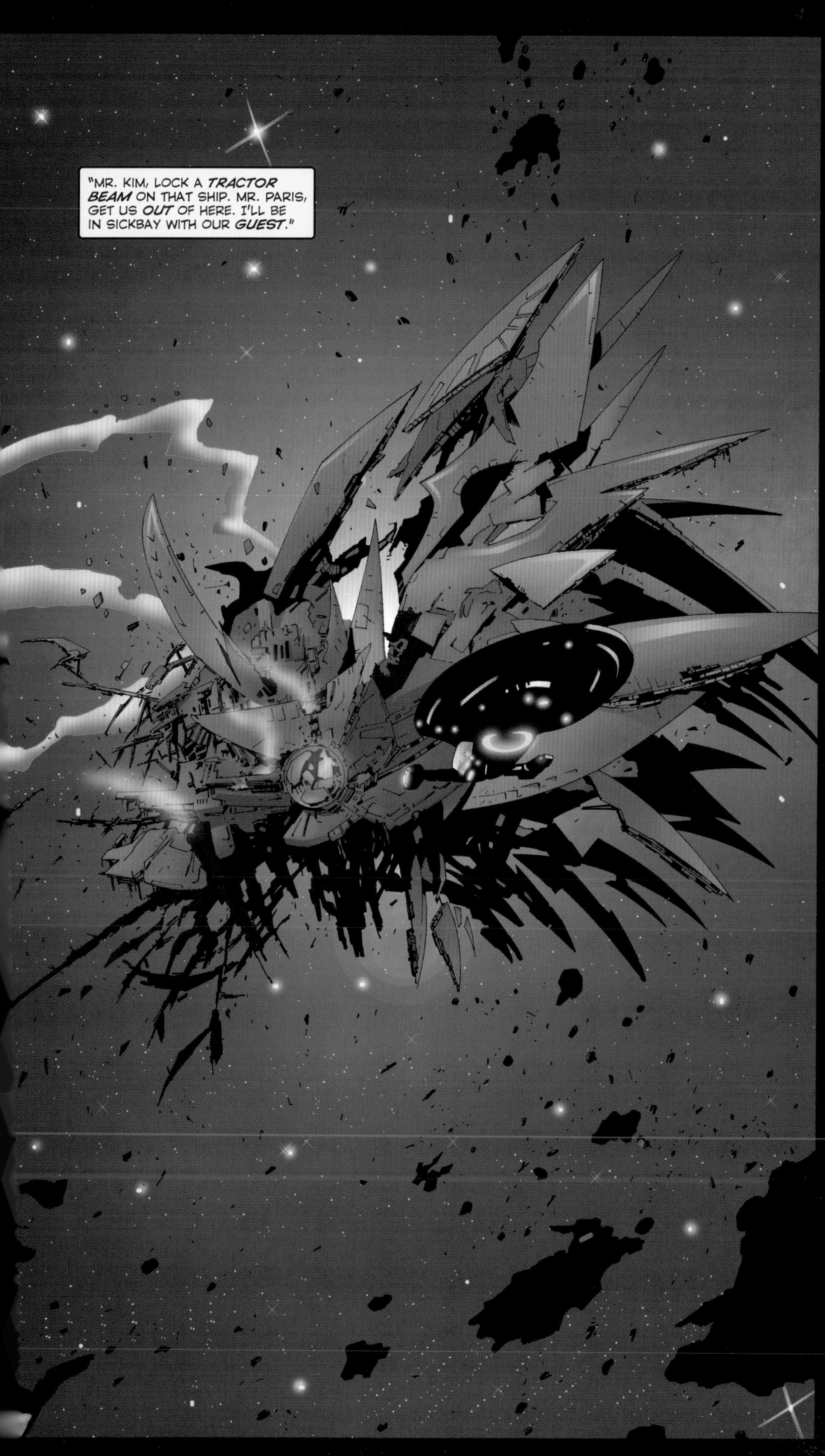
"MR. KIM, LOCK A TRACTOR BEAM ON THAT SHIP. MR. PARIS, GET US OUT OF HERE. I'LL BE IN SICKBAY WITH OUR GUEST."

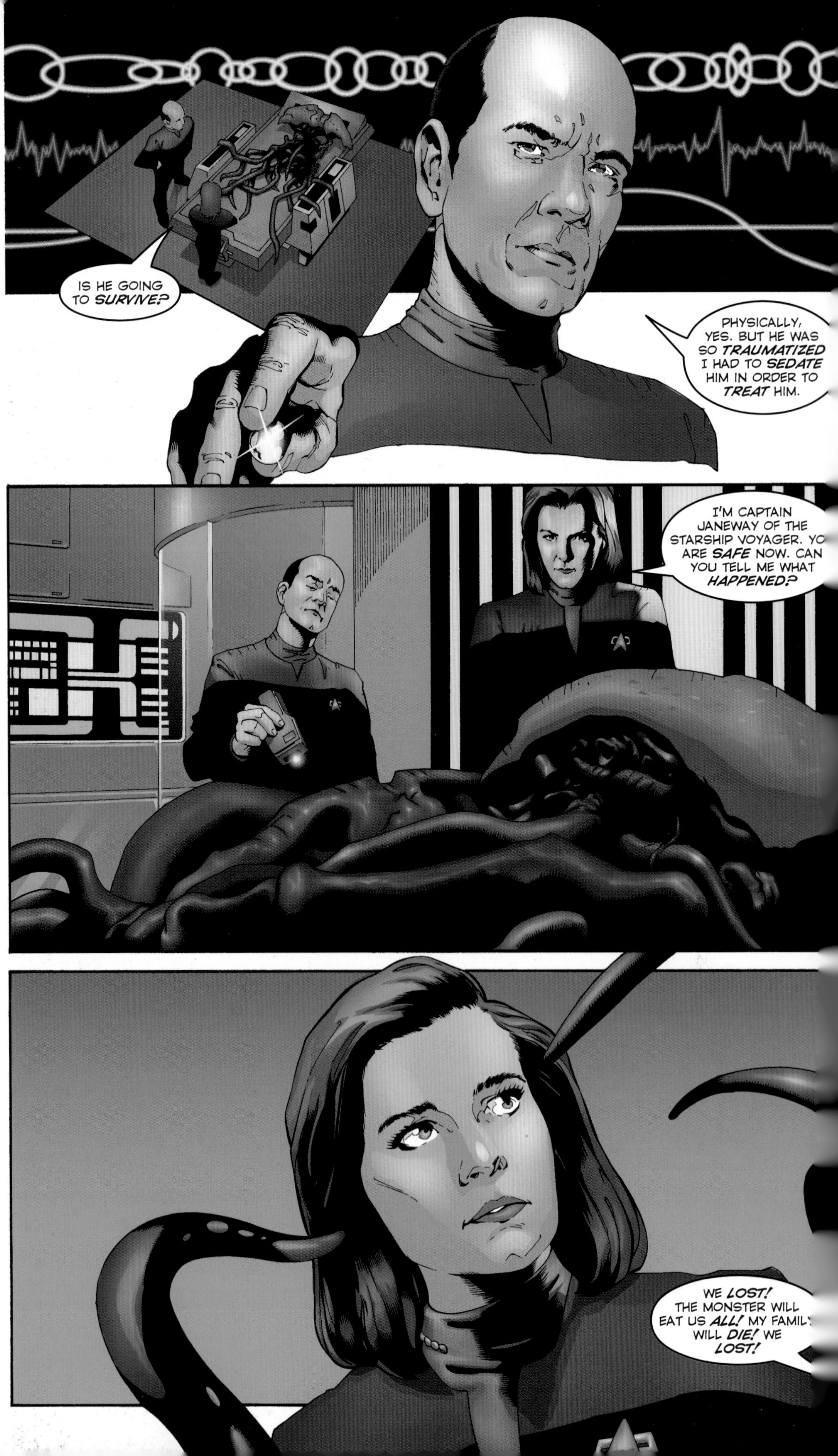

IS HE GOING TO *SURVIVE?*
PHYSICALLY, YES. BUT HE WAS SO *TRAUMATIZED* I HAD TO *SEDATE* HIM IN ORDER TO *TREAT* HIM.
I'M CAPTAIN JANEWAY OF THE STARSHIP VOYAGER. YO ARE *SAFE* NOW. CAN YOU TELL ME WHAT *HAPPENED?*
WE *LOST!* THE MONSTER WILL EAT US *ALL!* MY FAMIL WILL *DIE!* WE *LOST!*

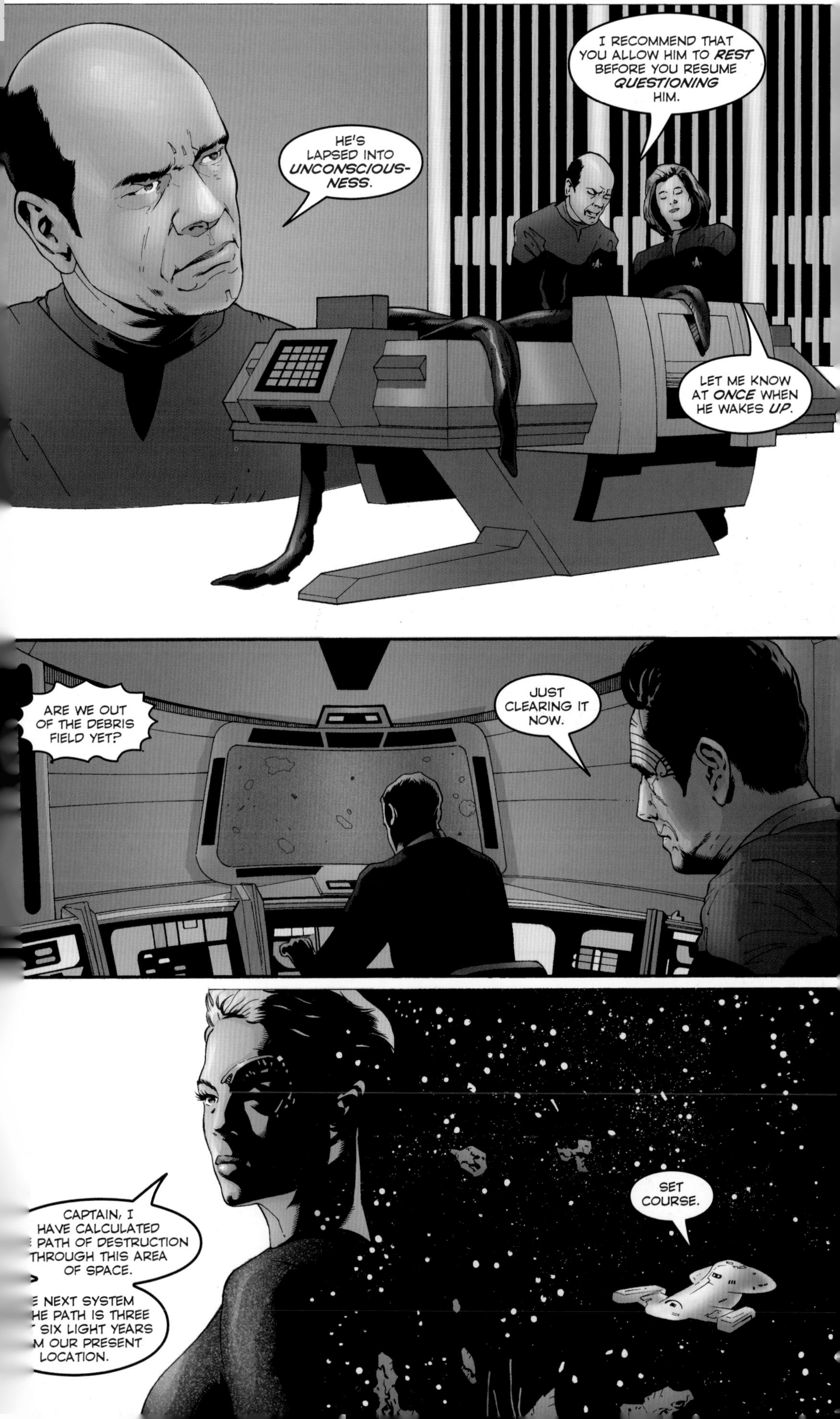
HE'S LAPSED INTO UNCONSCIOUSNESS.
I RECOMMEND THAT YOU ALLOW HIM TO REST BEFORE YOU RESUME QUESTIONING HIM.
LET ME KNOW AT ONCE WHEN HE WAKES UP.
ARE WE OUT OF THE DEBRIS FIELD YET?
JUST CLEARING IT NOW.
CAPTAIN, I HAVE CALCULATED E PATH OF DESTRUCTION THROUGH THIS AREA OF SPACE.
E NEXT SYSTEM HE PATH IS THREE T SIX LIGHT YEARS M OUR PRESENT LOCATION.
SET COURSE.

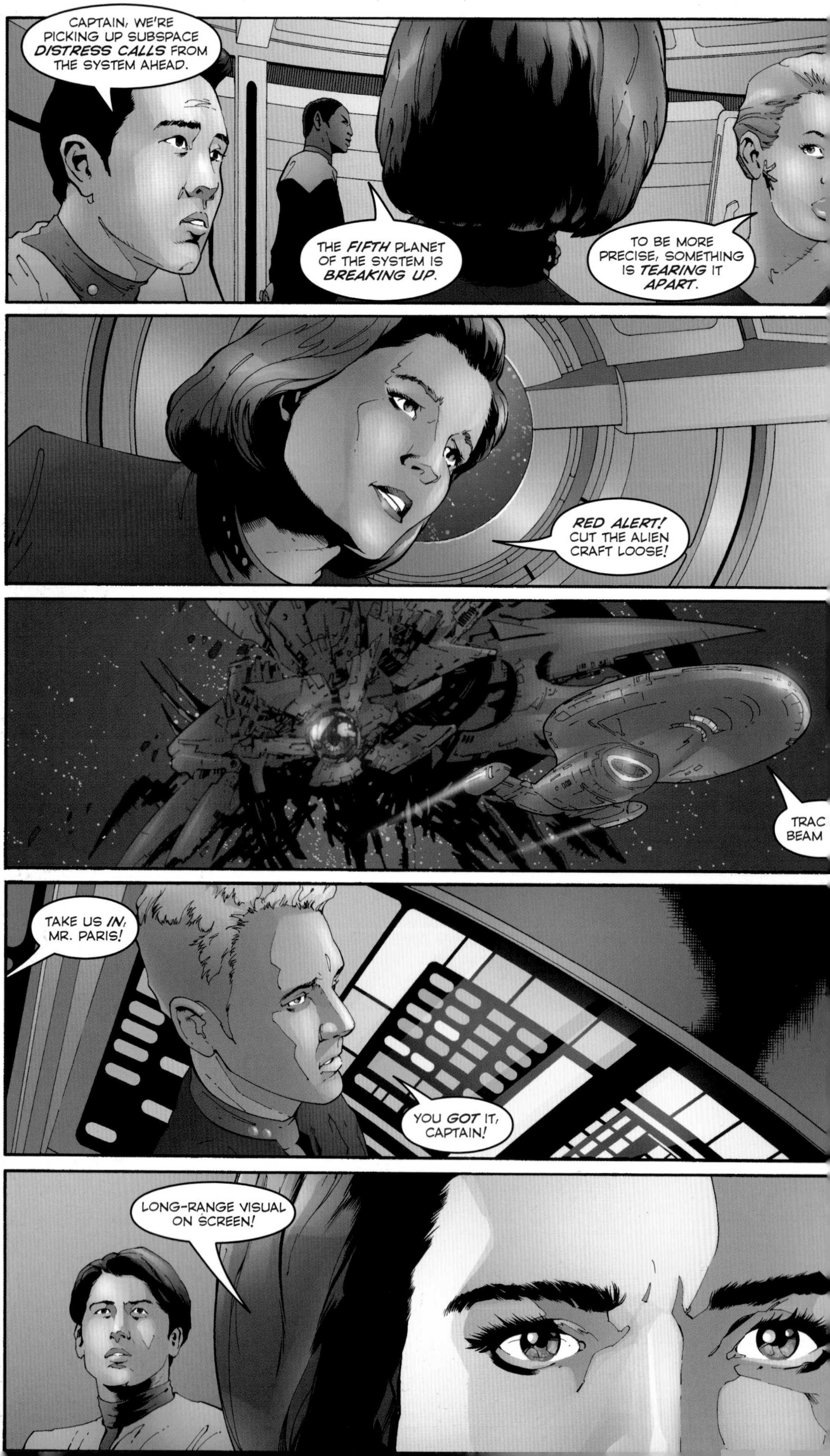
CAPTAIN, WE'RE PICKING UP SUBSPACE DISTRESS CALLS FROM THE SYSTEM AHEAD.
THE FIFTH PLANET OF THE SYSTEM IS BREAKING UP.
TO BE MORE PRECISE, SOMETHING IS TEARING IT APART.
RED ALERT! CUT THE ALIEN CRAFT LOOSE!
TRAC BEAM
TAKE US IN, MR. PARIS!
YOU GOT IT, CAPTAIN!
LONG-RANGE VISUAL ON SCREEN!

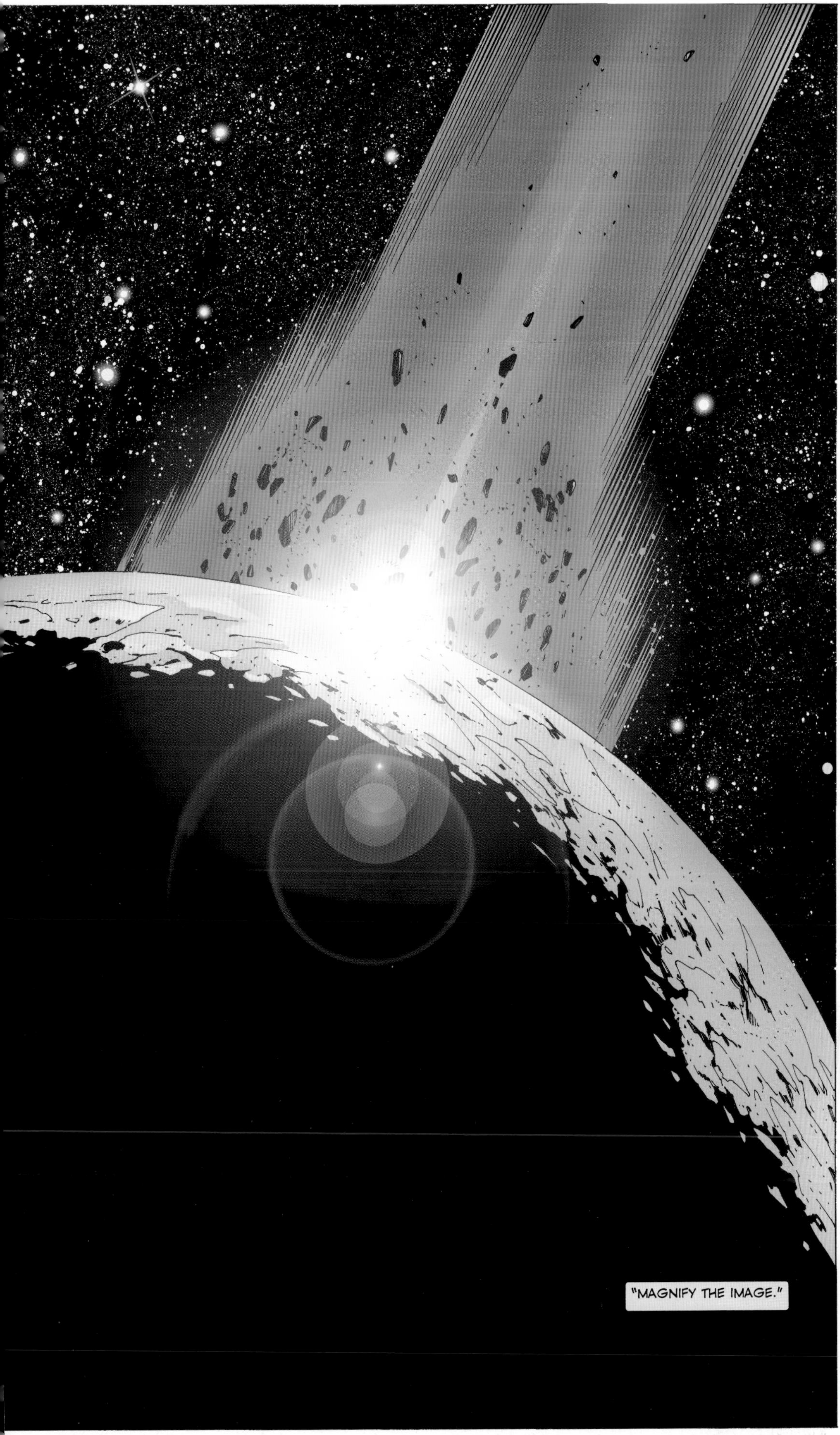
"MAGNIFY THE IMAGE."

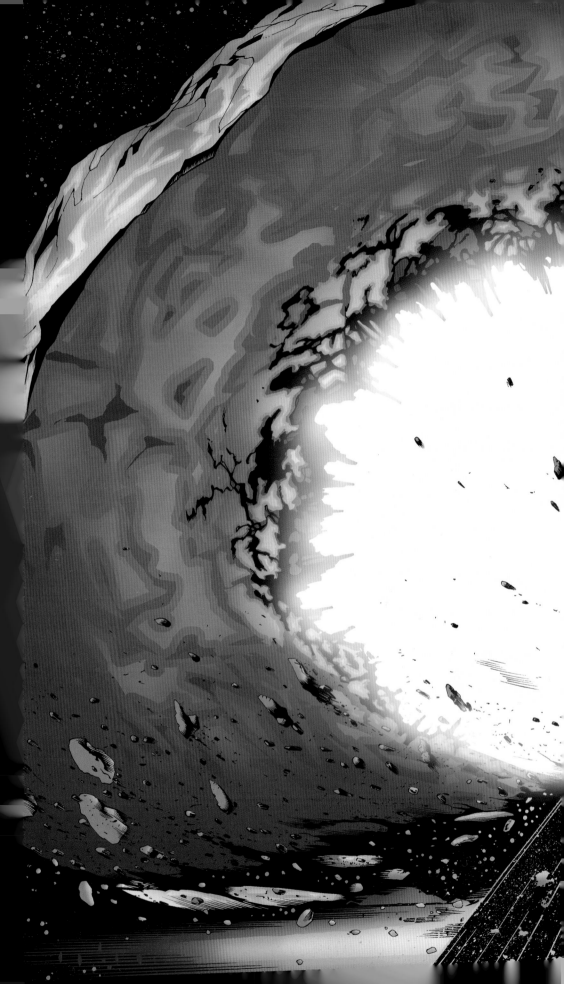

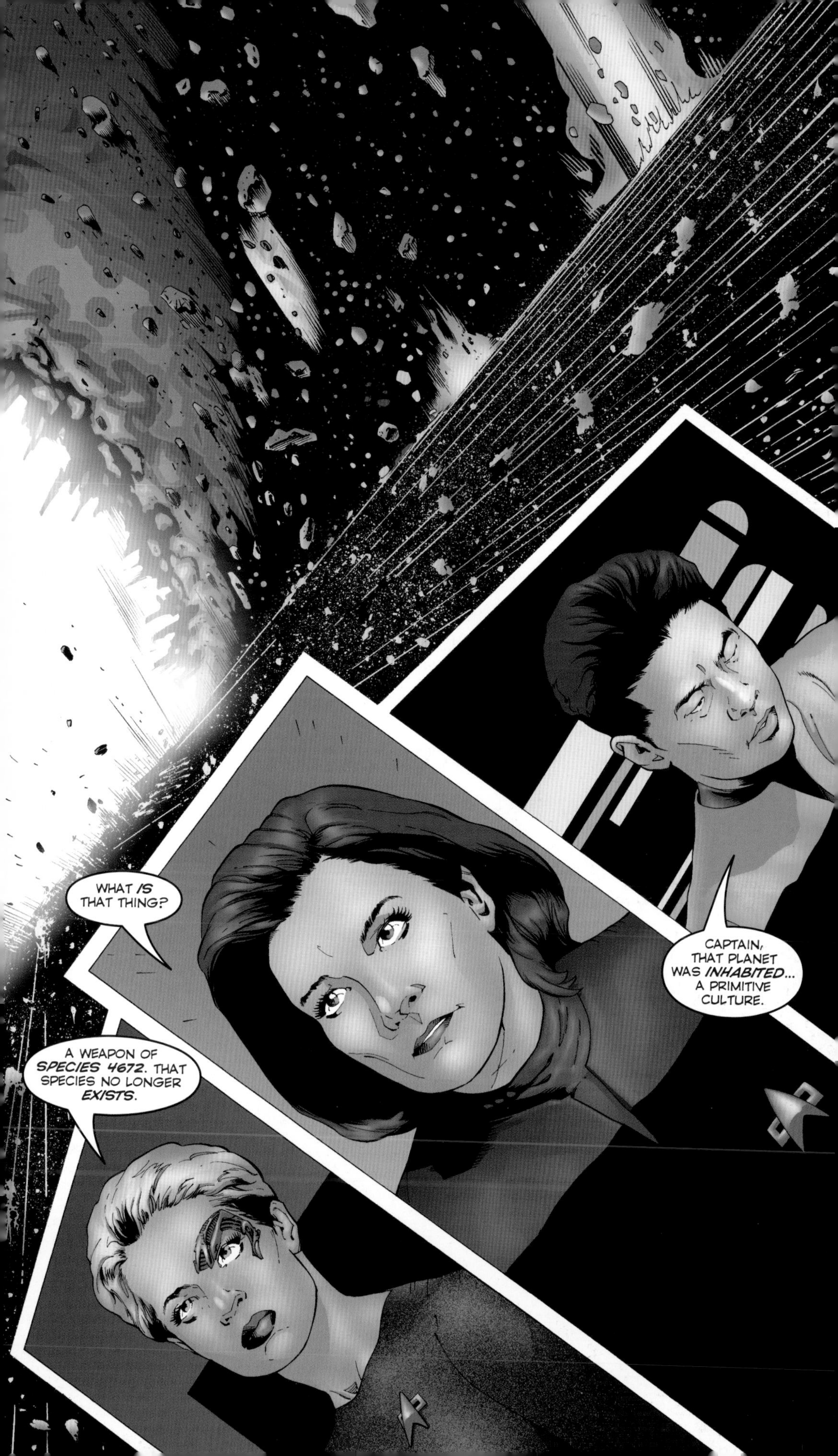
WHAT *IS* THAT THING?
CAPTAIN, THAT PLANET WAS *INHABITED*... A PRIMITIVE CULTURE.
A WEAPON OF *SPECIES 4672*. THAT SPECIES NO LONGER *EXISTS*.

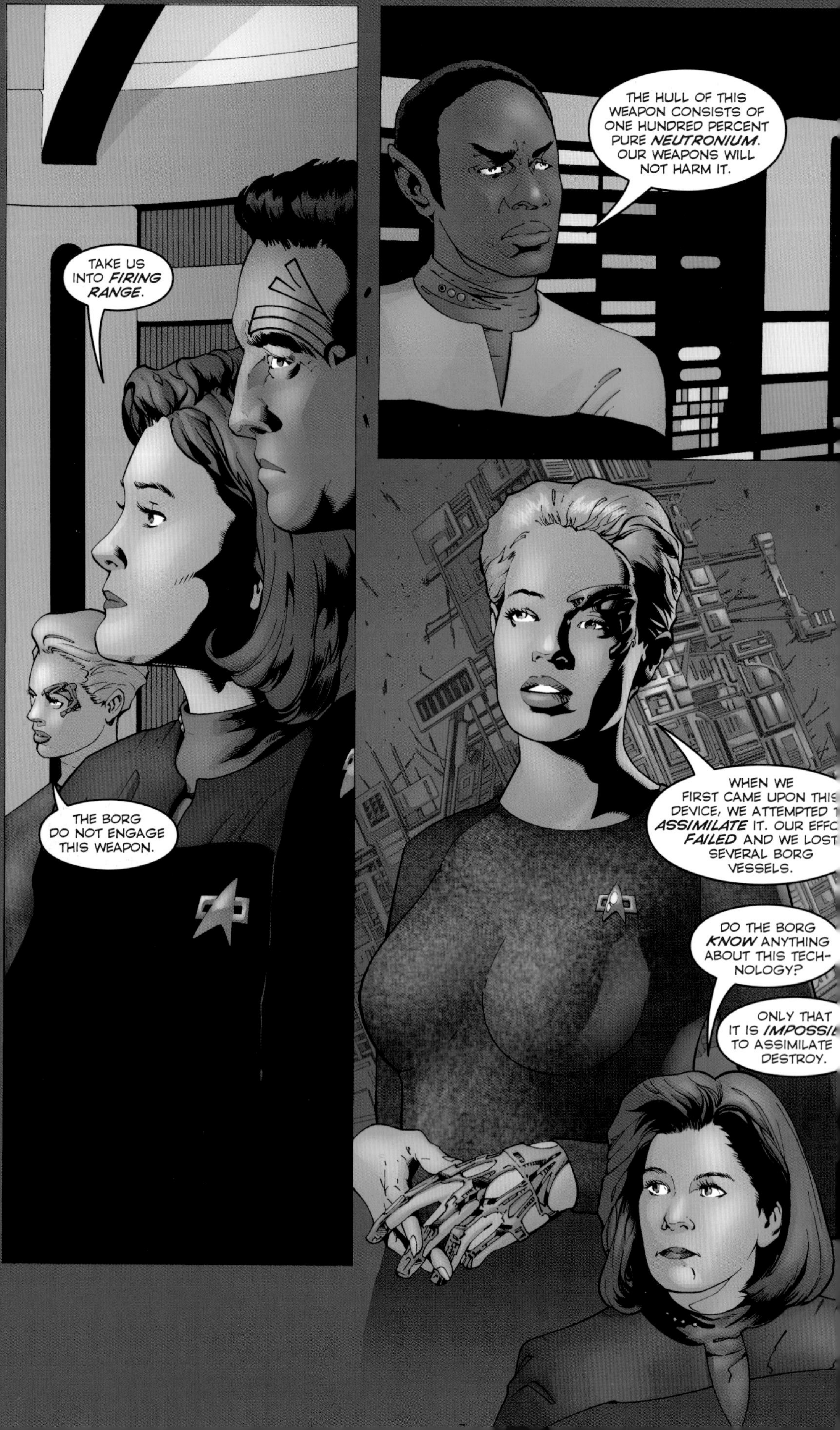
TAKE US INTO FIRING RANGE.
THE HULL OF THIS WEAPON CONSISTS OF ONE HUNDRED PERCENT PURE NEUTRONIUM. OUR WEAPONS WILL NOT HARM IT.
THE BORG DO NOT ENGAGE THIS WEAPON.
WHEN WE FIRST CAME UPON THIS DEVICE, WE ATTEMPTED T ASSIMILATE IT. OUR EFFC FAILED AND WE LOST SEVERAL BORG VESSELS.
DO THE BORG KNOW ANYTHING ABOUT THIS TECH-NOLOGY?
ONLY THAT IT IS IMPOSSI TO ASSIMILATE DESTROY.

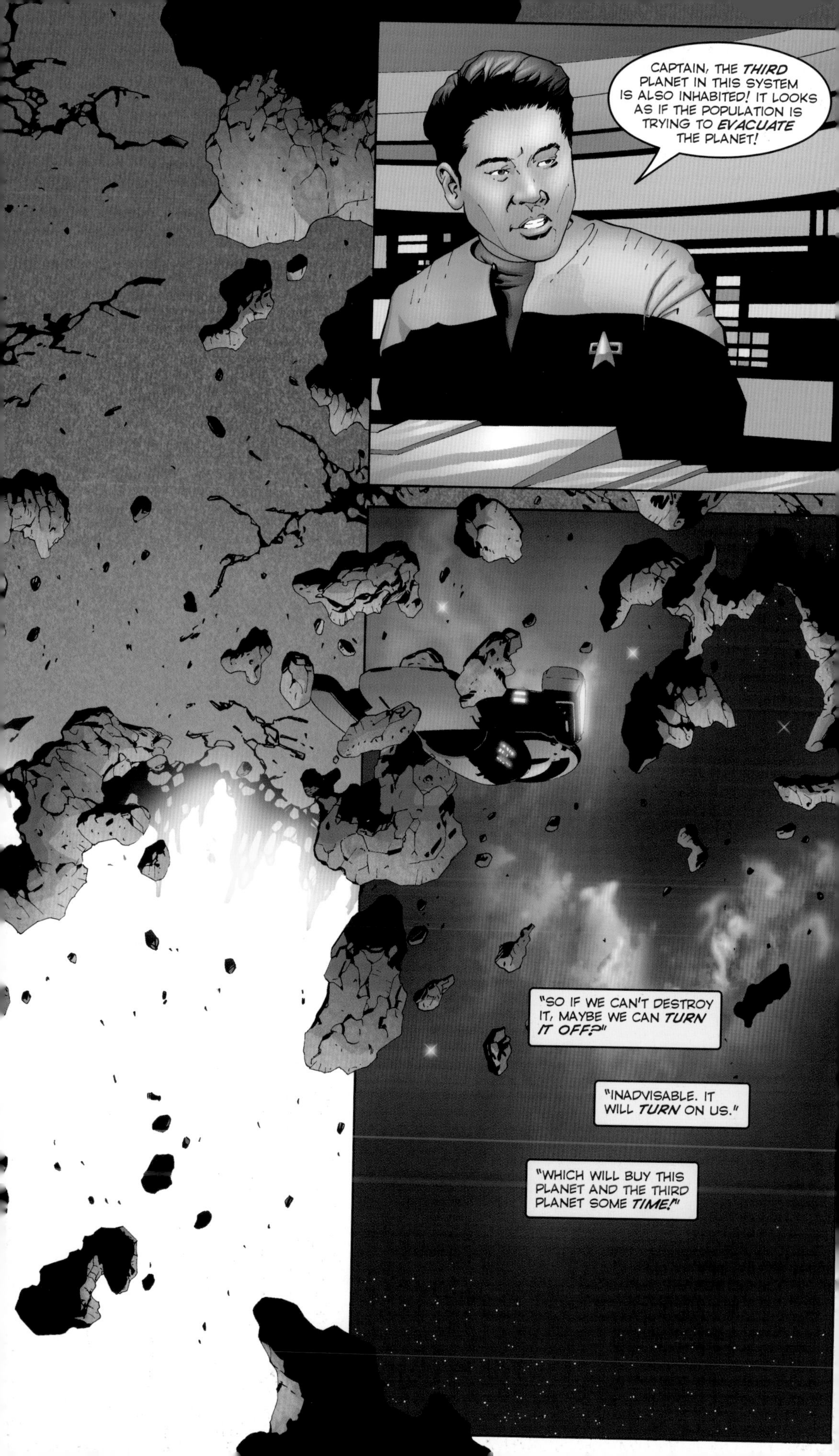

CAPTAIN, THE *THIRD* PLANET IN THIS SYSTEM IS ALSO INHABITED! IT LOOKS AS IF THE POPULATION IS TRYING TO *EVACUATE* THE PLANET!
"SO IF WE CAN'T DESTROY IT, MAYBE WE CAN *TURN IT OFF?*"
"INADVISABLE. IT WILL *TURN* ON US."
"WHICH WILL BUY THIS PLANET AND THE THIRD PLANET SOME *TIME!*"

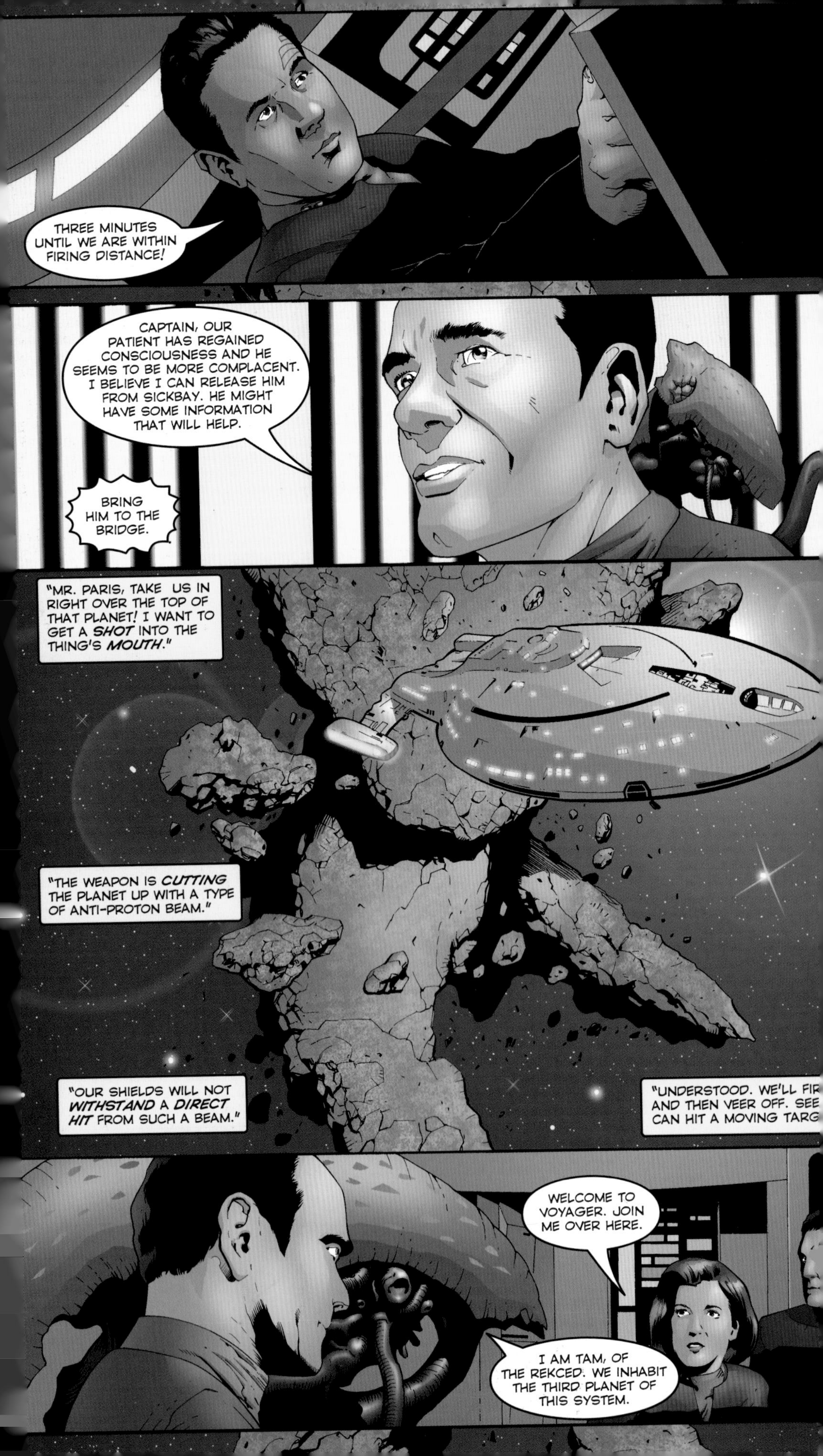
THREE MINUTES UNTIL WE ARE WITHIN FIRING DISTANCE!
CAPTAIN, OUR PATIENT HAS REGAINED CONSCIOUSNESS AND HE SEEMS TO BE MORE COMPLACENT. I BELIEVE I CAN RELEASE HIM FROM SICKBAY. HE MIGHT HAVE SOME INFORMATION THAT WILL HELP.
BRING HIM TO THE BRIDGE.
"MR. PARIS, TAKE US IN RIGHT OVER THE TOP OF THAT PLANET! I WANT TO GET A SHOT INTO THE THING'S MOUTH."
"THE WEAPON IS CUTTING THE PLANET UP WITH A TYPE OF ANTI-PROTON BEAM."
"OUR SHIELDS WILL NOT WITHSTAND A DIRECT HIT FROM SUCH A BEAM."
"UNDERSTOOD. WE'LL FIR AND THEN VEER OFF. SEE CAN HIT A MOVING TARG
WELCOME TO VOYAGER. JOIN ME OVER HERE.
I AM TAM, OF THE REKCED. WE INHABIT THE THIRD PLANET OF THIS SYSTEM.

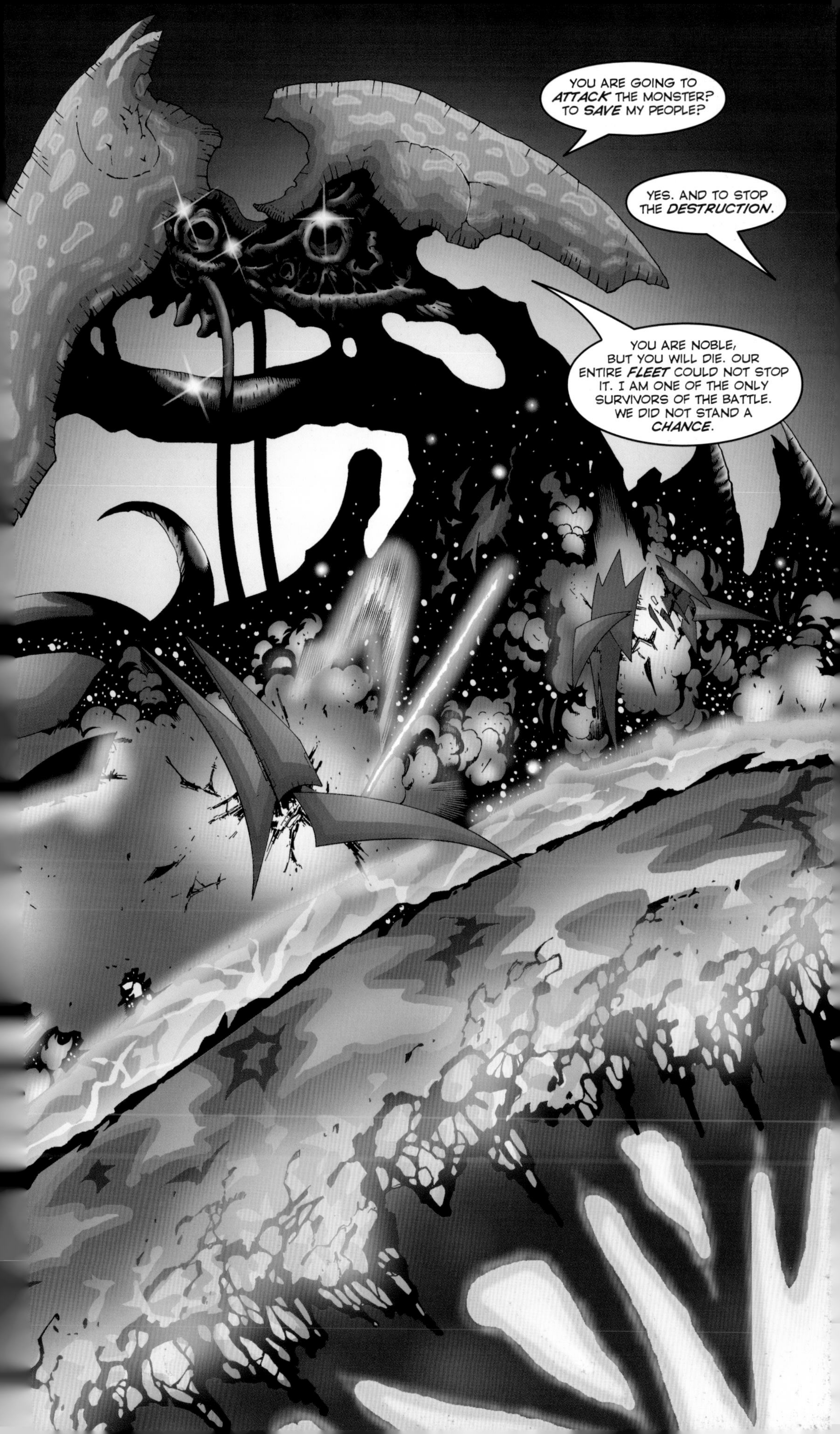
YOU ARE GOING TO ATTACK THE MONSTER? TO SAVE MY PEOPLE?
YES. AND TO STOP THE DESTRUCTION.
YOU ARE NOBLE, BUT YOU WILL DIE. OUR ENTIRE FLEET COULD NOT STOP IT. I AM ONE OF THE ONLY SURVIVORS OF THE BATTLE. WE DID NOT STAND A CHANCE.

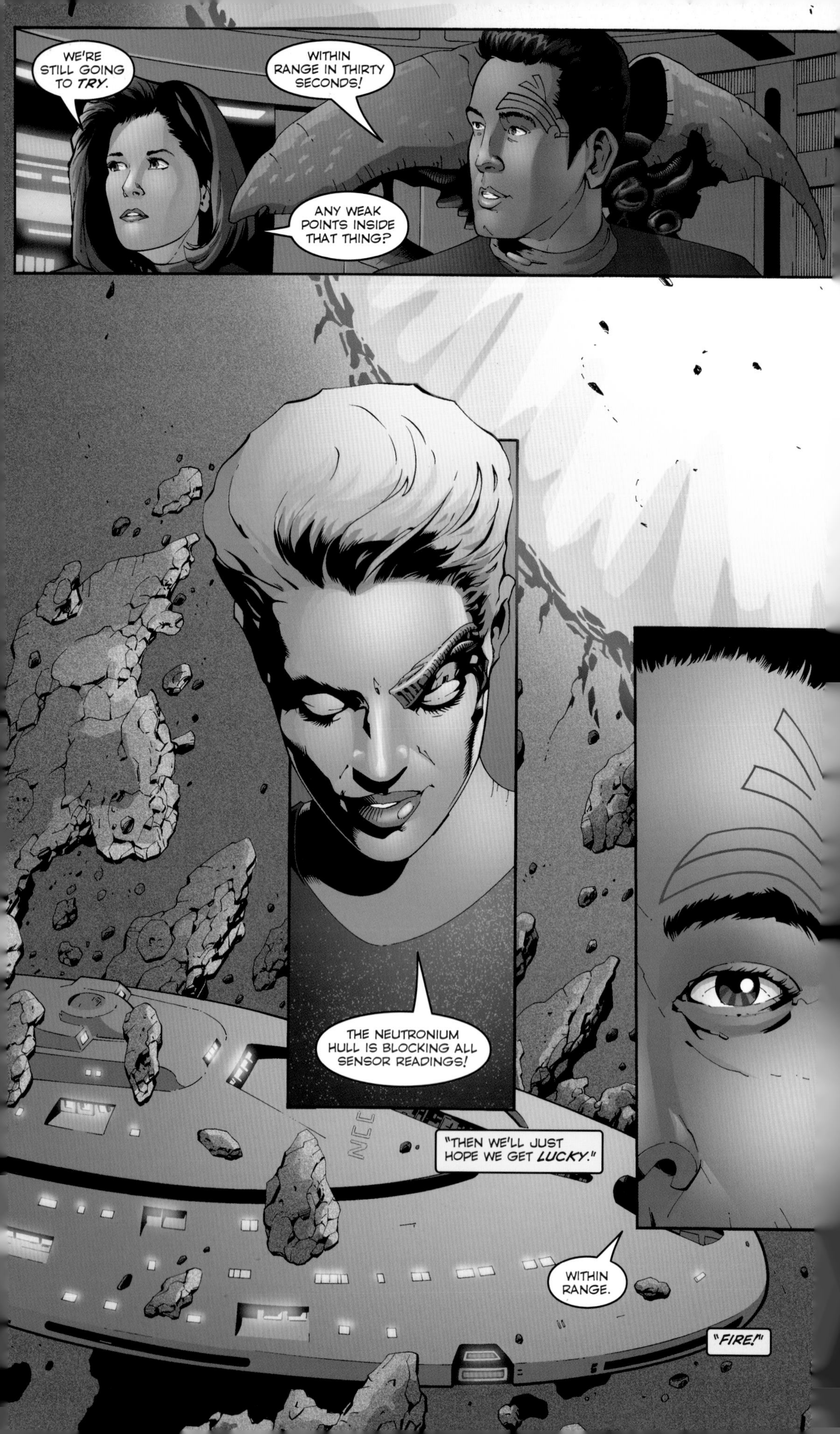
WE'RE STILL GOING TO *TRY*.
WITHIN RANGE IN THIRTY SECONDS!
ANY WEAK POINTS INSIDE THAT THING?
THE NEUTRONIUM HULL IS BLOCKING ALL SENSOR READINGS!
"THEN WE'LL JUST HOPE WE GET *LUCKY*."
WITHIN RANGE.
"*FIRE!*"

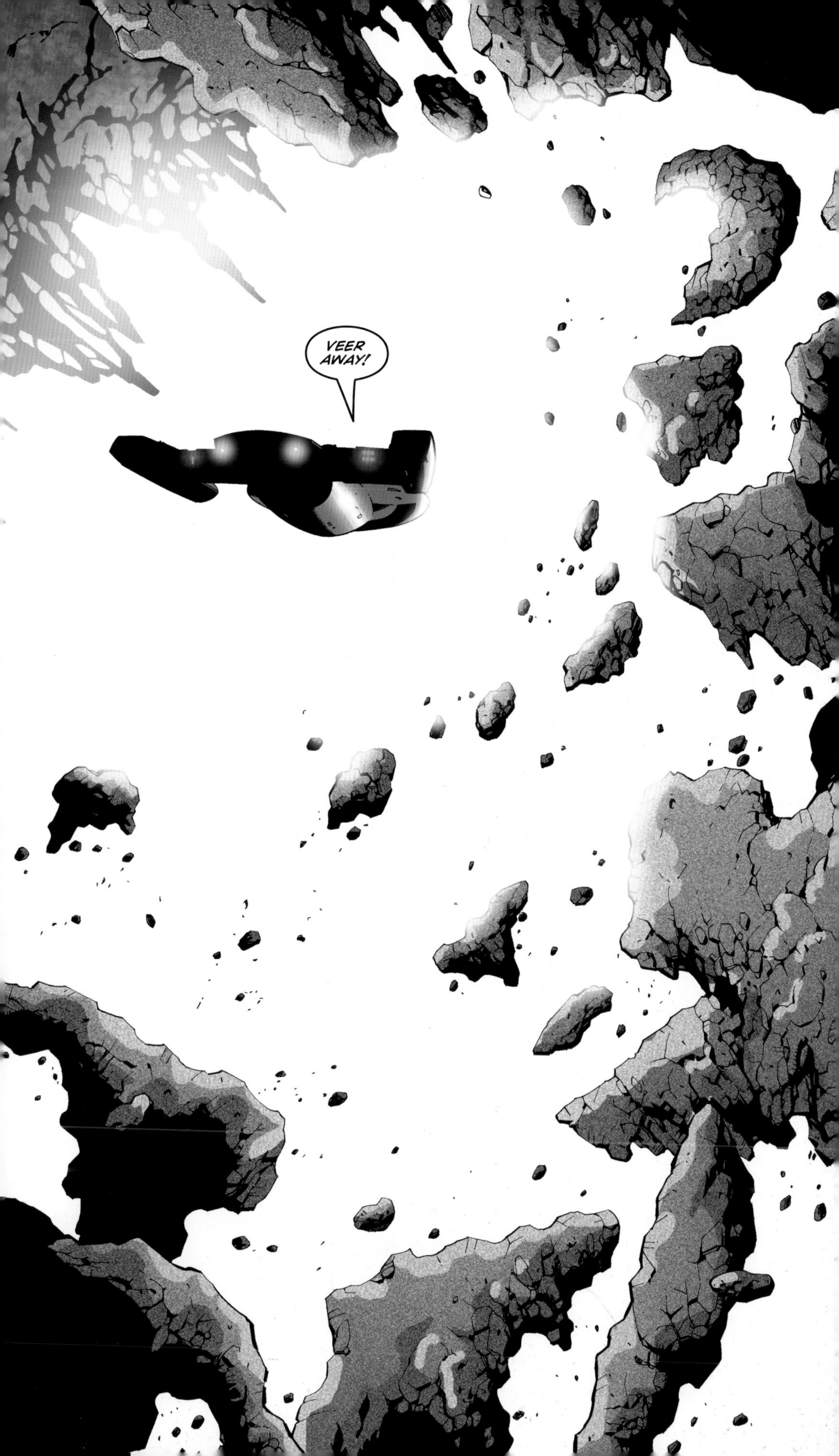
VEER AWAY!

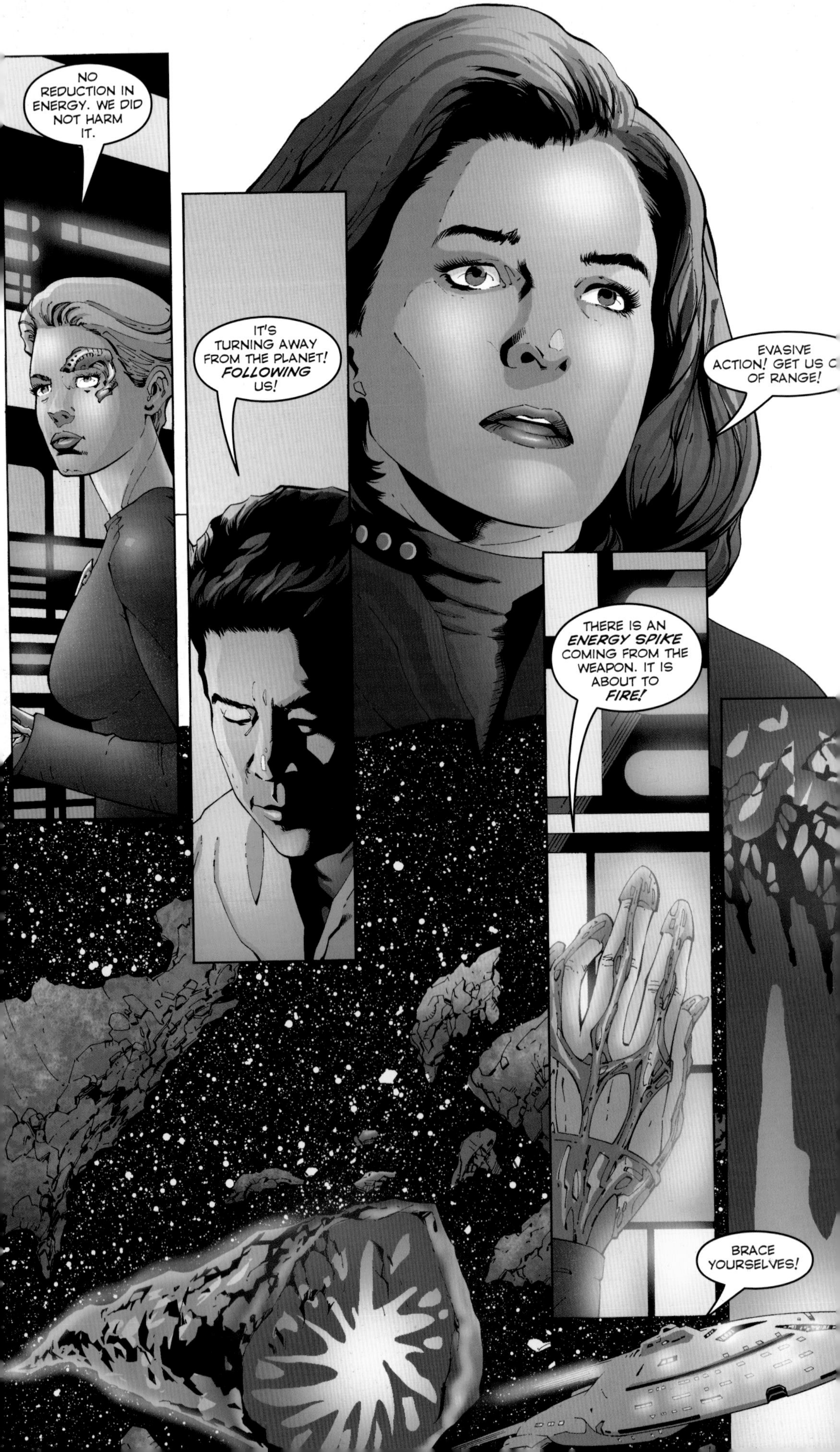
NO REDUCTION IN ENERGY. WE DID NOT HARM IT.
IT'S TURNING AWAY FROM THE PLANET! *FOLLOWING* US!
EVASIVE ACTION! GET US OF RANGE!
THERE IS AN *ENERGY SPIKE* COMING FROM THE WEAPON. IT IS ABOUT TO *FIRE!*
BRACE YOURSELVES!

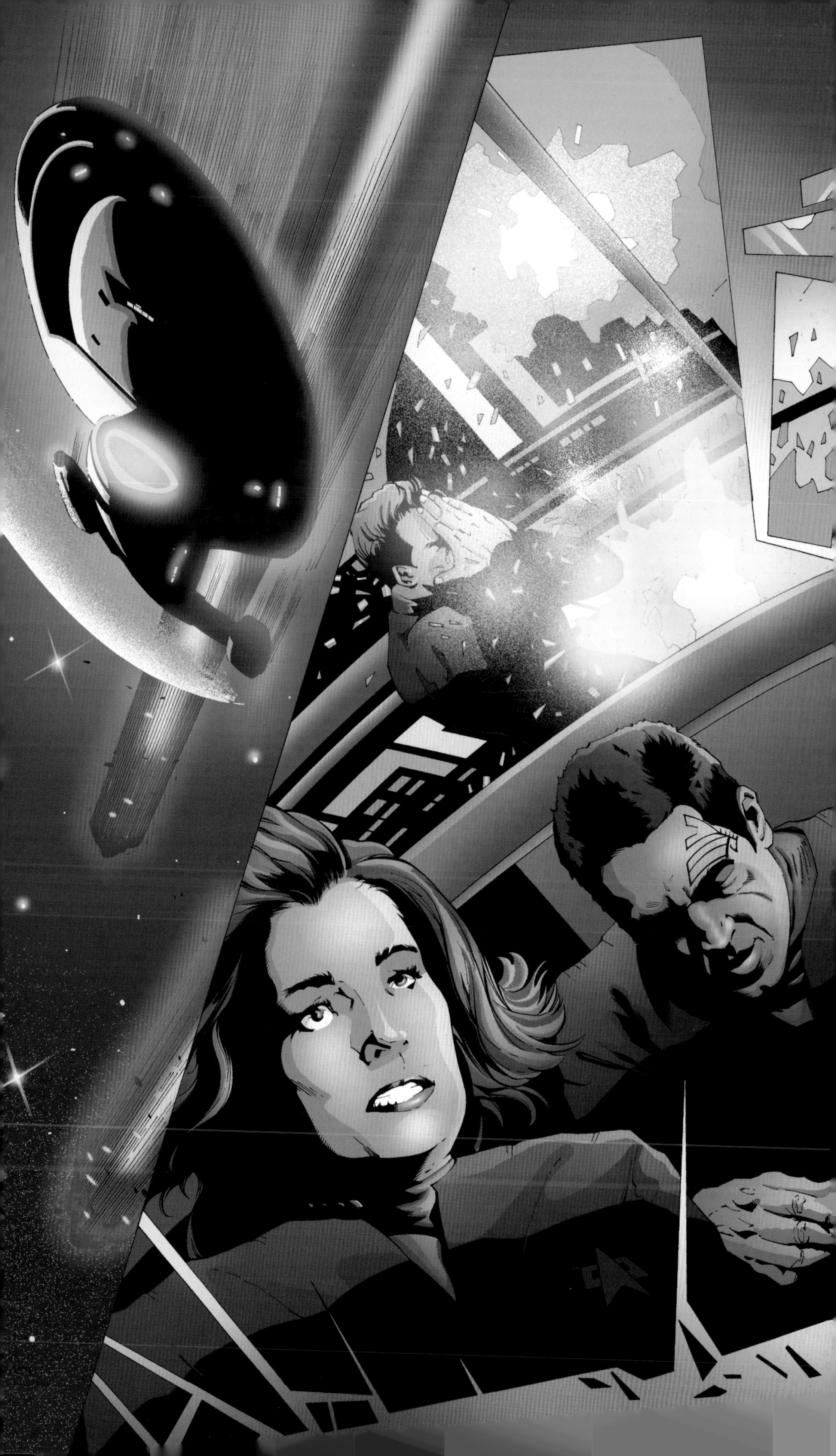

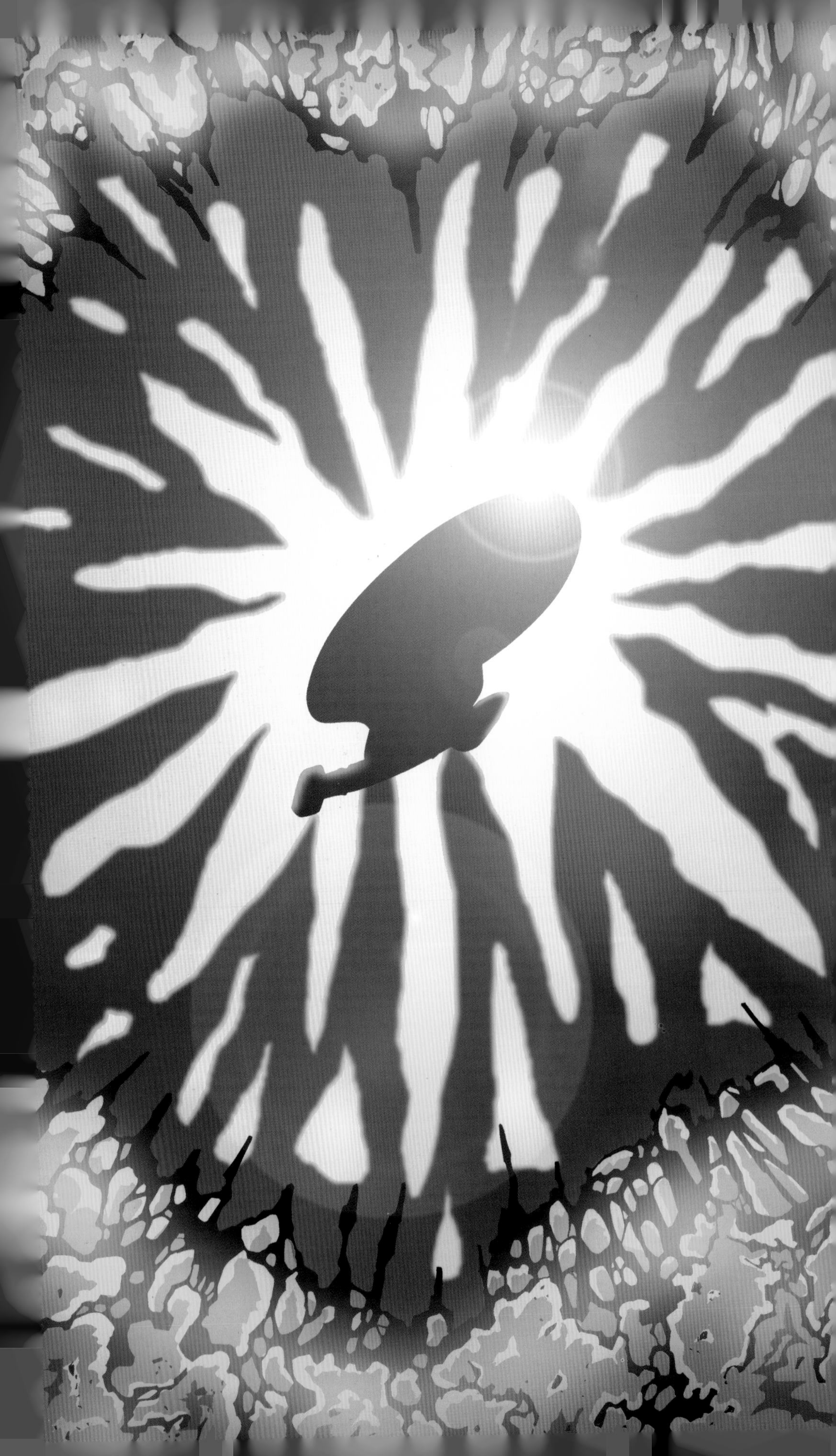

CHAPTER 2

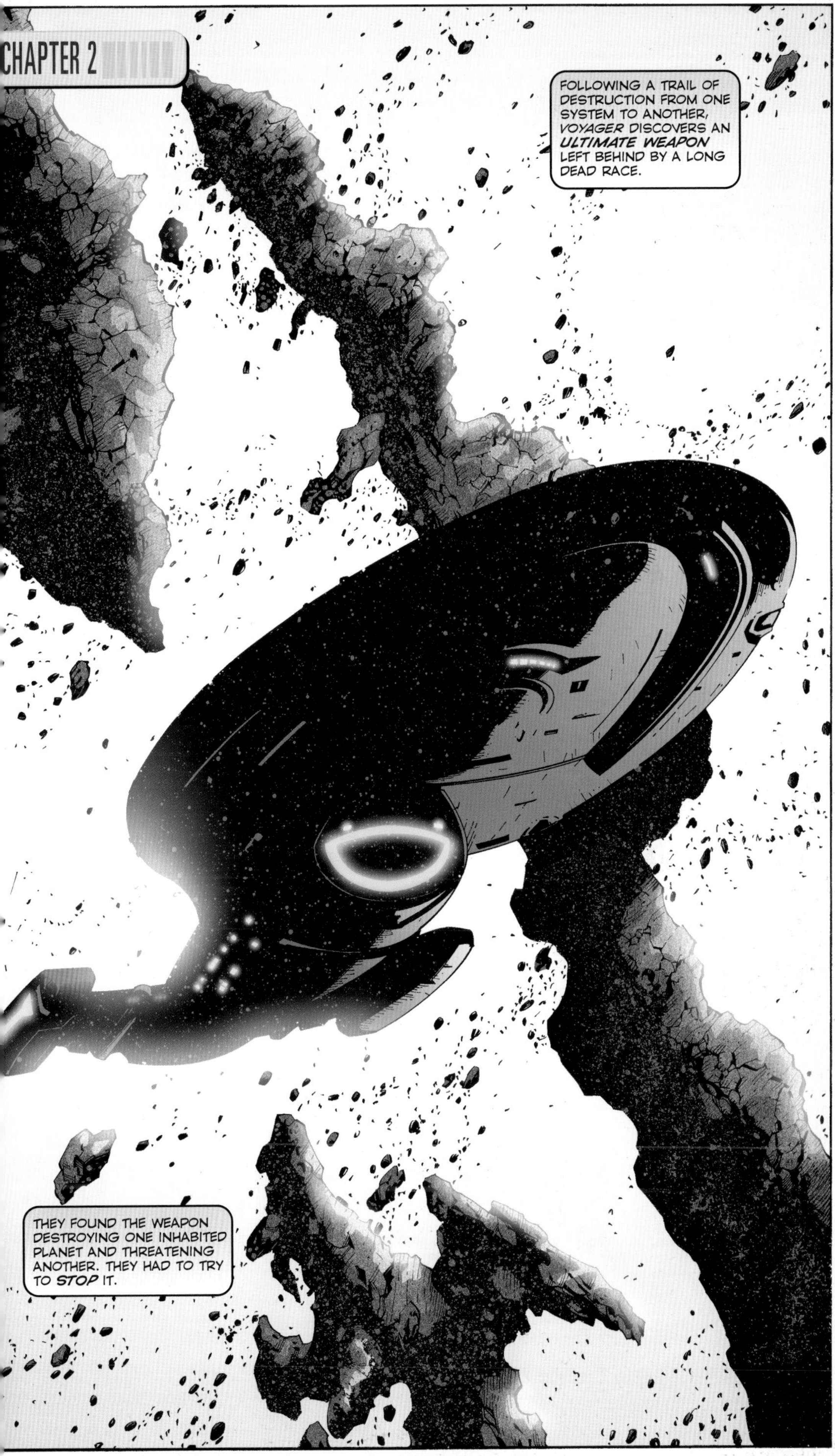
FOLLOWING A TRAIL OF DESTRUCTION FROM ONE SYSTEM TO ANOTHER, VOYAGER DISCOVERS AN ULTIMATE WEAPON LEFT BEHIND BY A LONG DEAD RACE.
THEY FOUND THE WEAPON DESTROYING ONE INHABITED PLANET AND THREATENING ANOTHER. THEY HAD TO TRY TO STOP IT.

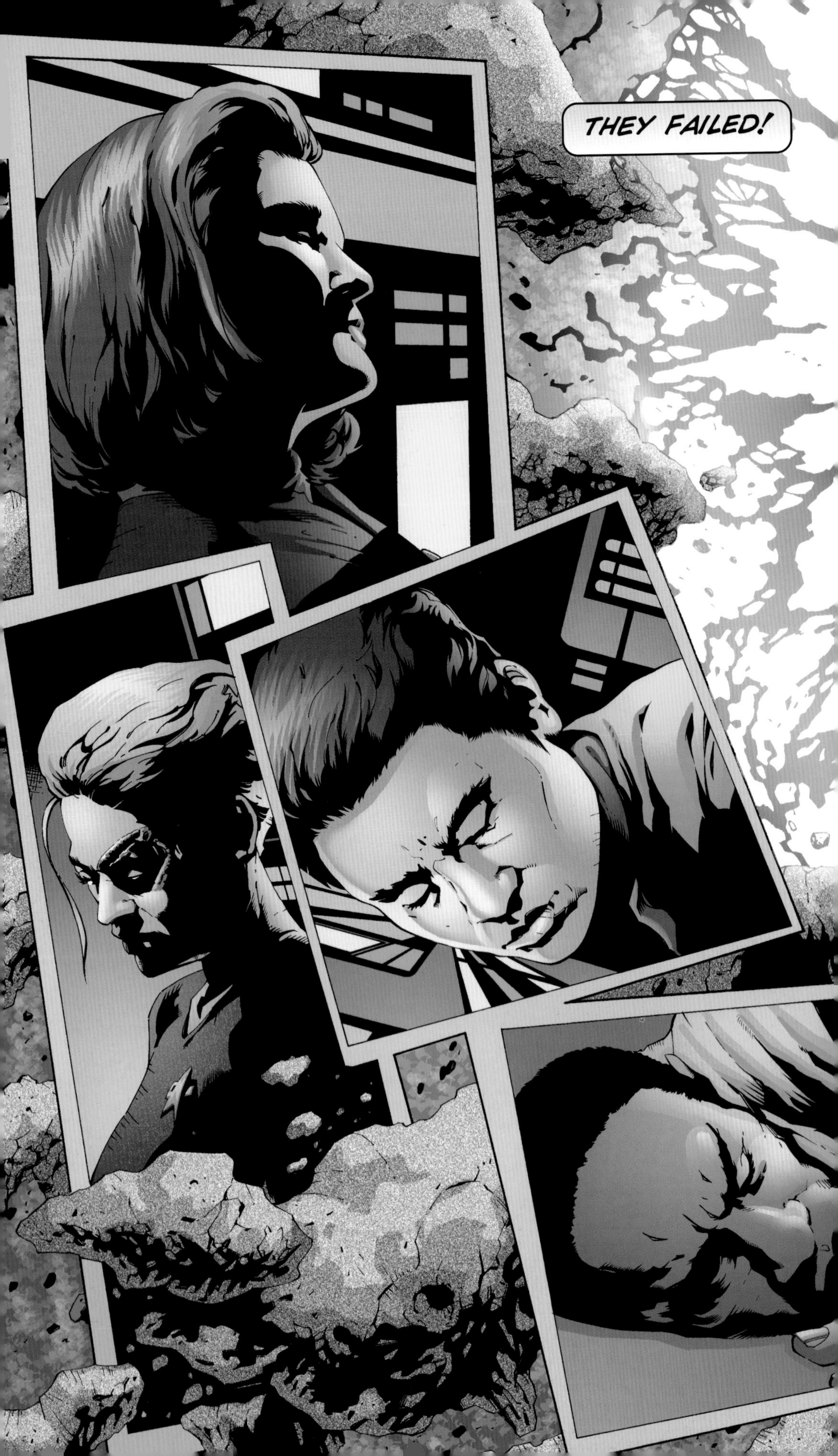
THEY FAILED!

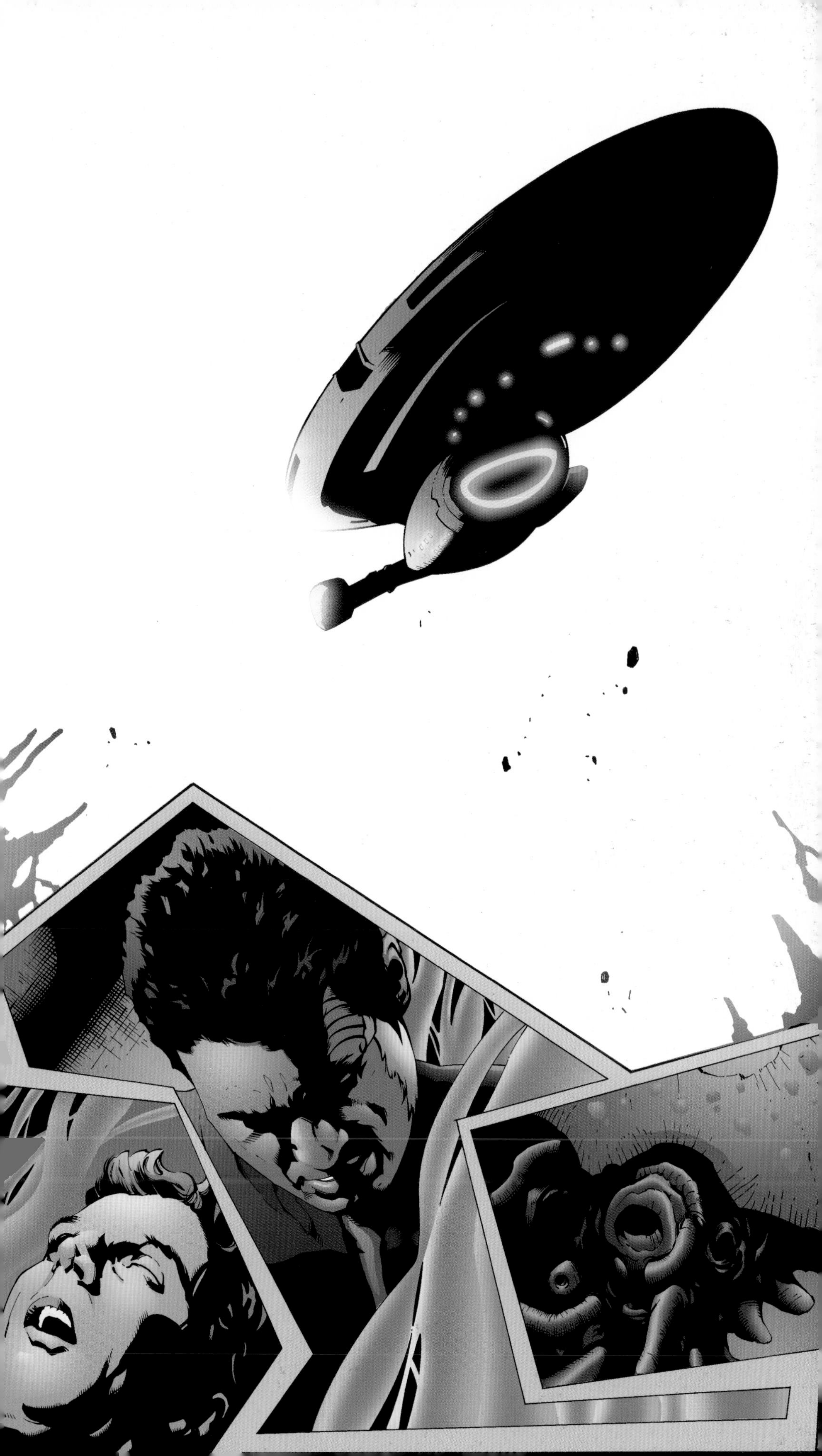

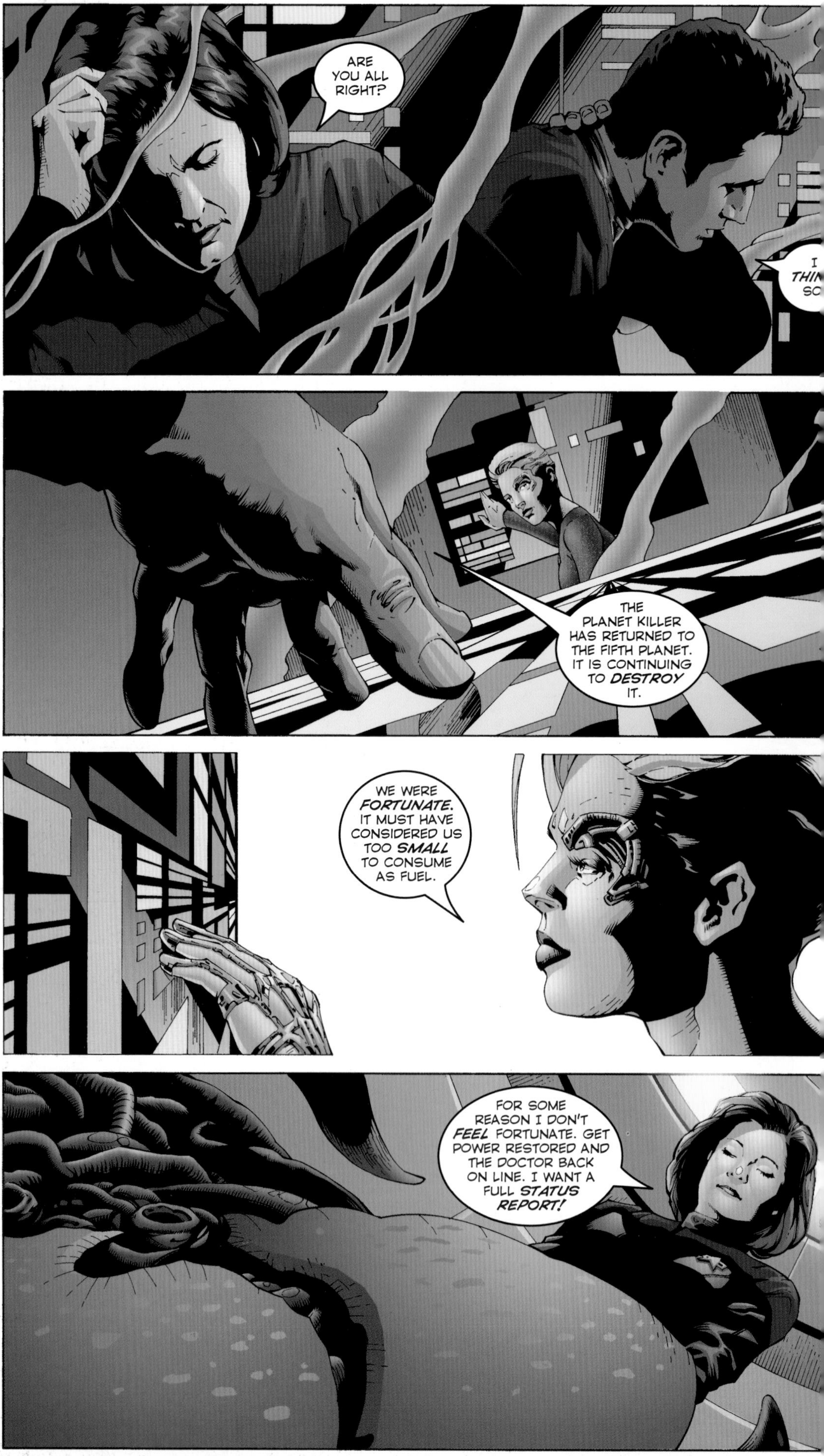
ARE YOU ALL RIGHT?
THE PLANET KILLER HAS RETURNED TO THE FIFTH PLANET. IT IS CONTINUING TO DESTROY IT.
WE WERE FORTUNATE. IT MUST HAVE CONSIDERED US TOO SMALL TO CONSUME AS FUEL.
FOR SOME REASON I DON'T FEEL FORTUNATE. GET POWER RESTORED AND THE DOCTOR BACK ON LINE. I WANT A FULL STATUS REPORT!

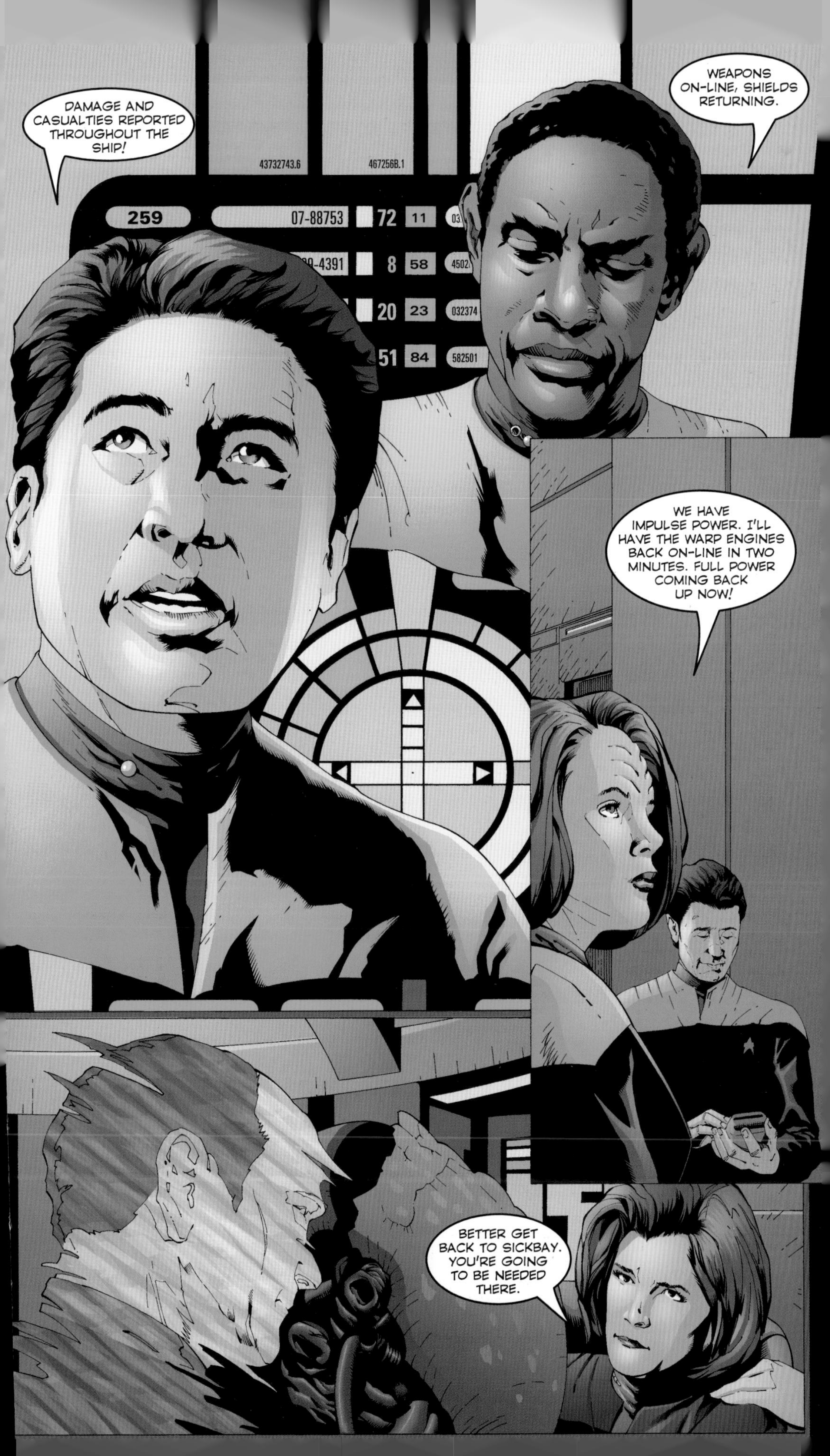
DAMAGE AND CASUALTIES REPORTED THROUGHOUT THE SHIP!
WEAPONS ON-LINE, SHIELDS RETURNING.
WE HAVE IMPULSE POWER. I'LL HAVE THE WARP ENGINES BACK ON-LINE IN TWO MINUTES. FULL POWER COMING BACK UP NOW!
BETTER GET BACK TO SICKBAY. YOU'RE GOING TO BE NEEDED THERE.

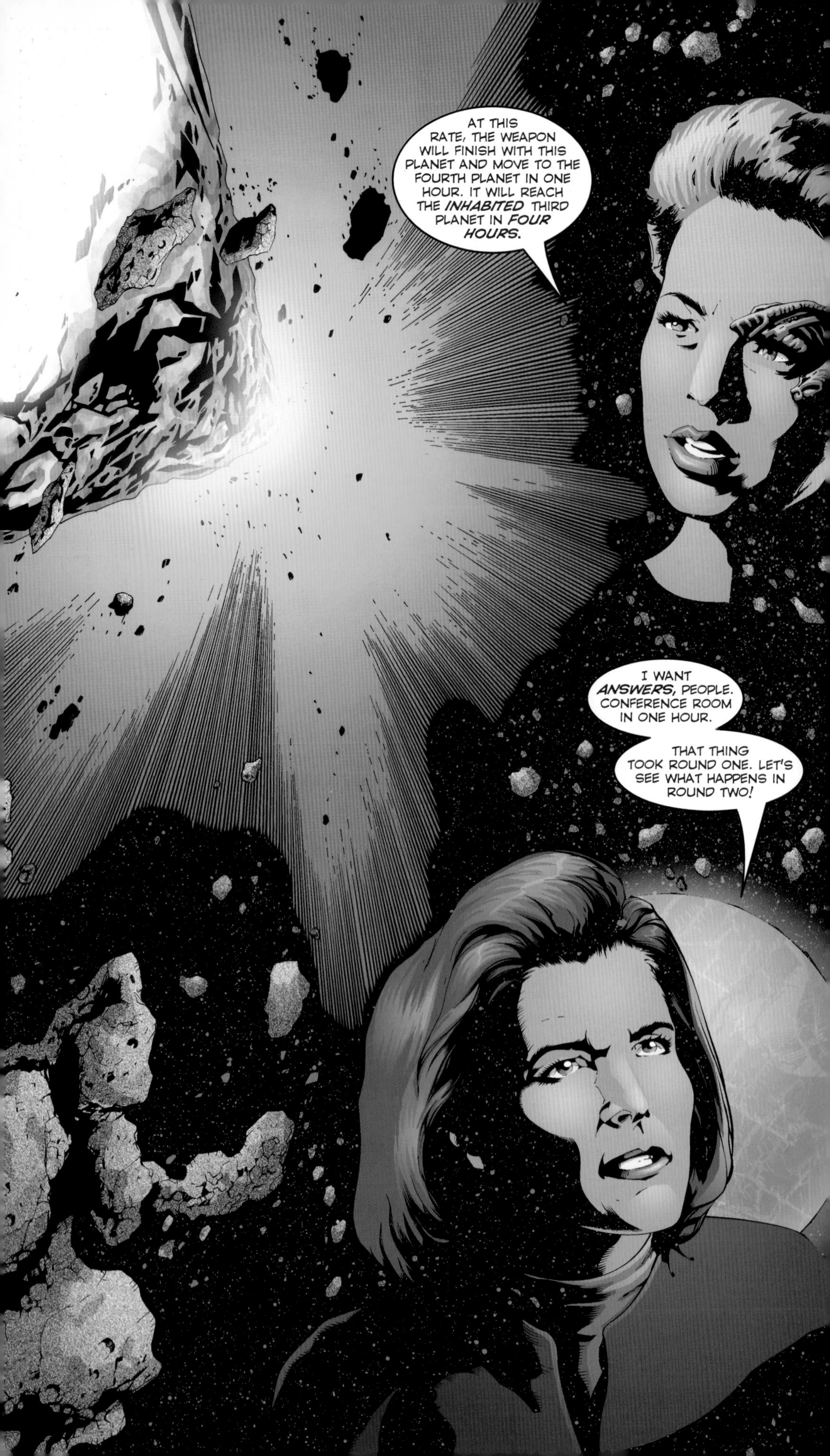
AT THIS RATE, THE WEAPON WILL FINISH WITH THIS PLANET AND MOVE TO THE FOURTH PLANET IN ONE HOUR. IT WILL REACH THE *INHABITED* THIRD PLANET IN *FOUR HOURS.*
I WANT *ANSWERS,* PEOPLE. CONFERENCE ROOM IN ONE HOUR.
THAT THING TOOK ROUND ONE. LET'S SEE WHAT HAPPENS IN ROUND TWO!

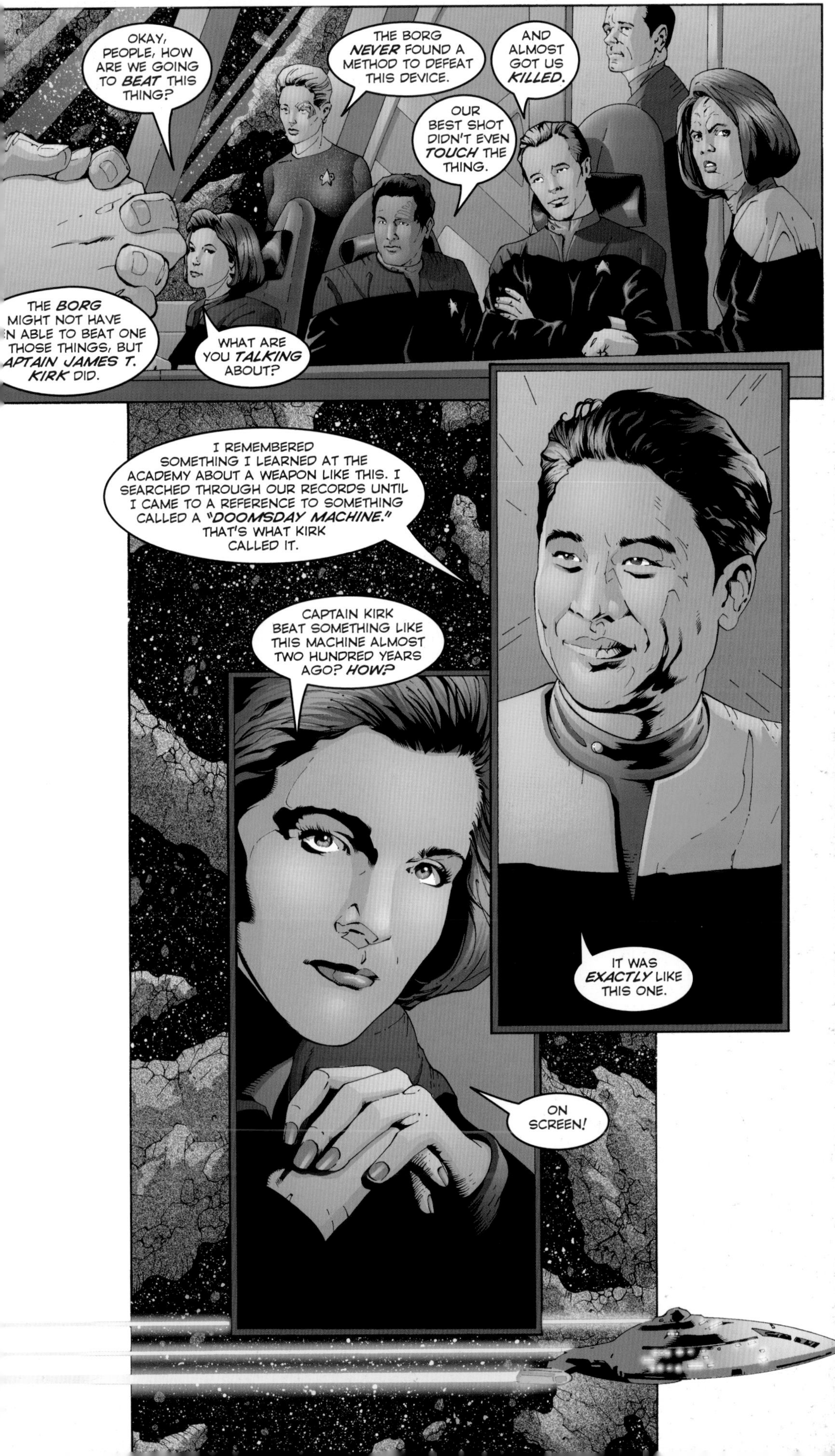
OKAY, PEOPLE, HOW ARE WE GOING TO BEAT THIS THING?
THE BORG NEVER FOUND A METHOD TO DEFEAT THIS DEVICE.
AND ALMOST GOT US KILLED.
OUR BEST SHOT DIDN'T EVEN TOUCH THE THING.
THE BORG MIGHT NOT HAVE N ABLE TO BEAT ONE THOSE THINGS, BUT APTAIN JAMES T. KIRK DID.
WHAT ARE YOU TALKING ABOUT?
I REMEMBERED SOMETHING I LEARNED AT THE ACADEMY ABOUT A WEAPON LIKE THIS. I SEARCHED THROUGH OUR RECORDS UNTIL I CAME TO A REFERENCE TO SOMETHING CALLED A "DOOMSDAY MACHINE." THAT'S WHAT KIRK CALLED IT.
CAPTAIN KIRK BEAT SOMETHING LIKE THIS MACHINE ALMOST TWO HUNDRED YEARS AGO? HOW?
IT WAS EXACTLY LIKE THIS ONE.
ON SCREEN!

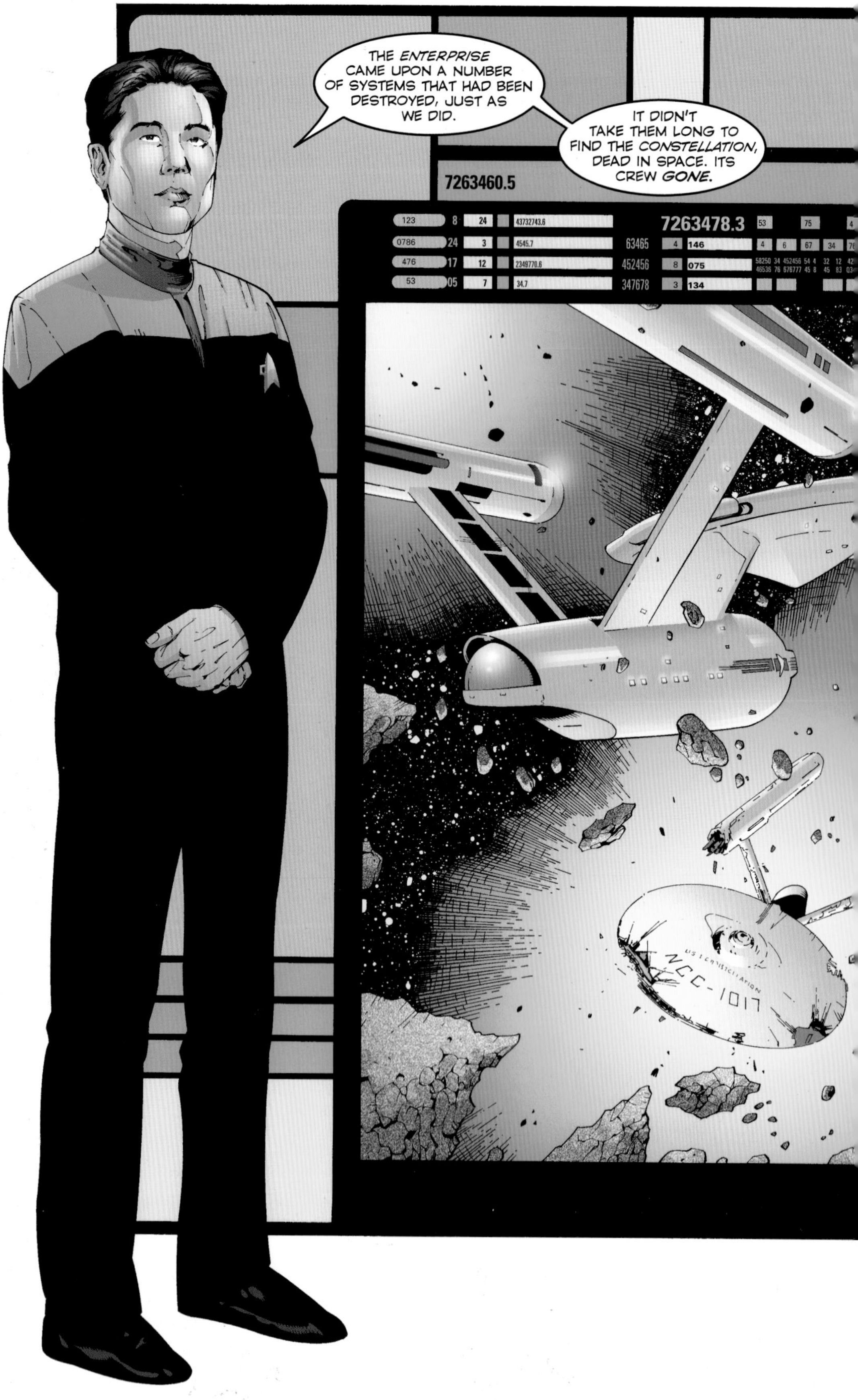
THE *ENTERPRISE* CAME UPON A NUMBER OF SYSTEMS THAT HAD BEEN DESTROYED, JUST AS WE DID.
IT DIDN'T TAKE THEM LONG TO FIND THE *CONSTELLATION*, DEAD IN SPACE. ITS CREW ***GONE***.
7263460.5
7263478.3
NCC-1017

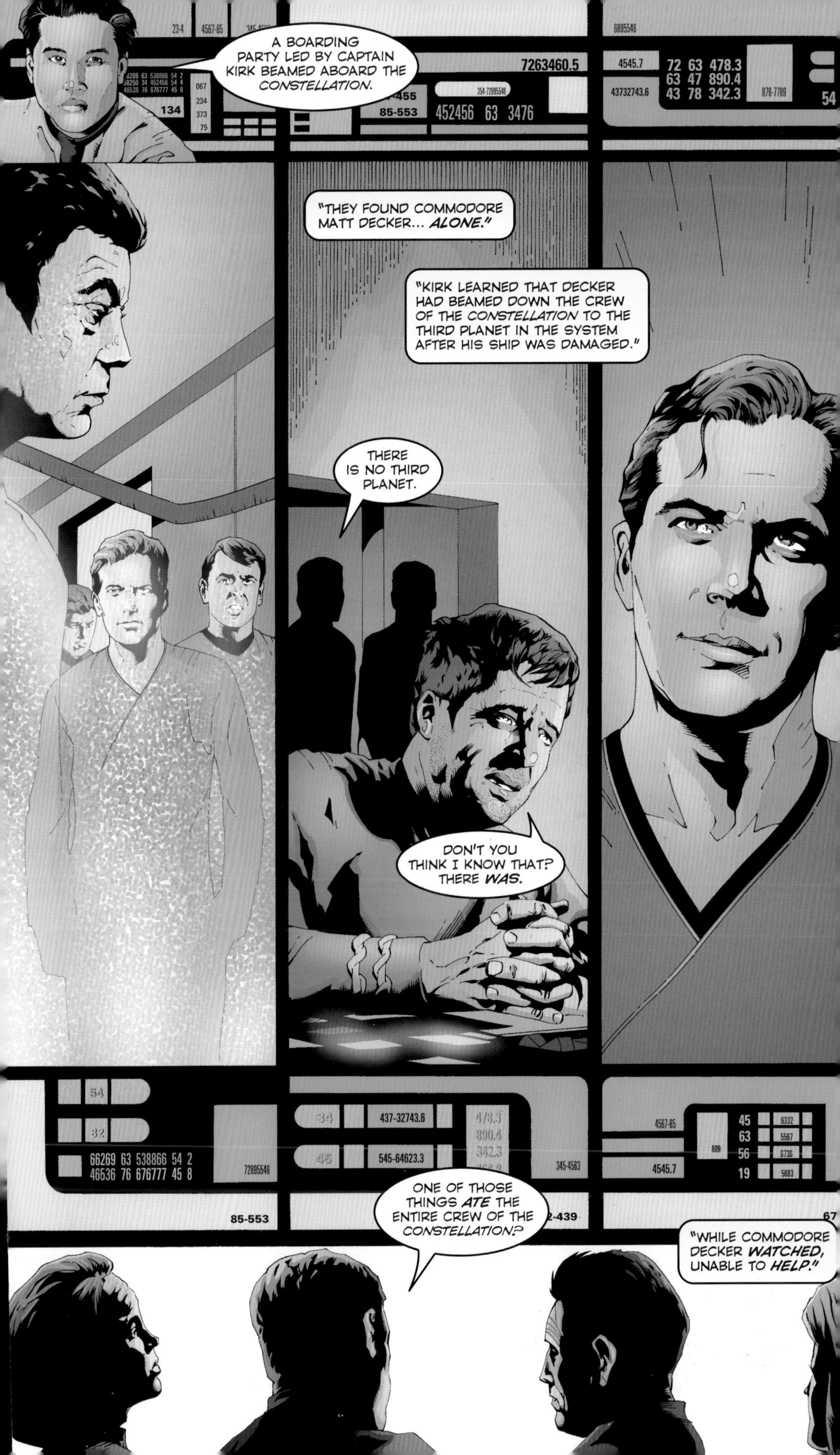
A BOARDING PARTY LED BY CAPTAIN KIRK BEAMED ABOARD THE CONSTELLATION.
"THEY FOUND COMMODORE MATT DECKER... ALONE."
"KIRK LEARNED THAT DECKER HAD BEAMED DOWN THE CREW OF THE CONSTELLATION TO THE THIRD PLANET IN THE SYSTEM AFTER HIS SHIP WAS DAMAGED."
THERE IS NO THIRD PLANET.
DON'T YOU THINK I KNOW THAT? THERE WAS.
ONE OF THOSE THINGS ATE THE ENTIRE CREW OF THE CONSTELLATION?
"WHILE COMMODORE DECKER WATCHED, UNABLE TO HELP."

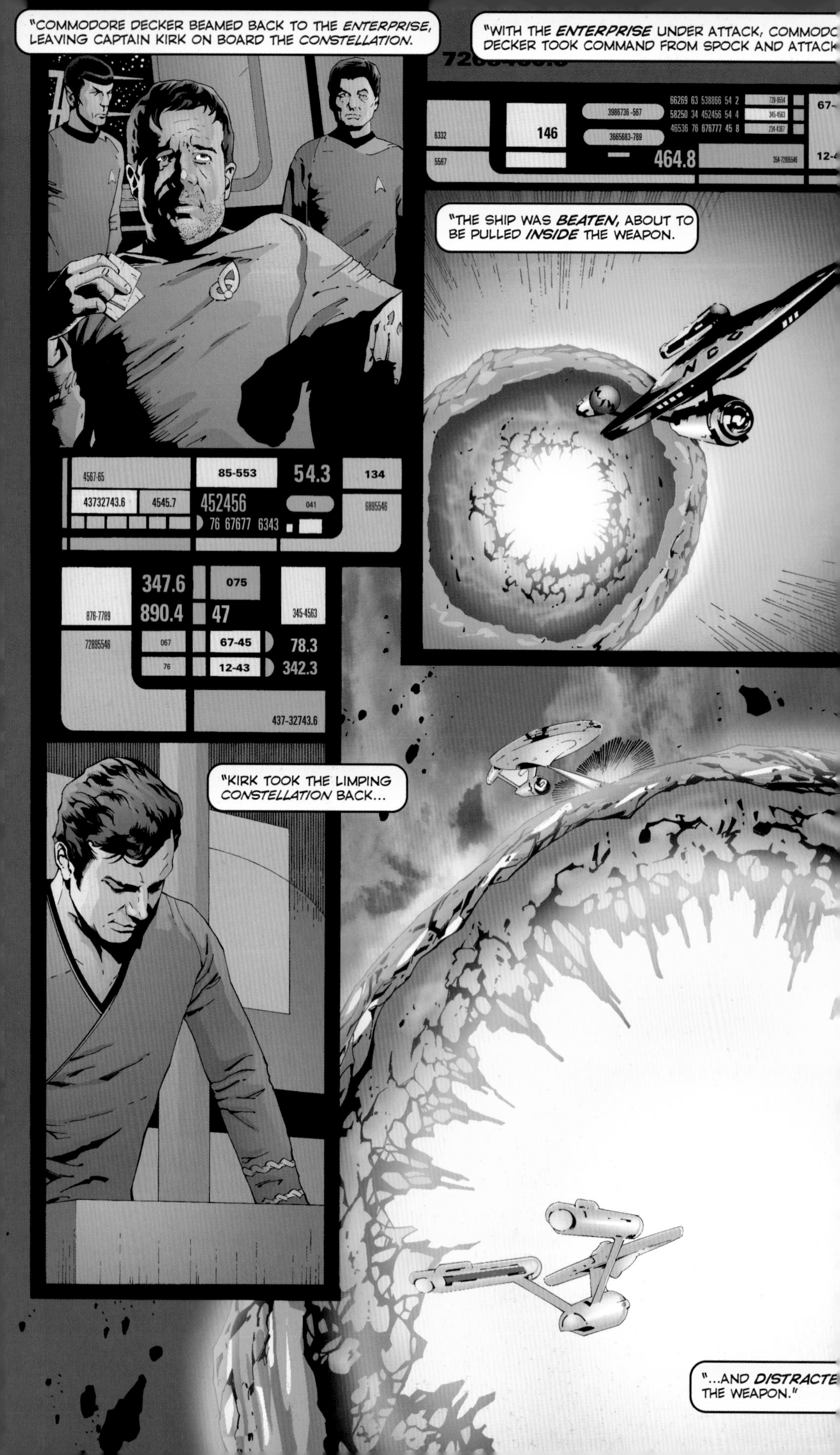
"COMMODORE DECKER BEAMED BACK TO THE *ENTERPRISE*, LEAVING CAPTAIN KIRK ON BOARD THE *CONSTELLATION*.
"WITH THE ***ENTERPRISE*** UNDER ATTACK, COMMODO
DECKER TOOK COMMAND FROM SPOCK AND ATTACK
146
464.8
"THE SHIP WAS ***BEATEN,*** ABOUT TO BE PULLED ***INSIDE*** THE WEAPON.
85-553
54.3
134
452456
347.6
075
890.4
47
67-45
78.3
12-43
342.3
"KIRK TOOK THE LIMPING *CONSTELLATION* BACK...
"...AND ***DISTRACTE***
THE WEAPON."

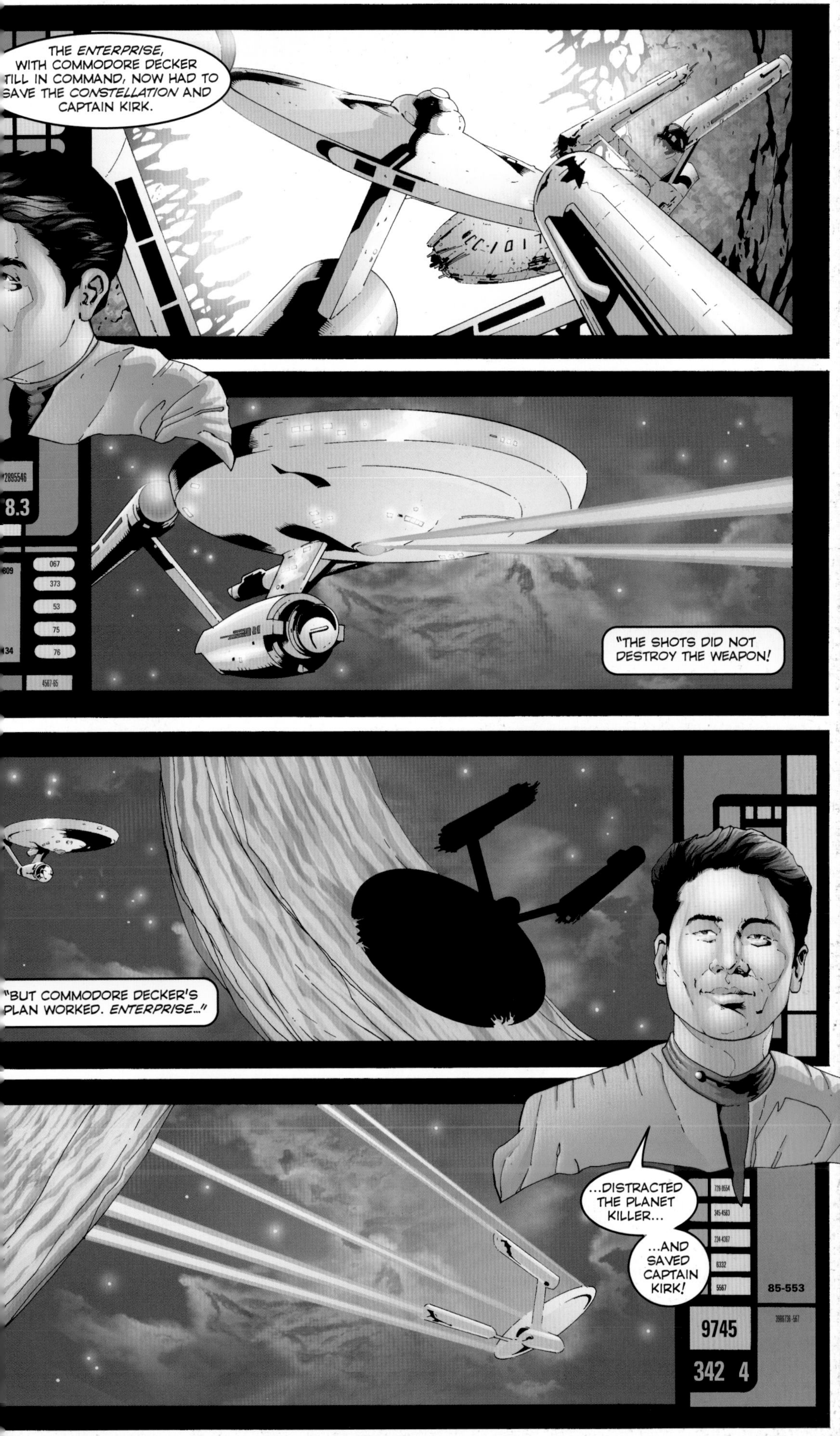
THE *ENTERPRISE*, WITH COMMODORE DECKER TILL IN COMMAND, NOW HAD TO SAVE THE *CONSTELLATION* AND CAPTAIN KIRK.
"THE SHOTS DID NOT DESTROY THE WEAPON!
"BUT COMMODORE DECKER'S PLAN WORKED. *ENTERPRISE*..."
...DISTRACTED THE PLANET KILLER...
...AND SAVED CAPTAIN KIRK!

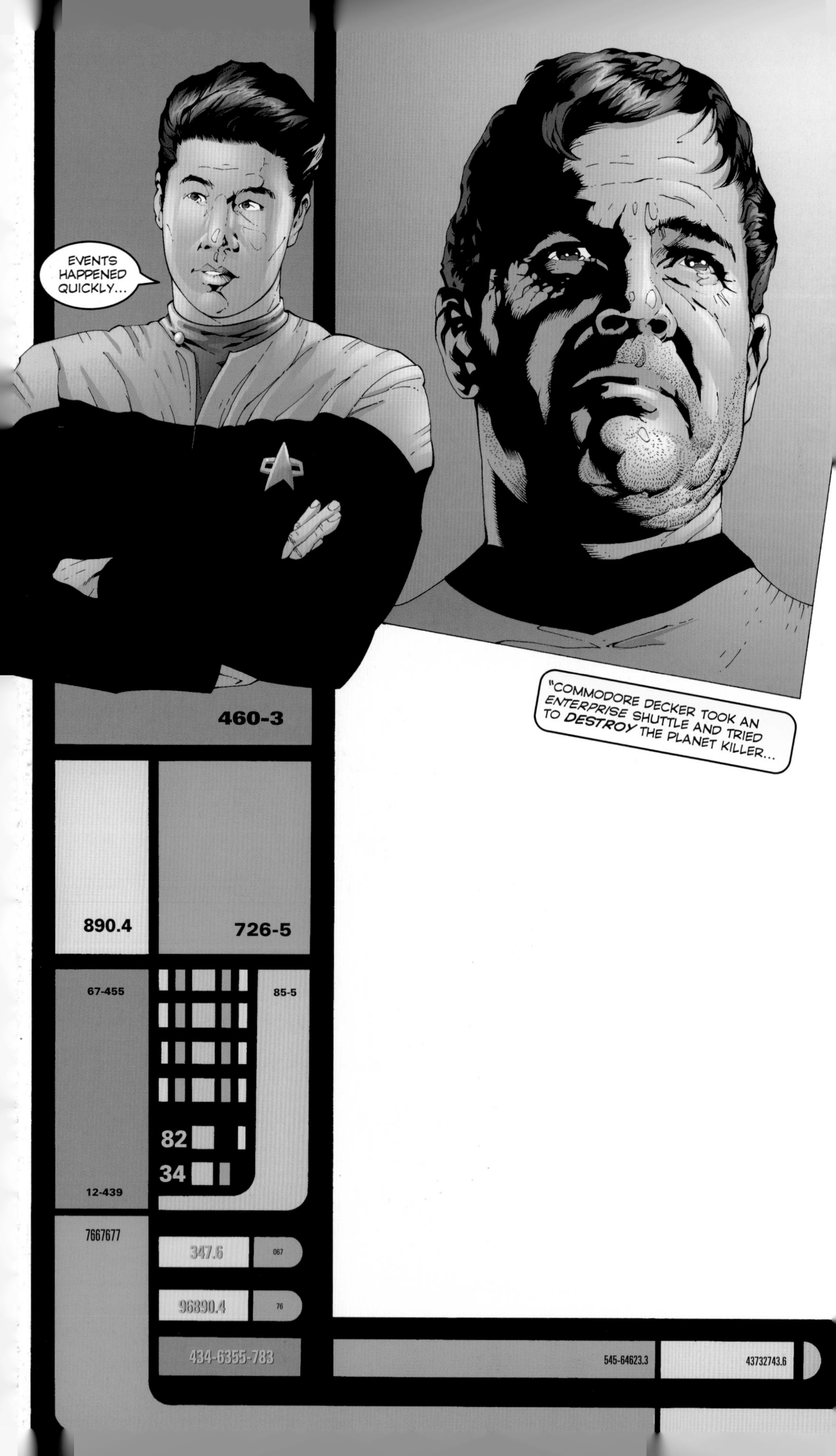
EVENTS HAPPENED QUICKLY...
"COMMODORE DECKER TOOK AN *ENTERPRISE* SHUTTLE AND TRIED TO ***DESTROY*** THE PLANET KILLER...
460-3
890.4
726-5
67-455
85-5
82
34
12-439
7667677
347.6
067
96890.4
76
434-6355-783
545-64623.3
43732743.6

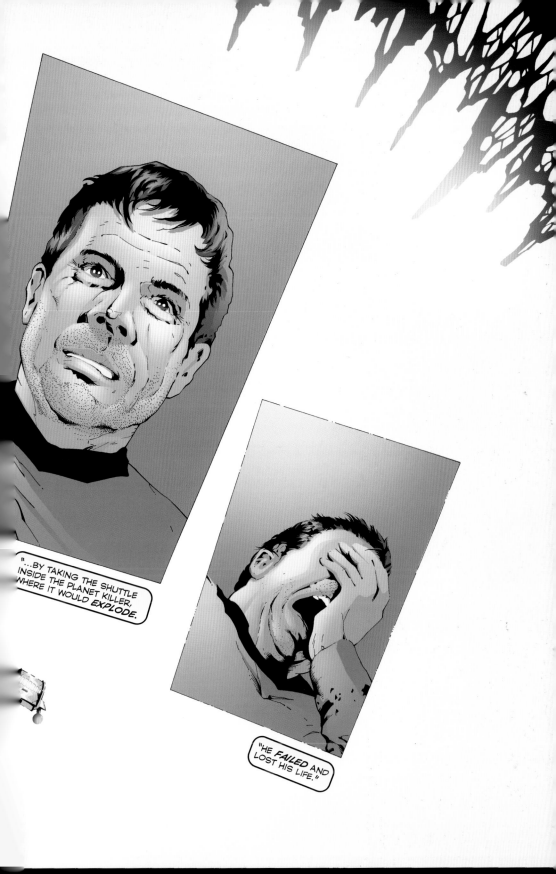

"...BY TAKING THE SHUTTLE INSIDE THE PLANET KILLER, WHERE IT WOULD *EXPLODE*.

"HE *FAILED* AND LOST HIS LIFE."

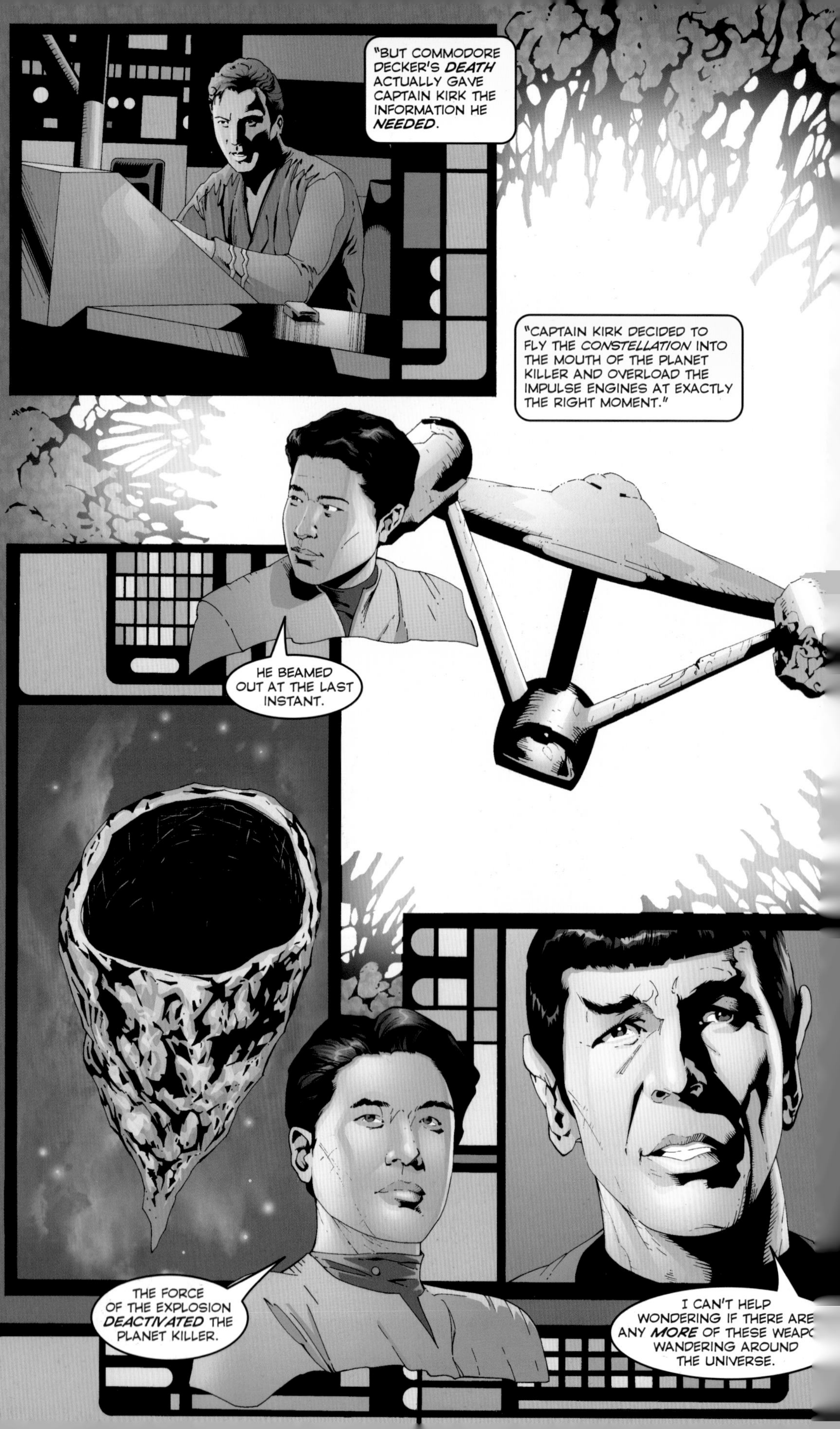
"BUT COMMODORE DECKER'S DEATH ACTUALLY GAVE CAPTAIN KIRK THE INFORMATION HE NEEDED.
"CAPTAIN KIRK DECIDED TO FLY THE CONSTELLATION INTO THE MOUTH OF THE PLANET KILLER AND OVERLOAD THE IMPULSE ENGINES AT EXACTLY THE RIGHT MOMENT."
HE BEAMED OUT AT THE LAST INSTANT.
THE FORCE OF THE EXPLOSION DEACTIVATED THE PLANET KILLER.
I CAN'T HELP WONDERING IF THERE ARE ANY MORE OF THESE WEAPO WANDERING AROUND THE UNIVERSE.

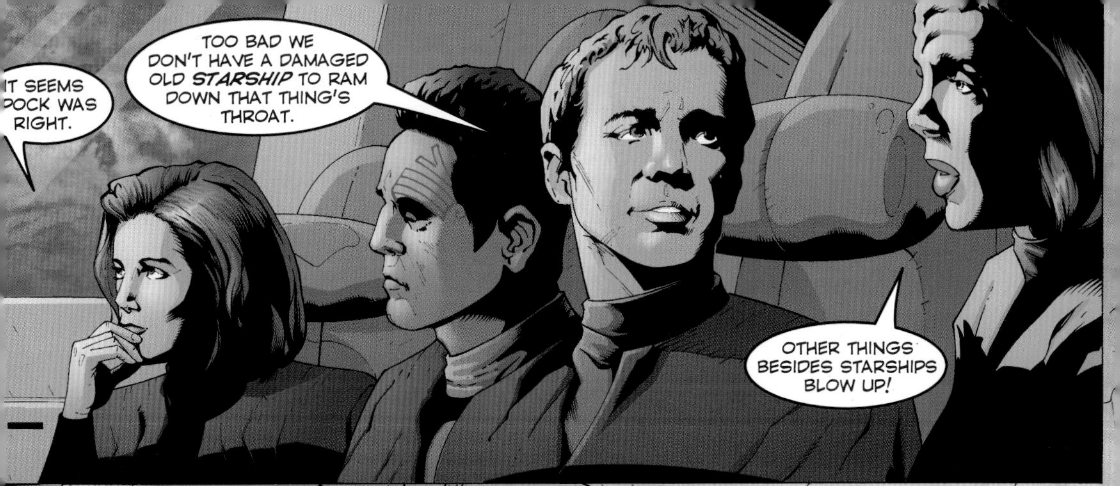
IT SEEMS POCK WAS RIGHT.
TOO BAD WE DON'T HAVE A DAMAGED OLD *STARSHIP* TO RAM DOWN THAT THING'S THROAT.
OTHER THINGS BESIDES STARSHIPS BLOW UP!

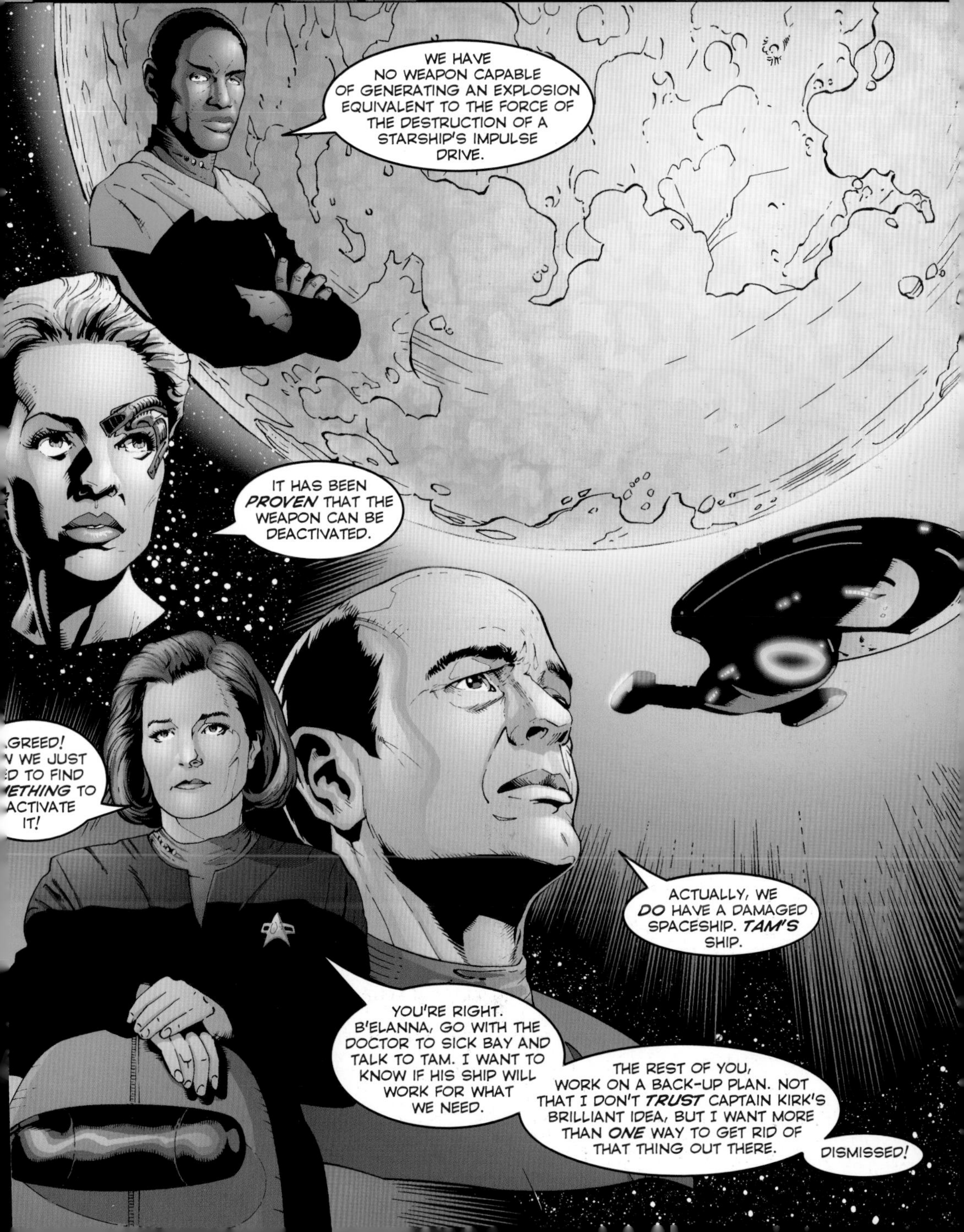
WE HAVE NO WEAPON CAPABLE OF GENERATING AN EXPLOSION EQUIVALENT TO THE FORCE OF THE DESTRUCTION OF A STARSHIP'S IMPULSE DRIVE.
IT HAS BEEN *PROVEN* THAT THE WEAPON CAN BE DEACTIVATED.
GREED! V WE JUST D TO FIND *METHING* TO ACTIVATE IT!
ACTUALLY, WE *DO* HAVE A DAMAGED SPACESHIP. *TAM'S* SHIP.
YOU'RE RIGHT. B'ELANNA, GO WITH THE DOCTOR TO SICK BAY AND TALK TO TAM. I WANT TO KNOW IF HIS SHIP WILL WORK FOR WHAT WE NEED.
THE REST OF YOU, WORK ON A BACK-UP PLAN. NOT THAT I DON'T *TRUST* CAPTAIN KIRK'S BRILLIANT IDEA, BUT I WANT MORE THAN *ONE* WAY TO GET RID OF THAT THING OUT THERE.
DISMISSED!

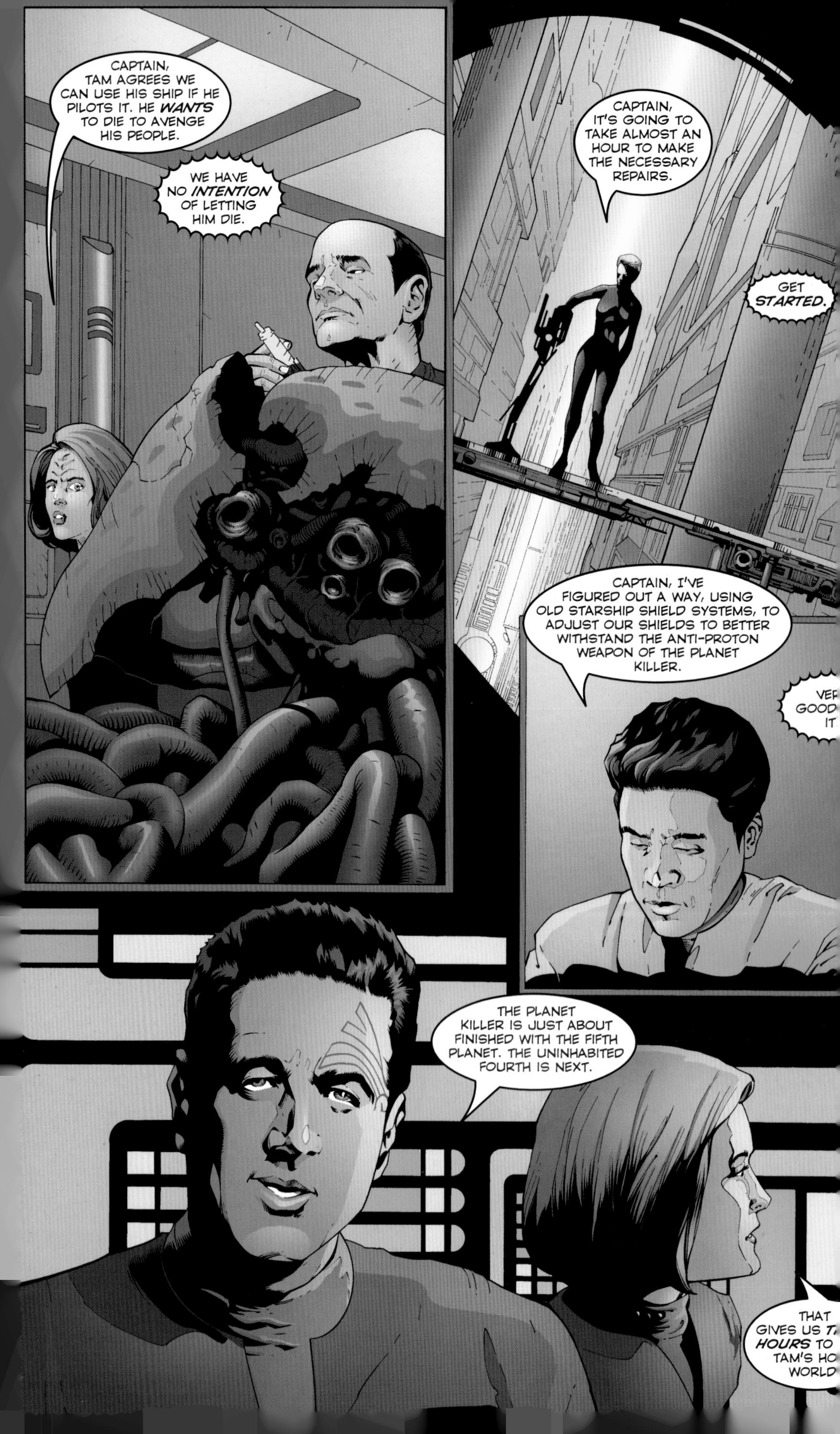
CAPTAIN, TAM AGREES WE CAN USE HIS SHIP IF HE PILOTS IT. HE *WANTS* TO DIE TO AVENGE HIS PEOPLE.
WE HAVE NO *INTENTION* OF LETTING HIM DIE.
CAPTAIN, IT'S GOING TO TAKE ALMOST AN HOUR TO MAKE THE NECESSARY REPAIRS.
GET *STARTED.*
CAPTAIN, I'VE FIGURED OUT A WAY, USING OLD STARSHIP SHIELD SYSTEMS, TO ADJUST OUR SHIELDS TO BETTER WITHSTAND THE ANTI-PROTON WEAPON OF THE PLANET KILLER.
VER GOOD IT
THE PLANET KILLER IS JUST ABOUT FINISHED WITH THE FIFTH PLANET. THE UNINHABITED FOURTH IS NEXT.
THAT GIVES US *T* *HOURS* TO TAM'S HO WORLD

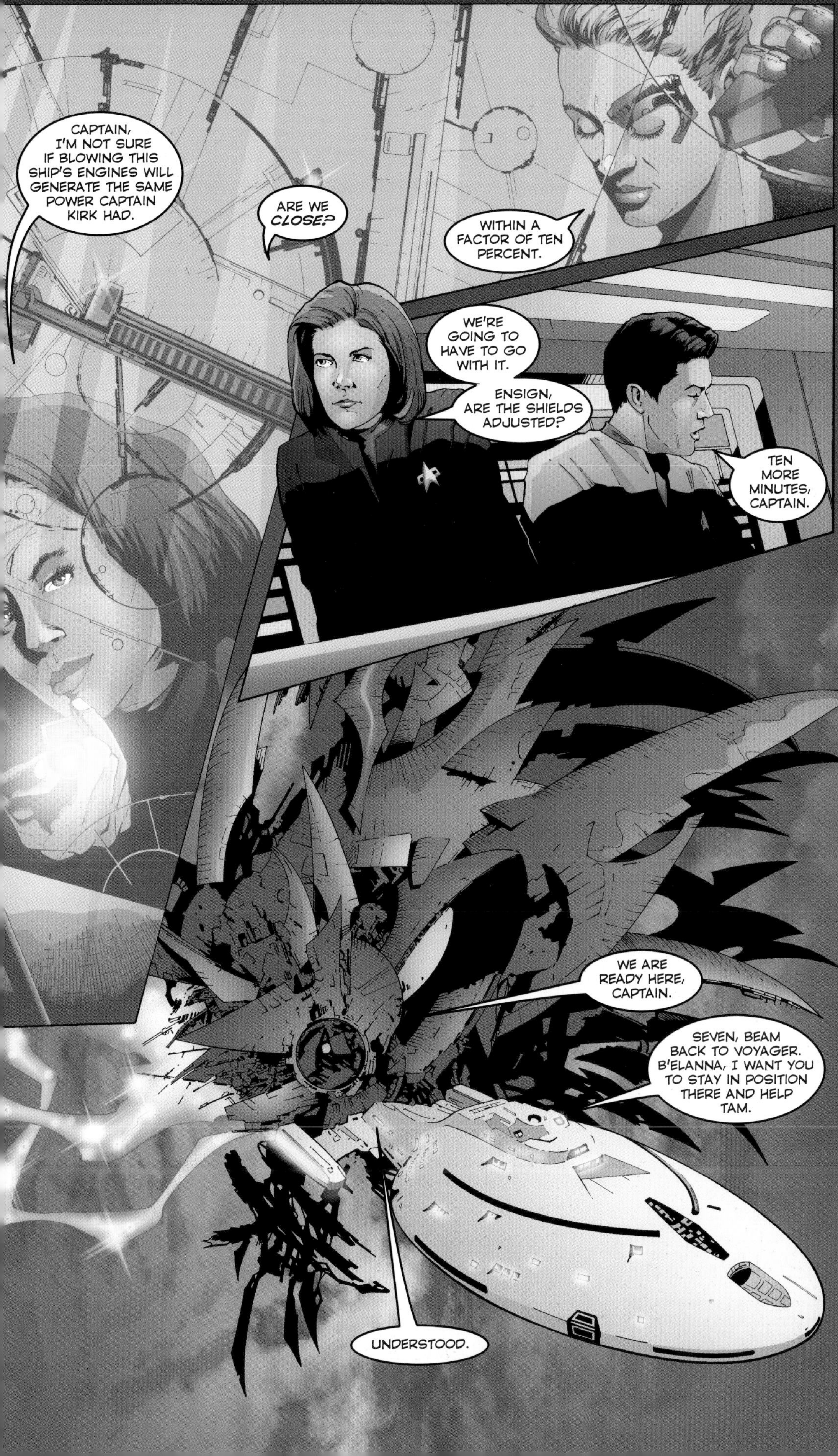
CAPTAIN, I'M NOT SURE IF BLOWING THIS SHIP'S ENGINES WILL GENERATE THE SAME POWER CAPTAIN KIRK HAD.
ARE WE *CLOSE?*
WITHIN A FACTOR OF TEN PERCENT.
WE'RE GOING TO HAVE TO GO WITH IT.
ENSIGN, ARE THE SHIELDS ADJUSTED?
TEN MORE MINUTES, CAPTAIN.
WE ARE READY HERE, CAPTAIN.
SEVEN, BEAM BACK TO VOYAGER. B'ELANNA, I WANT YOU TO STAY IN POSITION THERE AND HELP TAM.
UNDERSTOOD.

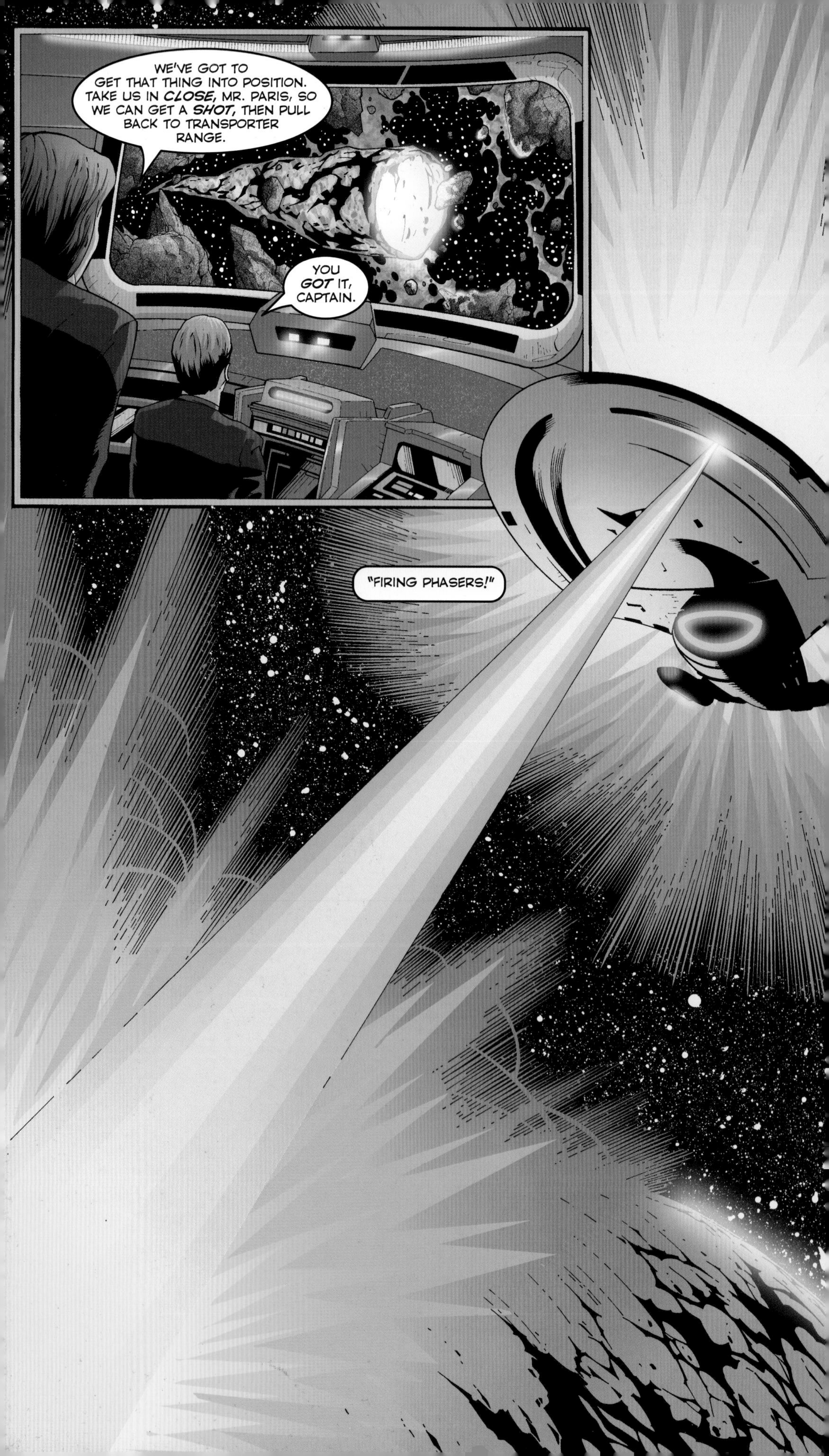
WE'VE GOT TO GET THAT THING INTO POSITION. TAKE US IN CLOSE, MR. PARIS, SO WE CAN GET A SHOT, THEN PULL BACK TO TRANSPORTER RANGE.
YOU GOT IT, CAPTAIN.
"FIRING PHASERS!"

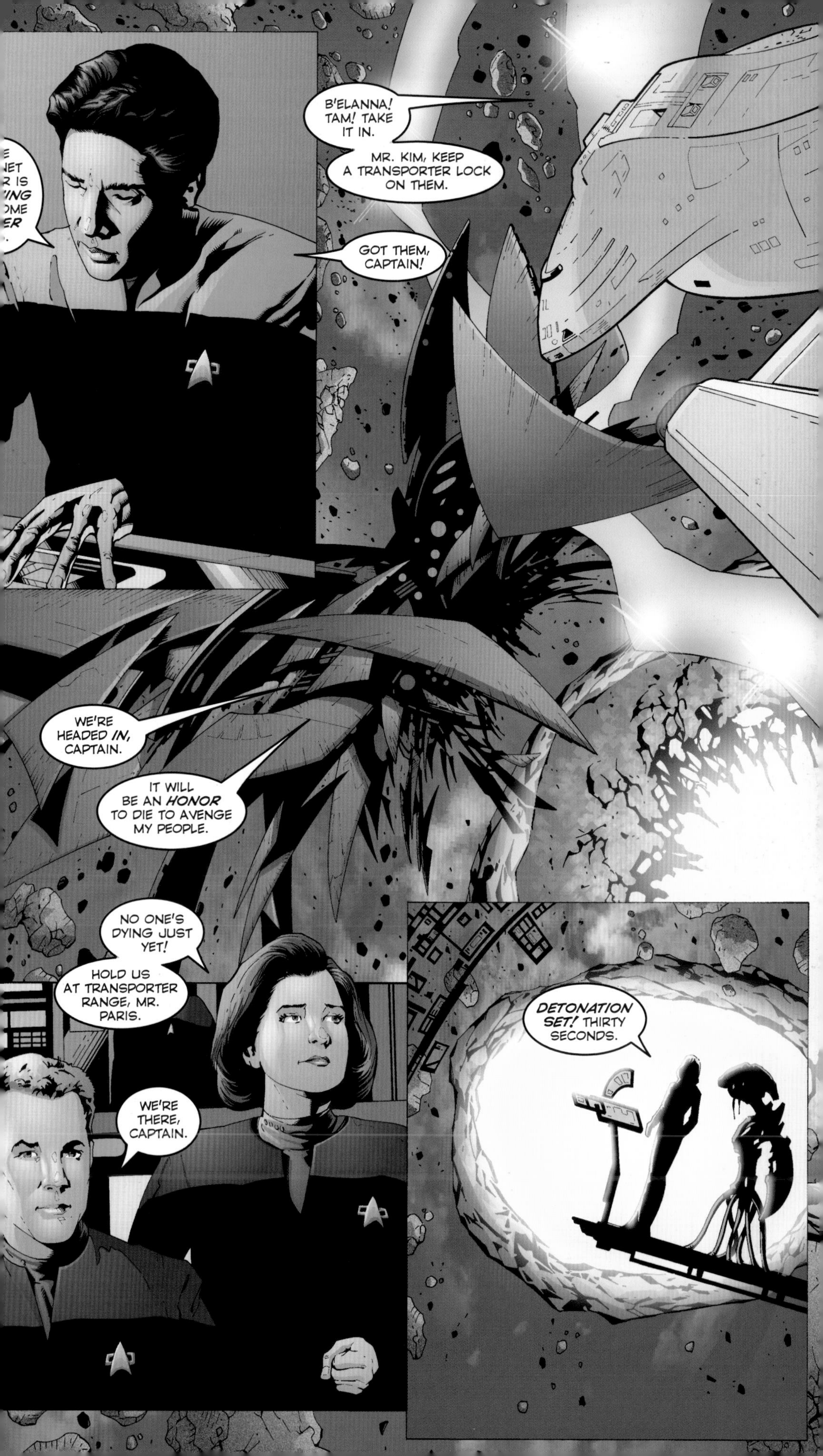
B'ELANNA! TAM! TAKE IT IN.
MR. KIM, KEEP A TRANSPORTER LOCK ON THEM.
GOT THEM, CAPTAIN!
WE'RE HEADED IN, CAPTAIN.
IT WILL BE AN HONOR TO DIE TO AVENGE MY PEOPLE.
NO ONE'S DYING JUST YET!
HOLD US AT TRANSPORTER RANGE, MR. PARIS.
WE'RE THERE, CAPTAIN.
DETONATION SET! THIRTY SECONDS.

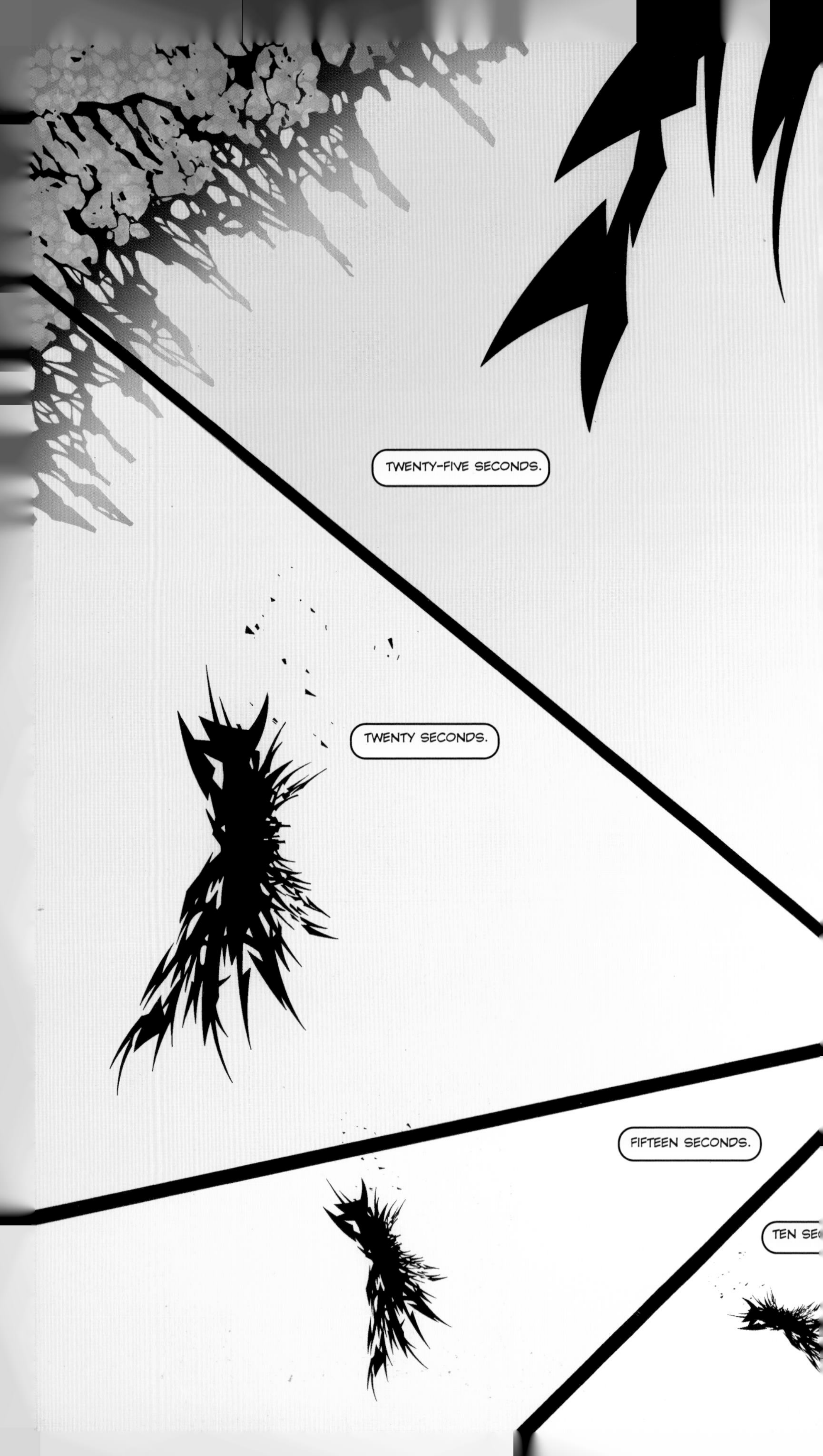
TWENTY-FIVE SECONDS.
TWENTY SECONDS.
FIFTEEN SECONDS.

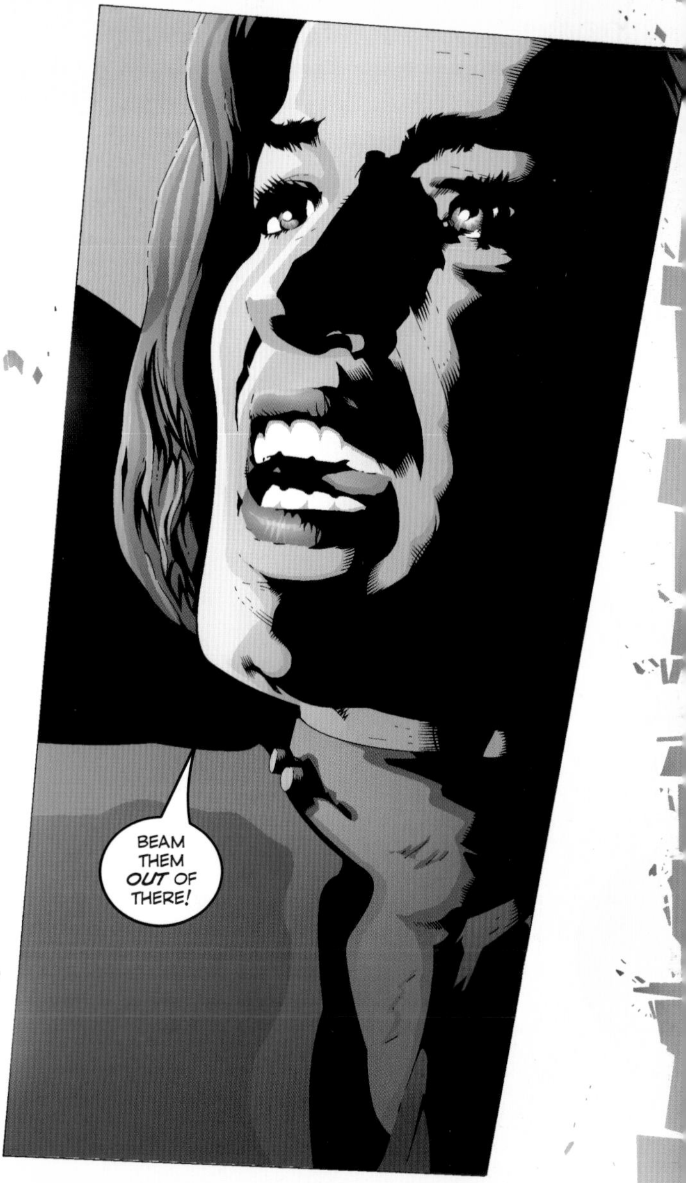
BEAM THEM OUT OF THERE!

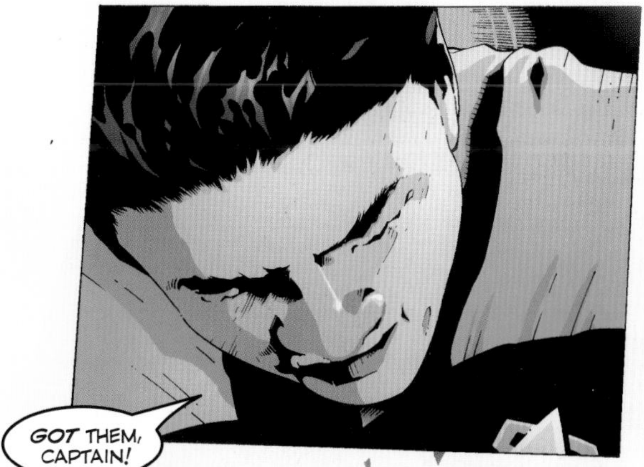
GOT THEM, CAPTAIN!

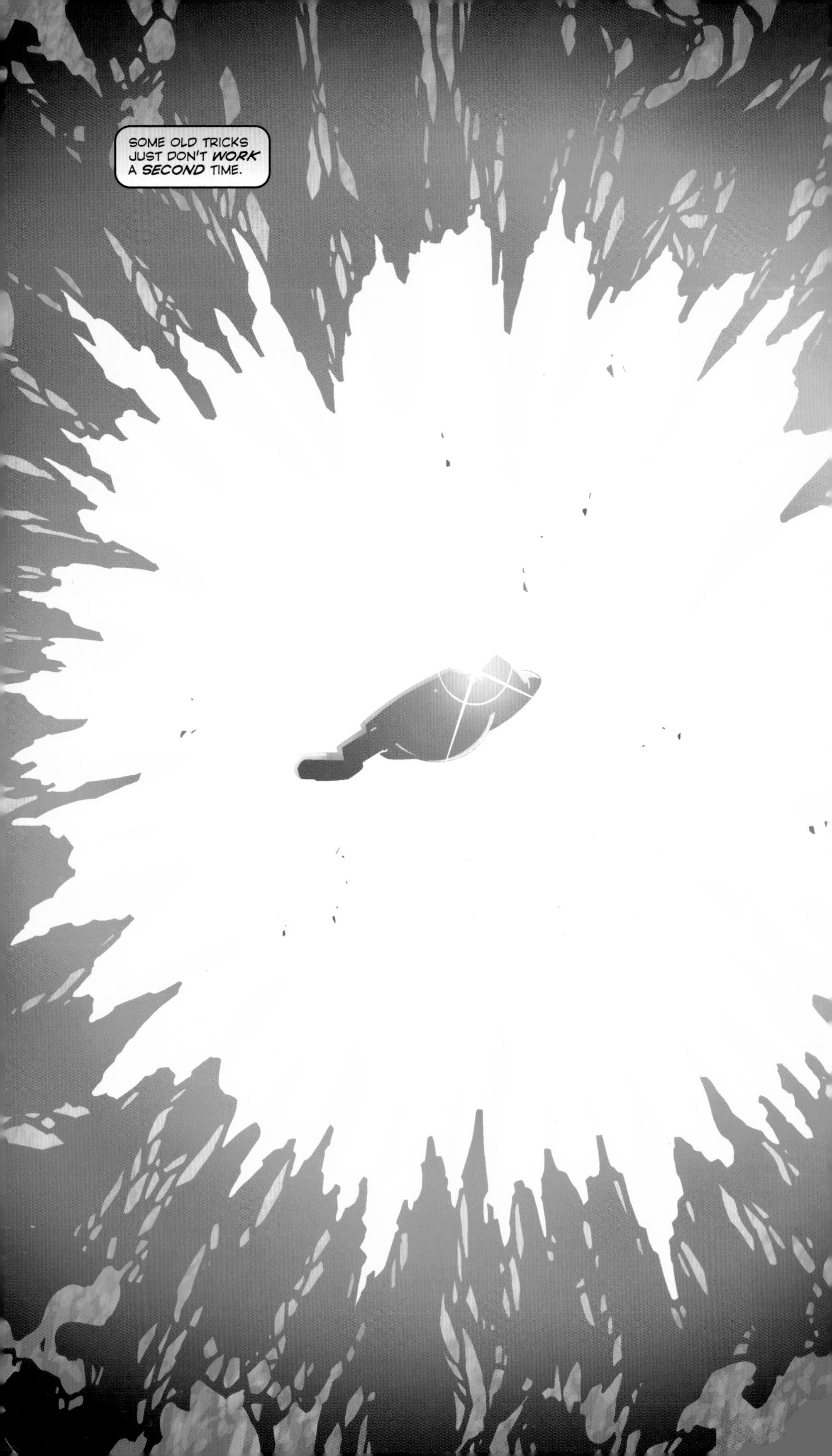
SOME OLD TRICKS JUST DON'T *WORK* A *SECOND* TIME.

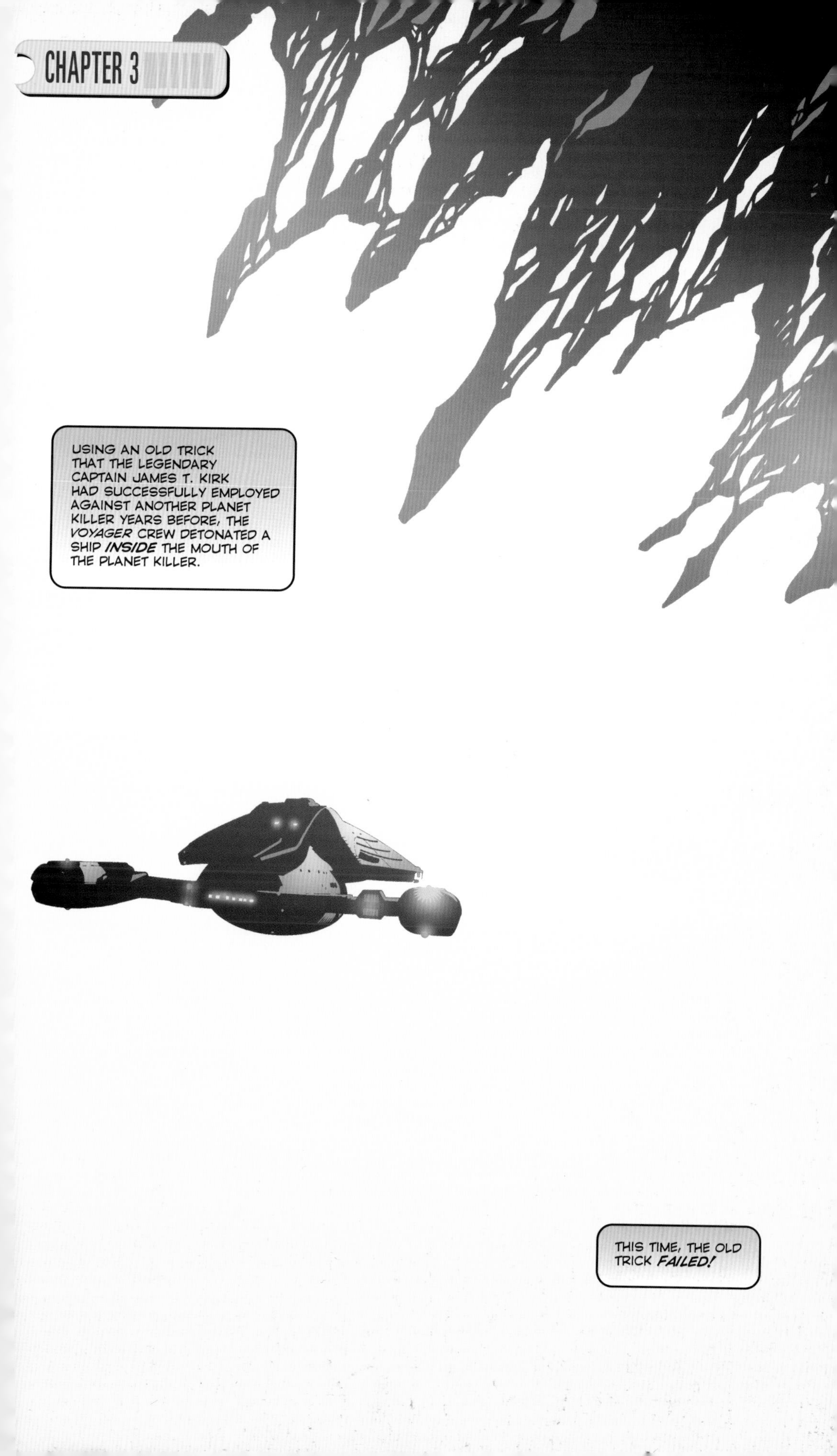
CHAPTER 3
USING AN OLD TRICK THAT THE LEGENDARY CAPTAIN JAMES T. KIRK HAD SUCCESSFULLY EMPLOYED AGAINST ANOTHER PLANET KILLER YEARS BEFORE, THE VOYAGER CREW DETONATED A SHIP INSIDE THE MOUTH OF THE PLANET KILLER.
THIS TIME, THE OLD TRICK FAILED!

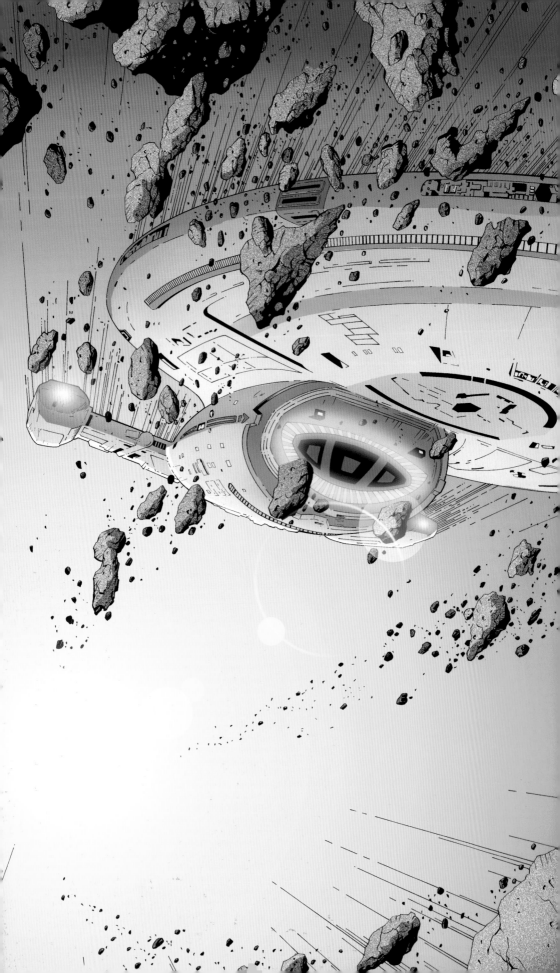

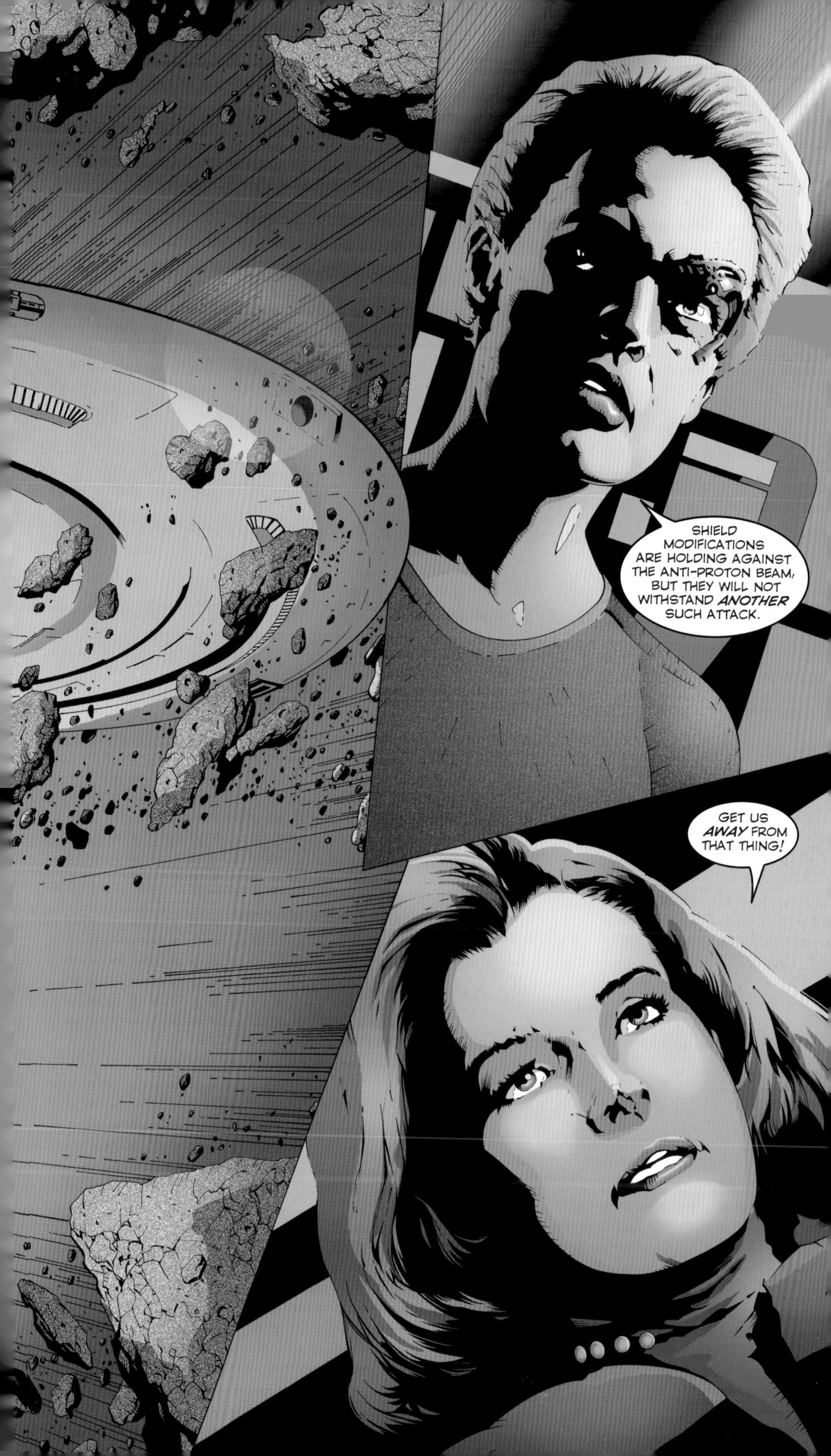
SHIELD MODIFICATIONS ARE HOLDING AGAINST THE ANTI-PROTON BEAM, BUT THEY WILL NOT WITHSTAND *ANOTHER* SUCH ATTACK.
GET US *AWAY* FROM THAT THING!

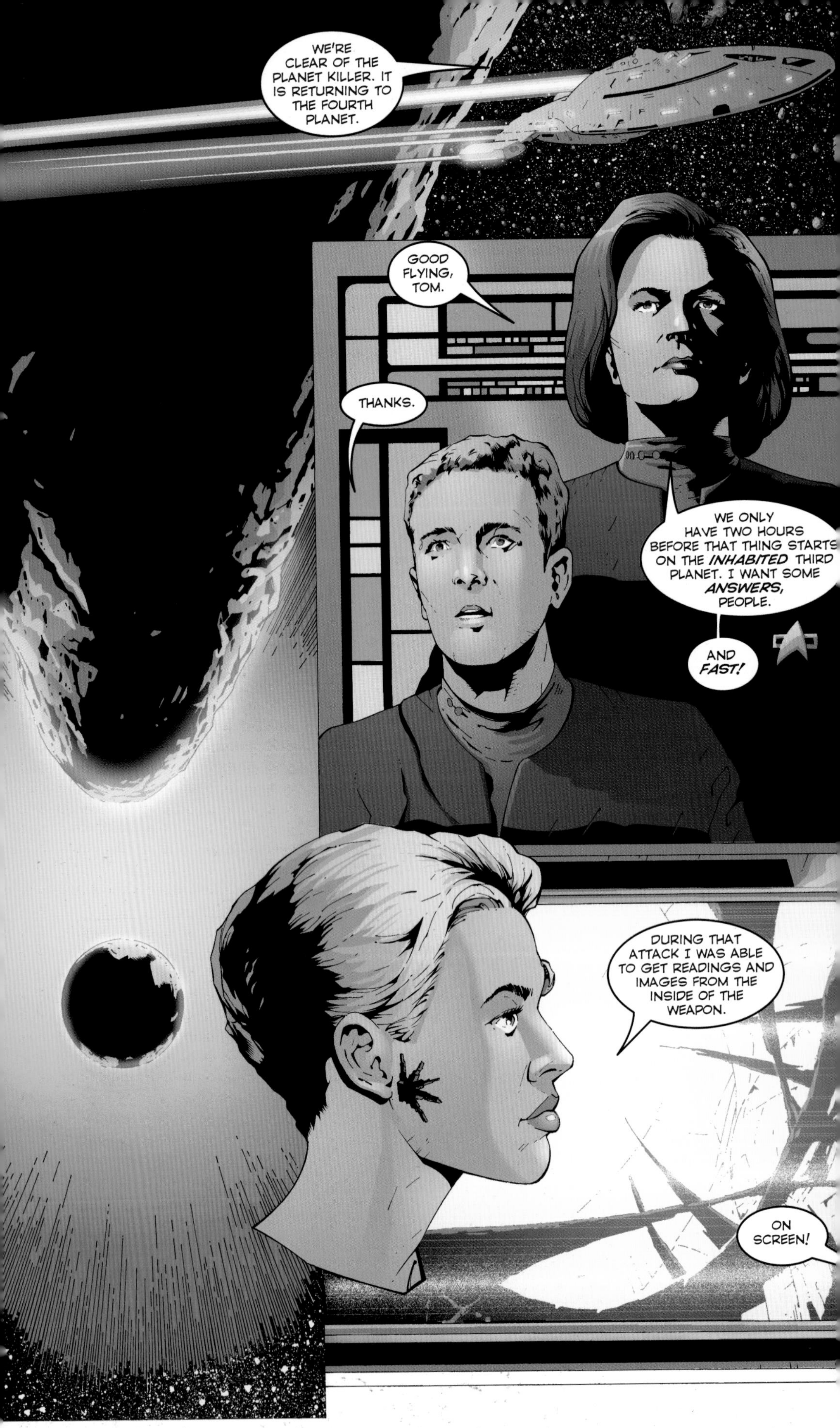
WE'RE CLEAR OF THE PLANET KILLER. IT IS RETURNING TO THE FOURTH PLANET.
GOOD FLYING, TOM.
THANKS.
WE ONLY HAVE TWO HOURS BEFORE THAT THING STARTS ON THE *INHABITED* THIRD PLANET. I WANT SOME *ANSWERS,* PEOPLE.
AND *FAST!*
DURING THAT ATTACK I WAS ABLE TO GET READINGS AND IMAGES FROM THE INSIDE OF THE WEAPON.
ON SCREEN!

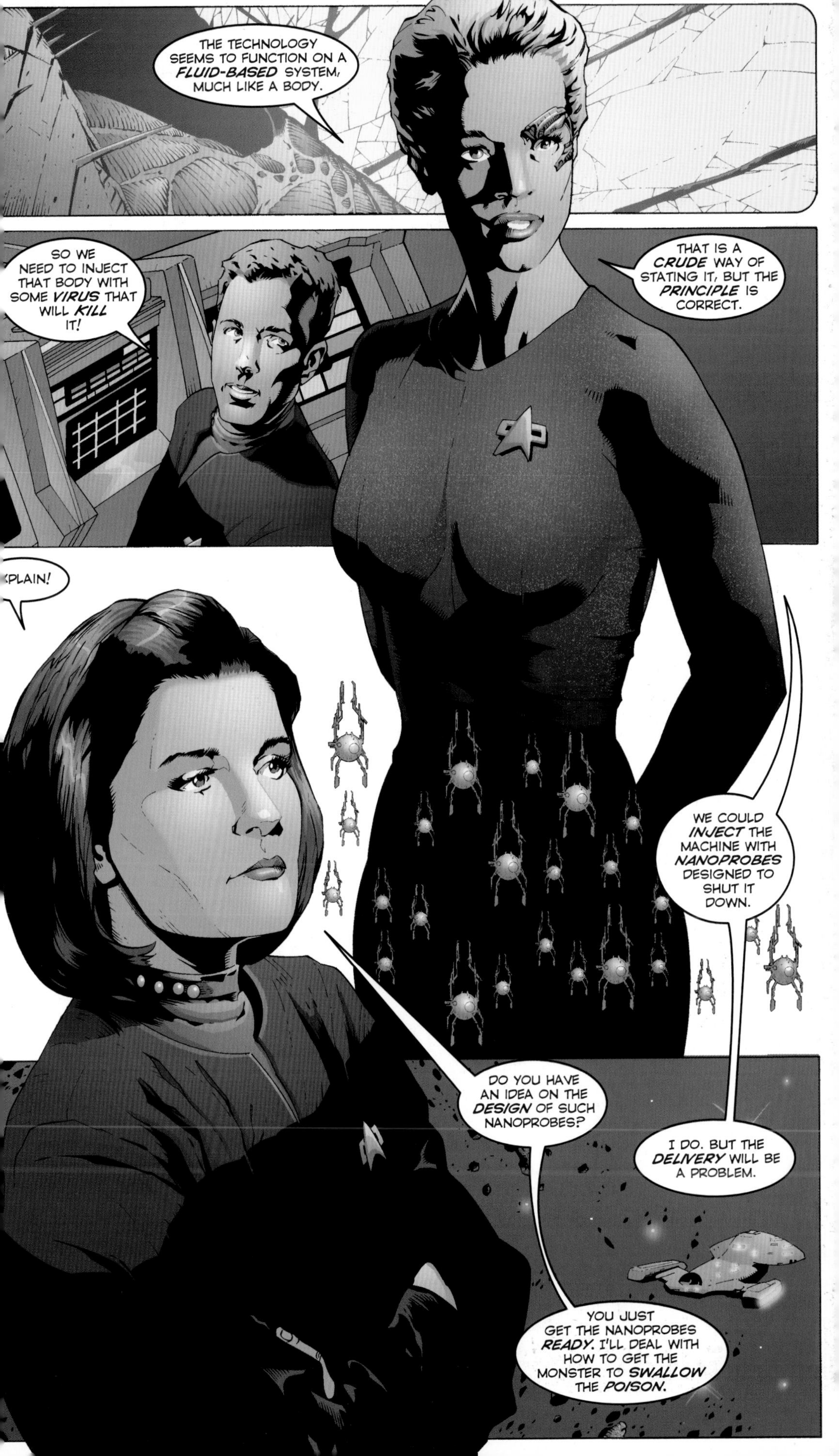
THE TECHNOLOGY SEEMS TO FUNCTION ON A FLUID-BASED SYSTEM, MUCH LIKE A BODY.
SO WE NEED TO INJECT THAT BODY WITH SOME VIRUS THAT WILL KILL IT!
THAT IS A CRUDE WAY OF STATING IT, BUT THE PRINCIPLE IS CORRECT.
XPLAIN!
WE COULD INJECT THE MACHINE WITH NANOPROBES DESIGNED TO SHUT IT DOWN.
DO YOU HAVE AN IDEA ON THE DESIGN OF SUCH NANOPROBES?
I DO. BUT THE DELIVERY WILL BE A PROBLEM.
YOU JUST GET THE NANOPROBES READY. I'LL DEAL WITH HOW TO GET THE MONSTER TO SWALLOW THE POISON.

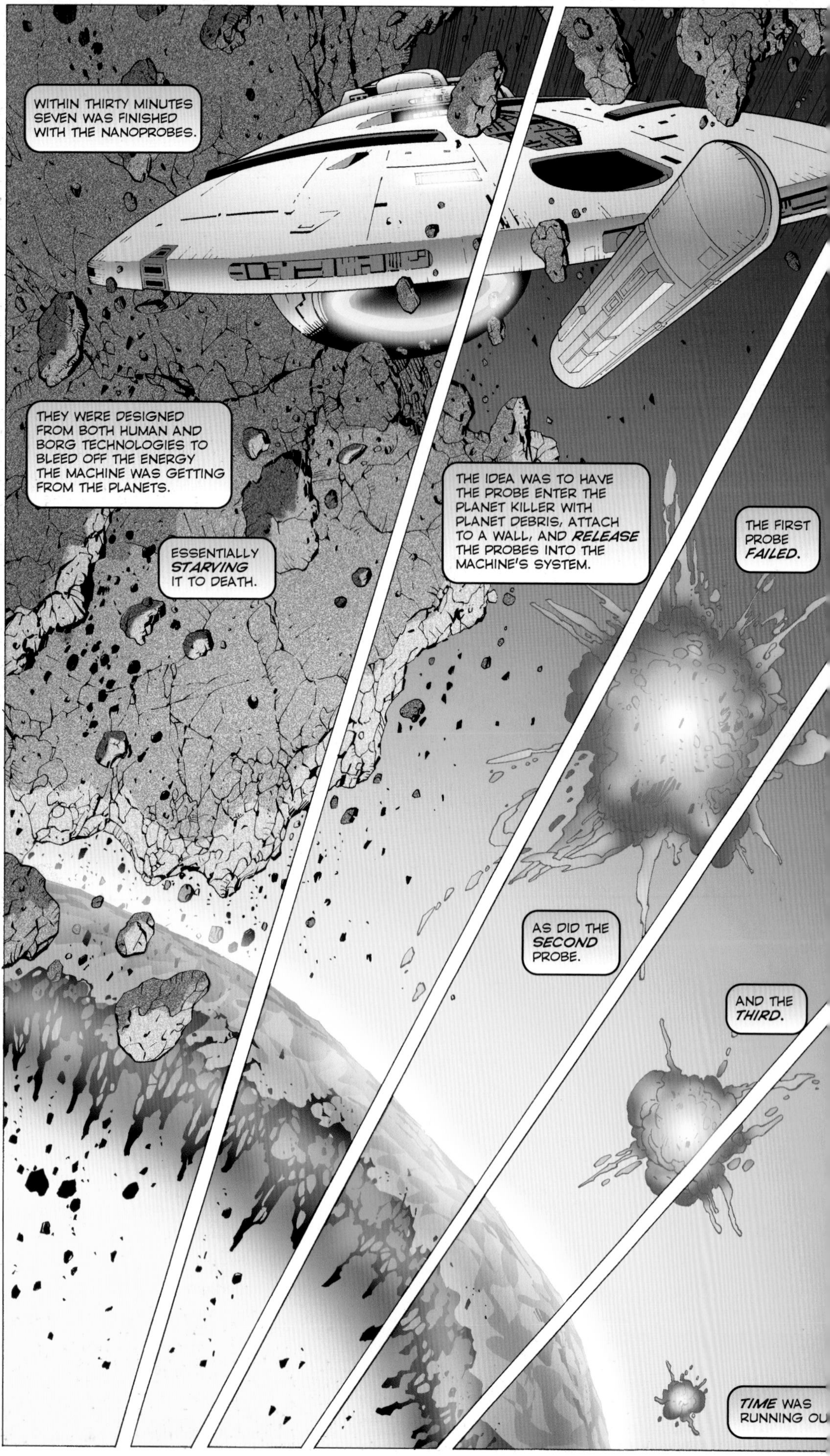

WITHIN THIRTY MINUTES SEVEN WAS FINISHED WITH THE NANOPROBES.
THEY WERE DESIGNED FROM BOTH HUMAN AND BORG TECHNOLOGIES TO BLEED OFF THE ENERGY THE MACHINE WAS GETTING FROM THE PLANETS.
ESSENTIALLY *STARVING* IT TO DEATH.
THE IDEA WAS TO HAVE THE PROBE ENTER THE PLANET KILLER WITH PLANET DEBRIS, ATTACH TO A WALL, AND *RELEASE* THE PROBES INTO THE MACHINE'S SYSTEM.
THE FIRST PROBE *FAILED*.
AS DID THE *SECOND* PROBE.
AND THE *THIRD*.
TIME WAS RUNNING OU

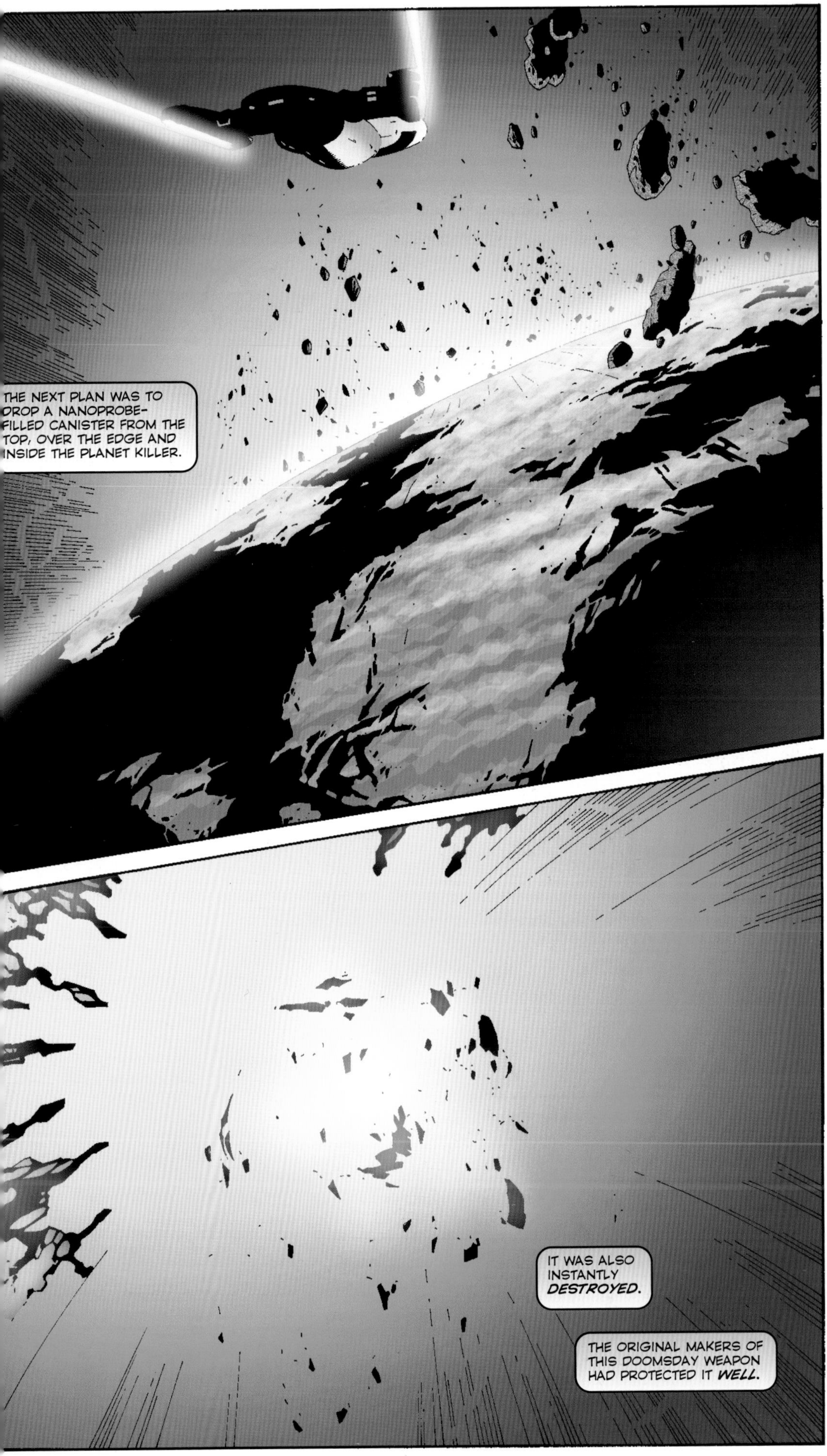
THE NEXT PLAN WAS TO DROP A NANOPROBE-FILLED CANISTER FROM THE TOP, OVER THE EDGE AND INSIDE THE PLANET KILLER.
IT WAS ALSO INSTANTLY *DESTROYED*.
THE ORIGINAL MAKERS OF THIS DOOMSDAY WEAPON HAD PROTECTED IT *WELL*.

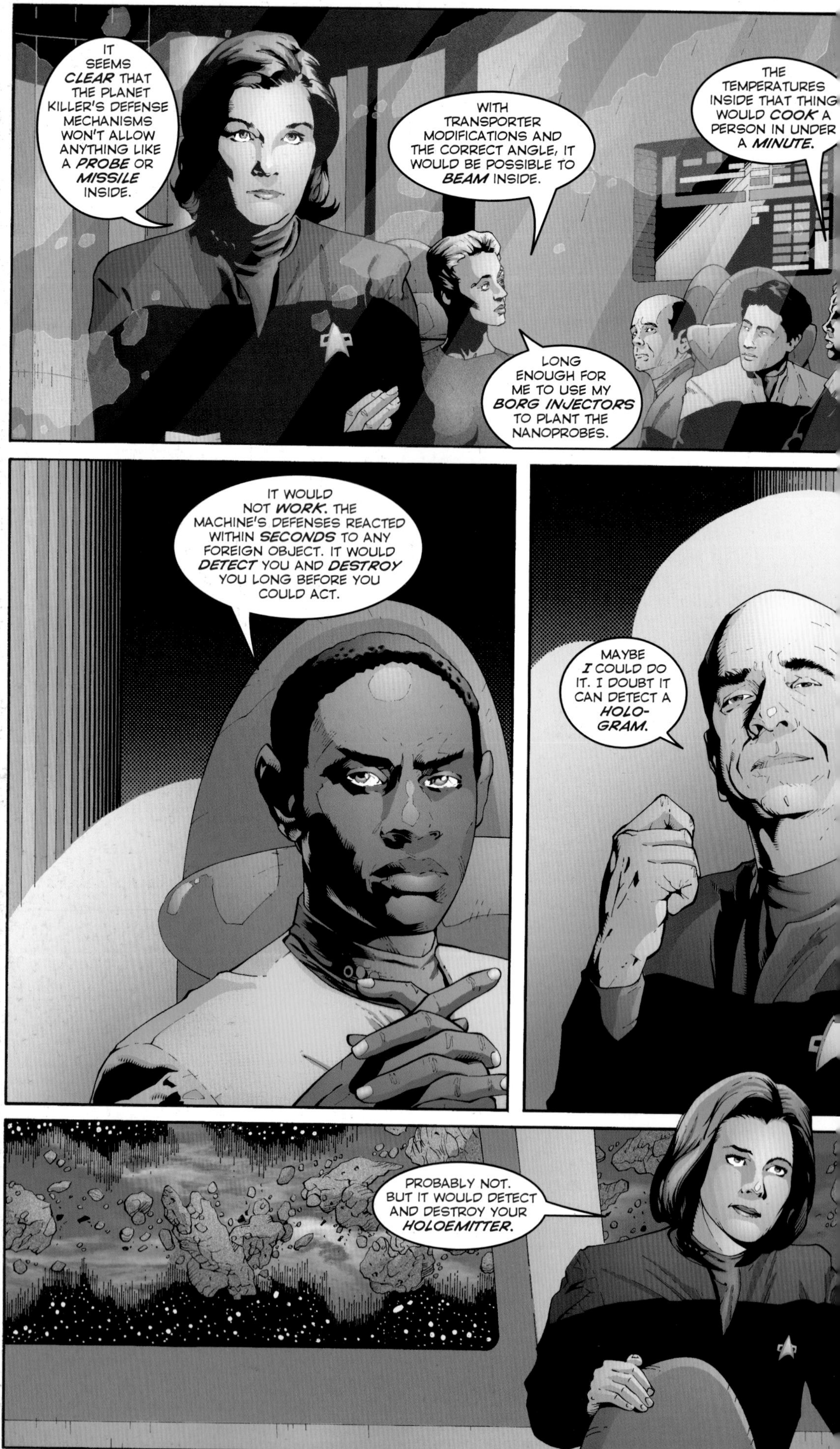
IT SEEMS CLEAR THAT THE PLANET KILLER'S DEFENSE MECHANISMS WON'T ALLOW ANYTHING LIKE A PROBE OR MISSILE INSIDE.
WITH TRANSPORTER MODIFICATIONS AND THE CORRECT ANGLE, IT WOULD BE POSSIBLE TO BEAM INSIDE.
THE TEMPERATURES INSIDE THAT THING WOULD COOK A PERSON IN UNDER A MINUTE.
LONG ENOUGH FOR ME TO USE MY BORG INJECTORS TO PLANT THE NANOPROBES.
IT WOULD NOT WORK. THE MACHINE'S DEFENSES REACTED WITHIN SECONDS TO ANY FOREIGN OBJECT. IT WOULD DETECT YOU AND DESTROY YOU LONG BEFORE YOU COULD ACT.
MAYBE I COULD DO IT. I DOUBT IT CAN DETECT A HOLOGRAM.
PROBABLY NOT. BUT IT WOULD DETECT AND DESTROY YOUR HOLOEMITTER.

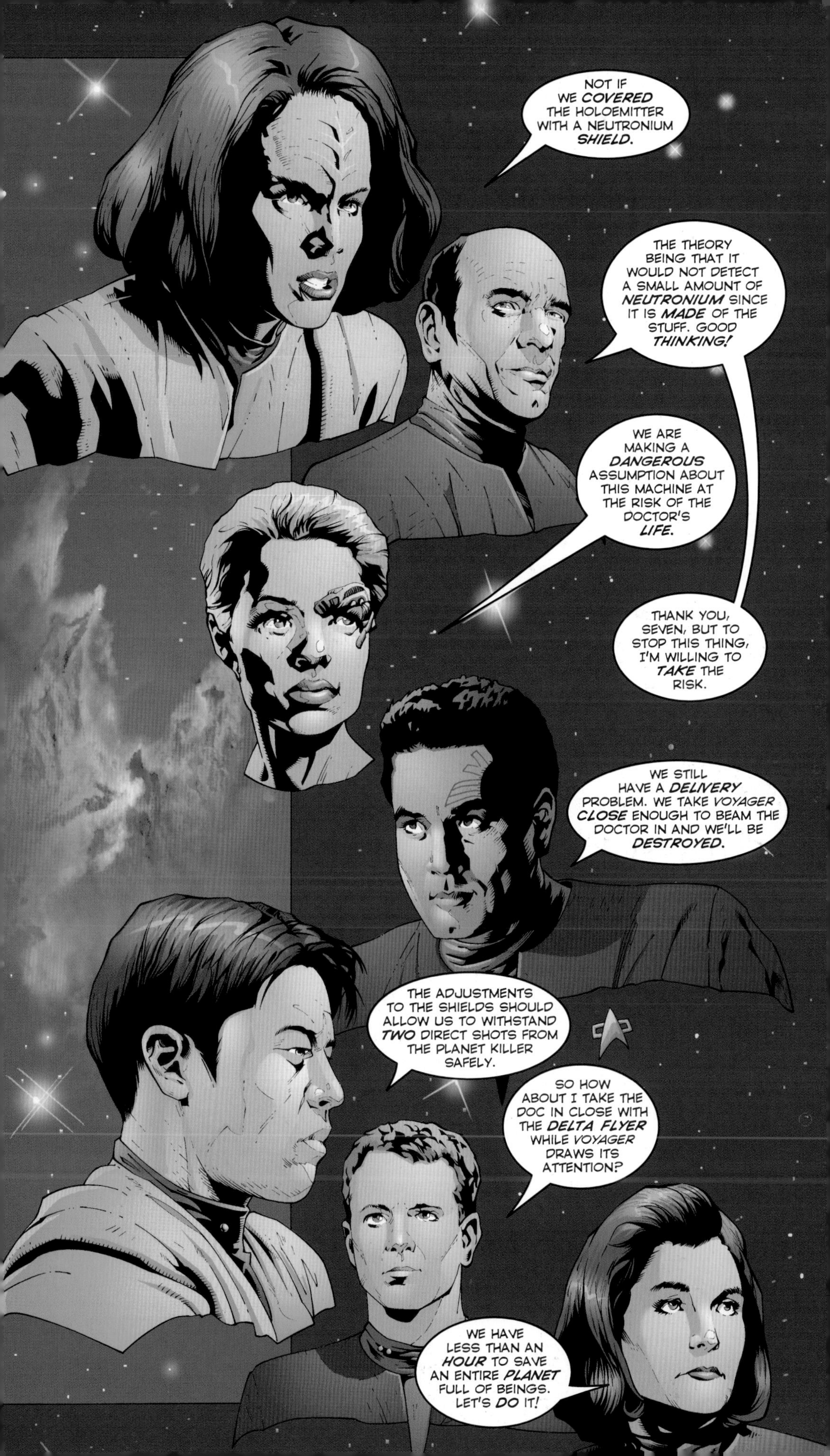
NOT IF WE COVERED THE HOLOEMITTER WITH A NEUTRONIUM SHIELD.
THE THEORY BEING THAT IT WOULD NOT DETECT A SMALL AMOUNT OF NEUTRONIUM SINCE IT IS MADE OF THE STUFF. GOOD THINKING!
WE ARE MAKING A DANGEROUS ASSUMPTION ABOUT THIS MACHINE AT THE RISK OF THE DOCTOR'S LIFE.
THANK YOU, SEVEN, BUT TO STOP THIS THING, I'M WILLING TO TAKE THE RISK.
WE STILL HAVE A DELIVERY PROBLEM. WE TAKE VOYAGER CLOSE ENOUGH TO BEAM THE DOCTOR IN AND WE'LL BE DESTROYED.
THE ADJUSTMENTS TO THE SHIELDS SHOULD ALLOW US TO WITHSTAND TWO DIRECT SHOTS FROM THE PLANET KILLER SAFELY.
SO HOW ABOUT I TAKE THE DOC IN CLOSE WITH THE DELTA FLYER WHILE VOYAGER DRAWS ITS ATTENTION?
WE HAVE LESS THAN AN HOUR TO SAVE AN ENTIRE PLANET FULL OF BEINGS. LET'S DO IT!

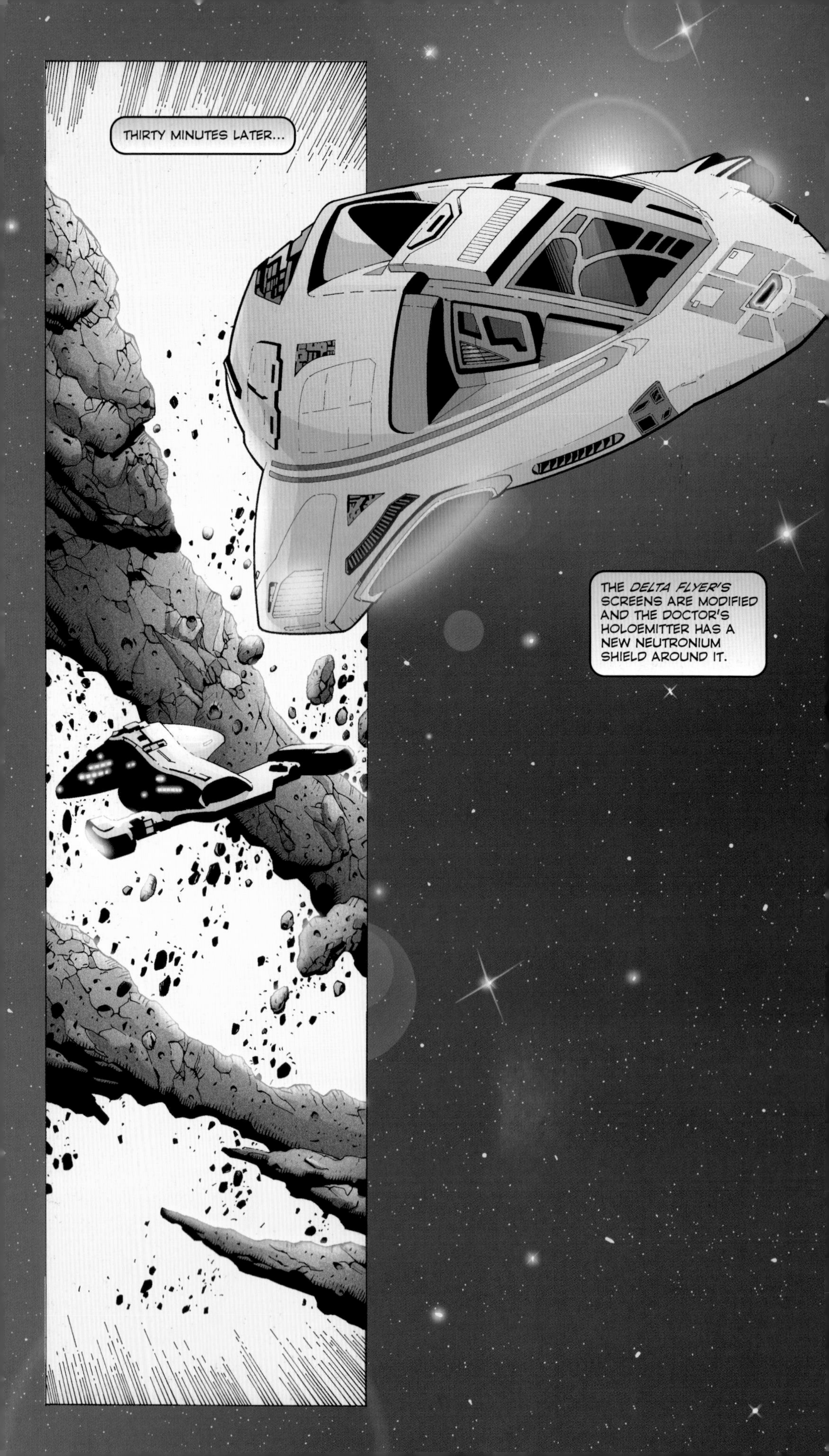
THIRTY MINUTES LATER...
THE *DELTA FLYER'S* SCREENS ARE MODIFIED AND THE DOCTOR'S HOLOEMITTER HAS A NEW NEUTRONIUM SHIELD AROUND IT.

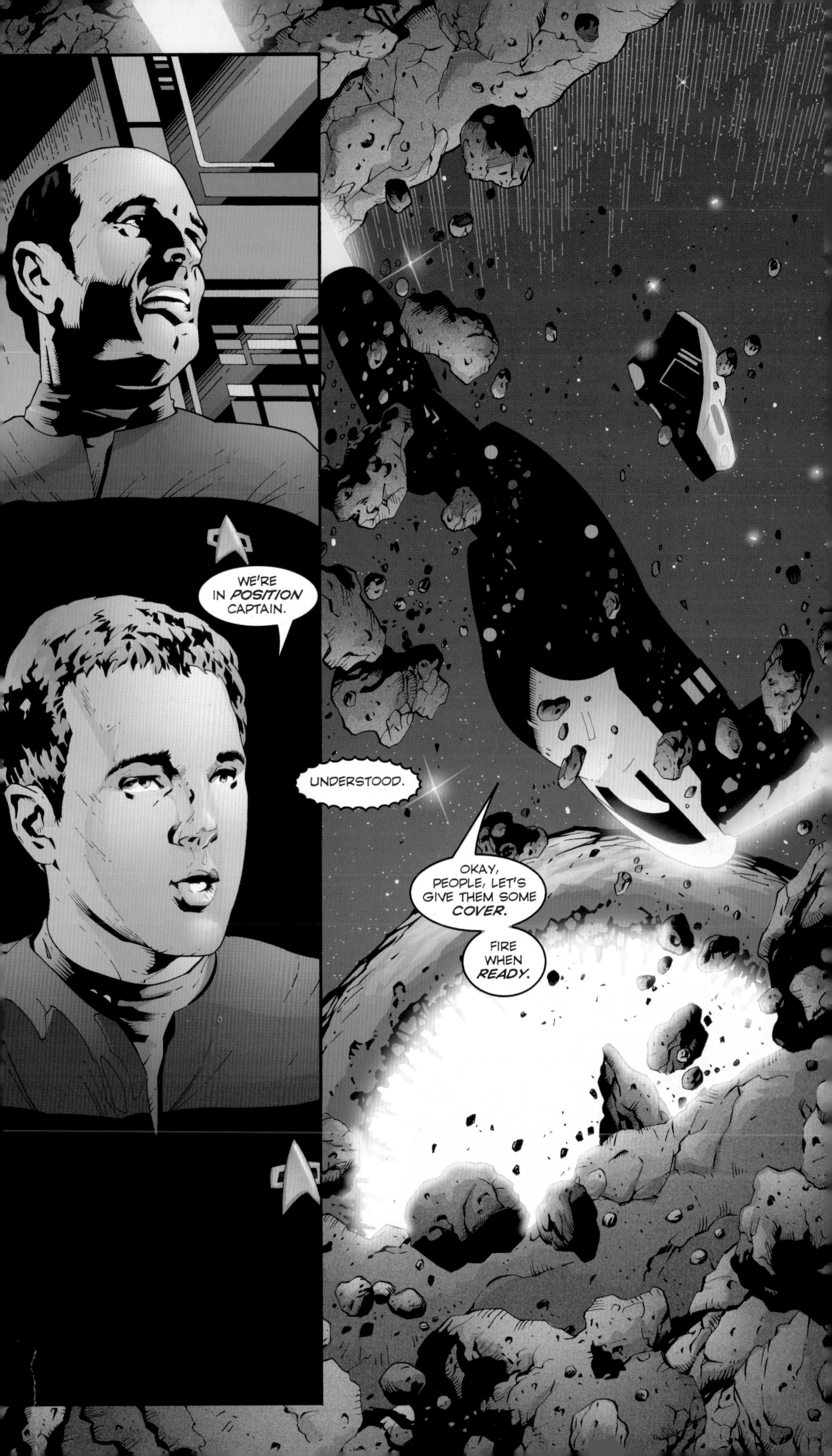
WE'RE IN *POSITION* CAPTAIN.
UNDERSTOOD.
OKAY, PEOPLE, LET'S GIVE THEM SOME *COVER*.
FIRE WHEN *READY*.

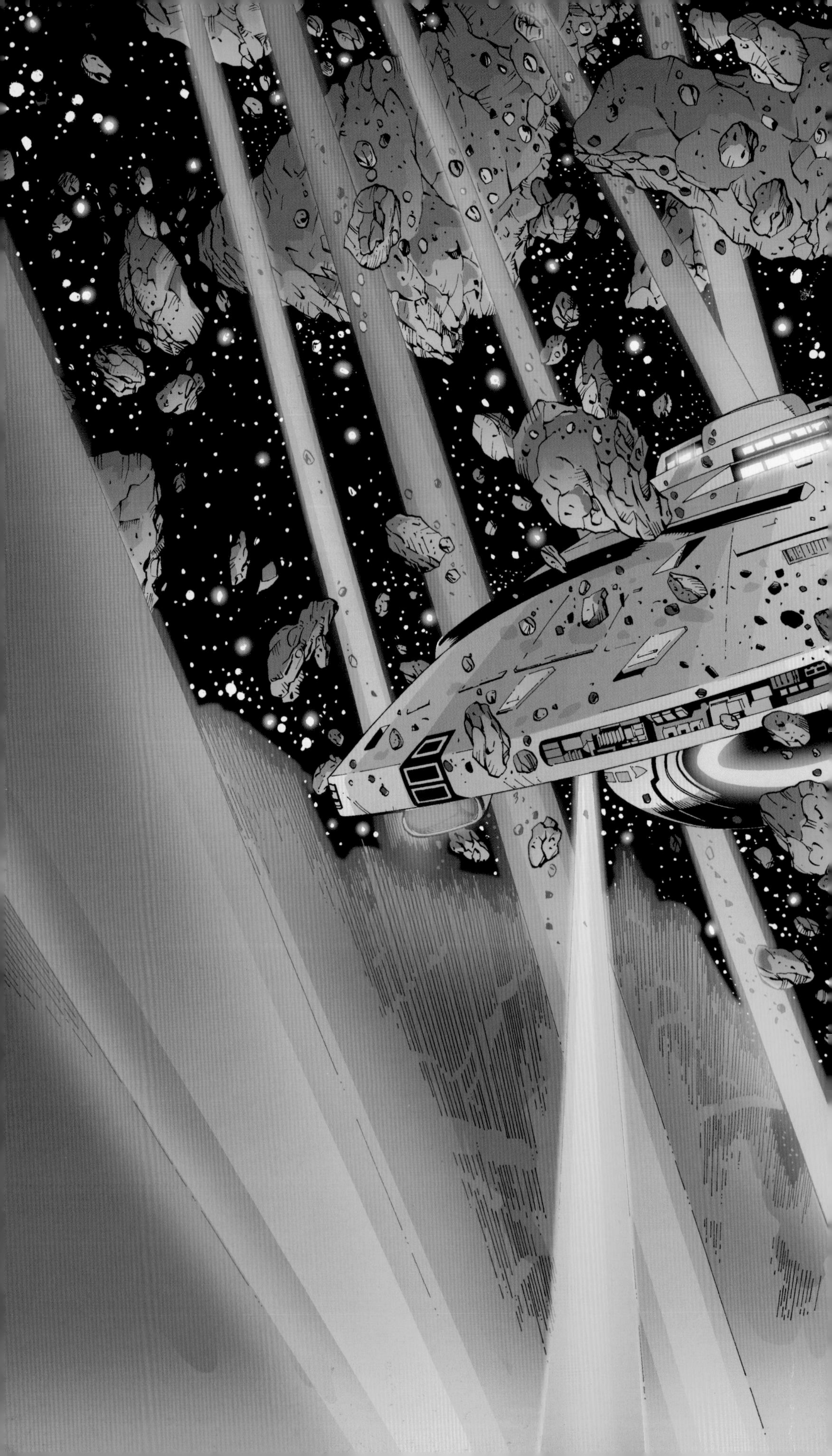

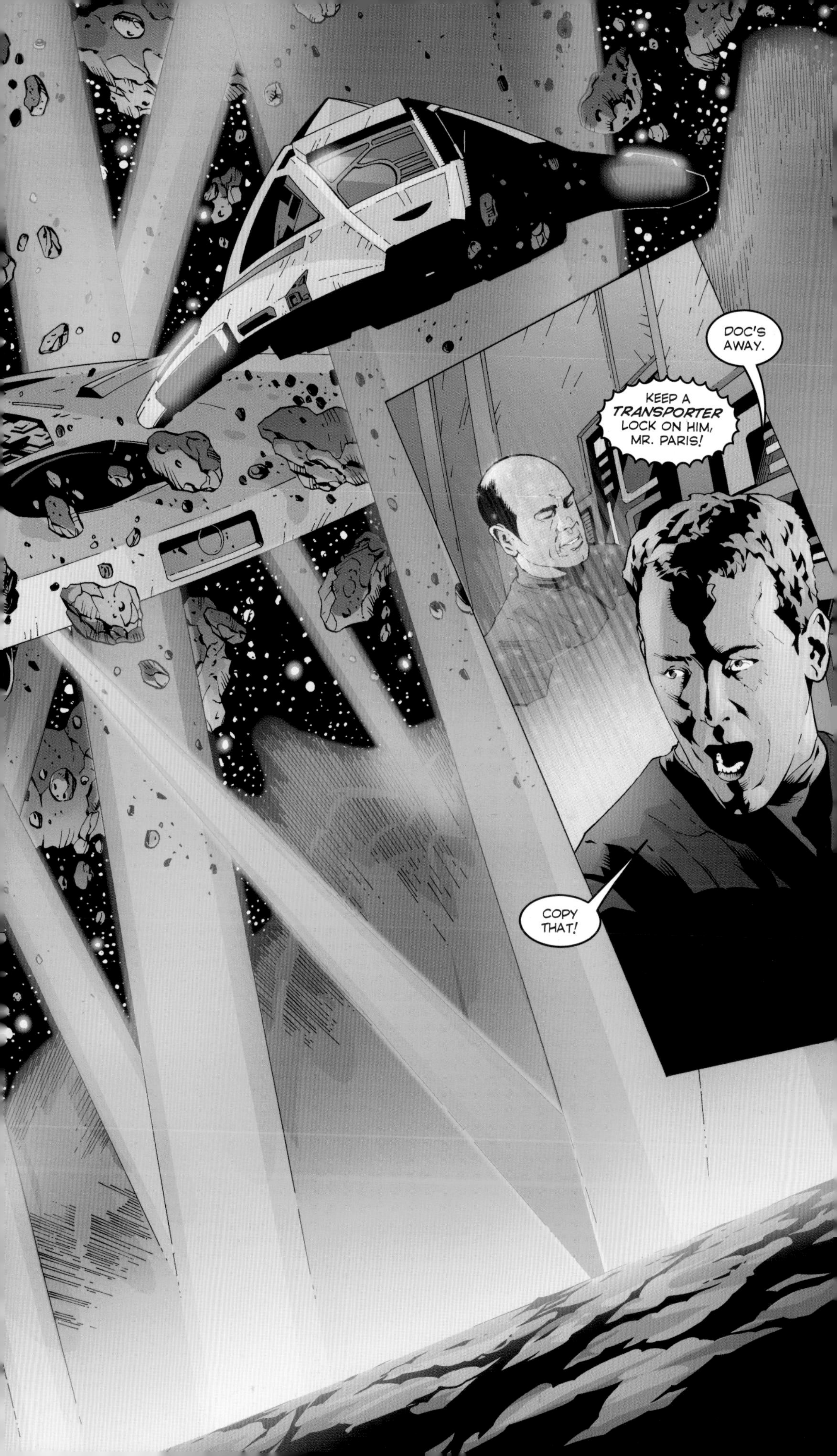
DOC'S AWAY.
KEEP A TRANSPORTER LOCK ON HIM, MR. PARIS!
COPY THAT!

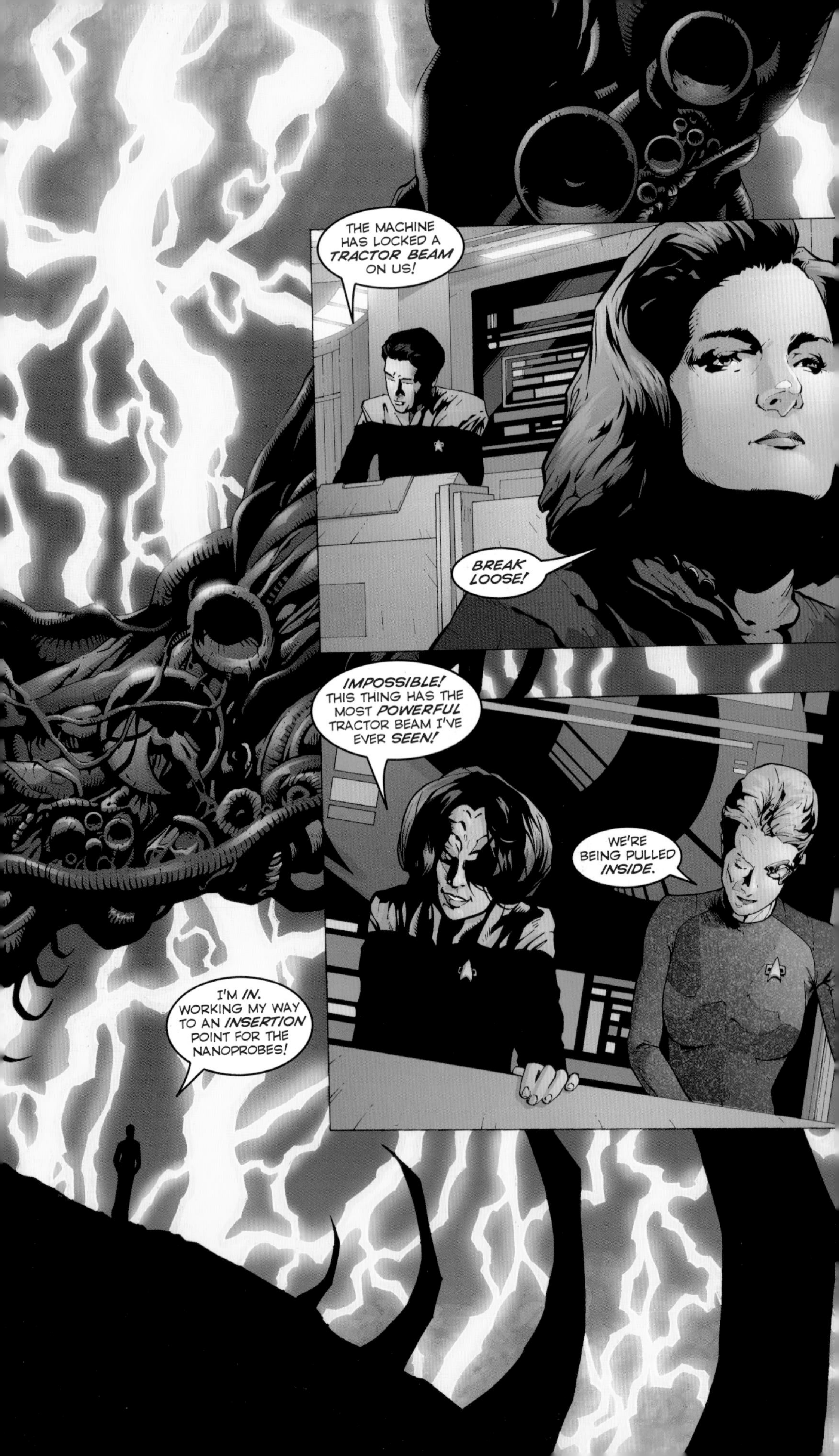
THE MACHINE HAS LOCKED A TRACTOR BEAM ON US!
BREAK LOOSE!
IMPOSSIBLE! THIS THING HAS THE MOST POWERFUL TRACTOR BEAM I'VE EVER SEEN!
WE'RE BEING PULLED INSIDE.
I'M IN. WORKING MY WAY TO AN INSERTION POINT FOR THE NANOPROBES!

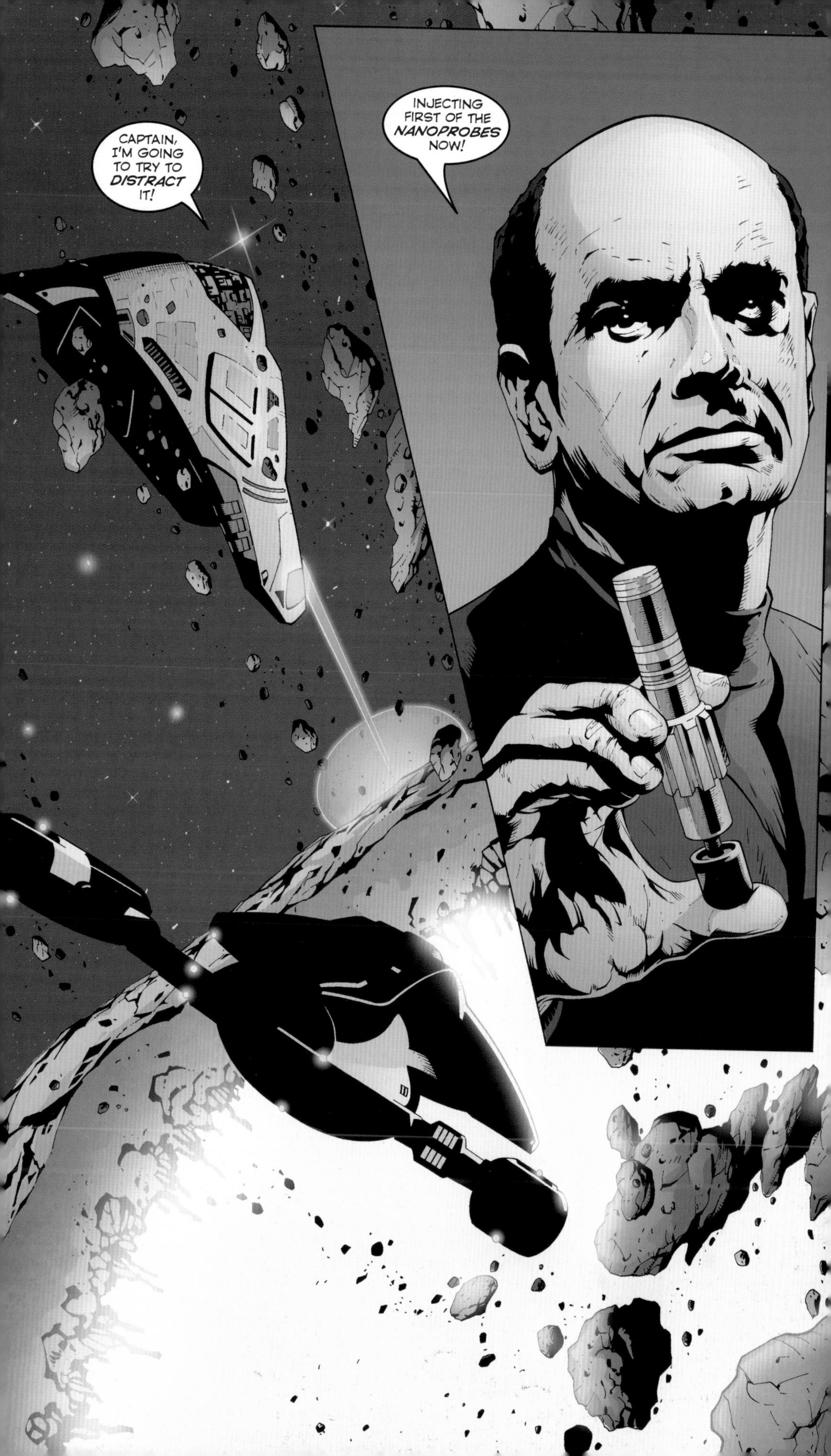
CAPTAIN, I'M GOING TO TRY TO DISTRACT IT!
INJECTING FIRST OF THE NANOPROBES NOW!

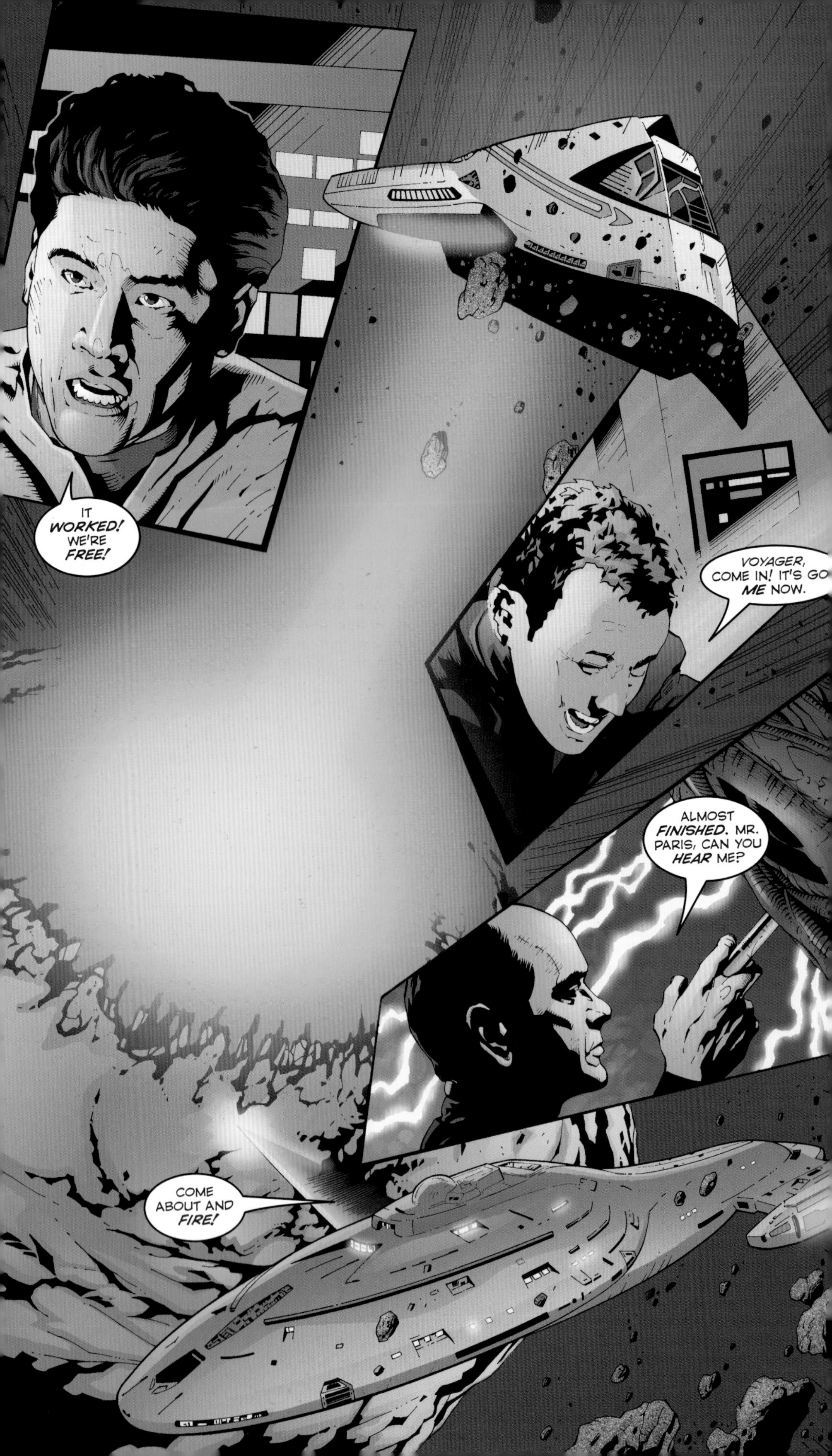
IT WORKED! WE'RE FREE!
VOYAGER, COME IN! IT'S GO ME NOW.
ALMOST FINISHED. MR. PARIS, CAN YOU HEAR ME?
COME ABOUT AND FIRE!

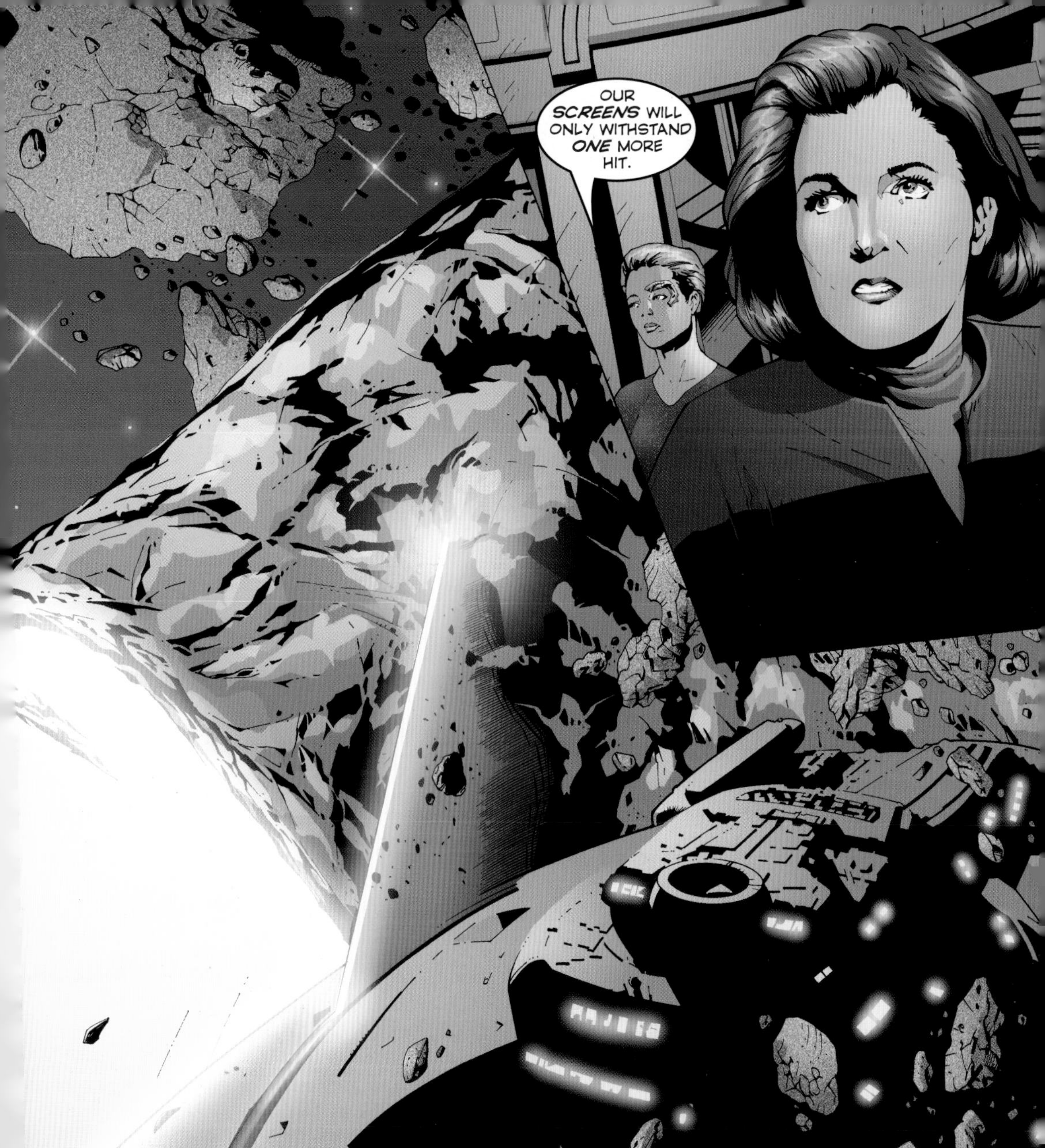
OUR SCREENS WILL ONLY WITHSTAND ONE MORE HIT.

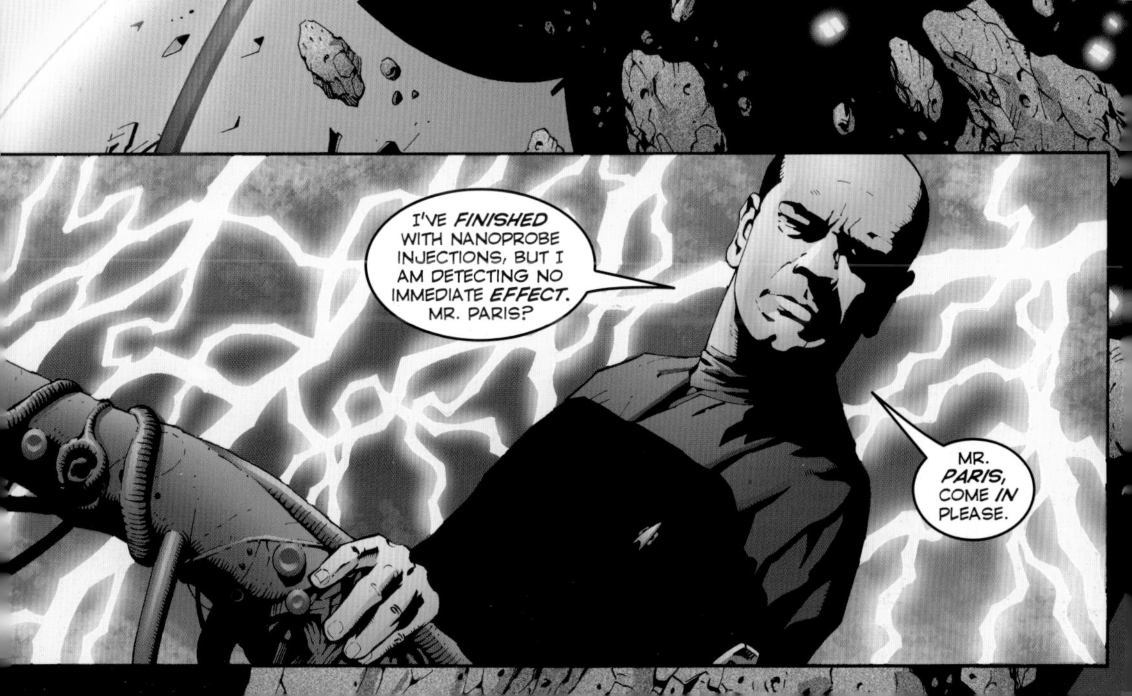
I'VE FINISHED WITH NANOPROBE INJECTIONS, BUT I AM DETECTING NO IMMEDIATE EFFECT. MR. PARIS?
MR. PARIS, COME IN PLEASE.

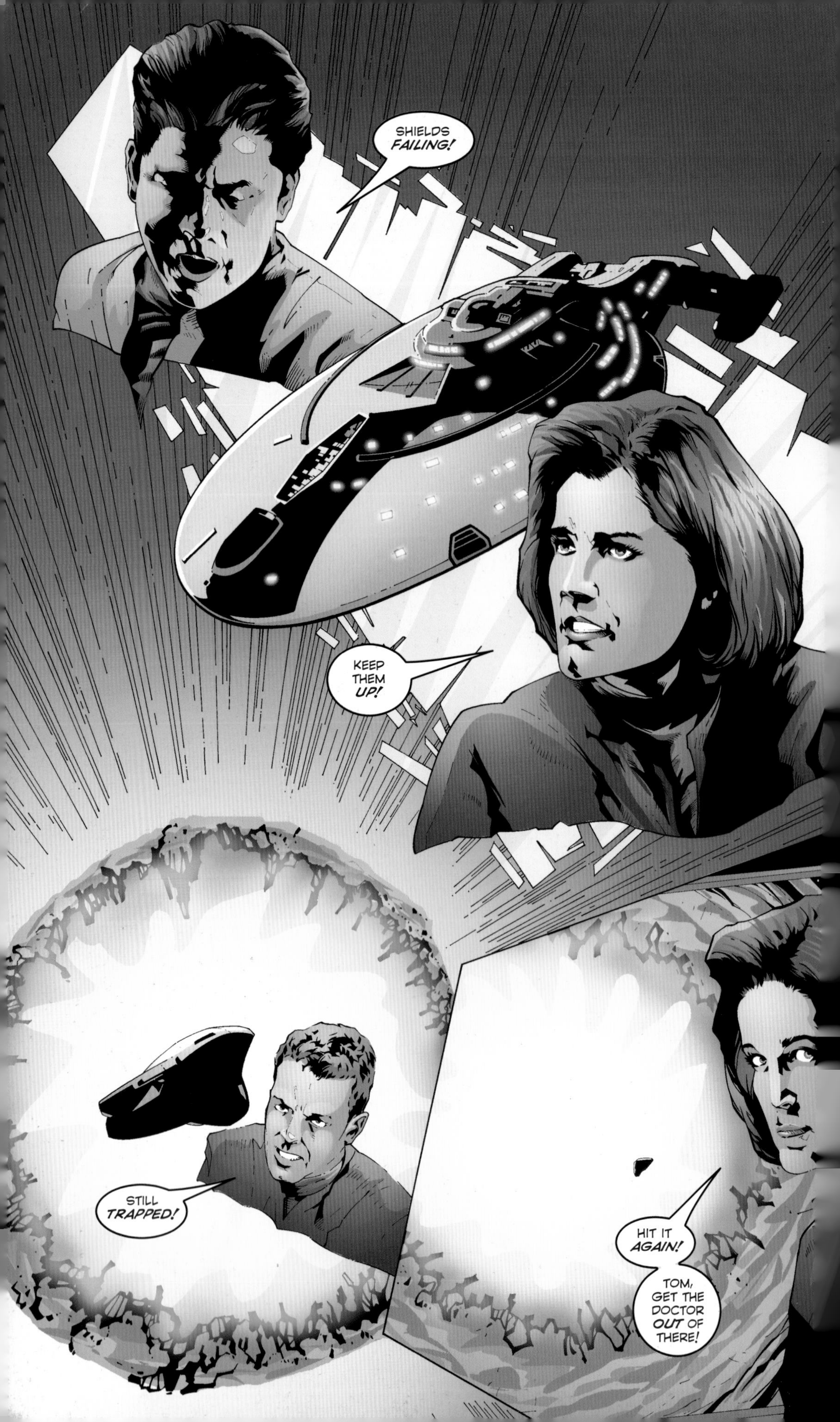
SHIELDS *FAILING!*
KEEP THEM *UP!*
STILL *TRAPPED!*
HIT IT *AGAIN!*
TOM, GET THE DOCTOR *OUT* OF THERE!

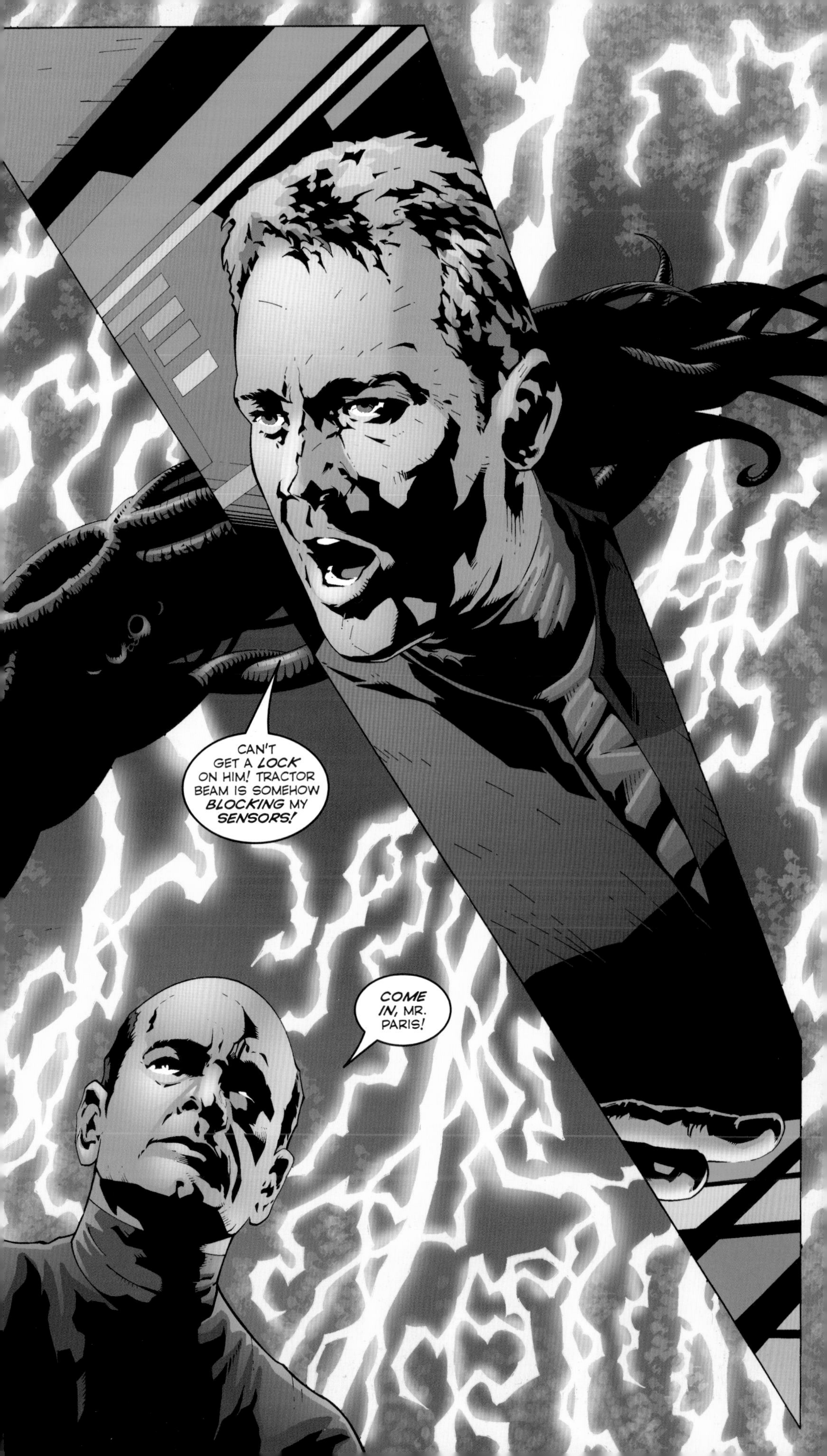
CAN'T GET A LOCK ON HIM! TRACTOR BEAM IS SOMEHOW BLOCKING MY SENSORS!
COME IN, MR. PARIS!

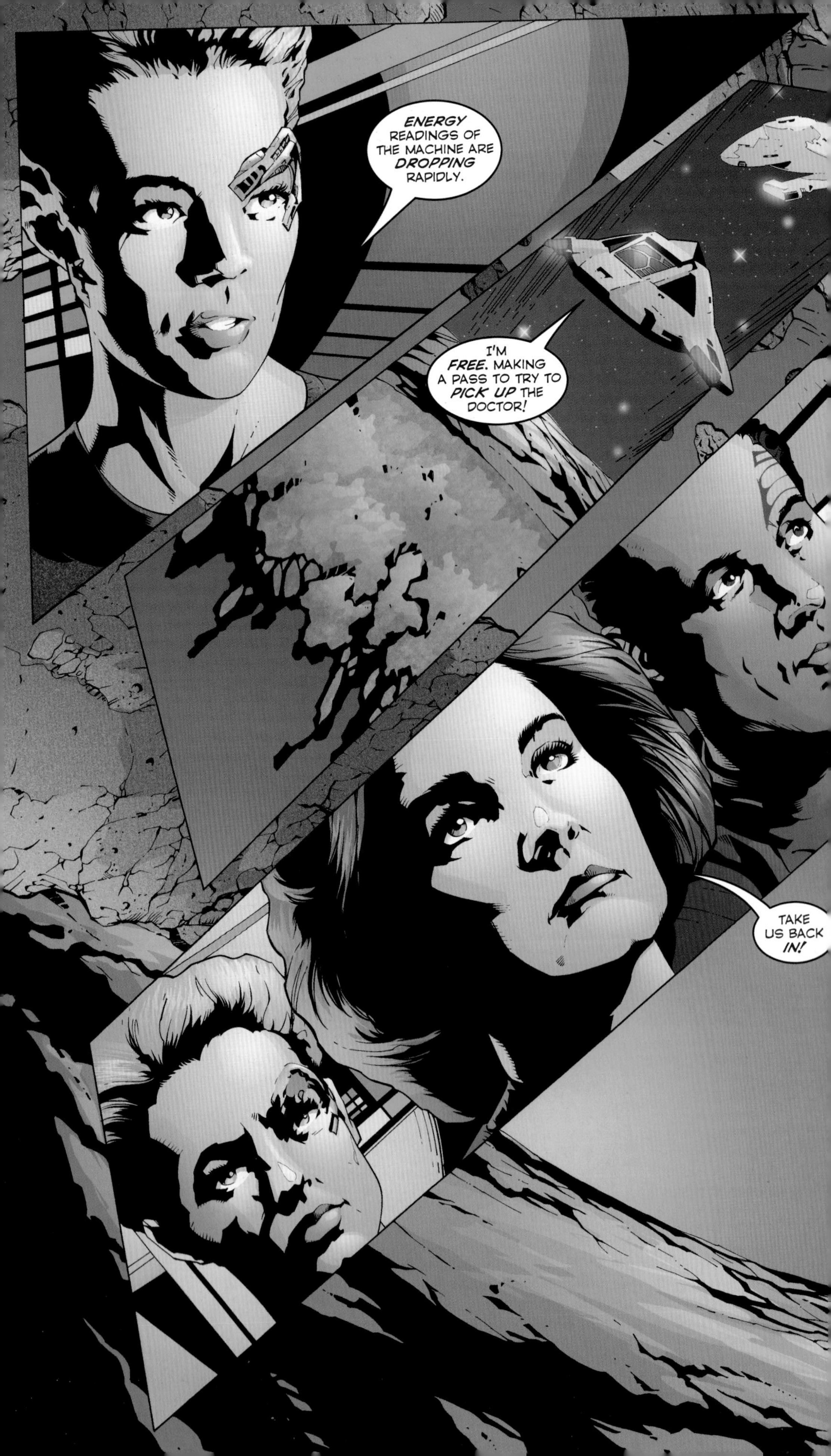
ENERGY READINGS OF THE MACHINE ARE DROPPING RAPIDLY.
I'M FREE. MAKING A PASS TO TRY TO PICK UP THE DOCTOR!
TAKE US BACK IN!

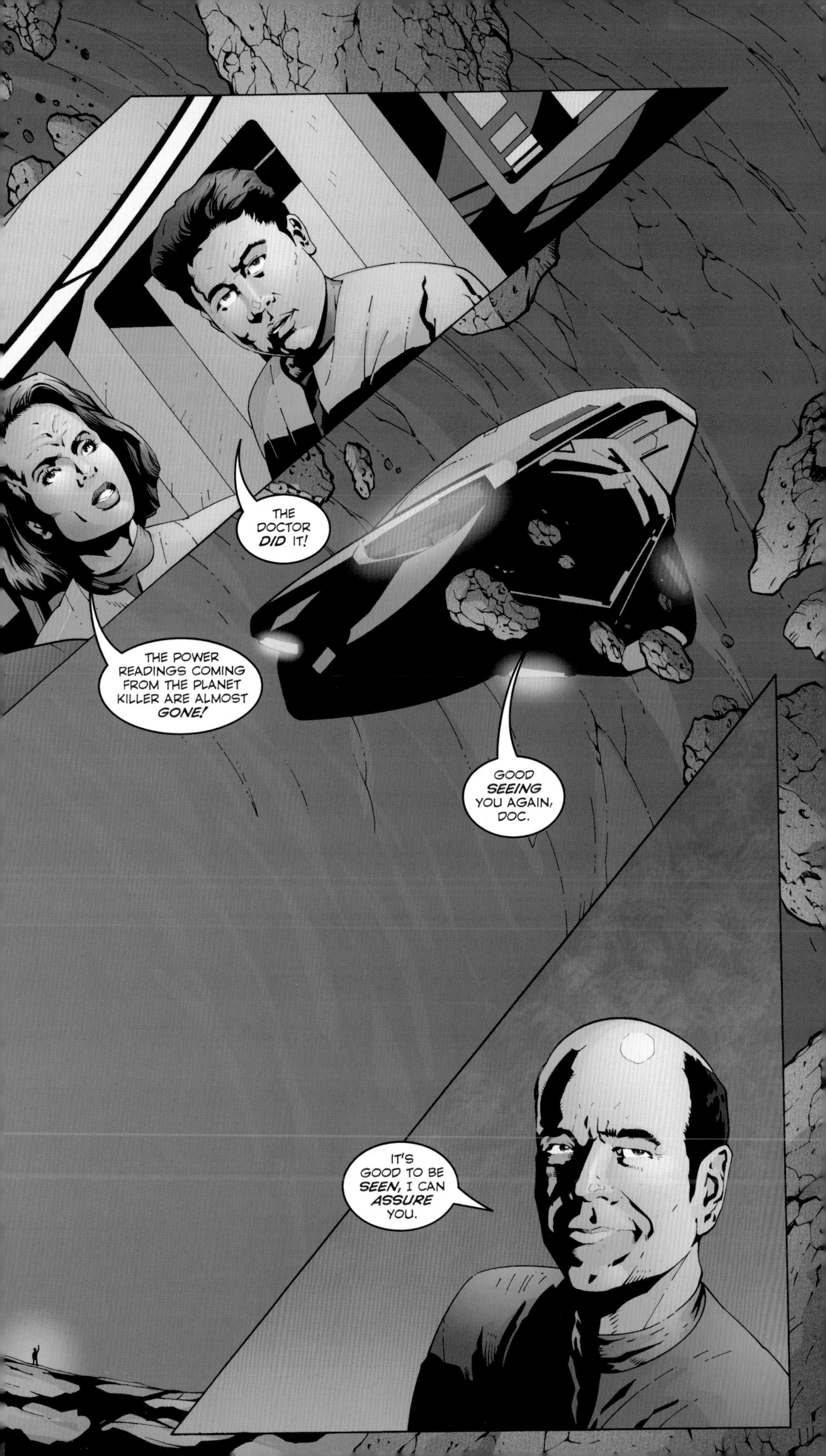
THE DOCTOR DID IT!
THE POWER READINGS COMING FROM THE PLANET KILLER ARE ALMOST GONE!
GOOD SEEING YOU AGAIN, DOC.
IT'S GOOD TO BE SEEN, I CAN ASSURE YOU.

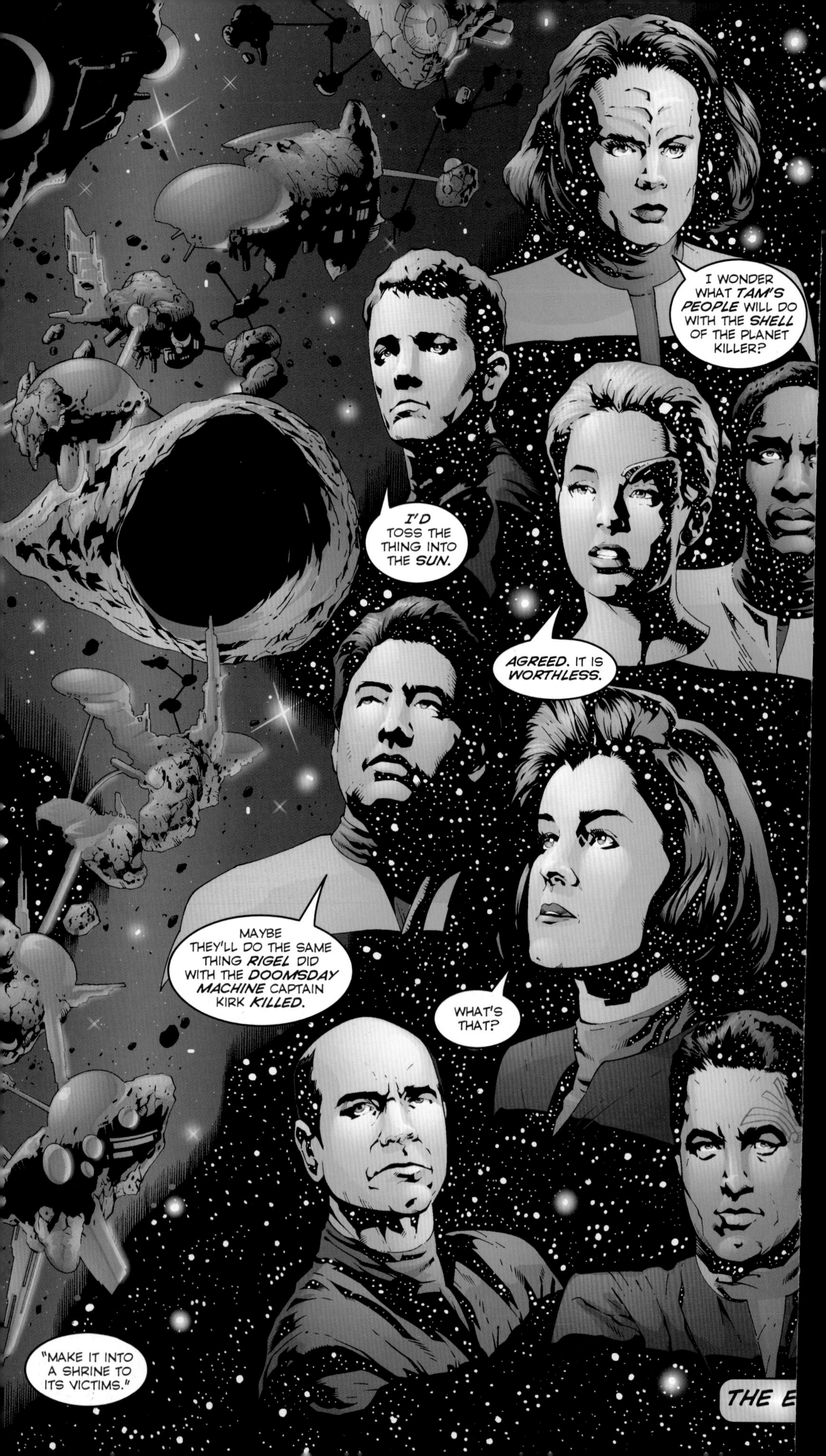
I WONDER WHAT TAM'S PEOPLE WILL DO WITH THE SHELL OF THE PLANET KILLER?
I'D TOSS THE THING INTO THE SUN.
AGREED. IT IS WORTHLESS.
MAYBE THEY'LL DO THE SAME THING RIGEL DID WITH THE DOOMSDAY MACHINE CAPTAIN KIRK KILLED.
WHAT'S THAT?
"MAKE IT INTO A SHRINE TO ITS VICTIMS."
THE E